PEARSON EDEXCEL INTERNATIONAL AS/A LEVEL

ECONOMICS

Student Book 1

Alan Hewison
Tracey Joad

Published by Pearson Education Limited, 80 Strand, London, WC2R 0RL.

www.pearsonglobalschools.com

Copies of official specifications for all Pearson Edexcel qualifications may be found on the website: https://qualifications.pearson.com

Text © Pearson Education Limited 2018
Designed by Pearson Education Limited 2018
Typeset by Tech-Set Ltd, Gateshead, UK
Original illustrations © Pearson Education Limited 2018
Edited by: Jeremy Toynbee, Jenny Hunt and Sarah Wright
Cover design by Pearson Education Limited 2018
Picture research by Aptara Inc.
Cover photo/illustration © **Getty Images:** DKart
Inside front cover photo: **Shutterstock**, Dmitry Lobanov

The rights of Alan Hewison and Tracey Joad to be identified as authors of this work have been asserted by them in accordance with the Copyright, Designs and Patents Act 1988.

First published 2018

24
14

British Library Cataloguing in Publication Data
A catalogue record for this book is available from the British Library

ISBN 978 1 29223 919 4

Printed and bound in Great Britain by Bell & Bain Ltd, Glasgow

Acknowledgements
The publisher would like to thank the following individuals and organisations for permission to reproduce photographs:

Photographs
(Key: b-bottom; c-centre; l-left; r-right; t-top)

123RF.com: 127, 209, Sean Pavone 281br; **Alamy Stock Photo:** Rob Lewine/Image Source 9t, Ton koene 9b, Taina Sohlman 72, Paris 94, Richard Ellis 102t, Palash khan 115, Thomas Cockrem 265t, Stanca Sanda 265b, Sue Heaton 269b; **Corbis:** Fancy Veer 17t; **Fotolia:** Georgios Kollidas 31; **Getty Images:** Glowimages vi, 2, Dougal Waters 17b, Maximilian Stock Ltd. 34, Alberto Incrocci 66, Tuul & Bruno Morandi/The Image Bank 75, Livia Corona/Stone 97, Martin Barraud/Caiaimage 121, Juan Barreto/AFP 132, Tuul & Bruno Morandi/The Image Bank 135, Westend61 190, 219, Matthew McVay/The Image Bank 231, Michael Reinhard/Corbis Documentary 253, Ricardo DeAratanha/Los Angeles Times 271, Howard Berman/The Image Bank 277; **Pearson Education:** 102b, Naki Kouyioumtzis 282tl; **Rex Features:** Quilai Shen 21, 207; **Shutterstock:** Jayakumar viib, 7, Carlos Yudica viit, 43, SunnyToys 5, Dziewul 10, Futurewalk 11, Monkey Business Images 13, Ae Cherayut 23t, Zurbagan 23c, Pics-xl 23b, David M G 28, A. Aleksandravicius 38, Jess Kraft 39, IMG_191 44, Zhao jian kang 45, Semen Lixodeev 47, Christian Draghici 57, TebNad 62, Oleksiy Mark 69, Sergey Ryzhov 77, I. Pilon 81l, bonchan 81r, Humphery 82, Rikard Stadler 84, Usoltceva Anastasiia 86, TTstudio 98, OlegD 99, kyrien 105, ChiccoDodiFC 106, Photka 108, hedgehog111 109, Ivan Kurmyshov 110, wong yu liang 111, zstock 117, Isantilli 118, Igor Grochev 120, MikeDotta 129, Lumppini 134, Photobac 147, Uber Images 150, Andresr 160, Tatiana Popova 170, Phonlamai Photo 177, Siriwat Sriphojaroen 197, Creativa Images 200, fotosunny 212, hkhtt hj 217, iurii 226, TTstudio 229, isak55 234, Marie Kanger Born 237, ksl 250, Pics721 269t, CLChang 273, Marcio Jose Bastos Silva 280, Osugi 281bl, Luciano Mortula 282tr, CP DC Press 291, Leonid Andronov 311, Gang Liu 316.
All other images © Pearson Education

The publisher would like to thank the following individuals and organisations for their approval and permission to reproduce their materials:

p. 47 AHDB Dairy; **pages 82, 83, 227** BP Statistical Review of World Energy June 2017; **p. 33** Central Intelligence Agency; **p. 250** DIW Berlin; **pages 19, 25, 28, 29, 38, 47, 57, 58, 61, 73, 74, 79, 81, 84, 87, 89, 95, 105, 117, 118, 120, 128, 129, 133, 134, 159, 162, 169, 175, 179, 189, 212, 216, 218, 235, 244, 245, 251, 252, 263, 264, 265, 267, 292, 296, 303, 305, 307, 308, 313, 315** © the Financial Times, All Rights Reserved; **p. 74** Globefish; pages gov.uk; **Pages 56, 84, 166, 167, 168, 169, 170, 212, 229, 245, 251, 256, 267** International Monetary Fund; **pages 9, 89 223** IFS Green budget; **p. 55** adapted from http://www.macrotrends.net/1369/crude-oilprice-history-chart; **pages 142, 157, 194, 195, 199, 203, 263,** Office for National Statistics; p. 63 adapted from http://oilprice.com /Energy/Energy -General/Electricity-Consumption-Continues-To-Fall.html; **pages 33, 69, 71, 139, 146, 148, 151, 154, 158, 161, 166, 180, 188, 195, 196, 197, 206, 212, 213, 216, 217, 218, 220, 221, 222, 229, 234, 242, 243, 244, 245, 258, 262, 264, 267, 268, 281, 283, 284, 285, 303, 305** Organization for Economic Co-operation and Development (OECD); **p.337** Resolution Foundation; **pages 87, 88** Society of Motor Manufacturers and Traders (SMMT); **pages 72, 74, 87, 296** Thomson Reuters DataStream; **pages 19, 74** United Nations; **p. 19** adapted from unstats.un.org, United Nations Statistics Division, © 2015 United Nations. Reprinted with the permission of the United Nations; **pages 39, 147, 153, 162, 170, 179, 189, 212** World Bank; **pages 56, 251, 256** World Economic Outlook; **pages 150, 153** World Happiness Report.

Endorsement statement
In order to ensure that this resource offers high-quality support for the associated Pearson qualification, it has been through a review process by the awarding body. This process confirms that this resource fully covers the teaching and learning content of the specification at which it is aimed. It also confirms that it demonstrates an appropriate balance between the development of subject skills, knowledge and understanding, in addition to preparation for assessment.

Endorsement does not cover any guidance on assessment activities or processes (e.g. practice questions or advice on how to answer assessment questions) included in the resource, nor does it prescribe any particular approach to the teaching or delivery of a related course.

While the publishers have made every attempt to ensure that advice on the qualification and its assessment is accurate, the official specification and associated assessment guidance materials are the only authoritative source of information and should always be referred to for definitive guidance.

Pearson examiners have not contributed to any sections in this resource relevant to examination papers for which they have responsibility.

Examiners will not use endorsed resources as a source of material for any assessment set by Pearson. Endorsement of a resource does not mean that the resource is required to achieve this Pearson qualification, nor does it mean that it is the only suitable material available to support the qualification, and any resource lists produced by the awarding body shall include this and other appropriate resources.

CONTENTS

UNIT 1: MARKETS IN ACTION

UNIT 2: MACROECONOMIC PERFORMANCE AND POLICY

ABOUT THIS BOOK

This book is written for students following the Pearson Edexcel International Advanced Level (IAL) Economics specification. It covers the first year of the International A Level qualification as well as the full International AS Level.

The book has been carefully structured to match the order of the topics in the specification, although teaching and learning can take place in any order, both in the classroom and in any independent learning. This book is organised into two units (Unit 1 Markets in action and Unit 2 Macroeconomic performance and policy), each with six topic areas.

Each topic area is divided into chapters to break the content down into manageable chunks. Each chapter begins by listing the key learning objectives and includes a getting started activity to introduce the concepts. There is a mix of learning points and activities throughout including global case studies that show a range of examples within real-life contexts. Checkpoint questions at the end of each chapter help assess understanding of the key learning objectives.

The content for Unit 1 is applicable to Paper 1 (Markets in action) and the content for Unit 2 is applicable to Paper 2 (Macroeconomic performance and policy). Knowing how to apply learning to both of these papers will be critical for exam success. There are exam questions at the end of each chapter to provide opportunity for exam practice. Answers are provided online in the teaching resource pack.

Topic openers
Introduce each of the key topics in the specification.

Learning objectives
Each chapter starts with a list of key assessment objectives.

Specification reference
The specification reference is given at the start of each chapter and in the running header.

SPECIFICATION 1.3.1 | 1 ECONOMICS AS A SOCIAL SCIENCE | 3

INTRODUCTORY CONCEPTS

The first part of Unit 1 looks at how economics defines itself as a social science and studies complex economic behaviour. It looks at the central economic problem of scarcity and how economic systems and agents make choices between competing alternatives. Some basic terms are introduced. The idea of markets and the role of money in the workings of an economic system is developed. Finally, the different types of economies – free market, mixed and command – are examined, along with a first look at the role of the state.

1 ECONOMICS AS A SOCIAL SCIENCE

UNIT 1
1.3.1

LEARNING OBJECTIVES

■ Understand that economics is a social science that uses the scientific method.
■ Understand that economists build models and theories based on assumptions.
■ Understand that the ceteris paribus assumption is used in building models and drawing conclusions.
■ Understand the distinction between positive statements and value judgements.

GETTING STARTED

'Governments should do more to help the unemployed'. Is this a fact or is it a value judgement? If you wanted to argue for or against this statement what factual arguments could you use? And what emotional ones could you put forward? Which of these arguments are economic and which are non-economic?

THE SCIENTIFIC METHOD

There are many sciences covering a wide field of knowledge. What links them all is a particular method of work or enquiry called the **scientific method.** The scientific method at its most basic is relatively easy to understand. A scientist postulates (puts forward) a **theory or model** – the scientist puts forward a **hypothesis** that is capable of being disproved (e.g. the Earth travels round the Sun). They then gather evidence to either support the theory or refute it. Observation of space gives evidence to support the theory that the Earth travels round the Sun, however, data refutes the idea that the Earth travels around the sun. They will gather evidence through controlled experiments. From this they will then accept, modify or refute the theory – the Earth does travel round the Sun.

Theories that gain universal acceptance are often called laws. Hence we have the law of gravity and, in economics, the laws of demand and supply.

ECONOMICS – THE SCIENCE

In natural sciences, such as physics or chemistry, it is relatively easy to use the scientific method. In physics, much of the work can take place in laboratories. Observations can be made with some degree of certainty. Control groups can be established. It then becomes relatively easy to accept or refute a particular hypothesis.

This is much more difficult in **social sciences** such as economics, sociology, politics and anthropology. In economics, it is often not possible to set up experiments to test hypotheses or establish control groups or conduct experiments in environments that enable one factor to be varied while other factors are kept constant. The economist has to gather data in the ordinary everyday world where many variables are changing over any given time period. It then becomes difficult to decide whether the evidence supports or refutes particular hypotheses.

Economists sometimes come to very different conclusions when considering a particular set of data as their interpretations may vary. For example, an unemployment rate of 6 per cent in one area of a country compared to a national average of 3 per cent may indicate a failure of government policy to help this area. Others may conclude that policy had been a success as unemployment may have been far greater without the use of policy.

It is sometimes argued that economics cannot be a science because it studies human behaviour and human behaviour cannot be reduced to scientific laws. There is an element of truth to this. It is very difficult to understand and predict the behaviour of individuals. However, nearly all economics is based on the study of the behaviour of groups of individuals. The behaviour of groups is often far more predictable than that of individuals. Moreover, we tend to judge a science on its ability to establish laws that are certain observations of space. Nonetheless, even in a hard science such as physics, it has become established that some laws can only be stated in terms of probabilities. In economics, much analysis is described using terms such as 'it is likely that' or 'this may possibly happen'. Economists use this type of language because they know they

Getting started
An activity to introduce the key concepts in each chapter. Questions are designed to stimulate discussion and use prior knowledge. These can be tackled as individuals, pairs, groups or the whole class.

Activity
Each chapter includes activities to embed understanding through case studies and questions.

Skills
Relevant exam questions are labelled with key skills, allowing for a strong focus on particular academic qualities. These transferable skills are highly valued in further study and the workplace.

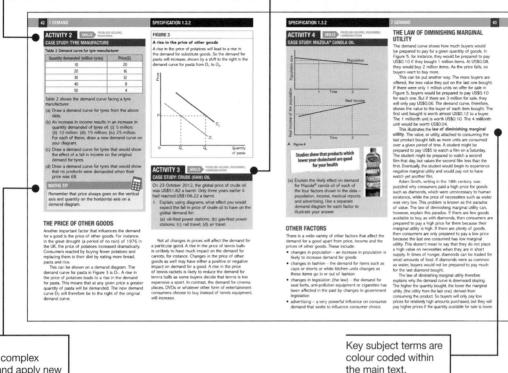

Maths tips
Help simplify complex calculations and apply new methods or formulae.

Key subject terms are colour coded within the main text.

Checkpoint
These questions check understanding of the key learning points in each chapter. These are NOT exam-style questions.

Exam practice
These questions are found at the end of each chapter. They are tailored to the Pearson Edexcel specification to allow for practice and development of exam writing technique. They also allow for practice responding to the command words used in the exams.

Thinking like an economist
Provide opportunities to explore an aspect of economics in more detail to deepen understanding.

Subject vocabulary
An alphabetical list of all the subject terms in each chapter with clear definitions for EAL learners. A collated glossary is provided in the eBook.

Exam hint
Give tips on how to answer the exam questions and guidance for exam preparation.

ASSESSMENT OVERVIEW

The following tables give an overview of the assessment for this course. You should study this information closely to help ensure that you are fully prepared for this course and know exactly what to expect in each part of the assessment.

PAPER 1	PERCENTAGE OF IAS	PERCENTAGE OF IAL	MARK	TIME	AVAILABILITY	STRUCTURE
MARKETS IN ACTION Written exam paper Paper code WEC11/01 Externally set and marked by Pearson Edexcel Single tier of entry Calculators can be used	50%	25%	80	1 hour 45 minutes	January, June and October First assessment: January 2019	Section A: six multiple-choice questions (6 marks), Section B: five short-answer questions (20 marks), Section C: a five-part question, based on data provided in a source booklet (34 marks), and Section D: one essay question from a choice of two (20 marks)

PAPER 2	PERCENTAGE OF IAS	PERCENTAGE OF IAL	MARK	TIME	AVAILABILITY	STRUCTURE
MACROECONOMIC PERFORMANCE AND POLICY Written exam paper Paper code WEC12/01 Externally set and marked by Pearson Edexcel Single tier of entry Calculators can be used	50%	25%	80	1 hour 45 minutes	January, June and October First assessment: June 2019	Section A: six multiple-choice questions (6 marks), Section B: five short-answer questions (20 marks), Section C: a five-part question, based on data provided in a source booklet (34 marks) and Section D: one essay question from a choice of two (20 marks).

ASSESSMENT OBJECTIVES AND WEIGHTINGS

ASSESSMENT OBJECTIVE	DESCRIPTION	% IN IAS	% IN IA2	% IN IAL
A01	Demonstrate knowledge of terms, concepts, theories and models to show an understanding of the behaviour of economic agents	27.5	18.8	23.1
A02	Apply knowledge and understanding to various economic contexts	30	22.5	26.3
A03	Analyse issues and evidence, showing an understanding of their impact on economic agents	22.5	28.8	25.6
A04	Evaluate economic arguments and use appropriate evidence to support informed judgements	20	30	25

Note: Percentages may not add up to 100 due to rounding.

RELATIONSHIP OF ASSESSMENT OBJECTIVES TO UNITS FOR THE INTERNATIONAL ADVANCE SUBSIDIARY QUALIFICATION

UNIT NUMBER	ASSESSMENT OBJECTIVE			
	A01	A02	A03	A04
Unit 1	13.8%	15%	11.3%	10%
Unit 2	13.8%	15%	11.3%	10%
Total for International Advanced Subsidiary	**27.5%**	**30%**	**22.5%**	**20%**
UNIT NUMBER	IAL SCORES			
Unit 1	6.9%	7.5%	5.6%	5%
Unit 2	6.9%	7.5%	5.6%	5%
Total for International Advanced Level:	**13.8%**	**15%**	**11.2%**	**10%**

Note: Percentages may not add up to 100 due to rounding.

RELATIONSHIP OF ASSESSMENT OBJECTIVES TO COMMAND WORDS

COMMAND	NUMBER OF MARKS	MARK SCHEME	AOS
Define	2	Points Based	AO1
Calculate	2	Points Based	AO2
Calculate	4	Points Based	AO1, AO2
Draw	4	Points Based	AO1, AO2
Explain what is meant by Explain the term Explain two characteristics	4	Points Based	AO1, AO2
Explain why Explain how Explain the likely impact Explain and illustrate	4	Points Based	AO1, AO2, AO3
Analyse	6	Points Based	AO1, AO2, AO3
Examine	8	Points Based	AO1, AO2, AO3, AO4
Discuss	14	Levels Based	AO1, AO2, AO3, AO4
Evaluate/ To what extent	20	Levels Based	AO1, AO2, AO3, AO4

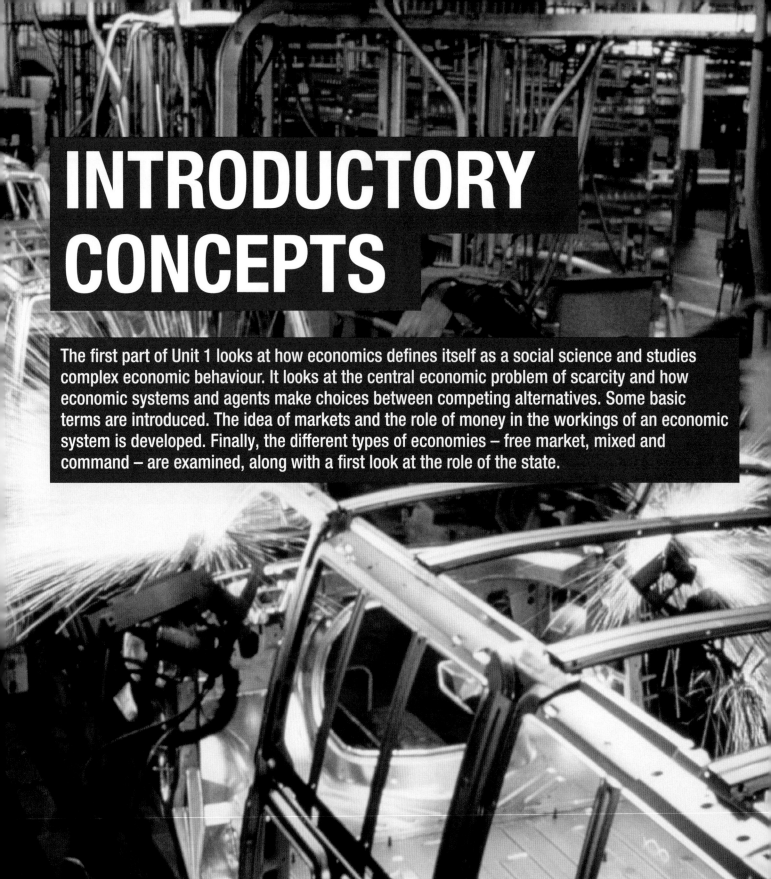

INTRODUCTORY CONCEPTS

The first part of Unit 1 looks at how economics defines itself as a social science and studies complex economic behaviour. It looks at the central economic problem of scarcity and how economic systems and agents make choices between competing alternatives. Some basic terms are introduced. The idea of markets and the role of money in the workings of an economic system is developed. Finally, the different types of economies – free market, mixed and command – are examined, along with a first look at the role of the state.

1 ECONOMICS AS A SOCIAL SCIENCE

LEARNING OBJECTIVES

- Understand that economics is a social science that uses the scientific method.
- Understand that economists build models and theories based on assumptions.
- Understand that the ceteris paribus assumption is used in building models and drawing conclusions.
- Understand the distinction between positive statements and value judgements.

GETTING STARTED

'Governments should do more to help the unemployed'. Is this a fact or is it a value judgement? If you wanted to argue for or against this statement what factual arguments could you use? And what emotional ones could you put forward? Which of these arguments are economic and which are non-economic?

THE SCIENTIFIC METHOD

There are many sciences covering a wide field of knowledge. What links them all is a particular method of work or enquiry called the **scientific method**. The scientific method at its most basic is relatively easy to understand. A scientist postulates (puts forward) a **theory or model** – the scientist puts forward a **hypothesis** that is capable of being disproved (e.g. the Earth travels round the Sun). They then gather evidence to either support the theory or refute it. Observation of space gives evidence to support the theory that the Earth travels round the Sun, however, data refutes the idea that the Earth travels around the sun. They will gather evidence through controlled experiments. From this they will then accept, modify or refute the theory – the Earth *does* travel round the Sun.

Theories that gain universal acceptance are often called **laws**. Hence we have the law of gravity and, in economics, the laws of demand and supply.

ECONOMICS – THE SCIENCE

In natural sciences, such as physics or chemistry, it is relatively easy to use the scientific method. In physics, much of the work can take place in laboratories. Observations can be made with some degree of certainty. Control groups can be established. It then becomes relatively easy to accept or refute a particular hypothesis.

This is much more difficult in **social sciences** such as economics, sociology, politics and anthropology. In economics, it is often not possible to set up experiments to test hypotheses or establish control groups or conduct experiments in environments that enable one factor to be varied while other factors are kept constant. The economist has to gather data in the ordinary everyday world where many variables are changing over any given time period. It then becomes difficult to decide whether the evidence supports or refutes particular hypotheses.

Economists sometimes come to very different conclusions when considering a particular set of data as their interpretations may vary. For example, an unemployment rate of 6 per cent in one area of a country compared to a national average of 3 per cent may indicate a failure of government policy to help this area. Others may conclude that policy had been a success as unemployment may have been far greater without the use of policy.

It is sometimes argued that economics cannot be a science because it studies human behaviour and human behaviour cannot be reduced to scientific laws. There is an element of truth to this. It is very difficult to understand and predict the behaviour of individuals. However, nearly all economics is based on the study of the behaviour of groups of individuals. The behaviour of groups is often far more predictable than that of individuals. Moreover, we tend to judge a science on its ability to establish laws that are certain observations of space. Nonetheless, even in a hard science such as physics, it has become established that some laws can only be stated in terms of probabilities. In economics, much analysis is described using terms such as 'it is likely that' or 'this may possibly happen'. Economists use this type of language because they know they have insufficient data to make firm predictions. In part it is because other variables may change at the same time, altering the course of events. However, it is also used because economists know that human behaviour, while broadly predictable, is not predictable to the last €1 spent or to the nearest US$1 of income.

THEORIES AND MODELS

The terms 'theory' and 'model' are often used to mean the same thing. There is no exact distinction to be made between the two. However, an economic theory is generally expressed in looser terms than a model. For instance, 'consumption is dependent upon income' might be an economic theory.

Theories can often be expressed in words; economic models, because they require greater precision in their specification, are often expressed in mathematical terms. For example, '$Ct = 567 + 0.852Yt$' where 567 is a constant, Ct is current consumption and Yt is current income, would be an economic model.

THE PURPOSE OF MODELLING

Why are theories and models so useful in science? The universe is complex. There is an infinite (endless) number of interactions happening at any moment in time. Somehow we all have to make sense of what is going on. For instance, we assume that if we put our hand into a flame, we will get burned. If we see a large hole in the ground in front of us, we assume that we will fall into it if we carry on walking in that direction.

One of the reasons we construct theories or models is because we want to know why something is as it is. Some people are fascinated by questions such as 'Why do we fall downwards and not upwards?' or 'Why can birds fly?'. More importantly we use theories and models all the time in deciding how to act. We keep away from fires to prevent getting burned. We avoid holes in the ground because we do not want to fall.

SIMPLIFICATION

One criticism made of economics is that economic theories and models are 'unrealistic'. This is true, but it is equally true of Newton's law of gravity, Einstein's theory of relativity or any theory or model. This is because any theory or model has to be a simplification of reality if it is to be useful. Imagine, for instance, using a map that described an area perfectly. To do this it would need to be a full-scale reproduction of the

entire area, which would give no practical advantage. Alternatively, drop a feather and a metal ball from the top of a tall building. You will find that they do not descend at the same speed, as one law in physics would predict, because that law assumes that factors, such as the drag effect caused by air, do not exist.

If a model is to be useful, it has to be simple. The extent of simplification depends on its use. If you wanted to go from Cape Town to Tokyo by air, it would not be very helpful to have maps that were on the same scale as your local maps. Whereas, if you wanted to visit a friend in a nearby town it wouldn't be very helpful to have a map of the world with you. A local town map is very much more detailed (that is, closer to reality) than a world map but this does not necessarily make it more useful or make it a 'better' model.

Simplification implies that some factors have been included in the model and some have been omitted. It could even be the case that some factors have been distorted to draw attention to particular points in a model. For instance, on a road map of Delhi, map makers will almost certainly not have attempted to name every small village or show the natural features of the area. In contrast, they will have marked in roads and highways that will appear several kilometres wide according to the scale of the map.

ASSUMPTIONS AND CETERIS PARIBUS

All sciences make assumptions when developing models and theories. In the case of the feather and the metal ball being dropped from a tall building, both would fall at equal speed if it were assumed that there was no drag effect caused by the air. Making assumptions allows the scientist to simplify a problem to make it easier to solve.

An important way in which economists simplify reality is to adopt the **ceteris paribus** condition. Ceteris paribus is Latin for 'all other things being equal' or 'all other things remaining the same'. For example, in demand theory, economists consider how price affects the amount demanded by buyers of a **good**. To isolate the price factor, they assume that all other factors that affect demand, such as income or the price of other goods, remain unchanged. Then economists see what happens to quantity demanded as the price of the good changes.

POSITIVE AND NORMATIVE ECONOMICS

Economics is concerned with two types of investigation. **Positive economics** is the scientific or objective study of the subject. It is concerned with finding out how economies and markets actually work. **Positive statements** are statements about economics that can be proven to be true or false. They can be supported or refuted by evidence. For example, the statement 'The Japanese economy is currently operating on its **production possibility frontier**' is a positive statement. Economists can search for evidence as to whether there are unemployed resources or not. If there are large numbers of unemployed workers, then the statement is refuted. If unemployment is very low, and we know that all market economies need some unemployment for the efficient workings of labour markets as people move between jobs, then the statement would be supported. Statements about the future can be positive statements too. For example, the hypothetical sentence 'The service sector in Singapore will grow by 15 per cent in size over the next five years' is a positive statement. Economists will have to wait five years for the proof to support or refute the statement to be available. However, it is still a statement that is capable of being proved or disproved.

Normative economics is concerned with value judgements. It deals with the study of and presentation of policy prescriptions about economics. **Normative statements** are statements that cannot be supported or refuted. Ultimately, they are viewpoints about how economies and markets should work. For example, 'The government should increase the state pension', or 'Manufacturing companies should invest more' are normative statements.

Economists tend to be interested in both positive and normative economics. They want to find out how economies work. But they also want to influence policy debates. Normative economics also typically contains positive economics within it. Take the normative statement 'The government should increase the state pension'. Economists putting forward this value judgement are likely to back up their opinion with positive evidence. They might state that 'The average pensioner has a **disposable income** of 40 per cent of the average worker' and 'The average pensioner only goes on holiday once every four years'. These are positive statements because they are capable of being proven or disproven. They are used to build up an argument that supports the final opinion that state pensions should be raised.

Normative statements tend to contain words like 'should' and 'ought'. However, sometimes positive statements also contain these words. 'Inflation should be brought down' is a normative statement because it is not capable of being refuted. 'Inflation should

reach 5 per cent by the end of the year' is a positive statement. At the end of the year, if inflation has reached 5 per cent, then the statement will have been proven to be correct.

ACTIVITY 1 SKILLS INTERPRETATION, COMMUNICATION

CASE STUDY: PUBLIC HEALTHCARE

India suffers from an extreme shortage of doctors, with just one physician for every 1800 people. The government is also reluctant about its public health spending, allocating just 1.4 per cent of gross domestic product, compared with 3.1 per cent in China. As a result, India's public healthcare system – on which working-class and poor Indians still rely – has neither the staff nor equipment to provide a reasonable standard of care for the seriously ill and injured patients seeking treatment.

Many patients are turned away from public hospitals for lack of beds, and even when they are seen, doctors have little time to spend with each patient. Waiting lists for emergency, life-saving surgery can be anything from six months to two years long. 'The majority of the Indian population is truly disenfranchised from access to healthcare,' says Dr Vivekanand Jha, executive director of the George Institute for Global Health, India. 'Public healthcare is completely broken. It's difficult for everyone to be given the kind of attention they deserve.'

(a) Explain which are the positive statements and which are the normative statements in this passage.

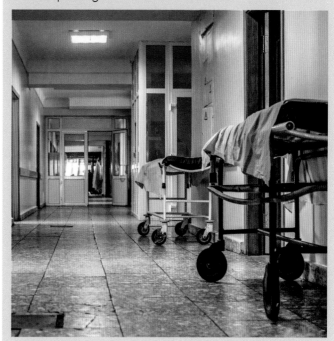

THINKING LIKE AN ECONOMIST

INCOME INEQUALITY

Whether income **inequality**, the relative gap between the rich and poor in an economy, is important or not is dependent on one's personal opinion. Some economic journalists have said that income inequality is not a problem while others assert that it is. The question of what level of income inequality is acceptable is a difficult one to answer, because it can be seen from a normative or positive perspective.

In economics, a normative statement is one that is subjective and value-based, while a positive statement is one that is objective and based on facts. From a normative perspective, the numbers are arbitrary (random). Looking at the economic data from a positive perspective, the conclusions are clearer.

From a positive perspective, there are some answers as to what is not an acceptable level of inequality, and there are non-partisan, economic implications of today's level of income inequality. Recent studies by the International Monetary Fund (IMF) suggest that income inequality can affect economic growth as measured by percentage change in gross domestic product (GDP).

If the share of income earned by the top 20 per cent increases, then GDP growth actually declines. In contrast, when the share of income of the bottom 20 per cent increases, there is higher GDP growth. The analysis from the IMF reveals that significant levels of income inequality cause GDP growth to decline.

The normative statement that 'rising income inequality is bad for the economy', becomes a positive statement when reinforced by analysis of data. Thus government actions such as cutting taxes would be counterintuitive to economic growth if it does nothing to address income inequality.

CHECKPOINT

1 What is the scientific method?

2 Why do economists use models?

3 Why do some people argue that economics is not a science?

4 What does ceteris paribus mean?

5 Why do economists use ceteris paribus?

6 What is the difference between a normative and a positive economic statement?

SUBJECT VOCABULARY

ceteris paribus all things being equal; the assumption that, while the effects of a change in one variable are being investigated, all other variables are kept constant.

disposable income the amount of money you have left to spend after you have paid your taxes, bills etc.

empirical based on scientific testing or practical experience, not on ideas.

good a thing that is produced in order to be sold.

hypothesis (plural: hypotheses) an idea that is suggested as an explanation for something, but that has not yet been proved to be true.

inequality an unfair situation, in which some groups in society have more money, opportunities, or power than others.

law a theory or model that has been verified by empirical evidence.

normative economics the study and presentation of policy prescriptions involving value judgements about the way in which scarce resources are allocated.

normative statements statements that cannot be supported or refuted because it is a value judgement.

positive economics the scientific or objective study of the allocation of resources.

positive statements statements that can be supported or refuted by evidence.

production possibility frontier shows how much an economy can produce given existing resources.

scientific method a method that subjects theories or hypotheses to being disproved by empirical evidence.

social science the study of societies and human behaviour using a variety of methods, including the scientific method.

theory or model a hypothesis that is capable of being refuted by empirical evidence.

EXAM PRACTICE

EDUCATION IN INDIA

SKILLS ▶ REASONING, INTERPRETATION

India has ambitions to reach the same level of educational standards as developed nations. However, according to a recent research paper by the Associated Chambers of Commerce and Industry of India, it could take at least six generations, or 126 years, if the country continues with its present level of spending.

The paper said that India's current spending of 3.83 per cent of its gross domestic product (GDP) on education was not sufficient to catch up, 'It will take six generations or 126 years to catch up with developed countries if we do not change our education system dramatically'.

By comparison, the USA spends 5.22 per cent of its GDP on education, Germany 4.95 per cent and the UK 5.72 per cent. The United Nations wants countries to spend at least 6 per cent of their GDP on education.

If India increases its spending on education, it could become a major supplier of skilled and qualified workers to the rest of the world, given the population advantage that it has. With over 315 million students, it has the largest number of pupils in the world.

The paper also noted that the educational sector in India faced major challenges, including a lack of teachers. At present, the shortage of teachers has been measured at 1.4 million. There are also concerns that some teachers do not measure up to the standards of the National Council for Teachers' Education (NCTE).

Also, because of an absence of focus on effective skill development, India is one of the least skilled countries. The paper said that only 4.7 per cent of the work force has any formal training, whereas the figure is 80 per cent for Japan, 95 per cent for South Korea, 75 per cent for Germany, 68 per cent for UK and 52 per cent for the USA.

Q

(a) Explain the difference between positive and normative statements. Illustrate your answer with one example of a positive statement from the data and one example of a normative statement.

(4 marks)

(b) Discuss the possible impact on the Indian economy if spending on education were to increase.

(14 marks)

EXAM HINT

Think of the main points about which you could write. These could include an increase in demand for more qualified Indian workers and the impact on their incomes. Indian businesses may become more competitive, more foreign companies may set up in India and this may have a beneficial impact on the Indian economy in terms of GDP and tax revenues.

You may then consider some of the possible drawbacks, such as where the extra money will come from, what other sectors of government spending may have to be cut to provide the funding, how long this will take to have an impact and the question of whether extra spending by itself will be enough to raise standards.

2 THE ECONOMIC PROBLEM

LEARNING OBJECTIVES

- Know that nearly all resources are scarce.
- Understand that human wants are infinite.
- Understand that scarce resources and infinite wants give rise to the basic economic problem – resources have to be allocated between competing uses.
- Know that allocation involves choices and each choice has an opportunity cost.
- Understand that an economy is a social organisation through which decisions about what, how and for whom to produce are made.
- Understand that the factors of production – land, labour capital and enterprise – are combined together to create goods and services for consumption.
- Understand that the rewards to the owners of the factors of production include rents, royalties, wages, interest and profit.

GETTING STARTED

What are you going to do tomorrow? What alternatives do you have? What could you do with your time? If it turns out you cannot do what you have planned, what is the next best alternative?

Just as your time tomorrow is a scarce resource, so is the money you have. How do you plan to spend it? What is the next best alternative purchase?

SCARCITY

It is often said that we live in a global village. The world's resources are finite; there are only limited amounts of land, water, oil, food and other resources on this planet. Economists therefore describe them as **scarce resources**.

Scarcity means that economic agents, such as individuals, firms, governments and international agencies, can only obtain a limited amount of resources at any moment in time. For instance, a family has to live on a fixed budget; it cannot have everything it wants. A firm might want to build a new factory but not have the resources to be able to do so. A government might wish to build new hospitals or devote more resources to its foreign aid programme but not have the finance to make this possible. Resources that are scarce are called **economic goods**.

Not all resources are scarce. There is more than enough air on this planet for everyone to be able to breathe as much as they want. Resources that are not scarce are called **free goods**. In the past, many goods such as food, water and shelter have been free, but as the population of the planet has expanded and as production has increased, so the number of free goods has diminished. Recently, for instance, clean beaches in many parts of the UK have ceased to be a free good to society. Pollution has forced water companies and seaside local authorities to spend resources cleaning up their local environment. With the destruction of the world's rain forests and increasing atmospheric pollution, the air we breathe may no longer remain a free good. Factories may have to purify (clean) the air they take from the atmosphere, for instance. This air would then become an economic good.

INFINITE WANTS

People have a limited number of **needs**, which must be satisfied if they are to survive as humans. Some are material needs, such as food, water, heat, shelter and clothing. Others are psychological and emotional needs, such as self-respect and being loved. People's needs are finite. However, no one would choose to live at the level of basic human needs if they could enjoy a higher standard of living.

This is because human **wants** are unlimited. It does not matter whether the person is a doctor in Africa, a manager in India, a farmer in the UK or the richest individual in the world, there is always something that person wants more of. This can include more food, a bigger house, a longer holiday, a cleaner environment, more friendship, better relationships, more self-respect, greater fairness or justice, peace, or more time to listen to music or cultivate the arts.

ACTIVITY 1

SKILLS | INTERPRETATION, REASONING, CRITICAL THINKING

CASE STUDY: SUNDAY SPIN

There was a time when people used to take their car out for a Sunday afternoon 'spin'. The newness of owning a car and the freedom of the road made driving a pleasant leisure activity. Today, with 35.8 million vehicles registered in the UK, a Sunday afternoon tour could easily turn into a nightmare traffic jam.

Of course, many journeys are trouble free. Traffic is so light that cars do not slow each other down. But most rush hour journeys today occur along congested (very busy) roads where each extra car on the road adds to the journey time of every other car. When London introduced a £5 a day 'congestion charge', a fee for cars to use roads in central London, the amount of traffic dropped by 17 per cent. This was enough to reduce journey times considerably.

Traffic congestion also greatly increases the amount of pollution created by cars. Our ecosystem can cope with low levels of emissions, but, as cities such as Paris and Beijing have discovered, high levels of traffic combined with the wrong weather conditions can lead to sharp increases in pollution levels. The car pollutes the environment anyway because cars produce polluting gases. Just over 20 per cent of global CO_2 emissions come from road transport.

Source: adapted from www.gov.uk.

(a) Explain whether roads are, in any sense, a 'free good' from an economic viewpoint.

ACTIVITY 2   **SKILLS**   PROBLEM-SOLVING, REASONING

CASE STUDY: DIFFERING HUMAN NEEDS

Draw up a list of minimum human needs for a teenager living in the USA today. How might this list differ from the needs of a teenager living in Ethiopia?

THE BASIC ECONOMIC PROBLEM

Resources are scarce but wants are infinite. It is this that leads to the **basic economic problem** and forces economic agents to make choices. They have to allocate their scarce resources between competing uses.

Economics is the study of this allocation of resources – the choices that are made by economic agents. Every **choice** involves a range of alternatives. For instance, should the government spend US$10 billion in tax revenues on defence, better schools or greater care for the elderly? Will you choose to become an accountant, an engineer or a teacher?

These choices can be graded in terms of the benefits to be gained from each alternative. One choice will be the 'best' one and a rational economic agent will take that alternative. But all the other choices will then have to be given up. The benefit lost from the next best alternative is called the **opportunity cost** of the choice. For instance, economics may have been your third choice at A level. Your fourth choice, one that you did not take up, might have been history. Then the opportunity cost of studying economics at A level is studying history at A level.

For consumers, opportunity cost is what has to be given up when spending on an item. For instance, the opportunity cost of a chocolate bar might be two packets of crisps. For producers, the opportunity cost of buying a machine might be the wages of four workers for three years. For government, the opportunity cost of a fighter plane might be building two new primary schools.

Free goods have no opportunity cost. No resources need be sacrificed when someone, say, breathes air or swims in the sea.

ACTIVITY 3   **SKILLS**   PROBLEM-SOLVING, ANALYSIS

CASE STUDY: COST OF EDUCATION

A recent report from HSBC, the banking corporation, shows that the cost to parents of educating a child from primary school through to the end of university ranges from US$8000 to nearly US$200,000 depending on where they live and how the state system subsidises education.

At the top of the list are the UAE and Singapore where parents can pay US$200,000. The global average is US$44,221, with early school costing US$12,820, secondary school US$15,111 and university or college US$16,290.

HSBC's data is based on how much parents report contributing towards tuition, books, transport and accommodation – including state or other subsidies.

(a) What might be the opportunity cost to parents of the global average of US$44,221?

(b) In non-financial terms, what is the opportunity cost to a student of going to a university or college?

WHAT IS AN ECONOMY?

Economic resources are scarce but human wants are infinite. An economy is a system that attempts to solve this basic economic problem. There are many different levels and types of economy. There is the household economy, the local economy, the national economy and the international economy. There are free market economies that attempt to solve the economic problem with the minimum intervention of government and command economies where the state makes most resource allocation decisions. Although these economies are different, they all face the same problem.

Economists distinguish three parts to the economic problem.

- **What** is to be produced? An economy can choose the mix of goods to produce. For instance, what proportion of total output should be spent on defence? What proportion should be spent on protecting the environment? What proportion should be invested for the future? What proportion should be manufactured goods and what proportion services?
- **How** is production to be organised? For instance, are smartphones to be made in the UK, Japan or China? Should car bodies be made out of steel or fibreglass? Would it be better to use machines on a production line or carry on using unskilled workers?
- **For whom** is production to take place? What proportion of output should go to workers? How much should pensioners get? What should be the balance between incomes in the UK and those in Bangladesh?

An economic system needs to provide answers to all these questions.

ECONOMIC RESOURCES

Economists commonly distinguish four types of resources available for use in the production process. They call these resources the **factors of production**.

Land is not only land itself but all natural resources below the earth, on the ground, in the atmosphere and in the sea. Everything from gold deposits to rainwater and natural forests are examples of land. **Non-renewable resources**, such as coal, oil, gold and copper, are land resources that once used will never be replaced. If we use them today, they are not available for use by our children or our children's children. **Renewable resources**, in contrast, can be used and replaced. Examples are fish stocks, forests or water. A forest is a renewable resource. However, it is only a renewable resource if it survives over time despite

economic activities, such as cutting wood or farming. It ceases to be a renewable resource if it is cleared to make way for a motorway. **Non-renewable resources** are resources that are diminishing over time due to economic exploitation. Oil is a non-renewable resource because it cannot be replaced.

Labour is the workforce of an economy – everybody from housepersons to doctors, teachers and politicians. Not all workers are the same. Each worker has a unique set of personal characteristics including intelligence, physical capability and emotional stability. But workers are also the products of education and training. The value of a worker is called their **human capital**. Education and training will increase the value of that human capital, enabling the worker to be more productive.

Capital is the manufactured stock of tools, machines, factories, offices, roads and other resources that are used in the production of goods and services.

ACTIVITY 4 — SKILLS ▶ PROBLEM-SOLVING, ANALYSIS

CASE STUDY: HOUSEHOLD ECONOMY

Consider your household economy.

(a) What is produced by your household (e.g. cooking services, cleaning services, accommodation, products outside the home)?

(b) How is production organised (e.g. who does the cooking, what equipment is used, when is the cooking done)?

(c) For whom does production take place (e.g. for mother, for father)?

(d) Do you think your household economy should be organised in a different way? Justify your answer.

Capital is of two types. **Working or circulating capital** is stocks of raw materials, semi-manufactured goods and finished goods that are waiting to be sold. These stocks circulate, or move, through the production process until they are finally sold to a consumer. **Fixed capital** is the stock of factories, offices, plant and machinery. Fixed capital is fixed in the sense that it will not be transformed into a final product as working capital will. It is used to transform working capital into finished products.

Enterprise or entrepreneurship is the fourth factor of production. It is the seeking out of profitable opportunities for production and taking risks in attempting to exploit these.

Entrepreneurs are individuals who:

- organise production – organise land, labour and capital in the production of goods and services
- take risks – with their own money and the financial capital of others; they buy factors of production to produce goods and services in the hope that they will be able to make a profit but in the knowledge that at worst they could lose all their money and go bankrupt.

Entrepreneurs are typically the owners of small- and medium-sized businesses who run those businesses on a day-to-day basis. However, managers in companies can also be entrepreneurial, if they both organise resources and take risks on behalf of their company.

THE REWARDS TO THE FACTORS OF PRODUCTION

Owners of the factors of production receive payments when they allow other economic agents to use them for a period of time. Owners of land may receive rent or lease payments. If 'land' is a resource like oil, copper or gold, owners may receive a royalty: a share of the money raised in sales of the resource.

In a modern economy, individuals may offer themselves for hire as workers. The reward to labour is the wage or earnings they receive.

Owners of capital, such as machinery, factories or hospitals, can earn a variety of types of income from renting or leasing these physical assets. They might receive rent or lease income. They might also receive a share of any profits made from their use.

Entrepreneurs earn profit from their activities, risking their financial capital and organising the factors of production to produce goods and services.

THINKING LIKE AN ECONOMIST

After A levels, students will have to decide whether to stay on in education, typically by doing a three-year university degree, or whether to try to find a job.

The opportunity costs of going to university are the lost benefits from the next best alternative. Getting a job at age 18 is not guaranteed, but if students can get a job they will be able to earn a wage and enjoy the spending power that goes with it. They are likely, in those three years, to have more money than their friends who have gone to university.

University students will miss out on three years of income, which they could have been earning, and will often build up a student debt to pay for tuition fees and their living expenses during this period. A study by the OECD, using data from the academic year 2008/09, highlighted the considerable differences in tuition fees charged to students across 25 countries in the world. The four countries with the highest average tuition fees were the USA, Korea, the UK and Japan. Some of the cheapest tuition fees included Sweden, Norway, the Czech Republic and Ireland. However, there are often well-developed student support schemes in the countries who charge the most, so students have access to grants and/or student loan schemes. In the UK, student loans are only paid back once earnings are above £21,000 per year.

However, data suggests that even with these debts, students on average will have more money over their lifetime. This is true even after any student debt has been taken from total earnings and the three years of potential earnings has been discounted. A report based on US data from the College Board, 'Education Pays 2013: The Benefits of Higher Education for Individuals and Society', states that in 2011 median earnings of individuals with an undergraduate degree were on average US$21,100 higher than those who did not continue their education after age 18. Graduates are also more likely to be employed, have better health and enjoy the experience. The opportunity costs of going to university – the lost benefits – are often lower than the lifetime rewards of being a graduate, even with rising tuition fees.

CHECKPOINT

1 What is scarcity in the economic sense?
2 What is a free good?
3 What is the difference between needs and wants?
4 What is meant by opportunity cost?
5 Give an example of opportunity cost from your own knowledge for (a) consumers, (b) firms and (c) governments.
6 What are the three questions that face every economy?
7 What is the difference between renewable and non-renewable resources?
8 What are the four factors of production?
9 What is the difference between working and fixed capital?

SUBJECT VOCABULARY

basic economic problem resources have to be allocated between competing uses because wants are infinite but resources are scarce.

capital as a factor of production is the stock of manufactured resources used in the production of goods and services.

choice economic choices involve the alternative uses of scarce resources.

economic goods goods that are scarce because their use has an opportunity cost.

enterprise or entrepreneurship as a factor of production is the seeking out of profitable opportunities for production and taking risks in attempting to exploit these.

entrepreneurs individuals who seek out profitable opportunities for production and take risks in attempting to exploit these.

factors of production the inputs to the production process: land, labour, capital and enterprise or entrepreneurship.

fixed capital economic resources, such as factories and hospitals, that are used to transform working capital into goods and services.

free goods goods that are unlimited in supply and therefore have no opportunity cost.

human capital the value of the productive potential of an individual or group or workers; it is made up of the skills, talents, education and training of an individual or group and represents the value of future earnings and production.

labour as a factor of production is the workforce.

land as a factor of production is all natural resources.

needs the minimum that is necessary for a person to survive as a human being.

non-renewable resources resources, such as coal or oil, which once exploited cannot be replaced.

non-sustainable resource a resource which that can be economically exploited in such as a way that its stock is being reduced over time.

opportunity cost the benefits of the next best alternative that are given up.

renewable resources resources, such as fish stocks or forests, that can be exploited over and over again because they have the potential to renew themselves.

scarce resources resources that are limited in supply so that choices have to be made about their use.

wants desires for the consumption of goods and services.

working or circulating capital resources that are in the production system waiting to be transformed into goods or other materials before being finally sold to the consumer.

EXAM PRACTICE

GOVERNMENTS FACING TOUGH CHOICES ACROSS THE WORLD

SKILLS REASONING, INTERPRETATION, ANALYSIS

THE NHS FACING TOUGH CHOICES

The National Health Service in the UK is one of the best in the world on international ratings. It is funded by the government through taxation.

However, this does not mean that tough choices do not have to be made. Politicians and health managers need to be more honest with the public, according to Sir Andrew Dillon, the head of NICE (National Institute for Health and Care Excellence). It is the responsibility of NICE to decide which drugs are value for money and can be offered by the NHS and which drugs will not be available to NHS patients.

In 2014, NICE ruled that two cancer drugs that extend lives – Zytiga R for prostate cancer and Kadcyla R for breast cancer – were not cost effective for the NHS, and were therefore rejected by the agency. Roche, the Swiss pharmaceuticals company, said the refusal to back its Kadcyla drug showed the UK's drug evaluation system was 'no longer fit for purpose' (working properly).

Sir Andrew Dillon said: 'The NHS has to exercise choices, sometimes to ensure its resources are allocated as fairly as possible.' Choosing to expand treatment in one area means that 'something else cannot be done'.

TRUMP: THE NEW PRESIDENT OF THE USA

In February 2017, President Donald Trump set out plans to increase spending on defence. The proposed budget for 2018 would see defence spending increase by US$54 billion, but this would be at the expense of other departments; particularly foreign aid and environmental. There are many critics of these proposals, but President Trump does not view environmental departments, such as climate change, as a priority for government spending. However, his critics would argue that this will lead to US firms using too much of the world's energy resources today, and negatively affecting future generations. They believe the environmental budget should be protected.

EXAM HINT

Make sure you clearly define the terms and make sure you find examples from the passage to explain each concept.

Q

1 The basic economic problem is:

  (a) What is to be produced, how it is to be produced and when it is to be produced.

  (b) How much is to be produced, what is to be produced and when it is to be produced.

  (c) How much is to be produced, how it is to be produced and for whom it is to be produced.

  (d) What is to be produced, how it is to be produced and for whom it is to be produced. **(1 mark)**

2 Define the term opportunity cost. **(2 marks)**

3 Explain why both the UK and US governments have to make choices. **(4 marks)**

4 Explain how the passage demonstrates the following concepts:

  (a) scarcity **(4 marks)**

  (b) choice **(4 marks)**

  (c) opportunity cost **(4 marks)**

  (d) positive and normative economics. **(4 marks)**

3 PRODUCTION POSSIBILITY FRONTIERS

LEARNING OBJECTIVES

■ Understand that the production possibility frontier (PPF) shows the maximum potential output of an economy.
■ Understand that growth in the economy will shift the PPF outwards, while a shift inwards of the PPF shows that the productive potential of an economy has declined.
■ Understand that consuming more in the present at the expense of producing capital goods can lead to lower growth of the potential output of an economy in the future.
■ Understand that production at a point inside the PPF indicates an underuse or an inefficient use of resources.
■ Understand that the PPF shows only what could be produced but not what should be produced.

GETTING STARTED

Your economics A level group decided to raise money for charity. It took each person a day to take part and you raised £500. You can give the money to two charities. Which two charities would you choose? How much would you give to each? If you give £100 more to one charity, how much less to do you give to the other? What would have been the likely outcome if half the group had given excuses and not taken part in the fund-raising activity? Answers to these questions illustrate opportunity cost, choice and production possibility frontiers.

THE PROBLEM OF SCARCITY

Over a period of time, resources are scarce and therefore only a finite amount can be produced. For example, an economy might have enough resources at its disposal to be able to produce 30 units of manufactured goods and 30 units of non-manufactured goods. If it were now to produce more manufactured goods, it would have to give up some of its production of non-manufactured items. This is because the production of a manufactured item has an opportunity cost – in this case the production of

non-manufactured items. The more manufactured goods that are produced, the less non-manufactured goods can be produced.

The different combinations are shown in Figure 1. The curved line is called the **production possibility frontier (PPF)** – other names for it include production possibility curve or boundary, and transformation curve. The PPF shows the different combinations of economic goods that an economy is able to produce if all resources in the economy are fully and efficiently employed. The economy therefore could be:
● at point C on its PPF, producing 30 units of manufactured goods and 30 units of non-manufactured goods
● at point D, producing 35 units of manufactured goods and 20 units of non-manufactured goods
● at point A, devoting all of its resources to the production of non-manufactured goods
● at points B or E, or anywhere else along the line.

FIGURE 1

The production possibility frontier
ABCDE is a PPF. It shows the different combinations of goods that can be produced if all resources are fully and efficiently utilised. The economy can produce at any point on the line. It cannot produce at G because the PPF shows the maximum that can be produced. It can produce within the PPF, such as at F, but less will be produced than the maximum possible.

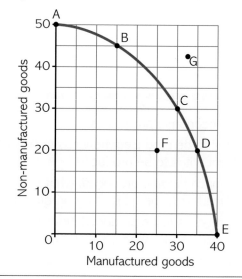

OPPORTUNITY COST

The production possibility frontier clearly illustrates the principle of opportunity cost. Assume that the economy is producing at point C in Figure 1 and that the aim is to move to point D. This means that the output of manufactured goods will increase from 30 to 35 units. However, the opportunity cost of that (i.e. what has to be given up because of that choice) is the lost output of non-manufactured goods, falling from 30 to 20 units. The opportunity cost at C of increasing manufacturing production by five units is 10 units of non-manufactured goods.

Another way of expressing this is to use the concept of the **margin**. In economics, the margin is a point of possible change. At point C in Figure 1, the economy could produce more manufactured goods, but at the cost of giving up non-manufactured goods. For example, the marginal cost of five more units of manufactured goods would be 10 fewer units of non-manufactured goods. This is shown by the movement from C to D along the boundary.

ACTIVITY 1

 SKILLS ▶ PROBLEM-SOLVING, REASONING

CASE STUDY: THE PRODUCTION POSSIBILITY FRONTIER

The production possibility frontier of an economy is as shown in Figure 1.
(a) (i) If the economy produces 15 units of manufactured goods, what is the maximum number of non-manufactured goods it can produce? (ii) How many manufactured goods could it produce if production of non-manufactured goods was 50 units?
(b) The economy is currently operating at point C. What is the opportunity cost of increasing production of non-manufactured goods by (i) 15 units; (ii) 20 units?
(c) The economy is at D. What is the marginal cost of increasing production of non-manufactured goods to point (i) C; (ii) B?

ECONOMIC GROWTH OR DECLINE

The economy cannot produce at any point outside its existing PPF. This is because the PPF shows the maximum potential output of an economy. In Figure 1, for example, the economy cannot produce at point G. However, the economy might be able to move to the right of its PPF in the future if there is economic growth. An increase in the productive potential of an economy is shown by a shift outwards of the PPF. In Figure 2 economic growth pushes the PPF from LL to MM, allowing the economy to increase its maximum level of production, say, from A to B.

FIGURE 2

Economic growth

An increase in the quantity or quality of the inputs to the production process means that an economy has increased its productive potential. This is shown by a shift to the right of the production possibility frontier from LL to MM. It would enable the economy to move production, for instance, from point A to point B.

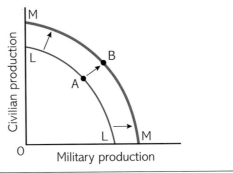

Growth in the economy can happen if:
- the quantity of resources available for production increases; for instance there might be an increase in the number of workers in the economy, or new factories and offices might be built
- there is an increase in the quality of resources; education will make workers more productive and technical progress will allow machines and production processes to produce more with the same amount of resources.

The PPF can shift inwards as well as outwards. The productive potential of an economy can fall. For example, war can destroy economic infrastructure. A rapid fall in the number of workers in a population can reduce potential output. Some environmentalists predict that global warming will damage world agriculture and this will then affect all production. Global warming could therefore lead to a shift inwards of the world's PPF.

Many economies experience high levels of unemployment of workers. Factories and machines may not be used when this occurs. Production then occurs *within* the boundary and not *on* the boundary such as at point F in Figure 1. If resources became fully used, the economy could move from inside the boundary to a point on the boundary. In Figure 1, this would mean a move from point F to, say, D or E.

CONSUMPTION VERSUS INVESTMENT

There is a potential conflict between consuming now and economic growth caused by investment. If an economy produces an extra £10 billion worth of restaurant meals for consumers, then they are better off today. If, however, that £10 billion had been spent on new factories, offices or new machinery, the productive potential of the economy is likely to increase. As a result, consumers may then be better off in the future.

This conflict can be shown in Figure 3. **Consumer goods**, such as food, holidays or DVDs, are shown on the vertical axis. **Capital goods**, such as factories, offices, roads, machines and equipment, are shown on the horizontal axis. Two economies, A and B, at the start are the same size in terms of overall production and population. However, country A produces more consumer goods and fewer capital goods than country B. So initially, country A produces at point C while country B produces at point D.

Over time, both economies grow. However, because country B has invested more, devoting more of its finite resources to capital goods, it grows faster. Ten years later, growth in country A has shifted its PPF to QQ and is producing at point E. However, the PPF of country B has shifted to RR and country B is producing at point F. At the start of the period, consumers in country A were wealthier than in country B because consumption of consumer goods was higher. But at the end, consumers in country B are wealthier. At point F, country B is producing more of both consumer and capital goods than country A, which produces at point E.

FIGURE 3

Consumption versus investment
Country B, which initially devotes more resources to investment (the production of capital goods), has a higher growth rate than country A, which initially produces more consumer goods.

Eventually, country B produces more capital and consumer goods than country A because of higher growth.

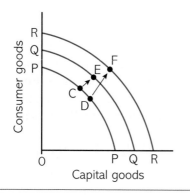

The production possibility frontiers in Figures 1 and 2 have been drawn concave to the origin (curving outwards), rather than as straight lines or convex lines. This is because it has been assumed that not all resources in the economy are as productive in one use compared to another.

EFFICIENCY

The production possibility frontier shows the maximum amount that can be produced from a given number of resources. Therefore, for an economy, the boundary shows the level of output where all resources are fully and efficiently employed. In Figure 1, there is full and efficient use of resources at all points along the boundary AE.

Efficiency on the boundary is of two types. There is productive efficiency, which means that production takes place at the lowest cost. Productive efficiency occurs when a given set of resources produces the maximum number of goods. All points on the boundary are productively efficient because they show a combination of goods produced at the lowest cost for that combination.

However, not all points on the boundary are **allocatively efficient**. Allocative efficiency occurs when social welfare is maximised. Not every combination of goods produced will maximise welfare and there could be just one point which does this.

ACTIVITY 2   **SKILLS**   ANALYSIS, PROBLEM-SOLVING, REASONING

CASE STUDY: DRAWING A PRODUCTION POSSIBILITY FRONTIER

Draw a production possibility frontier. The vertical axis shows the production of public sector goods and the horizontal axis shows production of private sector goods. The economy is currently producing at point A on the frontier where 50 per cent of all production is devoted to public sector goods and 50 per cent to private sector goods.

(a) Mark the following points on your drawing.
(i) Point A.
(ii) Point B, which shows production following the election of a government that increases government spending on both education and healthcare.
(iii) Point C, where unemployment is present in the economy.
(iv) Point D, where the government takes over production of all goods and services in the economy.

(b) Draw another diagram, putting the original production possibility frontier you drew for (a) on it, labelling it AA.

  (i) Draw a new production possibility frontier on the diagram, labelling it PP, which shows the position after a devastating war has hit the economy.

  (ii) Draw another PPF, labelling it QQ, which shows an increase in productivity in the economy such that output from the same amount of resources increases by 50 per cent in the public sector but twice that amount in the private sector.

CHOICE

The PPF by itself gives no indication of which combination of goods will be produced in an economy. All it shows is the combination of goods which an economy could produce if output were maximised from a given fixed amount of resources. It shows a range of possibilities and much of economics is concerned with explaining why an economy, ranging from a household economy to the international economy, chooses to produce at one point either on or within its PPF rather than another.

THINKING LIKE AN ECONOMIST

WATER SHORTAGES

In many circumstances, water is a free good. It falls from the sky or can be collected from rivers with no opportunity cost. However, with the world's population predicted to rise to over 11 billion, water is becoming an ever scarcer resource in many countries.

Scarcity is being felt not just by consumers but also by producers. For example, the world's oil and gas supplies could be transformed by the relatively new process of fracking – forcing liquid through rocks to release oil and a gas called 'shale' trapped in the rocks. But each US well (deep hole containing oil, water or gas) requires on average 2 million gallons (1 gallon = around 4.5 litres) of water to extract all the oil or gas in the well. Many wells are in areas of relative water shortage. Hence, Antero Resources,

a US shale gas company, is planning to spend US$525 million on a pipe to carry water to its operations to increase reliability of supplies.

Countries and industries where water is scarce therefore face a trade-off between investing in water facilities or using the money for other purposes. If there is not enough water, there is an immediate conflict between household consumption for drinking and cleaning, and its use by industry including farming and manufacturing. If industry faces water restrictions, in the short term there will be less production forcing the production possibility frontier inwards. In the long term, if there is too little investment in water infrastructure, production will be lower than if more had been invested today. In other words, the production possibility frontier will be to the left of where it might otherwise have been.

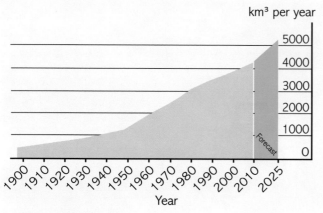

km³ per year

▲ **Figure 4 Global water use**

EXAM PRACTICE

SYRIA [SKILLS] REASONING, ANALYSIS, CRITICAL THINKING

In 2011, Syria descended into civil war. This led some Western governments to impose bans on exports to the country. Not surprisingly, output measured by gross domestic product has fallen quickly. Millions of people have been forced to flee their homes. Most have had to move within Syria, but several million have become refugees in neighbouring countries. Thousands of schools have been destroyed or are being used as shelter for displaced persons. A lack of access to healthcare and scarcity of medicines have led to disastrous health situations in several regions in Syria. In the meantime, spending on military defence has increased dramatically.

CHINA

Since the mid-1970s, many indicators have suggested that China's economy has been growing dramatically.

In 2014, it was growing by nearly 10 per cent per annum. This meant that output would be doubling roughly every seven years. It is not difficult to understand why the Chinese economy has been so successful. By the mid-1970s, it already had a relatively well-educated workforce compared to other poor developing countries. However, some sources suggested its economy was otherwise inefficient and undeveloped. From the mid-1970s, there was a gradual decrease in Communist control of the economy that allowed ordinary Chinese people to set up their own businesses in a more free market style economy. Exports began to be encouraged.

This linked China to the global economy. Finally, there was a considerable flow of investment money and technological knowledge into China. Foreign investors were keen to take advantage of cheap labour and found the promise of what would soon become the world's largest economy hard to resist.

Percentage					
	1971–80	1981–90	1991–2000	2001–11	2012–17
Yearly average growth in output (%)	6.3	9.4	10.5	10.3	6.8

▲ **Table 1 China, average annual growth in output (%), 1971–14**

THE UK

The UK currently has four nuclear-powered submarines (underwater ships), but they are coming to the end of their service life. It is estimated that replacing the four submarines will cost at least £25 billion.

Q

1 Define the term production possibility frontier.
(2 marks)

2 Using examples from the data, explain why a production possibility frontier might:
(a) shift inwards **(4 marks)**
(b) shift outwards. **(4 marks)**

3 A peace group has put forward a proposal that the UK should not replace its fleet of nuclear submarines. Using production possibility frontiers, discuss the possible economic implications of this proposal. **(14 marks)**

EXAM HINT

Identify the alternative ways in which the resources used to build a new fleet of replacement nuclear submarines could be used, including spending on alternative defence goods. Mention opportunity cost and choice. Which would be consumer goods and which would be capital goods? Which might be the best alternative uses and why?

4 SPECIALISATION AND THE DIVISION OF LABOUR

LEARNING OBJECTIVES

- Understand that specialisation and the division of labour give rise to large gains in productivity.
- Understand that the economy can be divided into three sectors: primary, secondary and tertiary. It can also be divided between the state sector and the private sector.
- Know that markets exist for buyers and sellers to exchange goods and services using barter or money.
- Know that money has four functions: as a medium of exchange; a unit of account; a store value; and a standard for deferred payment.
- Understand that near monies, such as time deposits in banks and building societies, are monies that are good units of account and stores of value but cannot be used immediately as a medium of exchange.

GETTING STARTED

Take any piece of clothing that you are wearing right now. Where was it sold? Where was it manufactured? Where did the raw materials for it come from? How many firms do you think might have been involved in getting it to you? Why do you think so many firms were involved in the chain of supply?

SPECIALISATION

Specialisation is the production of a limited range of goods by an individual, firm or country in co-operation with others so that together a complete range of goods is produced.

Specialisation can occur between nations. For instance, a country like Honduras produces bananas and trades those for cars produced in the USA. **Globalisation** is currently increasing this process of specialisation between nations. Specialisation can also occur within economies.

Specialisation by individuals is called the **division of labour**. Adam Smith, in a passage in his famous book *An Enquiry into the Nature and Causes of the Wealth of Nations* (1776), described the division of labour among pin workers. He wrote: '*A workman not educated to this business... could scarce... make one pin in a day, and certainly could not make twenty. But in the way in which this business is now carried on,... it is divided into a number of branches... One man draws out the wire, another straightens it, a third cuts it, a fourth points, a fifth grinds it at the top for receiving the head; to make the head requires two or three distinct operations; to put it on is a peculiar business, to whiten the pins is another; it is even a trade by itself to put them into the paper.*'

He pointed out that one worker might be able to make 20 pins a day if he were to complete all the processes himself. But ten workers together specialising in a variety of tasks could, he estimated, make 48,000 pins.

This enormous increase in **productivity** (output per unit of input employed) arises from both increases in **labour productivity** (output per worker) and **capital productivity** (output per unit of capital employed).

- Specialisation enables workers to gain skills in a narrow range of tasks. These skills enable individual workers to be far more productive than if they were responsible for a range of tasks. In a modern economy a person could not possibly hope to be able to take on every job that society requires.
- The division of labour makes it cost effective to provide workers with specialist tools. For instance, it would not be profitable to provide every farm worker with a vehicle. But it is possible to provide a group of workers with a vehicle that they can then share.
- Time is saved because a worker is not constantly changing tasks, moving around from place to place and using different machinery and equipment.
- Workers can specialise in those tasks to which they are best suited.

The division of labour has its limits. If jobs are divided up too much, the work can become tedious and monotonous. Workers do not feel connected to their work. This will result in poorer quality of work and less output per person. Workers will do everything possible to avoid work – going to the toilet, spending too long over breaks and reporting sick, for instance. The size of the market too will limit the division of labour. A shop owner in a village might want to specialise in selling health foods but finds that in order to survive she has to sell other products as well.

Over-specialisation also has its disadvantages. For example, in Europe, areas such as Wales, the Ruhr, Lorraine and the Basque Country have suffered high levels of unemployment since the 1950s as their traditional heavy industry, such as coal mining and steelmaking, declined and was not replaced by enough new service sector jobs. Another problem with specialisation is that a breakdown in part of the chain of production can cause chaos within the system. The Japanese earthquake of 2016 affected production not just in the local area, but also disrupted overseas production for many manufacturers, including Toyota®, Honda® and Sony®. Similarly, businesses in Mumbai are affected by frequent power cuts.

ACTIVITY 1   SKILLS ▶ INTERPRETATION, REASONING

CASE STUDY: SPECIALISATION

(a) Explain, with the help of the photograph, what is meant by 'specialisation'.

(b) What might be some of the (i) advantages to firms and (ii) disadvantages to workers of the division of labour shown in the photograph?

SECTORS OF THE ECONOMY

Economies are divided into three main sectors. In the **primary sector** of the economy, raw materials are extracted and food is grown. Examples of primary sector industries are agriculture, forest management, fishing, extracting oil and mining. In the **secondary or manufacturing sector**, raw materials are transformed into goods. Examples of secondary sector industries are motor manufacturing, food processing, furniture making and steel production. The **tertiary or service sector**

produces services such as transport, sport and leisure, distribution, financial services, education and health.

Most firms tend to operate in just one of these sectors, specialising in producing raw materials, manufactured goods or services. Some very large firms, such as BP, operate across all three sectors, from the extraction of oil to its refining (purifying) and sale to the public through petrol stations.

Economies can also be split into two sectors: the public sector and the private sector. The **public sector** is the state or government sector of the economy. Production of goods and services is achieved by organisations such as government departments, local authorities or state-owned businesses. The **private sector** is that part of the economy owned by private individuals, companies and charities. For example, in the UK, the public sector organises education for most children. So a state primary school is part of the public sector. However, some parents choose to pay for their children to go to schools that are in the private sector. Most healthcare is provided by the public sector through the National Health Service. However, there is also a smaller private healthcare sector where companies such as Nuffield Health and individual doctors provide patient services.

MARKETS

Markets play a crucial role in almost all economies today. Markets are where buyers and sellers meet. For economists, markets are not just street markets. Buying and selling can take place online, in newspapers and magazines, through mail order or over the telephone in financial deals or on industrial estates as well as in high street shopping centres. A **market** is any convenient set of arrangements by which buyers and sellers communicate to exchange goods and services.

Economists group buyers and sellers together. For instance, there is an international market for oil in which large companies and governments buy and sell oil. There are also national markets for oil. Not every company or government involved in the buying and selling of oil in Brazil, say, will be involved in the US or Malaysian oil markets. There are also regional and local markets for oil. In your area there will be a small number of petrol filling stations (sellers of petrol) where you (the buyers) are able to buy petrol. All these markets are interlinked (connected) but they are also separate. A worldwide increase in the price of oil may or may not result in an increase in the price of petrol at the pumps in your local area. Equally, petrol prices in your area may increase when prices at a national and international level remain constant. Sometimes, economists refer to **sub-markets**. This is a term used to describe a market within a larger market. For example, the market for diesel fuel in Brazil is a sub-market of the market for all oil-based fuels in Brazil. Equally the market for all oil-based fuels in Brazil is a sub-market of the international market for fuels.

How buyers and sellers are grouped together and therefore how markets are defined depends upon what is being studied. We could study the tyre industry or we could consider the market for cars and car components, which includes part but not all of the tyre industry. Alternatively, we might want to analyse the market for rubber, which would require a study of rubber purchased by tyre producers.

Many Western economists argue that specialisation, exchange and the market lie at the heart of today's economic prosperity in the industrial world. Although it is likely that the market system increases prosperity, we shall see that it does not always lead to the most efficient allocation of resources.

ACTIVITY 2 | SKILLS | INTERPRETATION, REASONING

CASE STUDY: COCHEM FOOD MARKET

Type	Number
Small independent food stores	1
Convenience food stores	1
Supermarket food stores	2

▲ **Table 1 Shops selling food items in Cochem**

Cochem is a town in Germany that has shops selling food items such as fresh vegetables, dairy products or canned food.

(a) Who might be the buyers and sellers in the local Cochem market for food products?

(b) What is the relationship between this market and the market for (i) meat and (ii) petrol?

MONEY AND EXCHANGE

Specialisation has enabled people to enjoy a standard of living that would be impossible to achieve through **self-sufficiency**. Specialisation, however, requires exchange. Workers can only specialise in refuse collecting, for instance, if they know that they will be able to exchange their services for other goods and services such as food, housing and transport.

Exchange for most of history has meant barter – swapping one good for another. However, barter has many disadvantages and it would be impossible to run a modern sophisticated economy using barter as a means or medium of exchange. It was

the development of money that enabled trade and specialisation to transform economies into what we know today. Money is anything that is widely accepted as payment for goods received, services performed, or repayment of past debt. In a modern economy, it ranges from notes and coins to money in bank accounts and deposits in building society accounts.

THE FUNCTIONS OF MONEY

Most people in the world today, if asked, 'What is money?', would reply, 'notes and coins'. What is it about notes and coins that make them money, and is there anything else that possesses these same properties? If something is to be money, it must fulfil four functions (i.e. it must do four things).

A medium of exchange This is the most important function of **money**. Money is used to buy and sell goods and services. A worker accepts payment in money because she knows that she will be able to use that money to buy products in the shops.

There is no money in a **barter** economy. Exchange is conducted directly by swapping one good with another. For instance, a farmer might pay 12 eggs for a new water jug or a woman might trade a carpet for a cow. This requires what is called a 'double coincidence of wants'. If the potter did not want eggs, then he might refuse to give the farmer the water jug. Barter requires that each party to the transaction wants what the other has to trade. This is costly and difficult, if not impossible, and therefore trade is discouraged. Without trade there can be no specialisation. Without specialisation, there can be little or no increase in living standards. So barter is associated with types of economy where individuals or small groups are self-sufficient, and the need for trade is small.

Money separates the two sides of a barter transaction. The potter will accept money for the water jug because he knows that he will be able buy the goods that he wants with the money.

A measure of value Money acts as a unit of account. If a dress costs US$30 and a skirt costs US$15, we know that the value of one dress equals the value of two skirts. At times of very high inflation, such as in Germany in 1923 or Zimbabwe in the early 2000s, money ceases to act as a unit of account. Prices may change by the hour. By 2009, inflation in Zimbabwe had reached 70,600 million per cent and the currency collapsed. High inflation therefore destroys the ability of money to perform this function. It is very difficult under a barter system to establish an agreed unit of account as people's opinions of the value of certain items differ greatly.

A store of value A worker who receives wages is unlikely to spend the money immediately. She may delay spending because it is more convenient to spend the money later. She will do this only if what she can buy in the future is approximately equal to what she can buy today. So money links the present and the future. It acts as a store of value. High inflation destroys this link because money in the future is worth far less than money today. In the German **hyperinflation** of 1923, people started to refuse payment in German money because it would lose so much value by the time they had spent it.

A method of deferred payment If people lend money today, they will only do so if they think that they will be able to buy roughly the same amount of goods when it is paid back. In trade, a company that accepts an order at a fixed price today for delivery and payment in a year's time will only do so if it is confident that the money it receives will have a value that can be assessed today. So again money must link different time periods when it comes to borrowed as well as saved money.

When money ceases to have this function, credit and borrowing collapse and this is very damaging to investment and economic growth in an economy.

ACTIVITY 3   SKILLS ▶ REASONING

CASE STUDY: IS IT MONEY?

(a) Explain which of these items might be considered 'money' and which would not.

FORMS OF MONEY IN A MODERN ECONOMY

In a modern economy there are a number of assets that can be classified as money.

Cash Cash means notes and coins. Cash is token (symbolic) money. It has little or no intrinsic (actual) value, unlike gold, which would be classified along with items such as cigarettes as commodity money. It is issued either by government or with the permission of government. Government reinforces the acceptability of cash by making it legal currency. This means that it must be accepted by law as a means of payment.

Cash is not an ideal form of money. In today's world, it is an almost ideal medium of exchange. But inflation affects three of the functions of money – those of a measure of value, a store of value and a method of deferred payment. In Venezuela, for example, on 1 January 2017, US$1 was worth VEF 3164 (bolivars, the Venezuelan currency). Just eight months later, at the start of August, it was worth VEF 10,389, meaning that the bolivar was worth less than one-third of its earlier value.

The higher the rate of inflation, the less it can be said that cash is a 'good' money.

Money in current accounts Banks and building societies offer customers current account facilities. Current accounts have two distinguishing features. First, cash can be withdrawn on demand from the account if it is in credit. So deposits can be immediately converted into money if the account holder, or owner, so wishes. Second, account holders are provided with a debit card and cheque book. Cheques and debit cards can be used to purchase goods and services. Cheque book money therefore is a medium of exchange. It is not perfect because people and firms can refuse to accept cheques and debit cards in a transaction. Moreover, little or no interest is offered on accounts and so current account deposits lose value over time with inflation, damaging their store of value function. But deposits in current accounts are nearly as good a form of money as cash.

Near monies Near monies are assets that fulfil some but not all of the functions of money. In particular, they act as measures of value and stores of value but cannot be used as mediums of exchange. However, they are convertible (changeable) into a medium of exchange quickly and at little cost. The ease with which an asset can be converted into money without loss of value is called **liquidity**. The more liquid an asset, the more easily it is changeable into money. The most obvious type of near monies is time deposits with savings banks. They pay higher rates of interest than current accounts. They are therefore used more for saving and less for making transactions than current accounts. Depositors need to give notice if they wish to withdraw from the account (hence the term 'time' deposit). Alternatively, many accounts offer instant access if an interest rate penalty is paid (i.e. the saver loses money for the privilege of instant withdrawal).

Non-money financial assets All financial assets can be converted into money. However, for most assets the potential penalties for doing this are great. There can be a long waiting time for withdrawal and there can be considerable loss of money from converting it. This damages their functions as measures of value and stores of value. Economists do not classify these assets as money. Shares, for instance, are easily sold, but it can take up to a month to receive the money from the sale. Shares can also change value rapidly and are therefore not a good store of value (when share prices fall) or a method of deferred payment (when share prices rise).

Money substitutes Money is not the only means of payment for goods and services. Charge cards and credit cards have become increasingly important over the past 40 years as a medium of exchange. But they are not stores of value. This is because possession of a card does not show that the person who owns the card has money in the card account. The card only represents an ability to borrow money instantly. So credit cards, for example, are not money but they are **money substitutes** (i.e. they are used instead of money).

ACTIVITY 4   SKILLS   PROBLEM-SOLVING

CASE STUDY: HOW MUCH MONEY?

Sayed Yazdani has EGP250 (Egyptian pounds) in a savings account. He owns a EGP270,000 apartment in Cairo but owes EGP150,000 in the form of a mortgage loan. His current account at his bank is in credit by EGP1500 and he has an overdraft facility of EGP1000. In his wallet he has EGP100 in cash. He has recently purchased EGP100 worth of goods using his credit card. His credit card limit is EGP3000.

(a) Explain how much money Sayed Yazdani has.

FINANCIAL MARKETS

A **financial market** is any convenient set of arrangements where buyers and sellers can buy or trade a range of services or assets that are monetary in nature. Financial markets are different from product markets or factor markets. Product markets exist for the buying and selling of physical goods and services. Factor markets exist for the buying and selling of land, labour and capital.

Financial markets exist for two reasons. One is to provide services demanded by households, firms and government. For example, households want to be able to spend money using a credit card. Firms want to be able to pay their suppliers. Governments want to be able to borrow money.

However, financial markets also exist because they allow participants to speculate and realise financial gains. Foreign exchange traders speculating on which way a currency might move in the next few seconds are not providing a service to a customer. They are hoping to make a profit. The combination of speculation and delivery of genuine services means that financial markets are prone to regular crises that cause significant damage to the real economy.

THE ROLE OF FINANCIAL MARKETS

Financial markets have a number of important roles to play in an economy. These include the following.

TO FACILITATE SAVING

Financial assets, such as money or stocks and shares, are a way of transferring spending power from the present into the future. For example, a worker is paid in July but wants to put aside some money to pay for a holiday in October. Another worker is 25 and wants to save some money for when he is retired. A household, currently renting property, wants to save $1000 a month for three years to put as a deposit on house. A firm has earned $6 million in profit. It wants to put that money aside in case trading falls and it has unexpected bills in the future. Facilitating saving is a key role of financial markets.

TO MAKE FUNDS AVAILABLE TO BUSINESSES AND INDIVIDUALS

Households, firms and governments all borrow money. For example, a household might borrow money on a credit card to finance the purchase of a new television. A firm might borrow money to buy equipment. A bank might borrow to lend more profitably to another financial institution. Or it may borrow to speculate on foreign currency. A government might borrow money to finance government spending which is not paid for by its receipts including taxes.

TO FACILITATE THE EXCHANGE OF GOODS AND SERVICES

Financial institutions play a vital role in creating payment systems for goods and services. Central banks, for example, mint coins and print paper money. **Retail banks** offer services such as debit cards and credit cards. More hidden from view are institutions which process trillions of cheque transactions per year. Visa, Amex and Mastercard are companies which offer credit card services to banks, retailers and individuals. Banks and bureau de changes buy and sell foreign currencies, exchanging notes, for example, or transferring money from one account into another bank account in a different country and a different currency. Firms might use a factor. This is a company which offers a variety of services, the most important being paying now for goods and services which have been delivered to another company and where the payment is only due in the future.

TO PROVIDE FORWARD MARKETS IN COMMODITIES AND CURRENCIES

Firms sometimes want to buy or sell forward. For example, farmers may want to sell the crop they are sowing at a guaranteed price. So they agree to sell 100 tonnes of a crop at $800 a tonne for delivery in six months' time. Food producers may want to even out price fluctuations by buying forward. A chocolate manufacturer, for example, may agree to buy 1000 tonnes of cocoa beans at $3000 per tonne for delivery in nine months' time. Forward markets exist in food commodities such as wheat, cocoa and soya beans. They also exist in other commodity markets such as copper or nickel. Foreign exchange such as dollars or euros can be bought and sold forward too.

TO PROVIDE A MARKET FOR EQUITIES

Equities are the shares of companies (in the USA, shares are called 'stocks' - hence the name stock exchange). Issuing shares, or **equity** finance, can be an important way in which companies, particularly those that are growing in size, can finance their expansion. Those buying new shares will get a share of profits made by the company. However, few would buy new shares if they could never sell them again. Locking up money forever in shares would be a very large risk for a saver. Not being able to sell means that the shares would be completely **illiquid**. Stock markets provide a way in which owners of shares can sell them to others. They create liquidity in the market. The greater the number of shares issued, and the more buyers and sellers in the market, the greater the liquidity. Having markets for second-hand shares therefore encourages buyers to purchase new shares when they become available.

THINKING LIKE AN ECONOMIST

SLAVE LABOUR AND THE SUPPLY CHAIN

Specialisation can have a dark side. According to the International Labour Organisation, about 21 million men, women and children are in slavery, including forced child labour. You might have bought something that was in part produced by what some people call 'slave labour'.

Few sellers will admit that their products have a slave labour component. However, according to a 2014 survey in the UK by the Chartered Institute of Purchasing and Supply, nearly three-quarters of managers responsible for buying products for their businesses admitted that they had 'zero visibility' (i.e. they did not know what was happening) on the early parts of their supply chain. The problem arises because of specialisation. Many goods and services sold in developed economies have very long supply chains. There may be hundreds of businesses involved in the production of a single item. A mobile phone seller, for example, might have a component of the phone made in China or India. That relatively unimportant component may have been made using slave labour in a manufacturing plant. Slave labour might have also been used in small-scale mining of the metal used in the component. Even in transport, there might be a trace of slave labour in the supply chain of the transport company. So at every stage, in primary, secondary and tertiary industries there is a risk.

Large companies selling directly to consumers are particularly vulnerable to bad publicity about slave labour. They are often the companies that attempt to investigate their supply chain and inspect production facilities across the world. But with so many separate businesses involved, it is usually impossible for them to guarantee that no slave labour has been used. Specialisation allows slavery to be a hidden problem to the consumer at the end of the production chain.

CHECKPOINT

1 What is specialisation?
2 Give two examples of specialisation from your own knowledge.
3 What is the difference between labour and capital productivity?
4 State two advantages and two disadvantages of the division of labour.

5 Give your own examples of industries in the primary, secondary ad tertiary sectors.
6 What is the difference between the private and public sectors?
7 What is the main disadvantage of a barter system?
8 What are the four functions of money?
9 What does liquidity mean in the economic sense?
10 Identify the five roles of financial markets.

SUBJECT VOCABULARY

barter swapping one good for another without the use of money.
capital productivity output per unit of capital employed.
division of labour specialisation by workers, who perform different tasks at different stages of production to make a good or service, in co-operation with other workers.
equity in a company, is the value of the assets owned by the shareholders.
financial market any convenient set of arrangements where buyers and sellers can buy or trade a range of services or assets that are fundamentally monetary in nature.
globalisation the tendency for the world economy to work as one unit, led by large international companies doing business all over the world.
hyperinflation a very fast rise in prices that seriously damages a country's economy.
illiquid difficult to convert an asset into cash. Completely illiquid means it is impossible to do so.
labour productivity output per worker.
liquidity the ability to change an asset into cash. The more liquid an asset is, the easier it is to do this.
market any convenient set of arrangements by which buyers and sellers communicate to exchange goods and services.
money any item, such as a coin or a bank balance, which fulfils four functions: a medium of exchange, a measure of value, a store of value and a method of deferred payment.

money substitutes anything that can be used as a medium of exchange but are not stores of value. Examples are charge cards or credit cards.
primary sector industries involving extraction and agriculture.
private sector the part of the economy owned by individuals, companies and charities.
productivity output per unit of input employed.
public sector the part of the economy where production is organised by the state or the government.
retail banks banks that provide services to individuals.
secondary or manufacturing sector industries involved in the production of goods, mainly manufactured goods.
self-sufficiency being able to provide all the things you need without help from other people.
specialisation a system of organisation where economic units such as households or nations are not self-sufficient but concentrate on producing certain goods and services and trading the surplus with others.
sub-market a market that is a distinct and identifiable part of a larger market.
tertiary or service sector industries involved in the production of services.

EXAM PRACTICE

THE iPHONE® SKILLS ▶ ANALYSIS, REASONING, CRITICAL THINKING

Apple®'s iPhone® is a truly international product. Although designed and developed at Apple's headquarters in the USA, production uses raw materials and components from all over the world. Each phone contains about 16 g of copper, much of which comes from Chile. Cobalt (a metal) is used in the batteries. Over half the world's supply comes from the Democratic Republic of Congo, and China produces most of the rare, earth elements that are crucial to high-tech products.

Companies from 34 countries manufacture the different parts that go into just one handset. For example, LG® from South Korea make the display

panels and Sony®, from Japan, make the cameras. Most iPhones are assembled (put together) in Foxconn's enormous factories in China before being shipped to the USA and then on to distribution centres and shops all over the world. In July 2016, Apple claimed to have sold its billionth iPhone.

Q

1 Explain why producing an iPhone involves the primary, secondary and tertiary sector. **(4 marks)**
2 Examine the benefits to Apple of using specialisation in producing iPhones. **(8 marks)**

5 TYPES OF ECONOMY

UNIT 1
1.3.1

LEARNING OBJECTIVES

- Understand that the function of an economic system is to resolve the basic economic problem.
- Understand that markets allocate resources determining what is to be produced, how it is to be produced and for whom production is to take place.
- Understand that resources can be allocated by planning rather than markets, as for example happens within firms and by governments.
- Know that free market economies, mixed economies and planned economies are three different types of economic system.
- Know that there are various ways in which economic systems can be evaluated including choice, quality and innovation, efficiency, economic growth, income distribution and risk.

GETTING STARTED

To what extent is your household a planned economy? Is all the spending controlled by one person or perhaps two people? Does anyone in the family get paid for doing jobs for the family like washing up, tidying their rooms or gardening? Would it be better if anyone who did a job within the house got paid? Would it be better if you had to pay rent for your room and money for the food you ate?

ECONOMIC SYSTEMS

The function of an economy is to resolve the basic economic problem – resources are scarce, but wants are infinite. Resources therefore need to be allocated. This allocation has three dimensions.

What is to be produced? Should it be pizzas, tanks or holidays, for example?

How is it to be produced? For example, is it going to be produced in Shenzen, China, or in Nairobi, Kenya? Is it going to be made using the latest technology or by hand? Is production going to be automated or is it going to be labour intensive?

For whom it is to be produced? Should products be equally distributed among the population? Should a small number of people be able to have 100 times the amount that the majority have? Should people living in developed economies enjoy 200 times the number of products available to people in an emerging economy?

An **economic system** is a complex network of individuals, organisations and institutions that allocates resources. This is done within social systems, such as the family or the local neighbourhood, and legal systems, such as the EU legal system.

Within an economic system, there are various 'actors'.

Individuals They are consumers and workers. They may own factors of production, which they supply for production purposes.

Groups Firms, political parties, families and charities are just some of the groups that might exist in an economic system.

Government Government might range from a local council, to a local police authority, to a national parliament or **supranational** organisation like the European Commission. One key role of government is to exercise power. It establishes or influences the relationships between individuals and groups, for instance, through the passing of laws or implementing those laws.

THE ALLOCATION OF RESOURCES

In rich industrialised economies, over the past 100 years, there have been two main ways in which resources have been allocated.

The market mechanism The market mechanism allocates resources through bringing together buyers and sellers who agree on a price for the product or resource being sold. In the market for chocolate bars, for example, chocolate manufacturers sell their products via shops and supermarkets to buyers like you. In the market for teachers, schools hire (i.e. buy the services of) teachers and teachers sell their labour. In the market for copper, copper mining companies sell to buyers, which include manufacturing companies.

Planning Planning allocates resources through administrative decisions. Planning occurs within families when individuals make decisions about who in the family is to get what. For example, adults will make decisions about children's birthday presents or how much the household spends on heating. Firms are also planned economies where managers decide how to allocate resources. At a national level, governments and government bodies allocate resources through planning. For example, in a budget, the finance minister will announce plans for how the government will spend money.

ACTIVITY 1   SKILLS ▶ COMMUNICATION, REASONING

CASE STUDY: BLACK FRIDAY

Black Friday is an American import. In America, on the last Friday of November, shops offer large discounts to encourage customers to spend and since 2013, UK retailers have copied the idea. In 2014, some supermarkets got more than they planned. The *Financial Times* reported that police were called to at least seven Tesco stores in the Manchester area after fights took place between customers competing for the bargains on offer. Online, websites for Tesco, Currys and Argos all struggled. Currys, the electrical retailer, left shoppers on its website waiting up to one hour in a virtual queue.

Source: adapted from © the *Financial Times*, 29.11.2014, All Rights Reserved.

(a) Explain, using the data as an example, how consumers, firms and government interact in a market economy like the UK.

TYPES OF ECONOMY

In rich, industrialised economies, three main types of economy can be distinguished.

Free market economies In **free market economies** (also called **free enterprise economies or capitalist economies or market economies**), the majority of resources are allocated through markets rather than through government and planning. There are no examples of pure free market economies in the world today. However, Singapore and the USA have a greater proportion of their resources allocated by the market than economies such as Sweden or Germany. In the USA, public (i.e. government) spending is around 37.5 per cent of total output. The government allocates resources, for example for education, defence, roads, policing and the justice system. Hong Kong (PRC) and the USA therefore tend to be called 'free market economies'.

Mixed economies In **mixed economies**, more resources are allocated through government planning than in free market economies. Typically between 40 per cent and 60 per cent of resources are allocated by government and the free market. Two key areas that distinguish free market and mixed economies are welfare benefits and healthcare. In mixed economies, there tends to be a greater reallocation of income through welfare benefits such as state pensions, unemployment and sickness benefits and child benefits. Mixed economies also tend to be ones where the healthcare system is administered and financed by the state. In pure free market economies, healthcare would be entirely financed by the private sector and, in theory, there would be no welfare benefit system.

Command economies In **command (or planned or centrally planned) economies**, most resources are allocated by the state and the market mechanism only plays a small part. The largest planned economy today is China, although it is moving towards a mixed economy. Cuba and The Democratic People's Republic of Korea (DPRK) are two other examples. Before 1990, the Soviet Union and Eastern European countries, such as Poland and Romania, were also planned economies.

ACTIVITY 2

SKILLS ▶ REASONING, ANALYSIS, CRITICAL THINKING

CASE STUDY: THE NORTH KOREAN (DPRK) ECONOMY

DPRK is one of the last remaining planned economies in the world. But it is slowly moving in a more market-orientated direction. In the 1990s, the break up of another planned economy, the Soviet Union, brought mass hunger to DPRK with an estimated 1 million deaths. The Soviet Union had been DPRK's main trading partner and had subsidised (funded) its economy. When that trade and subsidy disappeared, DPRK's income fell significantly. It was during this time that informal markets, particularly for food, appeared. Today, these informal markets provide an estimated two-thirds of the population with their main source of income. However, officially, agriculture is all collectivised, meaning that the state owns all farms and directs production. So too with industry. However, the government has established a small number of Special Economic Zones where foreign companies can set up and employ DPRK workers to produce goods for export. It wants to expand their number.

Source: adapted from © the *Financial Times*, 12.3.2014, 2.9.2014, All Rights Reserved.

(a) Explain what it might mean for DPRK as a planned economy to move 'in a more market-orientated direction'.

AN EVALUATION OF DIFFERENT TYPES OF ECONOMY

The different types of economy have advantages and disadvantages.

Choice Comparing the USA with the former Soviet Union in 1985, or DPRK or Cuba today, it is clear that individual citizens on average have more choice in free market economies. Planning tends to produce uniform products. So in the Soviet Union, everything from cars to shoes to food was mass-produced in large quantities but with little variety.

In a market economy, consumers can choose between thousands of different versions of cars. As workers, in a market economy, people have choices about which jobs to apply for. In planned economies, there tends to be much more direction with workers being allocated jobs. Citizens also have far less income after tax in planned economies than in free market economies. The amount they are free to spend on products of their choice is therefore much smaller. However, choice has its limitations. In free market economies, those with high incomes or high levels of education have far more choice than those with low incomes or low levels of education. Choice for an unemployed worker in a high-unemployment area might very limited indeed.

Quality and innovation One advantage claimed of a free market economy is that there are strong motivations built into the system to innovate and produce high-quality goods. Companies that fail to do both are likely to be driven out of business by more efficient firms. However, this assumes that consumers or buyers have the power to make free choices. In practice, many markets are dominated by a few large producers that direct the market through advertising and other forms of marketing in order to exploit the consumer. So while choice and innovation are greater than under planned systems, the advantages of free market economies may not be as great as it might at first seem.

Efficiency The planned economies of the Soviet Union and Eastern Europe proved to be inefficient. One major problem was that workers and managers had little incentive to work efficiently.

Usually guaranteed their jobs, they only had to meet their minimum work targets to stay safe. Markets tend to lead to greater efficiency because of competition. Firms in a competitive market have to be efficient to survive and make a profit. However, competition in many markets in mixed and free market economies is limited because a few large firms dominate those markets. Also, large firms are small planned economies in themselves and often struggle to maintain efficient production through planning in exactly the same way that planned economies such as the Soviet Union struggled to be efficient.

Economic growth One frequently made claim is that the more market-orientated an economy, the higher the rate of growth of its overall economy will be. Markets are assumed to be dynamic while government control is assumed to discourage innovation and best practice. The planned economies of the Soviet Union and Eastern Europe certainly fell behind in terms of growth. Planning the whole economy produced large inefficiencies. However, both mixed and free market economies at the same level of development seem to grow at very similar rates over the long term. Free market economies do not seem to have higher rates of growth than mixed economies over time.

Distribution of income and wealth Free market economies tend to have higher levels of inequality than mixed or planned economies. This is because resources produced by government through the planning process tend to be distributed more equally than would be the case in a free market. Higher income earners and wealth owners also tend to pay a larger proportion of tax in mixed compared to free market economies.

Risk Free market economies tend to expose their citizens to far more risk than mixed or planned economies. For example, there tends to be far less provision for risks associated with ill health, unemployment and old age in free market economies. The wealthy can afford to spend their way out of problems. However, the poor can be left with no healthcare, no job, no house and no food. In mixed and planned economies, there tend to be a birth-to-death group of services and benefits provided by government for citizens.

Political freedom All planned economies in the 20th and 21st century have limited political freedoms to enforce control. Almost all have been totalitarian police states. In contrast, both free market and mixed economies in the rich industrialised world have been associated with political freedom.

Since the 1950s, most planned economies have disappeared. Apart from DPRK, the few that remain, such as China, are moving towards a more market economy. Equally, there has been a tendency for the size of government in free market economies to grow. Among mixed economies, those such as Sweden and Norway, which at one point saw their government spending rise to over 60 per cent of GDP, have generally moved back towards a more market-orientated allocation of resources.

SMITH, HAYEK AND MARX

Three writers who have strongly influenced thinking about economic systems are Adam Smith, Friedrich Hayek and Karl Marx.

Adam Smith Adam Smith published his famous book, *An Enquiry into the Nature and Causes of the Wealth of Nations*, in 1776. In the book he explained how the 'invisible hand' of the market would allocate resources to everyone's advantage. He argued that the selfish desire for profit by every individual could lead to a whole economy where benefit was maximised. He attacked the economic system of his day, which restricted free trade through **protectionism**, economic restrictions and legal barriers. Adam Smith is often

seen as a supporter of free market economies and laissez-faire government. Laissez-faire means that the government should leave markets as much as possible to regulate themselves. However, there are many points in his writings where he recognises that the state has an important role to play in providing a structure within which free markets can operate. He saw that individuals and firms would attempt to distort markets to gain more for themselves. He also saw that the poor needed to be defended from those who owned property. For example, he argued that businesses would attempt to combine together to raise prices at the expense of the consumer. He wrote that employers would reduce wages as much as possible whether or not workers could survive on these incomes. He also argued that the state had to provide those goods and services that free markets would otherwise not provide. The whole legal and judicial structure for enforcing property law, for example, needed to be provided by the state. So too did goods such as roads and bridges.

Friedrich Hayek Friedrich Hayek was a 20th-century Austrian economist who moved to the UK in 1931. His most famous book is *The Road to Serfdom*, published in 1944. In it, he argued that ever-greater control of the economy by the state leads to totalitarianism and the loss of freedom by the individual. He was reacting to the loss of individual freedom in the Soviet Union under Joseph Stalin and Germany under Adolf Hitler. He correctly saw that individuals were forced to comply with state wishes through the threat of prison and death. However, he then said that greater state control over the economy in both the UK and the USA also led to a loss of freedom for the individual. For Hayek, the poor in the UK and the USA were better off than in Germany or the Soviet Union because at least they had their personal freedom. Proponents of free markets have used Hayek's thoughts to argue that free unregulated markets are better than regulated markets or direct state provision and control because the liberties of the individual are maintained in free markets. He also said that central planning by governments led to the will of a small minority of individuals being imposed on the whole of society. Critics would argue, however, that this occurs in free market economies too. Those who own property are able to impose their will on everyone else. In a free market economy, the poor have very few 'spending votes' compared to the rich. In free market economies, the rich are also able to buy influence over political processes, influencing political decision making. The poor then become politically powerless as well as being economically weaker.

Karl Marx Karl Marx was a 19th-century German thinker and writer and is often considered to be the founder of modern socialism. His most famous book is *Das Kapital*, the first part of which was published in 1867. He correctly saw that there was a great gap between the economic fortunes of the owners of property and workers in 19th-century Europe. He wanted to see that gap eliminated. He developed a theory which said that it was historically inevitable that workers, the proletariat, would rise up in revolution against property owners and seize control of the means of production. A new democratic society would arise, which would lead to equality and where property would be owned by everyone collectively. Karl Marx, although he advocated revolution, would probably not have approved of the Marxist state created by Joseph Stalin in the Soviet Union in the 1920s, 1930s and 1940s. The problem for Marxists was how to go from a capitalist free market economy to an ideal economy in which somehow everyone owned everything to the benefit of all. Joseph Stalin solved this problem by creating a command economy where the state owned most resources. Command economies ultimately have not been anywhere near as successful as free market and mixed economies at delivering economic benefit to their citizens. Also, as

Hayek pointed out, they came to rely on the abuse of political power to enforce their decisions.

▲ **Karl Marx**

THINKING LIKE AN ECONOMIST

MIXED ECONOMIES

The shape of today's UK economy was formed between 1945 and 1951 in the years following the Second World War. A Labour government created the Welfare State, including a free National Health Service and a system of birth-to-death benefits that eliminated the worst of the poverty seen before 1945.

In common with most industrialised economies, the UK saw the rate of growth government spending rise faster than national income in the 1950s, 1960s and 1970s. The result was that government spending as a percentage of GDP rose.

The 1980s saw an attempt by a Conservative government under Margaret Thatcher to reduce the role of the state significantly and move the economy back to being more market orientated. The 'Thatcher revolution' was influential throughout the industrialised world. It led to a debate that is still continuing today about what should be left for market forces to provide and what should be done by the state.

Sweden was one country that was influenced by this debate. Along with Norway and Denmark, it had

created a large welfare state, which helped create much greater equality in society than in, for example, the USA. However, in the early 1990s, it experienced a banking crisis and a major recession. This led to government spending soaring to 71 per cent of GDP. In the years that followed, Sweden recognised that its government spending was too high. By 2014, it had fallen to a little over 50 per cent, not much more than the average for the eurozone.

When the world experienced a banking crisis and major recession in 2008, like Sweden before, government spending as a proportion of GDP tended to rise in most countries. This was because government spending itself rose at a time when GDP was falling. In the UK, government spending as a proportion of GDP rose to 51 per cent in 2009. In 2010, a new coalition government with a Conservative Party chancellor (finance minister), George Osborne, promised to cut public spending. This was to reduce government borrowing. Following their win in the 2015 election the Conservative Party continued with this policy.

However, it was also designed to reduce the size of the state and shift the UK away from Scandinavian and other European mixed economies towards a more free market US-style mix of private and public sectors. The debate about whether the UK should be a mixed economy rather than a free market economy is therefore still very much alive.

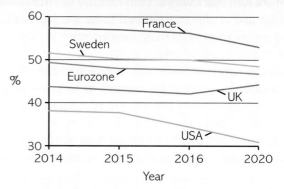

Note: Data for 2018–20 are estimates.

▲ **Figure 1 Government spending as a percentage of GDP, 2014–20**

CHECKPOINT

1 What are the three basic questions that all economic systems must address?

2 What is the market mechanism?

3 What is the main difference, in the allocation of resources, between a free market economy and a command economy?

4 How would you expect the following to differ between a free market economy and a command economy?
   – choice
   – quality and innovation
   – efficiency
   – economic growth
   – distribution of income and wealth.

SUBJECT VOCABULARY

command or planned or centrally planned economy an economic system where government, through a planning process, allocates resources in society.
economic system a complex network of individuals, organisations and institutions and their social and legal inter-relationships which allocate resources.
free market economy, or free enterprise economy or capitalist economy or market economy an economic system that resolves the basic economic problems mainly through the market mechanism.
mixed economy an economy where both the free market mechanism and the government planning process allocate significant proportions of total resources.
protectionism when a government tries to help industries in its own country by taxing or restricting foreign goods.
supranational involving more than one country.

EXAM PRACTICE

THE US ECONOMY   SKILLS   REASONING, ANALYSIS, CRITICAL THINKING

Money can buy lots of things in the USA for the ordinary foreign tourist. Prices are cheap and service is good. The free market means the tourist has the choice of everything from the most luxurious five-star hotel to a tent or caravan, a Michelin-star restaurant to a burger restaurant, or a walk in the countryside.

However, the US economy is a divided economy. Tourists tend to be served by the half of Americans who are on low wages. According to the 2015 US census, half of all households earn US$56,516 or less per year while one-fifth of households earn US$22,800 or less. The bottom half of Americans cannot expect to see much increase in their incomes over the coming decades. After all, as Figure 2 shows, since 1980, the bottom fifth of income earners have seen very little change in their before-tax income. Contrast that with the top 5 per cent who have seen their incomes grow 84 per cent. The top 1 per cent have seen their incomes rise by nearly 300 per cent. The USA is truly a winner-takes-all society.

Support for the free market is strong in the USA. The free market is supposed to deliver superior growth to the 'socialist' countries of Europe. But the evidence is not conclusive. At least some of the difference in growth rates is explained by the high immigration rates to the USA. More workers means more output and so higher GDP. But it does not mean higher output per person.

Free market supporters also criticise the government-financed healthcare systems of Europe. In America, it has been a strongly defended freedom to have so little money that you cannot afford to visit the doctor, let alone have a life-saving operation. This changed with the introduction of 'Obamacare', an insurance scheme designed to give medical access to all.

However, the free market medical care system, to date, has left life expectancy (length) in 2016 in the richest country in the world at only 79.8 years – ranked 42nd by the CIA *World Factbook*. For Sweden, it is 82.1 years and for Japan it is 85.0 years.

Note: *Income measured in CPI-U-RS adjusted dollars.

▲ **Figure 2 Growth in real household income* by income quintile (%) USA, 1980–2015**

Social promotion is also a real problem in the USA. Barack Obama was very unusual. He was the first person in living memory to be elected president who was not already a millionaire. Even then, he and his wife were in the top 1 per cent of income earners when he began to run for president in 2007. Just as in the UK or in Sweden, individuals in the USA can make it from poverty to riches. But most wealthy people are the sons and daughters of rich parents. The chances of a child from a poor background today making it to the top of the income pile are very low.

Source: with information from www.cia.gov

	GDP per head at constant purchasing power parities % increase at 2005 prices					GDP at constant purchasing power parity increase at 2005 prices
	1971–80	1981–90	1991–2000	2001–13	1971–2013	1971–2013
Canada	2.8	1.4	1.8	0.8	1.7	2.8
France	3.0	1.9	1.6	0.5	1.7	2.2
Germany	2.8	2.2	1.6	0.9	1.8	2.0
Italy	3.3	2.3	1.6	-0.5	1.5	1.8
Japan	3.2	4.1	0.9	0.7	2.1	2.6
Sweden	1.6	1.9	1.8	1.2	1.6	2.0
UK	1.8	2.6	2.8	0.8	1.9	2.2
USA	2.1	2.4	2.2	0.8	1.8	2.8

▲ **Table 1 Annual average real growth in GDP per head and GDP (%)**

Source: adapted from stats.oecd.org

Q

1 Analyse how resources are allocated in a free market economy such as the USA. **(6 marks)**

2 Evaluate the extent to which the economy of the USA performs better than mixed economies, such as Sweden's, when judged by (a) economic growth; (b) distribution of income and wealth; (c) risk for individuals? **(20 marks)**

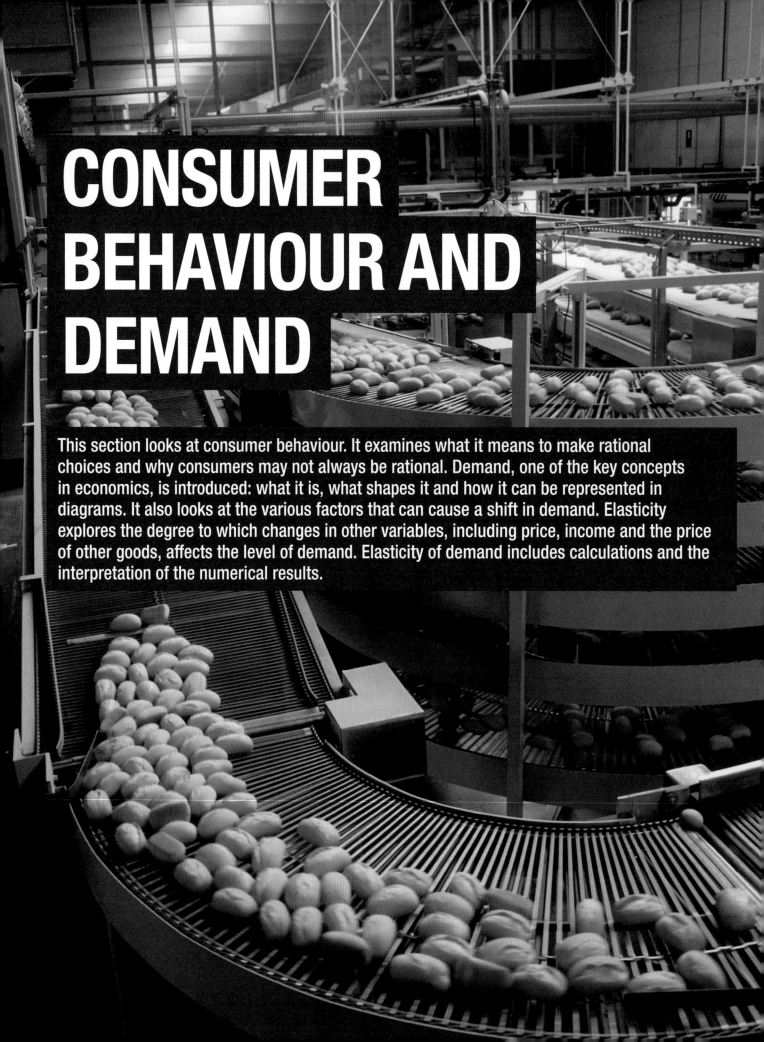

CONSUMER BEHAVIOUR AND DEMAND

This section looks at consumer behaviour. It examines what it means to make rational choices and why consumers may not always be rational. Demand, one of the key concepts in economics, is introduced: what it is, what shapes it and how it can be represented in diagrams. It also looks at the various factors that can cause a shift in demand. Elasticity explores the degree to which changes in other variables, including price, income and the price of other goods, affects the level of demand. Elasticity of demand includes calculations and the interpretation of the numerical results.

6 RATIONAL DECISION MAKING

LEARNING OBJECTIVES

- Understand the assumption of rationality in decision making.
- Understand the reasons why consumers may not aim to maximise utility.
- Understand framing and bias.

GETTING STARTED

In front of you is a bag of popcorn, a chocolate bar, a can of lemonade and a doughnut. If you could choose just one of these to eat or drink right now, which would you choose? What would be your second choice if that product was not available? Which would be your least favourite item? In real life, do you always act in a rational manner, maximising your net benefits from the money you spend?

RATIONAL ECONOMIC DECISION MAKING

Much of the economics that is taught at A level and on university degree courses is based on **neo-classical theory**. It is a body of economics that was developed from the 1870s onwards. In this book, almost all the **microeconomics** – the study of individual markets – is based on neo-classical theory. Equally, **macroeconomics** taught at A level is mainly a fusion of neo-classical theory with the ideas of John Maynard Keynes, a very famous economist of the 1920s and 1930s.

One of the key assumptions of neo-classical theory is that economic agents, such as individuals or firms, make decisions in a rational way. The word 'rational' has a precise meaning in neo-classical theory. It is that economic agents are able to rank the order of different outcomes from an action in terms of their net benefits to them. They then act in a way that will maximise these net benefits. For example, you might prefer salted popcorn to sweet popcorn. Assuming that all the other factors in the decision are the same, you are a rational economic decision maker if you choose a pack of salted popcorn when you have the option.

When making a decision, there is often a number of factors that will influence an economic agent. For example, you might want to buy a packet of popcorn now. You could buy it now from your nearest shop 2 minutes walk away at a cost of US$0.60 or you could go to a local supermarket 10 minutes walk away at a cost of US$0.40. Alternatively, you could simply not buy the packet of popcorn.

There are two costs here. One is the cost of the packet – US$0.40 or US$0.60. The other is the value of your time and effort to get the packet. If you value 8 minutes of your time at more than US$0.20, you will buy at the local shop. If you value 2 minutes of your time at, say, US$20, you probably will not buy a packet at all because the benefit from consuming them is probably not worth the US$20.60 it will cost at the local shop.

MAXIMISATION

Another key assumption of neo-classical theory is that economic agents act in a way that will maximise their net benefits.

Consumers Consumers are assumed to maximise their **economic welfare**, sometimes referred to or measured by **utility** or satisfaction from consuming goods. In a world where their resources are scarce, they have to make choices. So they have to compare the utility to be gained from consuming an extra unit of a product with its opportunity cost. If there is US$2 to be spent, would it be best spent on chocolate, a magazine or a gift to charity, for example.

Workers Workers are assumed in neo-classical theory to want to maximise their own welfare at work. Workers take a number of different considerations into account when deciding where to work and how long to work. Pay is usually a key consideration. But other factors, such as job security, how long it takes to commute to work, the satisfaction derived from doing a particular job with a particular group of other workers and the cost of looking for alternative employment, are all important too.

Firms Neo-classical theory assumes that the owners of firms want to maximise their reward from ownership. This means that firms will aim to maximise their profits.

Governments Governments are assumed to want to maximise the welfare of citizens. They take decisions that will lead to increased welfare for the country as a whole.

Neo-classical theory recognises that these assumptions about the goals of economic actors can be over-simplified. For example, large firms tend to be run not by their owners, the shareholders, but by managers. Not surprisingly, managers can often take decisions that will benefit themselves rather than the shareholders who have employed them. Governments tend to maximise the welfare of all citizens. However, governments around the world may be corrupt. They then take decisions that will tend to benefit the members of the government rather than citizens. Equally, governments tend to reward their own supporters at the expense of other citizens. In a democracy, there is little point in taking decisions that will reward those people who vote for other parties. Instead, decisions are made that will benefit those who always vote for you and those who might vote for you in an election.

ACTIVITY 1

SKILLS ▷ COMMUNICATING, REASONING, CRITICAL THINKING

CASE STUDY: NUDGING

In 2017, Richard Thaler won the Nobel Prize for economics for his contributions in the field of behavioural economics, examining how irrational instincts can often overrule rational choices.

In order to prevent this happening he has favoured something that has been called 'nudging'. By making small changes in government policy, people can be persuaded to do things that are more rational and in their long-term self-interest, such as saving for a pension, not missing hospital appointments and eating more healthily.

Nudging takes many forms and has spread out all over the world. In Australia, a government project gives people personalised suggestions on how to be more environmentally friendly when travelling. In Madrid, Spain, smart parking meters charge more for cars that pollute more and charge less for energy efficient vehicles. In Dhaka, Bangladesh, Coca-Cola® installed a video game machine that provides a free game in return for empty bottles. In Stockholm, Sweden, a speed camera not only records and fines speeding drivers but also records the safe drivers and enters them into a competition to win back some of the cash raised.

(a) Why might it be considered more rational to use less polluting vehicles?

(b) Are consumers who use more polluting vehicles being rational or irrational?

(c) How would designing public buildings with fewer lifts be an example of nudging people to behave in a more rational manner?

Neo-classical theory also recognises that not every decision will be made in a rational way. However, neo-classical economists would argue that their theories will be correct so long as most economic agents act in a rational way most of the time.

THE MARGIN

Some economic theories assume that economic agents will act rationally in a way that maximises their total net benefit. For example, consumers will act to maximise their total utility. However, there are problems with this approach. One of the key elements of neo-classical economic theory is that it is much simpler to assume that decisions are taken at the margin. For example, when you decide whether or not you want to buy a packet of popcorn now, you do not review all your spending decisions. What you do, according to neo-classical economists, is that you look at the one decision in isolation. What will give the greatest utility: to buy a packet of crisps now, or not to buy? For a firm, it may investigate whether to take on an extra worker. The firm does not review all its spending decisions when making this one decision. Instead, it considers whether or not profit will be increased by taking on the extra worker.

Marginal analysis is essential to the study of economics today both at A level and at university level. A quick look at the index of a standard economics textbook will show how many different marginal variables there are, for example, marginal utility, marginal cost, marginal benefit, marginal product, marginal rate of tax and the marginal propensity to consume.

RATIONALITY VERSUS BEHAVIOURAL ECONOMICS

It was explained above that neo-classical economics assumes that consumers are rational. They aim to maximise their own utility or economic welfare. They do this by buying a bundle of goods with their limited income. The bundle of goods is constructed so that it achieves maximum utility for the buyer. This then has implications for consumer behaviour. For example, consumers will always prefer to buy the same good at a lower price than a higher price. If they are offered a bundle of goods, with an additional good, X, they would prefer to buy it compared to just the bundle of goods without X.

Some economists, however, argue that the picture of **homo-economicus** offered by neo-classical economics of economic actors is incorrect. Economic agents, such as consumers, are not rational.

For example, they often do not buy at the cheapest price and their choices can be manipulated. This view is explored by a branch of economics called **behavioural economics**.

REASONS WHY CONSUMERS MAY NOT BEHAVE RATIONALLY

There are a number of reasons why behavioural economists argue that consumers may not behave rationally, including the following.

Consideration of the influence of other people's behaviour and the need to feel valued Rationality assumes that economic actors act individually in a way that will maximise their own benefits. However, evidence suggests that individuals often do not make free and independent choices. Instead, they make choices that are influenced by social norms. These are beliefs held by a group of people about how to behave. For example, a group of university students might be on a night out where the social norm is that everyone spends heavily. One individual does not want to spend much money. The social norm for the group is likely to make that one individual spend more than they might want. Or a teenager might insist that their parents buy very expensive branded trainers rather than unbranded trainers because the teenager wants to 'fit in' with a peer group and needs to feel valued.

The importance of habitual behaviour and inertia Habits are extremely important when making decisions. Habits may represent shortcuts in decision making. For example, using a rule of thumb saves time and effort. A rule of thumb is a quick way of assessing a situation that does not give an exact answer, but most of the time is sufficiently accurate to justify using it. Equally, consumers, as a habit, often do not gather together all the information they need to make a good decision 100 per cent of the time. This is because they know that good decisions can be made most of the time with only part of the information required. It is not worth the time and effort to get all the information needed. Everyone has habits, which firms learn to exploit. Supermarkets, for example, know that shoppers tend to concentrate on products that are displayed at eye level. They exploit this habit by tending to place high-profit goods at eye level and low-profit goods at the bottom and top of shelves. Habits can be particularly damaging when they become addictions. Most people who are addicted to tobacco or food know that it is in their long-term interests to control their addiction. However, they lack the self-control to give up or moderate a particular form of behaviour. Few people, for example, when they are overweight have enough self-control to change their diet, take exercise and lose weight. Lack of self-control then leads to economic agents making decisions that will not maximise their benefits.

Even when people are aware that there might be a better alternative they do not change their behaviour because of inertia. They may think that it is too much trouble and not worth the effort. Examples include people not wanting to change bank accounts to get a better service or energy providers to get a lower bill.

Consumer weakness at computation (calculation) Consumers are not always willing or able to make comparisons between prices and different goods on offer. Prices and offers are often presented in ways where consumers find it difficult to do the mathematics required for a comparison. Some firms deliberately exploit this weakness by presenting information in a disjointed way or simply not giving enough information to make a rational choice. For example, a shopper might want to buy some canned beans. On the shelves are individual cans and packs of six. The individual cans are priced at US$0.47. The pack of six is priced at US$2.99. Past experience tells the shopper that multipacks are usually cheaper than individual items. So, because the shopper cannot or will not make a calculation and habitually buys multipacks, it is the pack of six that goes into the shopping trolley. But it is actually US$0.17 cheaper to buy six individual cans. US$0.47 x 6 is not an easy calculation to make. Many consumers simply cannot multiply 47 by 6 in their heads. Most of the rest, can probably do the calculation, but will not try because it requires some mental effort. Yet, according to neo-classical economists, the supermarket will not sell any six packs of canned beans at these prices because consumers are rational.

FRAMING AND BIAS

Economic statements or choices can be worded in such a way as to influence the outcome. This can be done intentionally if someone is trying to achieve a particular result, which makes it harder to make rational choices. For example, if you are considering choosing between two businesses, would you prefer the one that claims '9 out of 10 customers are happy with our service' or one that claims '10% of our customers are not happy with our service'? Would you be persuaded to buy a €15,000 car for €18,000? Probably not, but what about 'Buy this car for only €500 a month in 36 easy payments'? In both cases the choices are exactly the same but one sounds better than the other.

Politicians and marketers understand what framing is all about and are very good at trying to influence our behaviour and perceptions. Framing questions in a particular way can bias the outcome according to the framer's particular needs. The minister for health might ask voters if they would rather spend money on hospitals for sick children or on the army – many voters will choose health. If the minister for defence asks the same voters if they think that spending on defence is important in maintaining a secure country to preserve peace and prosperity, most will probably agree. The rational economist needs to be aware of all these potential problems to make a truly rational choice.

THINKING LIKE AN ECONOMIST

RYANAIR

In 2014, the *Financial Times* reported that the budget airline company, Ryanair, had seen a fall in its net profits over the preceding 12 months. The company was quoted as saying that the results were 'disappointing' and announced a number of measures to improve future profitability.

Neo-classical economic theory assumes that shareholders expect their companies to maximise profits. In the case of Ryanair, the company has grown fast since it was founded in 1985. Its success is based on low prices and low costs. By having lower costs than most of its rivals, it can afford to offer lower priced air tickets to its customers and make a profit. Low airfares have been so attractive to customers that the company has grown to be one of the largest airlines in Europe.

Ryanair's customers are likely to be maximising their utility when they buy a Ryanair flight. Typically they shop around for the cheapest flight to their chosen destination. The *Financial Times* reported that Ryanair had been voted the worst of 100 big brands in the UK market for customer relations by the readers of the consumer magazine, *Which?*. In calculating their utility in a rational manner, customers who buy tickets are compensating for any negative

utility they may suffer from customer service with the savings in price on the airfare.

Following the announcement of lower profits, Ryanair announced that it would make improvements to its customer service in an attempt to increase sales and profits. Ryanair were perhaps acknowledging that some potential customers were not flying Ryanair because they valued better service more than saving, say, £40 on a flight.

Source: adapted from © the *Financial Times*, 19.5.2014, All Rights Reserved.

SUBJECT VOCABULARY

behavioural economics a branch of economics that accepts that consumers and other economic agents do not always act rationally and looks at why this might be so.

default to fail to pay money that you owe at the right time.

economic welfare the level of well-being or prosperity or living standards of an individual or group of individuals such as a country.

homo-economicus the rational human used by economists when constructing, explaining and verifying models.

macroeconomics the study of the economy as a whole, including inflation, growth and unemployment.

microeconomics the study of the behaviour of individuals or groups such as consumers, firms or workers, typically within a market context.

neo-classical theory a theory of economics that typically starts with the assumption that economic agents will maximise their benefits and act rationally, and that develops how resources will be allocated in markets and at what price through the forces of demand and supply; the margin is a key concept in neo-classical theory.

utility the satisfaction or benefit derived from consuming a good or a set of goods.

EXAM PRACTICE

SKILLS | PROBLEM SOLVING, REASONING, ANALYSIS

MICROFINANCE INITIATIVE

In India, a study was conducted of individuals who borrowed small sums of money through a microfinance initiative. One group of individuals met weekly to discuss how they were getting on. The other group met monthly, which was the norm for the scheme. Two years after the loans had been repaid, it was found that the individuals who met weekly had more informal social contact with each other than the individuals who met monthly. They were more willing to pool (share) risks and were three times less likely to **default** on their second loan.

Source: adapted from the World Bank, *World Development Report* 2014

ALDI

Following its ban on the sale of confectionery by checkouts in UK stores in 2015, the supermarket chain Aldi has announced that it will do the same in the USA. All 1500 of its American stores will stop selling sweets and confectionery next to the tills as it tries to move its customers towards healthier eating.

Source: adapted from https://www.confectionerynews.com/ Article/2016/03/02/How-chocolate-firms-should-react-to-candy-bans-Euromonitor

PESO LOANS

Low income individuals from Mexico City were invited to choose the best one-year MXN 10,000 (Mexican peso) loan product from a list of loan products typical of those available locally. Only 39 per cent of people could identify the lowest-cost product when given the information in the form of brochures designed by banks for their customers. In contrast, 68 per cent could pick out the lowest-cost product when using a simple summary sheet designed by the Consumer Financial Credit Bureau of Mexico.

Source: adapted from the World Bank, *World Development Report* 2014

Q

1 Define rationality in economics. **(2 marks)**

2 Illustrating your answer from the data, explain why consumers might not behave rationally because:

(a) they are influenced by other people's behaviour **(4 marks)**

(b) of habitual behaviour **(4 marks)**

(c) of weaknesses in computation. **(4 marks)**

7 DEMAND

LEARNING OBJECTIVES

- Understand the concept of 'demand'.
- Understand the distinction between movements along a demand curve and shifts of a demand curve.
- Understand the concept of diminishing marginal utility and its significance for the shape of the individual demand curve.
- Know the factors that may cause a shift in the demand curve.

GETTING STARTED

'Demand for rice fell by 5 per cent in Egypt last year.' What do you think is meant by 'demand'? What might have caused a drop in demand of 5 per cent?

DEMAND

A market exists wherever there are buyers and sellers of a particular good. Buyers demand goods from the market while sellers supply goods to the market.

Demand has a particular meaning in economics. Demand is the quantity of goods or services that will be bought at any given price over a period of time. For instance, approximately 2 million new cars are bought each month in the EU today at an average price of, say, €16,000. Economists would say that the monthly demand for cars at €16,000 would be 2 million units.

DEMAND AND PRICE

If everything else were to remain the same (this is known as the ceteris paribus condition), what would happen to the quantity demanded of a product as its price changed? If the average price of a car were to fall from €16,000 to €8000, then it is not difficult to guess that the quantity demanded of cars would rise. On the other hand, if the average price rose to €40,000, very few cars would now be sold.

This is shown in Table 1. As the price of cars rises then, ceteris paribus, the quantity of cars demanded will fall. Another way of expressing this is shown in Figure 1. Price is on the vertical axis and quantity demanded over time is on the horizontal axis. The curve is downward sloping showing that as price falls, quantity demanded rises. This **demand curve** shows

Price (€)	Demand (million units per month)
4000	4.0
8000	2.0
16,000	1.0
40,000	0.4

▲ Table 1 The demand schedule for cars

the quantity that is demanded at any given price. When price changes there is said to be a movement along the curve. For instance, there is a movement along the curve from point A to point B, a fall of 1 million cars a year, when the price of cars rises from €8000 to €16,000. There is an **extension of demand** when the quantity demanded rises. There is a **contraction of demand** when the quantity demanded falls.

It is important to remember that the demand curve shows **effective demand**. It shows how much would be bought (i.e. how much consumers can afford to buy and would buy) at any given price and not how much buyers would like to buy if they had unlimited resources.

FIGURE 1

The demand curve

The demand curve is downward sloping, showing that the lower the price, the higher will be the quantity demanded of a good. In this example, only 0.4 million cars per month are demanded at a price of £40,000 each, but a reduction in price to £4000 increases quantity demanded to 4 million units per month.

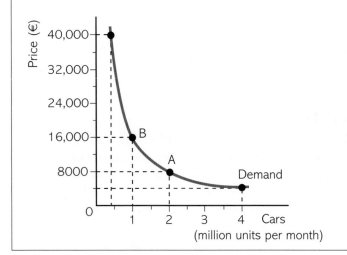

Economists have found that in almost all cases, rises in price lead to falls in quantity demanded. The demand curve is therefore almost always downward sloping. Mathematically, it means that there is an inverse (opposite) relationship between price and quantity demanded.

CONDITIONS OF DEMAND

Changes in price will lead to a change in quantity demanded. These changes are shown by movements along the demand curve. However, there are many other factors apart from price that can cause demand for a product to change. These other factors are collectively called the **conditions of demand**. Changes in the conditions of demand cause a **shift in the demand curve** either to the right or to the left.

ACTIVITY 1   SKILLS   PROBLEM-SOLVING, REASONING, COMMUNICATION

CASE STUDY: INDIAN RAILWAYS

Indian Railways is responsible for rail transport in India. It charges different prices to different passengers for the same journeys depending, for instance, on when they travel, their age, whether they are making a single or return journey or whether they have a season ticket. Using a demand curve diagram, explain what happens in each of the following examples.

(a) Students are charged half price for a rail journey instead of being charged full price.

(b) The reduction given to senior citizens is reduced.

(c) Indian Railways increases its prices on a route by 5 per cent.

(d) Indian Railways currently offer 53 different reductions but increases the number to 60.

DEMAND AND INCOME

One condition of demand is income. Demand for a normal good rises when income rises. For instance, a rise in income leads consumers to buy more cars. A few goods, known as inferior goods, fall in demand when incomes rise.

The effect of a rise in income on demand is shown in Figure 2. Buyers are purchasing OA of clothes at a price of OE. Incomes rise and buyers react by purchasing more clothes at the same price. At the higher level of income they buy, say, OB of clothes. A new demand curve now exists, D_2. It will be to the right of the original demand curve because at any given price more will be demanded at the new higher level of income.

FIGURE 2

A change in income

An increase in income will raise demand for a normal good. At a price of OE, for instance, demand will rise from OA to OB. Similarly, at all other prices, an increase in income will result in a level of demand to the right of the existing demand curve. So the demand curve will shift to the right from D_1 to D_2. A fall in income will result in less being demanded at any given price. Hence the demand curve will shift to the left, from D_1 to D_3.

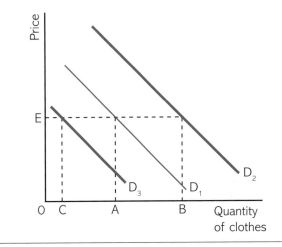

Economists say that a rise in income will lead to an *increase in demand* for a normal good such as clothes. An increase in demand is shown by a shift in the demand curve. (Note that an increase in quantity demanded would refer to a change in quantity demanded resulting from a change in price and would be shown by a movement along the curve.) In Figure 2, the original demand curve D_1 shifts to the right to its new position D_2. Similarly, a fall in income will lead to a *fall in demand* for a normal good. This is shown by a shift to the left of the demand curve from D_1 to D_3. For instance, at a price of OE, demand will fall from OA to OC.

Two points need to be made. First, the demand curves in Figure 2 have been drawn as straight lines. These demand curves drawn show a hypothetical (or imaginary) position. They are drawn straight purely for convenience and do not suggest that actual demand curves for real products are straight. Second, the shifts in the demand curves are drawn as parallel shifts. Again this is done for convenience and neatness but it is most unlikely that a rise or fall in income for an actual product would produce a precisely parallel shift in its demand curve.

ACTIVITY 2 ▸ SKILLS ▸ PROBLEM-SOLVING, REASONING

CASE STUDY: TYRE MANUFACTURE

Quantity demanded (million tyres)	Price(£)
10	20
20	16
30	12
40	8
50	4

▲ Table 2 Demand curve for tyre manufacturer

Table 2 shows the demand curve facing a tyre manufacturer.

(a) Draw a demand curve for tyres from the above data.

(b) An increase in income results in an increase in quantity demanded of tyres of: (i) 5 million; (ii) 10 million; (iii) 15 million; (iv) 25 million. For each of these, draw a new demand curve on your diagram.

(c) Draw a demand curve for tyres that would show the effect of a fall in income on the original demand for tyres.

(d) Draw a demand curve for tyres that would show that no products were demanded when their price was £8.

MATHS TIP

Remember that price always goes on the vertical axis and quantity on the horizontal axis on a demand diagram.

THE PRICE OF OTHER GOODS

Another important factor that influences the demand for a good is the price of other goods. For instance, in the great drought (a period of no rain) of 1976 in the UK, the price of potatoes increased dramatically. Consumers reacted by buying fewer potatoes and replacing them in their diet by eating more bread, pasta and rice.

This can be shown on a demand diagram. The demand curve for pasta in Figure 3 is D_1. A rise in the price of potatoes leads to a rise in the demand for pasta. This means that at any given price a greater quantity of pasta will be demanded. The new demand curve D_2 will therefore be to the right of the original demand curve.

FIGURE 3

A rise in the price of other goods

A rise in the price of potatoes will lead to a rise in the demand for substitute goods. So the demand for pasta will increase, shown by a shift to the right in the demand curve for pasta from D_1 to D_2.

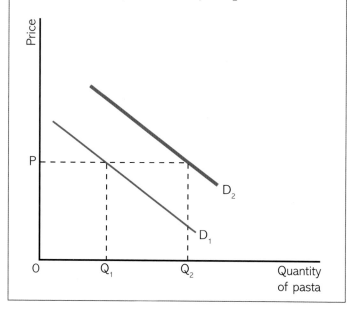

ACTIVITY 3 ▸ SKILLS ▸ PROBLEM-SOLVING, REASONING, COMMUNICATION

CASE STUDY: CRUDE (RAW) OIL

On 23 October 2012, the global price of crude oil was US$51.82 a barrel. Only three years earlier it had reached US$106.22 a barrel.

1. Explain, using diagrams, what effect you would expect the fall in price of crude oil to have on the global demand for:

   (a) oil-fired power stations; (b) gas-fired power stations; (c) rail travel; (d) air travel.

Not all changes in prices will affect the demand for a particular good. A rise in the price of tennis balls is unlikely to have much impact on the demand for carrots, for instance. Changes in the price of other goods as well may have either a positive or negative impact on demand for a good. A rise in the price of tennis rackets is likely to reduce the demand for tennis balls as some buyers decide that tennis is too expensive a sport. In contrast, the demand for cinema places, DVDs or whatever other form of entertainment consumers choose to buy instead of tennis equipment, will increase.

ACTIVITY 4　SKILLS ▶ PROBLEM-SOLVING, REASONING, COMMUNICATION

CASE STUDY: MAZOLA® CANOLA OIL

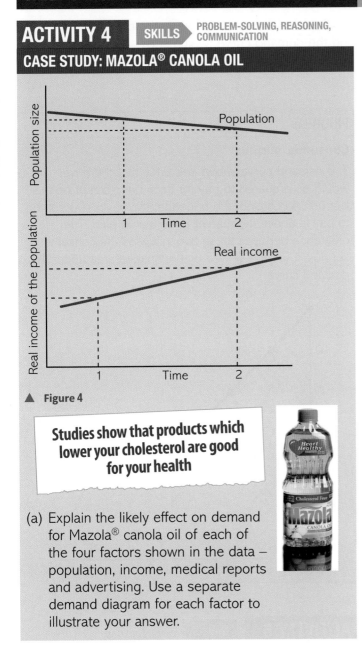

▲ Figure 4

Studies show that products which lower your cholesterol are good for your health

(a) Explain the likely effect on demand for Mazola® canola oil of each of the four factors shown in the data – population, income, medical reports and advertising. Use a separate demand diagram for each factor to illustrate your answer.

OTHER FACTORS

There is a wide variety of other factors that affect the demand for a good apart from price, income and the prices of other goods. These include:

- changes in population – an increase in population is likely to increase demand for goods
- changes in fashion – the demand for items such as caps or shorts or white kitchen units changes as these items go in or out of fashion
- changes in legislation (the law) – the demand for seat belts, anti-pollution equipment or cigarettes has been affected in the past by changes in government legislation
- advertising – a very powerful influence on consumer demand that seeks to influence consumer choice.

THE LAW OF DIMINISHING MARGINAL UTILITY

The demand curve shows how much buyers would be prepared to pay for a given quantity of goods. In Figure 5, for instance, they would be prepared to pay US$0.10 if they bought 1 million items. At US$0.08, they would buy 2 million items. As the price falls, so buyers want to buy more.

This can be put another way. The more buyers are offered, the less value they put on the last one bought. If there were only 1 million units on offer for sale in Figure 5, buyers would be prepared to pay US$0.10 for each one. But if there are 3 million for sale, they will only pay US$0.06. The demand curve, therefore, shows the value to the buyer of each item bought. The first unit bought is worth almost US$0.12 to a buyer. The 1 millionth unit is worth US$0.10. The 4 millionth unit would be worth US$0.04.

This illustrates the **law of diminishing marginal utility**. The value, or utility, attached to consuming the last product bought falls as more units are consumed over a given period of time. A student might be prepared to pay US$5 to watch a film on a Saturday. The student might be prepared to watch a second film that day, but values the second film less than the first. Eventually, the student would begin to experience negative marginal utility and would pay not to have watch yet another film.

Adam Smith, writing in the 18th century, was puzzled why consumers paid a high price for goods such as diamonds, which were unnecessary to human existence, while the price of necessities such as water was very low. This problem is known as the paradox of value. The law of diminishing marginal utility can, however, explain this paradox. If there are few goods available to buy, as with diamonds, then consumers are prepared to pay a high price for them because their marginal utility is high. If there are plenty of goods, then consumers are only prepared to pay a low price because the last one consumed has low marginal utility. This doesn't mean to say that they do not place a high value on necessities when they are in short supply. In times of hunger, diamonds can be traded for small amounts of food. If diamonds were as common as water, buyers would not be prepared to pay much for the last diamond bought.

The law of diminishing marginal utility therefore explains why the demand curve is downward sloping. The higher the quantity bought, the lower the marginal utility (the utility from the last one) derived from consuming the product. So buyers will only pay low prices for relatively high amounts purchased, but they will pay higher prices if the quantity available for sale is lower.

ACTIVITY 5 REASONING, ANALYSIS, COMMUNICATION

CASE STUDY: DIMINISHING MARGINAL UTILITY

Samira loves clothes. The first pair of jeans that she bought herself, she really liked. Then she bought another pair of jeans but she did not wear them as much as her first pair of jeans. Two years later, she had five pairs of jeans in her wardrobe. When she went out shopping, she did not really look at jeans any more and spent her money on other items for her wardrobe. Samira's brother, Intzar, had one pair of jeans, which he wore frequently. When his mum suggested that he might like to buy another pair, he said he had better things to spend his money on. He would only buy another pair when his existing pair had fallen apart.

(a) How does this illustrate the law of diminishing marginal utility?

CONSUMER SURPLUS

Figure 5 can be used to explain the concept of **consumer surplus**. This is the difference between the value to buyers and what they actually pay. Assume in Figure 5 that all buyers pay a price of US$0.06 for a product. The buyer who bought the millionth unit would have been prepared to pay US$0.10 for that unit. So that buyer has gained a consumer surplus of US$0.04 (US$0.10 – 0.06) on that unit. The buyer who bought the 2 millionth unit would have been prepared to pay US$0.08 for the unit. So the consumer surplus on the 2 millionth unit is US$0.02 (US$0.08 – 0.06). The buyer who bought the 3 millionth unit gained no consumer surplus. The price paid was exactly equal to the value or utility of US$0.06 placed by the buyer on the unit.

The total consumer surplus at a price of US$0.06 is shown by the shaded area in Figure 5. It is the sum

of all the vertical lines between the price of US$0.06 and the demand curve, which shows the value that buyers are placing on marginal units purchased.

FIGURE 5

Consumer surplus

The demand curve shows the price that the buyer would be prepared to pay for each unit. Except on the last unit purchased, the price that the buyer is prepared to pay is above the market price that is paid. The difference between these two values is the consumer surplus. It is represented by the shaded area under the demand curve.

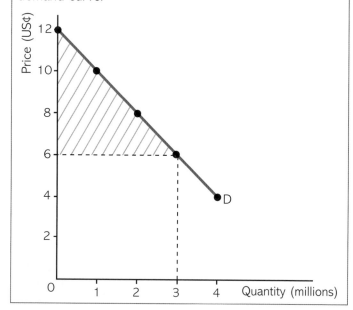

ACTIVITY 6 PROBLEM-SOLVING, REASONING, COMMUNICATION

CASE STUDY: DEMAND AND CONSUMER SURPLUS

Demand for a good is zero at US$200. It then rises to 50 million units at US$100 and 75 million at US$50.

(a) Draw the demand curve for prices between 0 and US$200.

(b) Shade the area of consumer surplus at a price of US$60.

(c) Is consumer surplus larger or smaller at a price of US$40 compared to US$60? Explain your answer.

THINKING LIKE AN ECONOMIST

Growth in global demand for steel is forecast to slow in 2018, with some developing countries' consumption reducing as their economies shift from manufacturing to services.

Overall demand for the commodity will increase 1.6 per cent to 165 billion tonnes in 2018, according to estimates by the World Steel Association (WSA). That compares with an underlying growth rate of 2.8 per cent in 2017.

Despite the slowdown, the figures mark an improvement compared with earlier estimates by the trade body, of 1.3 per cent demand growth this year and 0.9 per cent in 2018.

Steel is often viewed as an economic barometer (measuring tool) because it is used in carmaking, construction and manufacturing.

'The global steel demand recovery is solid and progress in the global steel market this year to date has been encouraging,' said T.V. Narendran, chairman of the worldsteel Economics Committee. 'We have seen the cyclical upturn broadening and firming throughout the year, leading to better than expected performances for both developed and developing economies, although the Middle East and North Africa region and Turkey have been an exception,' he added.

All geographic regions are expected to witness demand growth in 2018, while only Africa and the grouping of non-EU European countries will consume less this year, according to the WSA.

As the producer of nearly half of the world's steel tonnage, China exerts a huge influence on industry dynamics through domestic consumption and exports.

Seth Rosenfeld, an analyst at Jefferies, said he believed that China's steel production would stagnate in 2018, roughly in line with domestic demand, as Beijing pressed ahead with plans to close unneeded steel factories. 'Chinese steel exports have plunged 30 per cent [so far in 2017], reversing years of export growth that painfully took share from western steelmakers. It seems clear that Chinese steelmakers no longer view exports as a necessary release valve,' said Mr Rosenfeld.

With Chinese mills operating at high utilisation rates, their exports should continue to decline, supporting 'robust' (strong) western steel prices and profit margins, added Mr Rosenfeld.

Elsewhere, steel demand growth in India, where the government wants to more than double production capacity by 2030 as it pursues a massive infrastructure programme, was downgraded for this year and next. This was partly down to the impact of last year's removal of large amounts of banknotes from currencies.

CHECKPOINT

1　What is effective demand?

2　What does a demand curve show.

3　Explain the difference between an extension of demand and a contraction of demand.

4　List four factors that will affect the demand for a good.

5　Create a diagram to show the impact of the following scenarios on the demand for Hyundai cars:
- an increase in the number of advertisements for Hyundai cars
- an increase in petrol prices
- a decrease in consumers' incomes.

6　What is marginal utility?

7　Create a diagram to show the area of consumer surplus.

SUBJECT VOCABULARY

conditions of demand factors other than price, such as income or the price of other goods, which lead to changes in demand and are associated with shifts in the demand curve.

consumer surplus the difference between how much buyers are prepared to pay for a good and what they actually pay.

contraction of demand when quantity demanded for a good falls because its price rises; it is shown by a movement up the demand curve.

demand curve the line on a price/quantity diagram that shows the level of effective demand at any given price.

demand or effective demand the quantity purchased of a good at any given price, given that other factors of demand remain unchanged.

extension of demand when quantity demanded for a good increases because its price falls; it is shown by a movement down the demand curve.

law of diminishing marginal utility the value or utility that individual consumers gain from the last product consumed falls the greater the number consumed. So the marginal utility of consuming the sixth product is lower than the second product consumed.

shift in the demand curve a movement of the whole demand curve to the right or left of the original caused by a change in any variable affecting demand except price.

underlying growth rate the long-run average growth rate for an economy over a period of time.

EXAM PRACTICE

BOOMING DEMAND LEADS TO HIGHER MILK PRICES

SKILLS REASONING, ANALYSIS, COMMUNICATION

In March 2014 it was reported that UK dairy farmers were doing well. Costs of production had been falling, while the prices they received for their milk had been rising significantly. This was despite the fact that UK consumers have seen a cut in their spending power over the past four years due to recession, which has in itself cut demand for dairy products. Rising food prices in general and rising prices for dairy products in UK supermarkets have also decreased demand.

However, demand for dairy products has been rising globally. Low- and middle-income countries, such as China, have been growing fast. Their populations have used their growing incomes in part to finance a more varied diet. This includes substantially increasing their consumption of products such as milk and cheese. China might be a long way away from a dairy farm in Devon, but the dairy market is a global market. Products such as dried milk powder and cheese are traded globally. To meet this demand, Dairy Crest has recently invested £45 million in its cheese factory in Cornwall to increase production of milk powder for export to Asia.

Demand for milk from UK farms has also been increasing domestically. Dairy producers have been investing in new facilities in the UK. The aim is to produce more in the UK of what is bought in UK supermarkets by customers. This will cut imports of dairy products such as butter and yoghurts into the UK. For example, Arla, the Danish co-operative that makes Lurpak® butter and is the UK's largest dairy operation, has created the world's biggest fresh milk processing factory in Aylesbury. Müller Wiseman, another of Britain's major milk processors, has spent £17 million on a butter factory in Shropshire.

Part of the reason for wanting to produce more in the UK has been recent food safety scares. In 2013, demand for minced beef products fell dramatically when it was found that some products had horse meat in them rather than beef. Being able to trace a dairy product back to a UK farm reassures British customers.

If the UK became self-sufficient in dairy products and cut out all imports, British dairy farmers would have to increase yearly production from the current 14 billion litres to between 17 billion and 19 billion litres. On top of that, the National Farmers' Union forecasts that global demand for dairy production will grow by 2.3 per cent per year for the next decade.

▲ Figure 6 Milk prices (UK) (farmgate, pence per litre)

Source: Adapted from AHDB Dairy

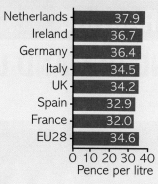

▲ Figure 7 European milk prices (farmgate, pence per litre), 2014

Source: Adapted from AHDB Dairy

Q

1 Consumer surplus is the difference between:
   (a) the price and the value to the buyer
   (b) the price to the buyer and the total cost
   (c) the reduced price and the normal price to the buyer
   (d) the price and the marginal utility to the buyer.
   (1 mark)

2 The data describes a number of factors that might have influenced demand for farm milk in the UK in recent years. Draw a demand curve diagram for each example, explaining the effect on demand of the changes in:
   (a) the price of dairy products in UK supermarkets
   (4 marks)
   (b) incomes of UK consumers **(4 marks)**
   (c) world demand for dairy products **(4 marks)**
   (d) scares about the quality of food purchased in the UK. **(4 marks)**

3 Analyse, with the aid of a demand curve diagram, the impact of 'rising prices for dairy products in UK supermarkets' on the consumer surplus enjoyed by UK consumers on dairy products.
   (6 marks)

4 Discuss whether British dairy farmers should have increased the size of their herds of dairy cattle in 2014. **(14 marks)**

8 PRICE ELASTICITY OF DEMAND

LEARNING OBJECTIVES

- Understand the concept of 'price elasticity of demand'.
- Understand how to use formulae to calculate price elasticity of demand.
- Understand the interpretation of numerical values of price elasticity of demand.
- Know the factors influencing price elasticity of demand.
- Understand how price elasticity of demand varies along a straight line demand curve.
- Know how to calculate total revenue.
- Understand the relationship between price elasticity of demand and total revenue.
- Understand the significance of price elasticity of demand for firms, consumers and the government.

GETTING STARTED

How much is the price of your favourite chocolate bar? If it goes up in price by 10 per cent, what do you think will be the change in quantity bought by all its buyers? How much is the price of a cinema ticket for a 17- or 18-year-old student? If it goes up in price by 10 per cent, what do you think will be the change in the number of tickets bought? In thinking about this, you are thinking about what economists call 'price elasticity of demand'.

THE MEANING OF DEMAND ELASTICITY

The quantity demanded of a good is affected by changes in the price of the good, changes in price of other goods, changes in income and changes in other relevant factors. Elasticity is a measure of how much the quantity demanded is affected by changes in price, income or other factors.

Assume that the price of gas increases by 1 per cent. If quantity demanded falls by 20 per cent as a result of this price change, then there is a large drop in quantity demanded in comparison to the change in price. The price elasticity of gas would be said to be very high. If quantity demanded falls by 0.01 per cent,

then the change in quantity demanded is relatively insignificant compared to the large change in price and the price elasticity of gas would be said to be low.

Different elasticities of demand measure the proportionate response of quantity demanded to a proportionate change in the variables that affect demand. So price elasticity of demand measures the responsiveness of quantity demanded to changes in the price of the good. Income elasticity measures the responsiveness of quantity demanded to changes in consumer incomes. Cross elasticity measures the responsiveness of quantity demanded to changes in the price of another good. Economists could also measure population elasticity, tastes elasticity or elasticity for any other variable that might affect quantity demanded, although these measures are rarely calculated.

PRICE ELASTICITY OF DEMAND

Economists choose to measure responsiveness in terms of proportionate or percentage changes. So **price elasticity of demand** – the responsiveness of changes in quantity demanded to changes in price – is calculated by using the formula:

$$\frac{\text{percentage change in quantity demanded}}{\text{percentage change in price}}$$

Sometimes, price elasticity of demand is called **own price elasticity of demand** to distinguish it from cross price elasticity of demand.

Table 1 shows a number of calculations of price elasticity. For instance, if an increase in price of 10 per cent leads to a fall in quantity demanded of 20 per cent, then the price elasticity of demand is 2. If an increase in price of 50 per cent leads to a fall in quantity demanded of 25 per cent then price elasticity of demand is 0.5.

Percentage change in quantity demanded	Percentage change in price	Elasticity
20	10	2
25	50	0.5
28	7	4
3	9	0.333

▲ Table 1 Price elasticity

Elasticity is sometimes difficult to understand at first. It is essential to memorise the formulae for elasticity. This will allow the idea of elasticity to be used easily and its importance to be understood.

ACTIVITY 1   SKILLS   PROBLEM-SOLVING

CASE STUDY: CALCULATING PED (1)

	Percentage change in quantity demanded	Percentage change in price
(a)	10	5
(b)	60	20
(c)	4	8
(d)	1	9
(e)	5	7
(f)	8	11

▲ Table 2 Price elasticity of demand

(a) Calculate the price elasticity of demand from the data in Table 2.

ALTERNATIVE FORMULAE

Data to calculate price elasticities is often not presented in the form of percentage changes. These have to be worked out. Calculating the percentage change is relatively easy. For example, if consumers have 10 apples and buy another 5, the percentage change in the total number of apples is 50 per cent. This answer is worked out by dividing the change in the number of apples they have (i.e. 5) by the original number of apples they possessed (i.e. 10) and multiplying by 100 to get a percentage figure. So the formula is:

$$\text{percentage change} = \frac{\text{new value} - \text{original value}}{\text{original value}}$$

$$= \frac{\text{change}}{\text{original value}} \times 100\%$$

Price elasticity of demand is measured by dividing the percentage change in quantity demanded by the percentage change in price (percentage change in price is denoted by this symbol Δ). Therefore an alternative way of expressing this is $\Delta Q_D / Q_D \times 100$ (the percentage change in quantity demanded Q_D) divided by $\Delta P/P \times 100$ (the percentage change in price P). The 100s cancel each other out, leaving a formula of:

$$\frac{\Delta Q_D}{Q_D} \div \frac{\Delta P}{P} \quad \text{or} \quad \frac{\Delta Q_D}{Q_D} \times \frac{P}{\Delta P}$$

This can also be written as:

$$\frac{P}{Q_D} \times \frac{\Delta Q_D}{\Delta P}$$

Examples of calculations of elasticity using the above two formulae are given in the following worked examples.

WORKED EXAMPLE

CALCULATIONS OF ELASTICITY OF DEMAND

Example 1

Quantity demanded originally is 100 at a price of £2. There is a rise in price to £3 resulting in a fall in demand to 75.

Therefore, the change in quantity demanded is 25 and the change in price is £1.

The price elasticity of demand is:

$$\frac{\Delta Q_D}{Q_D} \div \frac{\Delta P}{P} = \frac{-25}{100} \div \frac{1}{2} = -\frac{1}{2}$$

Example 2

Quantity demanded originally is 20 units at a price of £5000. There is a fall in price to £4000 resulting in a rise in demand to 32 units.

Therefore, the change in quantity demanded is 12 units resulting from the change in price of £1 000. The price elasticity of demand is:

$$\frac{P}{Q_D} \times \frac{\Delta Q_D}{\Delta P} = \frac{5000}{20} \times \frac{12}{1000} = -3$$

ACTIVITY 2   SKILLS   PROBLEM-SOLVING

CASE STUDY: CALCULATING PED (2)

	Original values		New values	
	Quantity demanded	Price (£)	Quantity demanded	Price (£)
(a)	100	5	120	3
(b)	20	8	25	7
(c)	12	3	16	0
(d)	150	12	200	10
(e)	45	6	45	8
(f)	32	24	40	2

▲ Table 3 Price elasticity of demand

(a) Calculate the price elasticity of demand for the data in Table 3.

MATHS TIP

Price elasticity of demand is a concept where it is essential to memorise the formula. If you do not, you cannot put the numbers in the right place to calculate an answer

ELASTIC AND INELASTIC DEMAND

Different values of price elasticity of demand are given special names. These values ignore minus signs and just refer to the number itself.

- Demand is price **elastic** if the value of elasticity is greater than one. If demand for a good is price elastic, then a percentage change in price will bring about an even larger percentage change in quantity demanded. For example, if a 10 per cent rise in the price of tomatoes leads to a 20 per cent fall in the quantity demanded of tomatoes, then price elasticity is 20 ÷ 10 or 2. Therefore the demand for tomatoes is elastic. Demand is said to be *perfectly elastic* if the value of elasticity is infinity (i.e. a fall in price would lead to an infinite increase in quantity demanded while a rise in price would lead to the quantity demanded becoming zero).

- Demand is price **inelastic** if the value of elasticity is less than one. If demand for a good is price inelastic then a percentage change in price will bring about a smaller percentage change in quantity demanded. For example, if a 10 per cent rise in the price of tickets for the Beijing subway resulted in a 1 per cent fall in journeys made, then price elasticity is 1 ÷ 10 or 0.1. Therefore, the demand for subway travel is inelastic. Demand is said to be *perfectly inelastic* if the value of elasticity is zero (i.e. a change in price would have no effect on quantity demanded).

- Demand is of **unitary elasticity** if the value of elasticity is exactly 1. This means that a percentage change in price will lead to an exact and opposite change in quantity demanded. For instance, a good would have unitary elasticity if a 10 per cent rise in price led to a 10 per cent fall in quantity demanded. These terms are summarised in Table 4.

	Description of the response to a change in price	Numerical measure of elasticity (ignoring the minus sign)	Changes in total expenditure/ revenue as price rises
Perfectly inelastic	Quantity demanded does not change at all as price changes	0	Increases
Inelastic	Quantity demanded changes by a smaller percentage than does price	Between 0 and 1	Increases
Unitary elasticity	Quantity demanded changes by exactly the same percentage as does price	1	Constant
Elastic	Quantity demanded changes by a larger percentage than does price	Between 1 and infinity	Decreases
Perfectly elastic	Buyers are prepared to purchase all they can obtain at some given price but none at all at a higher price	Infinity	Decreases to zero

▲ **Table 4 Elasticity: summary of key terms**

GRAPHICAL REPRESENTATIONS

Figure 1 shows a straight line graph. It is a common mistake to conclude that elasticity of a straight line demand curve is constant all along its length. In fact nearly all straight line demand curves vary in elasticity along the line.

- At point A, price elasticity of demand is infinity. Here quantity demanded is zero. Putting $Q = 0$ into the formula for elasticity:

$$\frac{\Delta Q_D}{Q_D} \div \frac{\Delta P}{P}$$

we see that zero is divided into ΔQ_D. Mathematically there is an infinite number of zeros in any number.

- At the point C, price elasticity of demand is zero. Here price is zero. Putting $P = 0$ into the formula for elasticity, we see that P is divided into ΔP, giving an answer of infinity. Infinity is then divided into the fraction $\Delta Q_D \div Q_D$. Infinity is so large that the answer will approximate to zero.

- At point B, exactly halfway along the line, price elasticity of demand is 1.

ACTIVITY 3   **SKILLS**   PROBLEM-SOLVING, REASONING

CASE STUDY: ELASTIC OR INELASTIC IN DEMAND?

Explain whether you think that the following goods would be elastic or inelastic in demand if their price increased by 10 per cent while all other factors remained constant:
(a) petrol
(b) fresh tomatoes
(c) holidays offered by a major tour operator
(d) a Hyundai car
(e) a branded chocolate bar
(f) a well-known fashion magazine.

FIGURE 1

Price elasticity along a straight demand curve

Price elasticity varies along the length of a straight demand curve, moving from infinity, where it cuts the price axis, to (−)1 half way along the line, to 0 where it cuts the quantity axis.

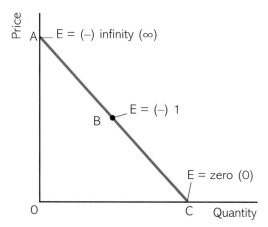

FIGURE 2

Perfectly elastic and inelastic demand curves and unitary elasticity

A vertical demand curve (a) is perfectly inelastic, while a horizontal demand curve (b) is perfectly elastic. A curve with unitary elasticity (c) is a rectangular hyperbola with the formula $PQ = k$ where P is price, Q is quantity demanded and k is a constant value.

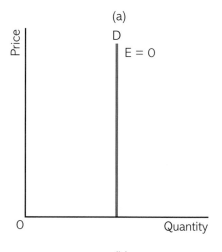

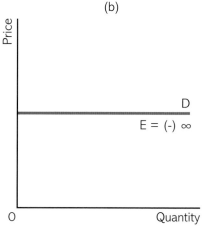

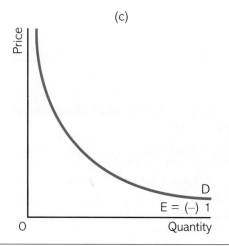

It is worth noting that the elasticity of demand at a point can be measured by dividing the distance from the point to the quantity axis by the distance from the point to the price axis, BC ÷ AB. In Figure 1, B is halfway along the line AC and so BC = AB and the elasticity at point B is −1.

Two straight line demand curves discussed earlier do not have the same elasticity all along their length. Figure 2(a) shows a demand curve that is perfectly inelastic. Whatever the price, the same quantity will be demanded. Figure 2(b) shows a perfectly elastic demand curve. Any amount can be demanded at one price or below it while nothing will be demanded at a higher price. Figure 2(c) shows a demand curve with unitary elasticity. Mathematically it is a rectangular hyperbola. This means that any percentage change in price is offset by an equal and opposite change in quantity demanded.

Another common mistake is to assume that steep demand curves are always inelastic and demand curves that have a shallow slope are always elastic. In Figure 3, two demand curves are drawn. In Figure 3(a), the demand curve has a very shallow slope. The part that is drawn is elastic but this is only because it is just the top half of the line which is drawn. If the whole line were drawn, the bottom half would be inelastic even though the slope of the line is shallow. Similarly, in Figure 3(b), the demand curve has a very steep slope. The part that is shown is indeed price inelastic but this is only because it is the bottom half of the line. The top half of the steep line would be elastic.

FIGURE 3

Slopes of straight line demand curves

Figure 4(a) shows an elastic demand curve but it is only elastic because it is the top half of the line, not because it has a shallow slope. Similarly, Figure 4(b) shows an inelastic demand curve but it is only inelastic because it is the bottom half of the line, not because it has a steep slope.

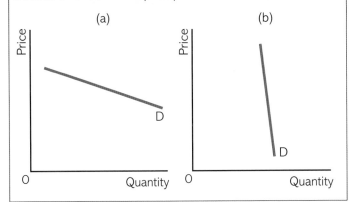

TWO TECHNICAL POINTS

In general, price elasticity of demand is written as a positive number. In fact any downward sloping demand curve always has a negative elasticity. This is because a rise in one variable (price or quantity) is always matched by a fall in the other variable. A rise is positive but a fall is negative and a positive number divided by a negative one (or vice versa) is always negative. However, economists often find it convenient to omit the minus sign in price elasticity of demand because it is easier to deal in positive numbers while accepting that the value is really negative.

A second point relates to the fact that elasticities over the same price range can differ. For example, at a price of US$2, demand for a good is 20 units. At a price of US$3, demand is 18 units. Price elasticity of demand for a rise in price from US$2 to US$3 is:

$$\frac{P}{Q_D} \times \frac{\Delta Q_D}{\Delta P} = \frac{2}{20} \times \frac{-2}{1} = -\frac{1}{5}$$

However, price elasticity of demand for a fall in price from US$3 to US$2 is:

$$\frac{P}{Q_D} \times \frac{\Delta Q_D}{\Delta P} = \frac{3}{18} \times \frac{-2}{1} = -\frac{1}{3}$$

The price elasticity for a rise in price is therefore less than for a fall in price over the same range.

ACTIVITY 4   SKILLS   PROBLEM-SOLVING, REASONING

CASE STUDY: DEMAND

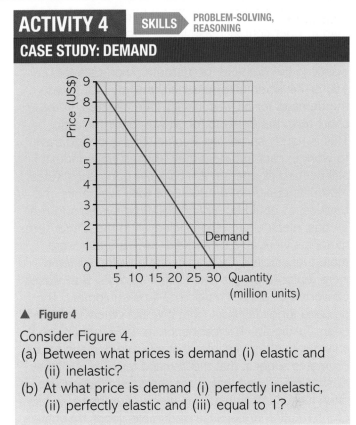

▲ Figure 4

Consider Figure 4.
(a) Between what prices is demand (i) elastic and (ii) inelastic?
(b) At what price is demand (i) perfectly inelastic, (ii) perfectly elastic and (iii) equal to 1?

THE DETERMINANTS OF PRICE ELASTICITY OF DEMAND

The exact value of price elasticity of demand for a good is determined by a wide variety of factors. Economists, however, argue that two factors in particular can be isolated: the availability of substitutes and time.

The availability of substitutes The better the substitutes for a product, the higher the price elasticity of demand will tend to be. For instance, salt has few good substitutes. When the price of salt increases, the demand for salt will change little and therefore the price elasticity of salt is low. Whereas, pasta has many good substitutes, from other types of pasta, to rice, potatoes, bread, and other foods. A rise in the price of pasta, assuming that all other food prices remain constant, is likely to have a significant effect on the demand for pasta. Hence the elasticity of demand for pasta is likely to be higher than that for salt.

Width of market definition The more widely the product is defined, the fewer substitutes it is likely to have. Pasta has many substitutes, but food in general has none. Therefore the elasticity of demand for pasta is likely to be higher than that for food. Similarly the elasticity of demand for mints is likely to be higher than for sweets in general. A 5 per cent increase in the price of mints with all other prices remaining constant, is likely to lead to a much larger fall in demand for mints than a 5 per cent increase in the price of all sweets.

Time The longer the period of time, the more price elastic is the demand for a product. For instance, in 1973–74 when oil prices increased by four times, the demand for oil was initially little affected. In the short term the demand for oil was price inelastic. This is hardly surprising. People still needed to travel to work in cars and heat their houses while industry still needed to operate. Oil had few good substitutes. Motorists could not put fuel into their fuel tanks and businesses could not change oil-fired systems to run on gas, electricity or coal. However, in the longer term motorists were able to, and did, buy cars that were more fuel efficient. Oil-fired central heating systems were replaced by gas and electric systems. Businesses converted or did not replace oil-fired equipment. The demand for oil fell from what it would otherwise have been. Taking the 10-year period to 1985, and given the changes in other variables that affected demand for oil, estimates suggest that the demand for oil was slightly elastic. It is argued that in the short term, buyers are often locked into spending patterns through habit, lack of information or because of durable goods that have already been purchased. In the longer term, they have the time and opportunity to change those patterns.

It is sometimes argued that necessities have lower price elasticities than luxuries. Necessities by definition have to be bought whatever their price in order to stay alive. So an increase in the price of necessities will barely reduce the quantity demanded. Luxuries, on the other hand, are by definition goods that are not essential to existence. A rise in the price of luxuries should therefore produce a proportionately large fall in demand. There is no evidence, however, to suggest that this is true. Food, usually viewed as a a necessity, does not seem to have a lower elasticity than holidays or large cars, which are both usually viewed as luxuries. Part of the reason for this is that it is very difficult to define necessities and luxuries in real life. Some food is a necessity but a significant proportion of what we eat is unnecessary for survival. It is not possible to distinguish between what food is consumed out of necessity and what is a luxury.

It is also sometimes argued that goods that form a relatively low proportion of total expenditure have lower elasticities than those that form a more significant proportion. A large car manufacturer, for instance, would continue to buy the same number of pens even if the price of pens doubled because it is not worth its while to bother changing to an alternative. In contrast, its demand for steel would be far more price elastic. There is no evidence to suggest

that this is true. Examples given in textbooks, such as salt and matches, have low price elasticities because they have few good substitutes. In the case of pens, manufacturers of pens would long ago have raised prices substantially if they believed that price had little impact on the demand for their product.

ACTIVITY 5 — SKILLS ▸ PROBLEM-SOLVING, REASONING

CASE STUDY: UNDERSTANDING DEMAND

	Price elasticity of demand
Nuts	−0.7
Fresh vegetables	−1.0
Fish	−0.5
Milk	−0.7
Poultry	−0.9
Fresh fruit	−1.0
Eggs	−0.6

▲ Table 5 Estimates of price elasticities of demand for selected household foods

Source: adapted from *Family Food* 2011, Defra

(a) Using the data in the table, calculate the percentage change in quantity demanded if the price of (i) nuts goes up by 10 per cent; (ii) fresh vegetables falls by 7.6 per cent; (iii) poultry goes up by 2 per cent.

(b) Calculate the change in total revenue for sellers if the price of (i) a unit of fresh fruit goes up by US$0.04 from an average price of US$1 when one million units were being sold before the price change; (ii) a dozen eggs goes up US$0.10 from an average price of US$2 when 2 million units were being sold before the price change.

(c) An increase in the price of which foods shown in the data would be most likely to lead to (i) the greatest and (ii) the least change in household expenditure? Explain your answer.

(d) Suggest reasons why the demand for some foods in Table 5 is more price inelastic than the demand for others.

PRICE ELASTICITY OF DEMAND AND TOTAL REVENUE/EXPENDITURE

Price elasticity of demand and changes in **total revenue** or **total expenditure** of a product are linked. Total expenditure is the amount that buyers spend on the product. Total revenue is the amount that sellers receive from selling the product. It will be assumed here that the two are the same amounts, although in practice they may be different if, for example, there are taxes on the sale of the product. Total expenditure or total revenue can be calculated by multiplying price and quantity:

Total expenditure = quantity purchased × price

or

Total revenue = quantity sold × price

For instance, if you bought five apples at US$0.10 each, your total expenditure would be US$0.50 and the total revenue of the seller would be US$0.50. If the price of apples went up, you might spend more, less, or the same on apples depending upon your price elasticity of demand for apples. Assume that the price of apples went up 40 per cent to US$0.14 each. You might react by buying fewer apples. If you now buy four apples (i.e. a fall in demand of 20 per cent), the price elasticity of demand is 20 ÷ 40 or 0.5. Your expenditure on apples will also rise (from US$0.50 to

US$0.56). If you buy two apples (i.e. a fall in quantity demanded of 60 per cent), your elasticity of demand is 60 ÷ 40 or 1.5 and your expenditure on apples will fall (from US$0.50 to US$0.28).

These relationships are what should be expected. If the percentage change in price is larger than the percentage change in quantity demanded (i.e. elasticity is less than 1, or inelastic), then expenditure will rise when prices rise. If the percentage change in price is smaller than the percentage change in quantity demanded (i.e. elasticity is greater than 1 or elastic), then spending will fall as prices rise. If the percentage change in price is the same as the change in quantity demanded (i.e. elasticity is unitary), expenditure will remain unchanged because the percentage rise in price will be equal and opposite to the percentage fall in demand. These relationships are summarised in Table 4 on page 51.

THINKING LIKE AN ECONOMIST

THE PRICE OF OIL

Oil is a key world commodity. In the 1950s and 1960s, the price of oil was relatively stable at around US$2 a barrel. Since 1970, however, the price of oil has changed rapidly and often. Both the actual price of oil (i.e. at current prices) and the real price of oil adjusted for inflation (i.e. at constant prices) have changed, but overall have increased dramatically, as can be seen in Figure 5. There have been a number of large upward price movements in that period.

- Between 1972 and 1974, there was a surge in world demand for oil as economies grew rapidly. At the same time, a 1973 conflict in the Middle East led Arab countries to restrict the supply of oil. Following the conflict, Arab countries realised that, through OPEC, the oil cartel, they could keep the price of oil high by agreeing to restrict output.
- Between 1978 and 1980, the sharp increase in price was caused by political upheaval in Iran, a major world oil producer, which saw a sharp fall in Iranian oil output.
- In the 1980s, OPEC found it difficult to maintain discipline in terms of restricting output of oil. The sharp rises in the price of oil had substantially reduced world demand for oil. The fall in UK demand can be seen in Figure 6. In 1990, however, another conflict, the first Gulf War against Iraq, led to fears that oil output would fall and produce another spike in the oil price.

- In the 2000s, growing demand for oil from China, combined with tight supply, led to a price surge. The world recession of 2008–10 led to a fall in world demand and prices. However, in 2011, oil prices regained their pre-recession levels as demand increased again and supply remained tight. From 2014 onwards, increased supply from OPEC and falling global demand saw the price of crude oil fall to almost one-half its previous level and in real terms was the same as the mid to late 1970s.

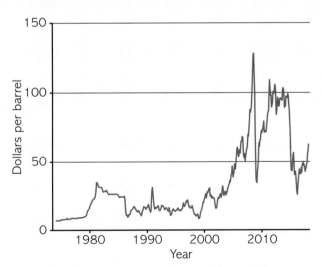

▲ **Figure 5 Spot crude oil price, US$ per barrel at current and constant (2012 US$) price**

Source: http://www.macrotrends.net/1369/ crude-oil-price-history-chart

PRICE ELASTICITY OF DEMAND FOR OIL

As we have seen previously, the actual price of crude oil has varied greatly over the last 50 years. Normally, when the price of a good increases we expect demand to fall and when price decreases consumption should increase. This is also true for oil but the large changes in price have had little if any impact on the global demand for oil. It has maintained a slow and steady growth rate apart from a few brief periods of severe financial instability. The last time a price change had any significant effect on global demand was after the sudden price rises of the 1970s (see Figure 6).

Part of the reason for this very price inelastic demand for oil is that it has had, up until now, few realistic substitutes. It is a source of fuel for transportation and heating and an important raw material in the chemical and plastics industries. Even when more developed economies have produced more fuel-efficient vehicles, developing economies have been growing and increasing the overall demand for oil. We may be about to see a change in the future as electric vehicles become more widespread and the production of renewable energy continues to increase, but at the moment the price elasticity of demand for oil remains very inelastic.

Table 6 shows estimates of the price elasticity of demand for oil for high income countries (OECD economies such as Germany or the USA) and middle and low income countries (non-OECD countries such as Brazil or Tanzania). Demand is highly inelastic for both groups of countries.

	Short term	Long term
OECD	−0.025	−0.093
Non-OECD	−0.007	−0.035

▲ **Table 6 Estimated price elasticities of demand for oil**

Source: adapted from *World Economic Outlook*, April 2011, IMF

SHORT-TERM AND LONG-TERM PRICE ELASTICITIES

In the short term, demand for oil is likely to be highly price inelastic. This is supported by the estimates shown in Table 6. Consumers of oil have little choice but to buy oil to run their cars, trains or heating systems. In the longer term, demand for oil is likely to be less inelastic. This is what Table 6 would suggest. This is partly because consumers can substitute oil for other forms of energy such as gas and coal. It is also because of energy-saving measures that become cost effective, for example, to replace old and inefficient light bulbs or develop more fuel-efficient cars.

OPEC and some of its member countries like Saudi Arabia are aware that too high a price for oil could result in a long-term decline in demand for oil despite rising world incomes. A large-scale switch from petrol-driven vehicles to ones powered by an alternative fuel such as hydrogen, could bring the price of oil down to below US$10 a barrel. This would have a significant impact on economies such as Saudi Arabia, which are highly dependent on oil revenues for their prosperity. It is in the interests of these countries to have an oil price that is as high as possible but is not so high that it encourages the long-term development of technologies that considerably reduce the demand for oil.

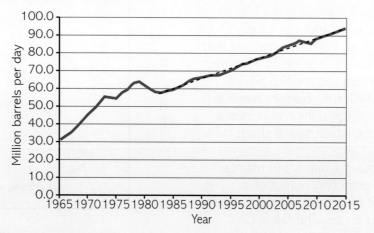

▲ **Figure 6 Global crude oil demand, 1965–2015**

The demand for crude oil has increased steadily each year. In 2014, the average daily demand was 36 million barrels per day higher than it was in 1986. During those 28 years, demand only dipped slightly three times but quickly recovered to maintain the historical growth rate.

CHECKPOINT

1 State the formula for price elasticity of demand.

2 If a good has a price elasticity of demand of −2.5, state whether it is price elastic or inelastic and explain why.

3 What is unitary elasticity?

4 Give three determinants of price elasticity of demand.

5 Create two diagrams to show the difference between a price elastic and a price inelastic demand curve.

6 Give two examples of price elastic products and price inelastic products, for each explain why.

7 State the formula for total revenue.

8 What happens to total revenue when the price of a price inelastic good increases?

SUBJECT VOCABULARY

elastic (demand) where the price elasticity of demand is greater than 1. The responsiveness of demand is proportionally greater than the change in price. Demand is perfectly elastic if price elasticity of demand is infinity.

inelastic (demand) where the price elasticity of demand is less than 1. The responsiveness of demand is proportionally less than the change in price. Demand is perfectly inelastic if price elasticity of demand is zero.

price elasticity of demand or own price elasticity of demand the proportionate response of changes in quantity demanded to a proportionate change in price, measured by the formula:

$$\frac{P}{Q_D} \times \frac{\Delta Q_D}{\Delta P}$$

total expenditure quantity bought multiplied by the average price of a product.

total revenue quantity sold multiplied by the average price of a product.

unitary elasticity where the value of price elasticity of demand is 1. The responsiveness of demand is proportionally equal to the change in price.

EXAM PRACTICE

FATTY FOOD CLAMPDOWN

Food and drink manufacturers are fighting fiercely against measures that would restrict sales of their foods. The mayor of New York, Michael Bloomberg, announced a ban 10 days ago on the sale of 'supersized' sugary drinks in restaurants, cinemas and stadiums. Hungary, France and Denmark have imposed higher taxes on unhealthy foods in order to discourage demand. In Denmark, for example, its 'fat tax' of DKK16 (Danish krone) (US$2.88) per kilogram of unhealthy saturated fat in a product will increase the price of a burger by about US$0.18 and a small pack of butter by about US$0.40.

Industry representatives say that measures such as these simply raise prices for consumers but have little effect on their eating habits. They also hit poor consumers hardest. Health experts say that restricting availability of unhealthy foods and raising their prices sharply will lead to healthier diets and fewer health problems.

Campaigners for health food eating have suffered setbacks as well as triumphs. In November 2012, the Danish government announced it was withdrawing its 'fat tax'. Apart from being unpopular with consumers, it said that retailers had found it difficult to administer

Source: adapted from © the *Financial Times*, 4.10.2011 and 9.6.2012

the tax. It also said that too many Danish consumers were now shopping across the border in Sweden and Germany for products subject to the fat tax. In 2013, Michael Bloomberg's ban on supersized sugary drinks was declared illegal in court. This was not before the ban was widely protested and became the subject of many jokes on late-night comedy shows.

Source: adapted from © the *Financial Times*, 20.11.2013
All Rights Reserved

	Price elasticity
Cheeses	-0.6
Fats (e.g. butter)	-0.5
Sweets	-0.5
Drink	-0.8
Fresh fruit	-1.0
Fresh vegetables	-1.0

▲ **Table 7 Estimates of price elasticities of demand for selected foods**

Source: adapted from *Family Food 2011*, Defra

Q

1 Define price inelastic demand. **(2 marks)**

2 Explain why cheeses and sweets have low price elasticities of demand. **(4 marks)**

3 Assume that the price elasticity of demand for butter is –0.5 and that for a sugary drink is –0.8. There is a rise in taxes on butter and sugary drinks.

Calculate by how much quantity demanded would fall if there were a rise in the price of:

(a) butter by 20 per cent **(2 marks)**

(b) sugary drinks by 50 per cent. **(2 marks)**

4 Examine whether 'fat taxes' are likely to benefit those on low incomes. **(8 marks)**

EXAM HINT

In your answer to Question 3, you need to explain **both** the costs and benefits of a fat tax to those on low incomes. Which costs and which benefits are the most important? Then in your conclusion, explain whether the benefits outweigh the costs or vice versa. Overall, will they be net beneficiaries of a fat tax? Include information both from the data and your own knowledge. Make sure you use Table 7 to assess the statement by food and drink manufacturers that raising prices will have 'little effect' on eating habits.

9 INCOME AND CROSS-ELASTICITIES

UNIT 1
1.3.2

LEARNING OBJECTIVES

- Understand the concept of 'income elasticity of demand'.
- Know how to use formulae to calculate income elasticity of demand.
- Understand the interpretation of numerical values of income elasticity of demand.
- Understand the difference between normal and inferior goods.
- Understand the significance of income elasticity of demand for firms, consumers and the government.
- Understand the concept of 'cross-elasticity of demand'.
- Know how to use formulae to calculate cross-elasticity of demand.
- Understand the interpretation of numerical values of cross-elasticity of demand.
- Understand the significance of cross-elasticity of demand for firms, consumers and the government.

GETTING STARTED

What is the good or service on which you spend the most? It might be chocolate, downloads or clothes for example. If your income went up by 50 per cent, what do you think would happen to the number and percentage of these items you would buy? If the price of these items went up by one-quarter (25 per cent), what would happen to your spending on the item on which you spend the next highest amount?

INCOME ELASTICITY OF DEMAND

The demand for a good will change if there is a change in consumers' incomes. **Income elasticity of demand** is a measure of that change. If the demand for housing increased by 20 per cent when incomes increased by 5 per cent, then the income elasticity of demand would be said to be positive and relatively high. If the demand for food were unchanged when income rose, then income elasticity would be 0. A fall in demand for a good when income rises gives a negative value to income elasticity of demand.

The formula for measuring income elasticity of demand is:

$$\frac{\text{percentage change in quantity demanded}}{\text{percentage change in income}}$$

So the numerical value of income elasticity of a 20 per cent rise in demand for housing when incomes rise by 5 per cent is +20/+5 or +4. The number is positive because both the 20 per cent and the 5 per cent are positive. In contrast, a rise in income of 10 per cent which led to a fall in quantity demanded of a product of 5 per cent would have an income elasticity of −5/+10 or −0.5. The minus sign in −5 shows the fall in quantity demanded of the product. Examples of items with a high income elasticity of demand are holidays and leisure activities, whereas washing up liquid tends to have a low income elasticity of demand.

Just as with price elasticity, it is sometimes easier to use alternative formulae to calculate income elasticity of demand. The above formula is equivalent to:

$$\frac{\Delta Q}{Q} \div \frac{\Delta Y}{Y}$$

where Δ is change, Q is quantity demanded and Y is income. Rearranging the formula gives another two alternatives:

$$\frac{Y}{Q} \times \frac{\Delta Q}{\Delta Y} \quad \text{or} \quad \frac{\Delta Q}{Q} \times \frac{Y}{\Delta Y}$$

Examples of the calculation of income elasticity of demand are given in Table 1. Some economists use the terms 'elastic' and 'inelastic' with reference to income elasticity. Demand is income inelastic if it lies between +1 and −1. If income elasticity of demand is greater than +1 or less than −1, then it is elastic.

Original quantity demanded	New quantity demanded	Original income (£)	New income (£)	$\frac{\Delta Q}{Q}$	÷	$\frac{\Delta Y}{Y}$	Numerical value
20	25	16	18	5/20	÷	2/16	+2
100	200	20	25	100/100	÷	5/20	+4
50	40	25	30	−10/50	÷	5/25	−1
60	60	80	75	0/60	÷	5/80	0
60	40	27	30	−20/60	÷	3/27	−3

The last two columns are headed by **Income elasticity of demand**.

▲ **Table 1 Calculation of income elasticity of demand**

ACTIVITY 1 SKILLS ▶ PROBLEM-SOLVING

CASE STUDY: CALCULATING IED

	Original		New	
	Quantity demanded	Income £	Quantity demanded	Income £
(a)	100	10	120	14
(b)	15	6	20	7
(c)	50	25	40	35
(d)	12	100	15	125
(e)	200	10	250	11
(f)	25	20	30	18

▲ **Table 2 Income elasticity of demand**

(a) Calculate the income elasticity of demand from the data in Table 2.

NORMAL AND INFERIOR GOODS

The pattern of demand is likely to change when income changes. It would be reasonable to assume that consumers will increase their demand for most goods when their income increases. Goods for which this is the case are called **normal goods**.

However, an increase in income will result in a fall in demand for other goods. These goods are called **inferior goods**. There will be a fall in demand because consumers will react to an increase in their income by purchasing products that are perceived to be of better quality. Common examples of inferior goods are:

- bread – consumers switch from this cheap, filling food to more expensive meat or convenience foods as their incomes increase
- canned tomatoes – consumers switch from cheaper canned to the more expensive fresh tomatoes
- bus transport – consumers switch from buses to their own cars when they can afford to buy their own car.

A good can be both a normal and an inferior good depending on the level of income. Bread may be a normal good for people on low incomes (i.e. they buy more bread when their income increases). But it may be an inferior good for higher income earners.

Normal and inferior goods are shown on Figure 1. D_1 is the demand curve for a normal good. It is upward sloping because demand increases as income increases. D_2 is the demand curve for an inferior good. It is downward sloping, showing that demand falls as income increases. D_3 is the demand curve for a good that is normal at low levels of income, but is inferior at higher levels of income.

FIGURE 1

Normal and inferior goods

On the quantity-income diagram, a normal good such as D_1 has an upward sloping curve, while an inferior good such as D_2 has a downward sloping curve. D_3 shows a good that is normal at low levels of income but is inferior at higher levels of income.

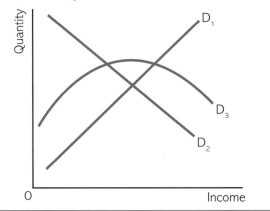

ACTIVITY 2 SKILLS ▶ PROBLEM-SOLVING, REASONING

CASE STUDY: NORMAL AND INFERIOR GOODS

	Grams per person per week			
	1980	1990	2000	2012
Sugar	392	211	132	91
Chicken and other poultry	141	164	170	192
Bananas	91	130	214	214
White bread	668	451	461	266
Fresh potatoes	1176	1008	727	478
Butter	106	42	37	41

▲ **Table 3 Quantity of food purchased by households: average per person per week, grams**

Source: adapted from *Family Food Statistics*, Defra

(a) Household incomes per person rose between each of the years shown in the table. Assuming that all other factors remained constant, which of the goods shown in Table 3 are normal goods and which are inferior goods?

INFERIOR GOODS AND INCOME ELASTICITY

Inferior goods can be distinguished from normal goods by their income elasticity of demand. The formula for measuring income elasticity is:

$$\frac{\text{percentage change in quantity demanded}}{\text{percentage change in income}}$$

A normal good will always have a positive income elasticity because quantity demanded and income either both increase (giving a plus divided by a plus) or both decrease (giving a minus divided by a minus). An inferior good, however, will always have a negative elasticity because the signs on the top and bottom of the formula will always be opposite (a plus divided by a minus or a minus divided by a plus, giving a minus answer in both cases).

For instance, if the demand for bread falls by 2 per cent when incomes rise by 10 per cent then it is an inferior good. Its income elasticity is −2/+10 or −0.2.

Greggs, the UK bakery chain, did well out of the recession starting in 2008 with growing sales and profit. Its 1500 stores found an eager market of customers who were seeing their incomes decline. Budget breakfasts and low-cost pastries, value sandwiches and a national network of stores helped it grow its sales while their more expensive competitors struggled.

As the economy began to climb out of recession in 2013, its sales actually fell. Greggs responded with a turnround plan. It concentrated on redecorating outlets rather than opening new ones to make them more attractive. Menus were changed to include better coffee and more breakfast options to attract better off customers who might otherwise buy from chains like Pret or even the supermarkets. It also added 'Balanced Choice', a range of healthy sandwiches designed to appeal to better off customers.

Source: adapted from © the *Financial Times*, 15.3.2012, 1.7.2014, 30.7.2014, All Rights Reserved.

(a) Why might the data suggest that many of Greggs' products are inferior goods?

(b) Explain why these products would have negative income elasticities.

(c) Suggest why Greggs changed its sales strategy when incomes began to rise as the economy moved out of recession in 2013. In your answer, explain the difference between inferior and normal goods.

NECESSITIES AND LUXURIES

Some economists distinguish between necessities (or basic goods) and luxuries (or superior goods). They state that necessities have an income elasticity

of less than +1 while luxury goods have an income elasticity of greater than +1. The problem with this distinction is that many products that have an income elasticity of less than +1 would hardly be classified as 'necessities' by most consumers. For example, most foods have an income elasticity of less than +1 and would therefore all be classified as necessities. Yet should fruit juice be just as much a necessity as tea, milk or meat? While it can be useful to discuss necessities and luxuries in theory, putting a precise value on these in terms of income elasticity of demand may not be particularly helpful.

CROSS ELASTICITY OF DEMAND

Cross elasticity of demand or cross-price elasticity of demand measures the proportionate response of the quantity demanded of one good to the proportionate change in the price of another. For example, it is a measure of the extent to which demand for goat increases when the price of beef goes up.

The formula for measuring cross elasticity of demand for good X with respect to the price of good Y is:

$$\frac{\text{percentage change in quantity demanded of good X}}{\text{percentage change in price of good Y}}$$

For example, if the quantity demanded of good X falls by 20 per cent as a result of a 10 per cent rise in the price of good Y, then the cross elasticity for good X with respect to the price of good Y is −2 (−20 per cent ÷ 10 per cent). More examples of the calculation of cross elasticity of demand are given in Table 4.

Some economists use the terms 'elastic' and 'inelastic' with reference to cross elasticity. If cross elasticity of demand is greater than +1 or less than −1, then it is elastic. If it lies between +1 and −1, then it is inelastic.

Original quantity demanded of good X	New quantity demanded of good X	Original price of good Y	New price of good Y	$\frac{\Delta Q_X}{Q_X}$	÷	$\frac{\Delta P_Y}{P_Y}$	Numerical value
16	20	8	10	4/16	÷	2/8	+1
50	30	10	11	−20/50	÷	1/10	−4
36	26	9	8	−10/36	÷	−1/9	+2.5
24	36	12	14	12/24	÷	2/12	+3
57	57	9	11	0/57	÷	2/9	0

▲ Table 4 Calculation of cross elasticity of demand

ACTIVITY 4 **SKILLS** PROBLEM-SOLVING

CASE STUDY: CALCULATING XED

	Original		New	
	Quantity demanded of good X	Price of good Y £	Quantity demanded of good X	Price of good Y £
(a)	100	5	180	6
(b)	40	40	13	17
(c)	200	10	170	13
(d)	90	6	30	4
(e)	72	12	54	13
(f)	126	18	140	16

▲ **Table 5 Cross elasticity of demand**

(a) For (a) to (f), calculate the cross elasticity of demand of good X with respect to the price of good Y from the data in Table 5.

SUBSTITUTES AND COMPLEMENTS

The quantity demanded for some goods can be significantly affected by changes in the price of some other goods.

Substitutes A rise in the price of a good such as lamb would increase the quantity demanded of chicken. This is because chicken is a **substitute** for lamb. A substitute is a good that can be replaced by another good. Examples of substitutes for European consumers are:

- Coca-Cola® and Pepsi-Cola®
- a holiday in Spain and a holiday in Turkey
- Asian food and Mexican food.

Two goods that are substitutes will have a positive cross elasticity. An increase (positive) in the price of one good such as a holiday in Spain, leads to an increase (positive) in the quantity demanded of a substitute such as a holiday in Turkey.

Complements A rise in price of a good such as cars would lead to a fall in the quantity demanded of a good such as petrol. This is because cars and petrol are **complements**. A complement is a good that is demanded because it is used with another good. Examples of complements are:

- tennis rackets and tennis balls
- washing machines and soap powder
- foreign holidays and sun cream
- tablets and apps.

Two goods that are complements will have a negative cross elasticity. An increase (positive) in the price of one good such as foreign holidays leads to a fall (negative) in demand for a complement such as sun cream.

However, for many products, the quantity demanded is little affected by the price of some other goods. For example, a rise in the price of soap powder is likely to have little impact on the demand for foreign holidays.

Goods that are not related The demand for some products is unlikely to be affected by the price of other products. For example, a rise in the price of glue is unlikely to have any impact on the demand for chocolate bars. The cross elasticity of two goods that have little relationship to each other would be 0. So a rise in the price of glue of 10 per cent is likely to have no effect (i.e. 0 per cent change) on the demand for chocolate bars. The cross elasticity of demand for glue to the price of chocolate bars is 0 per cent ÷ 10 per cent, which is 0.

THINKING LIKE AN ECONOMIST

ELECTRICITY CONSUMPTION CONTINUES TO FALL

In the USA in 2016, electricity sales fell for the sixth time in 10 years. Despite rising incomes and falling real prices, America's electricity users managed to do with less. Industrial firms made the sharpest cuts in their electricity usage. Their consumption fell in seven of the previous 10 years.

The 1.3 per cent drop in total consumption in 2016 looks small but it came despite real economic growth and the lower real price of electricity. In the past, electric sales always used to go up when the price of electricity declined and the economy grew.

In economic language, electricity had a negative price elasticity of demand and a positive income elasticity of demand. Previously, a 1.6 per cent improvement in income as measured by real gross domestic product (GDP) and a 2.5 per cent real price decrease together should have caused consumers to use at least 1–2 per cent more electricity. But, with similar conditions in both 2015 and 2016, sales declined in both years. So, either the price elasticity of demand for electricity fell or income elasticity of demand fell in those years. Or it could be that both became more inelastic.

Source: adapted from http://oilprice.com/Energy/Energy-General/Electricity-Consumption-Continues-To-Fall.html

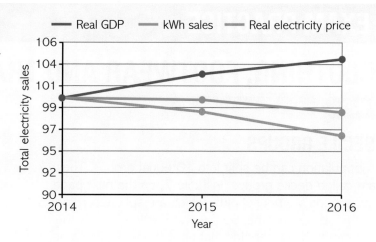

▲ Figure 2 Index of total electricity sales, real GDP and real price of electricity (2014 = 100)

1 State the formulas for income and cross elasticity of demand.

2 What is the difference between normal and inferior goods?

3 Give your own example of each of the goods in question 2.

4 What is the difference between necessities and luxuries?

5 Give your own example of each of the items in question 4.

6 What is the difference between complements and substitutes?

7 Give your own example of each of the items in question 6.

SUBJECT VOCABULARY

complements goods that are purchased with other goods to satisfy a want. Complements have a negative cross elasticity of demand with each other.

cross elasticity or **cross-price elasticity of demand** a measure of the responsiveness of quantity demanded of one good to a change in price of another good. It is measured by dividing the percentage change in quantity demanded of one good by the percentage change in price of the other good.

income elasticity of demand a measure of the responsiveness of quantity demanded to a change in income. It is measured by dividing the percentage change in quantity demanded by the percentage change in income.

inferior goods goods for which demand falls when income increases (i.e. it has a negative income elasticity of demand).

normal goods goods for which demand increases when income increases (i.e. has a positive income elasticity of demand).

substitutes goods that can be replaced by another to satisfy a want. Substitutes have a positive cross elasticity of demand with each other.

EXAM PRACTICE

CLOTHING, FOOTWEAR AND TRANSPORT

SKILLS ANALYSIS, COMMUNICATION, REASONING

DECILE GROUPS

A population can be split into 10 equal groups. These are called decile groups. In Table 7, on the next page, the groups are households, which are split according to their gross income. So the first decile group is the one-tenth of households that have the lowest income. The fifth decile group is the one-tenth of households between 40 and 50 per cent of the total, while the tenth decile group is made up of the highest 10 per cent of households by gross income. Data for the other seven decile groups is available, but is not printed here in order to simplify the data.

MEASURING INCOME ELASTICITY OF DEMAND

Income elasticity of demand is measured by dividing the percentage change in quantity demanded of a good or a basket of goods by the percentage change in income of consumers. Quantity demanded is a physical number, like 100 washing machines or 1000 shirts. However, when data for quantity is not available, a good substitute variable is expenditure. This is quantity multiplied by price. If prices remain the same as expenditure changes, then the percentage change in quantity will be the same as the percentage change in expenditure.

GROSS AND DISPOSABLE INCOME

Gross income is income before income tax, national insurance contributions and welfare benefits have been taken into account.

Disposable income is equal to gross income minus income tax and employees' national insurance contributions plus welfare benefits.

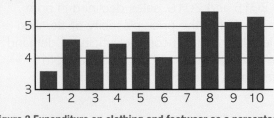

▲ Figure 3 Expenditure on clothing and footwear as a percentage of total expenditure by gross income decile group, 2012

Source: adapted from ONS, *Family Spending* 2013

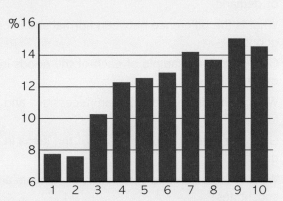

▲ Figure 4 Expenditure on transport as a percentage of total expenditure by gross income decile group, 2012

Source: adapted from ONS, *Family Spending* 2013

	Clothing and footwear %	Transport %	Real disposable income per household
1980	8.1	14.6	100
1995–96	5.9	14.9	129
2012	4.8	13.1	177

▲ Table 6 Clothing and footwear and transport as a percentage of total household expenditure, real disposable income per household, 1980 to 2012

Source: adapted from ONS, *Family Spending* 2013

	First decile	Fifth decile	Tenth decile
Men's outer garments	1.60	3.40	14.20
Men's under garments	0.10	0.40	0.80
Women's outer garments	2.50	7.30	18.50
Women's under garments	0.50	1.10	2.20
Boys' outer garments (5–15)	0.20	0.50	1.60
Girls' outer garments (5–15)	0.30	1.20	1.90
Infants' outer garments (under 5)	0.20	0.70	1.10
Children's under garments (under 16)	0.10	0.50	0.70
Accessories	0.20	0.70	1.90
Sewing equipment and clothing hire	0.00	0.10	0.40
Dry cleaners, laundry and dyeing	0.10	0.20	1.10
Footwear	1.30	3.80	11.80
Total clothing and footwear	**7.10**	**19.90**	**56.20**
Purchase of vehicles	2.40	14.10	48.30
Petrol, diesel and other motor oils	5.10	22.10	47.30
Other motoring costs	3.60	10.80	29.00
Rail and tube fares	0.90	1.90	11.70
Bus and coach fares	0.80	1.40	1.60
Combined fares	0.40	0.20	2.30
Other travel and transport	1.30	2.00	13.90
Total transport	**14.50**	**52.50**	**154.10**
Total expenditure per household on all goods and services £	189.30	422.60	1065.60
Range of total gross income per household £	0–169	438–541	1397+

▲ **Table 7 Average weekly expenditure per household on clothing and footwear and transport (£) by gross income decile group, 2012**

Source: adapted from ONS, *Family Spending* 2013

EXAM TIP

Look at Table 7 to see what happens to spending on bus and coach fares as different income groups are compared. Does this suggest that bus and coach travel is an inferior good? In the future, average incomes are likely to rise (they have doubled over the past 30 years). Is demand for bus and coach travel likely to rise with this rise in incomes? Looking at Table 7, is car and rail transport likely to replace bus and coach travel?

Q

1 The income elasticity of demand for bananas is estimated at +1.4. Which of the following best describes bananas?
  (a) A normal good with income inelastic demand.
  (b) An inferior good with income inelastic demand.
  (c) A normal good with income elastic demand.
  (d) An inferior good with income elastic demand.　**(1 mark)**

2 Explain how spending on clothing and footwear and transport
  (a) varies with income　　　　　　　　　**(4 marks)**
  (b) has changed over time.　　　　　　　**(4 marks)**

3 Using the data, explain whether 'clothing and footwear' is likely to have a higher income elasticity of demand than transport.　　　　　　　　　　　　**(4 marks)**

4 Using Table 7, analyse which components of clothing and footwear and transport are likely to have the highest income elasticities.　　　　　　**(6 marks)**

5 Using the data in Table 7 and the concept of income elasticity of demand, discuss whether bus and coach transport has a future in the UK.　**(14 marks)**

SUPPLY

Supply is the complementary concept to demand. Together they form a powerful model that is used for economic analysis. Supply looks at the producer, what determines the amount they produce at a given price and how it can be represented in diagrams. Price elasticity of supply explores the degree to which changes in price affect the level of supply. Price elasticity of supply also includes calculations and the interpretation of numerical results. Finally, the difference between the short run and the long run is examined.

10 SUPPLY AND PRICE ELASTICITY OF SUPPLY

LEARNING OBJECTIVES

- Understand the concept of 'supply'.
- Understand the distinction between movements along a supply curve and shifts of a supply curve.
- Understand factors that may cause a shift in the supply curve.
- Understand the concept of 'price elasticity of supply'.
- Understand calculation and interpretation of numerical values of price elasticity of supply.
- Understand factors that influence price elasticity of supply.
- Understand the distinction between the short run and long run in economics and its significance for price elasticity of supply.

GETTING STARTED

A large mining company is deciding whether to develop a new gold mine in West Africa on land that has been found to contain gold ore deposits. What factors do you think will determine whether it goes ahead with the project and starts to produce gold?

SUPPLY

In any market there are buyers and sellers. Buyers demand goods while sellers supply goods. **Supply** in economics is defined as the quantity of goods that sellers are prepared to sell at any given price over a period of time. For instance, in June 2017, UK farmers sold 1230 million litres of milk at an average price of 26.7 pence per litre. So economists would say that the supply of milk at 26.7 pence per litre over the one month period was 1230 million litres.

SUPPLY AND PRICE

If the price of a good increases, how will producers react? Assuming that no other factors have changed, they are likely to expand production to take advantage of the higher prices and the higher profits that they can now make. In general, quantity supplied will rise (there will be an extension of supply) if the price of the good also rises, assuming that other variables remain the same.

This can be shown on a diagram using a supply curve. A supply curve shows the quantity that will be supplied over a period of time at any given price. Consider Figure 1, which shows the supply curve for wheat. Wheat is priced at £110 per tonne. At this price only the most efficient farmers grow wheat. They supply 110 million tonnes per year. However, if the price of wheat rose to £140 per tonne, farmers already growing wheat might increase the amount of their land used for wheat production, while other non-wheat growing farmers might start to grow wheat. Farmers would do this because at a price of £140 per tonne it is possible to make a profit on production even if costs are higher than at a production level of 110 million units.

FIGURE 1

The supply curve

The supply curve is upward sloping, showing that firms increase production of a good as its price increases. This is because a higher price enables firms to make profit on the increased output whereas at the lower price they would have made a loss on it. Here, an increase in the price of wheat from £110 to £140 per tonne increases quantity supplied from 110 million tonnes to 150 million tonnes per year.

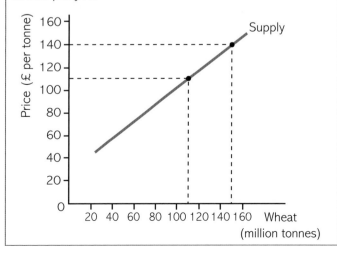

ACTIVITY 1   SKILLS ▷ PROBLEM-SOLVING

CASE STUDY: SUPPLY CURVES

Price (£)	Quantity supplied (million units per year)
5	5
10	8
15	11
20	14
25	17

▲ **Table 1 Price and quantity supplied**

(a) Draw a supply curve from the above data.

(b) Draw new supply curves assuming that quantity supplied at any given price:
(i) increased by 10 units; (ii) increased by 50 per cent; (iii) fell by 5 units; (iv) halved.

A fall in price will lead to a fall in quantity supplied, or *contraction of supply*. This is shown by a movement along the supply curve. At a lower price, some firms will reduce relatively unprofitable production while others will stop producing completely. Some of the latter firms may even go out of business, unable to cover their costs of production from the price received.

An upward sloping supply curve assumes that:

- firms are motivated to produce by profit – so this model does not apply, for instance, to much of what is produced by government

- the cost of producing a unit increases as output increases (a situation known as rising marginal cost) – this is not always true but it is likely that the prices of factors of production to the firm will increase as firms bid for more land, labour and capital to increase their output, thus pushing up costs.

CONDITIONS OF SUPPLY

Changes in price will lead to a change in quantity supplied. These changes are shown by movements along the supply curve. However, there are many other factors apart from price that can cause supply of a product to change. These other factors are, as a group, called the **conditions of supply**. Changes in the conditions of supply cause a shift in the supply curve either to the right or to the left. The conditions of supply include the costs of production, technology and the prices of other goods.

COSTS OF PRODUCTION

The supply curve is drawn on the assumption that the general costs of production in the economy remain constant (part of the ceteris paribus condition). If other things change, then the supply curve will shift. If the costs of production increase at any given level of output, firms will attempt to pass on these increases in the form of higher prices. If they cannot charge higher prices then profits will fall and firms will produce less of the good or might even stop producing it altogether. A rise in the costs of production will therefore lead to a decrease in supply.

This can be seen in Figure 2. The original supply curve is S_1. A rise in the costs of production means that at any given level of output firms will charge higher prices. At an output level of OA, firms will increase their prices from OB to OC. This increase in prices will be true for all points on the supply curve. So the supply curve will shift upwards and to the left to S_2 in Figure 2. There will have been a fall in supply. (Note that a fall in quantity supplied refers to a change in *quantity supplied* because of a change in price and would be shown by a movement along the supply curve.) On the other hand, a fall in the costs of production will lead to an increase in supply of a good. This is shown by a shift to the right in the supply curve.

FIGURE 2

A rise in the costs of production

A rise in the costs of production for a firm will push its supply curve upwards and to the left, from S_1 to S_2. For any given quantity supplied, firms will now want a higher price to compensate them for the increase in their costs.

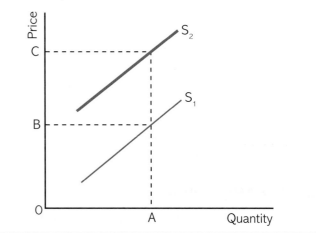

TECHNOLOGY

Another factor that affects supply of a particular good is the state of technology. The supply curve is drawn on the assumption that the state of technology remains unchanged. If new technology is introduced to the production process it should lead to a fall in the costs of production. This greater productive efficiency will encourage firms to produce more at the same price or produce the same amount at a lower price or some combination of the two. The supply curve will shift downwards and to the right. It would be unusual for firms to replace more efficient technology with less efficient technology. However, this can occur at times of conflict or natural disasters. If new technical equipment is destroyed, firms may have to use less efficient means of production, reducing supply at any given price, resulting in a shift in the supply curve to the left.

ACTIVITY 2    SKILLS   REASONING, INTERPRETATION
CASE STUDY: SHIFTING SUPPLY CURVES

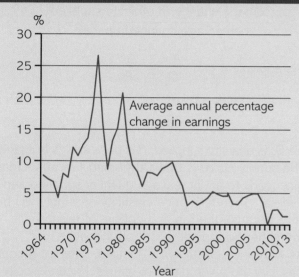

▲ **Figure 3 Average annual percentage change in earnings, 1964–2013 (UK earnings)**

Source: adapted from www.oecd.org

(a) Explain how a change in earnings can shift the supply curve of a product to the left.

(b) Discuss in which years the supply curves for goods made in the UK are likely to have shifted (i) furthest and (ii) least far to the left according to the data.

THE PRICES OF OTHER GOODS

Changes in the prices of some goods can affect the supply of a particular good. For instance, if the price of wood increases substantially there will be an increase in the quantity of wood supplied. More trees will be planted and grown. As a result there will be an increase in the supply of wood (saw) dust used for animal bedding. At the same price, the quantity of wood dust supplied to the market will increase.

An increase in the price of wood therefore leads to an increase in the supply of wood dust. However, an increase in tree planting is likely to be at the expense of production of wheat or sheep farming. So an increase in wood production is likely to lead to a fall in the supply of other agricultural products as landowners switch production to take advantage of higher profits in wood.

ACTIVITY 3   SKILLS   REASONING, COMMUNICATION
CASE STUDY: THE CHANGING PRICE OF TECHNOLOGY

Explain, using supply curves, why it cost US$10,000 in 1970 for a machine that could do the same as a calculator which cost US$100 in 1975 and US$5 today.

OTHER FACTORS

A number of other factors affect supply. These include:
- the goals of sellers – if for some reason there is a change in the profit levels that a seller expects to receive as a reward for production, then there will be a change in supply; for instance, if an industry such as the book retailing industry went from one made up of many small sellers more interested in selling books than making a profit to one where the industry was dominated by a few large profit-seeking companies, then supply would fall
- government legislation – anti-pollution controls that raise the costs of production, the removal of legal barriers to setting up business in an industry, or tax changes, are some examples of how government can change the level of supply in an industry
- expectations of future events – if firms expect future prices to be much higher, they may restrict supplies and stockpile goods; if they expect disruptions to their future production because of a strike they may stockpile raw materials, paying for them with borrowed money, thus increasing their costs and reducing supply
- the weather – in agricultural markets, the weather plays a crucial role in determining supply, bad weather reducing supply, good weather producing bumper yields
- producer cartels – in some markets, producing firms or producing countries band together, usually to restrict supply; this allows them to raise prices and increase their profits or revenues; the best known cartel today is OPEC, which restricts the supply of oil onto world markets.

ACTIVITY 4 — SKILLS ▸ REASONING, ANALYSIS, COMMUNICATION

CASE STUDY: EFFECTS ON SUPPLY

Explain, using diagrams, how you would expect supply of the following goods to be affected by the events stated, assuming that other variables remain the same.

(a) **Rubber.** Rubber crops in Laos begin to yield natural rubber.

(b) **Office space in London.** The government introduced new regulations allowing office space to be converted into homes.

(c) **Corn.** US farmers respond to rising prices for soya by increasing their planting soya on land that was used to grow corn.

PRODUCER SURPLUS

FIGURE 4

Producer surplus
The supply curve shows how much will be supplied at any given price. Except on the last unit supplied, the supplier receives more for the good than the lowest price at which it is prepared to supply. This difference between the market price and lowest price at which a firm is prepared to supply is producer surplus. Total producer surplus is shown by the shaded area above the supply curve.

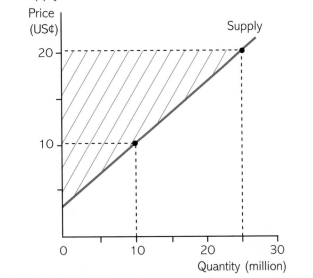

In Figure 4, firms will supply 10 million units at US$0.10, whereas they will supply 25 million units at US$0.20. Assume that the price that firms receive is actually US$0.20. Some firms will then receive more than the lowest price at which they are prepared to supply. For instance, one firm was prepared to supply the 10 millionth unit at US$0.10. The firm receives

US$0.20, which is US$0.10 more. This US$0.10 is **producer surplus**. It is the difference between the market price, which the firm receives, and the price at which it is prepared to supply. The total amount of producer surplus earned by firms is shown by the area between the supply curve and horizontal line at the market price. It is the sum of the producer surplus earned at each level of output.

PRICE ELASTICITY OF SUPPLY

Price elasticity of demand measures the responsiveness of changes in quantity demanded to changes in price. Equally, the responsiveness of quantity supplied to changes in price can also be measured – this is called price elasticity of supply. The formula for measuring the price elasticity of supply is:

$$\frac{\text{percentage change in quantity supplied}}{\text{percentage change in price}}$$

This is equivalent to: $\dfrac{\Delta Q_s}{Q_s} \div \dfrac{\Delta P}{P}$

or $\dfrac{P}{Q_s} \times \dfrac{\Delta Q_s}{\Delta P}$

where Q_s is quantity supplied, P is price and Δ is change.

The supply curve is upward sloping (i.e. an increase in price leads to an increase in quantity supplied and vice versa). Therefore price elasticity of supply will be positive because the top and bottom of the formula will be either both positive or both negative.

As with price elasticity of demand, different ranges of elasticity are given different names. Price elasticity of supply is:

- **perfectly inelastic (0)** if there is no response in quantity supplied to a change in price
- **inelastic (between 0 and 1)** if there is a less than proportionate response in quantity supplied to a change in price
- **unitary (1)** if the percentage change in quantity supplied equals the percentage change in price
- **elastic (between 1 and infinity)** if there is a more than proportionate response in quantity supplied to a change in price
- **perfectly elastic (infinite)** if producers are prepared to supply any amount at a given price.

These various elasticities are shown in Figure 5. It should be noted that any straight line supply curve passing through the origin has an elasticity of supply equal to 1. This is best understood if we take the formula:

$$\frac{P}{Qs} \times \frac{\Delta Qs}{\Delta P}$$

$\Delta Qs/\Delta P$ is the inverse of (i.e. 1 divided by) the slope of the line, while P/Qs, assuming that the line passes through the origin, is the slope of the line. The two multiplied together must always equal 1.

FIGURE 5

Elasticity of supply

The elasticity of supply of a straight line supply curve varies depending upon the gradient of the line and whether it passes through the origin.

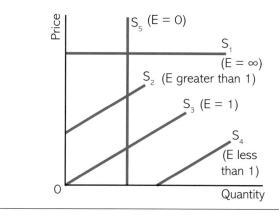

DETERMINANTS OF ELASTICITY OF SUPPLY

As with price elasticity of demand, there are four factors that determine supply elasticity across a wide range of products.

Availability of substitutes Substitutes here are not consumer substitutes but producer substitutes. These are goods that a producer can easily produce as alternatives. For instance, one model of a car is a good producer substitute for another model in the same range because the car manufacturer can easily switch resources on its production line. In contrast, carrots are not substitutes for cars. The farmer cannot easily switch from the production of carrots to the production of cars. If a product has many substitutes then producers can quickly and easily alter the pattern of production if its price rises or falls. Hence its elasticity of supply will be relatively high. However, if a product has few or no substitutes, then producers will find it difficult to respond flexibly to variations in price. If there is a fall in price, a producer may have no alternative but either to carry on producing much the same quantity as before or withdraw from the market. Price elasticity of supply is therefore low.

Time The shorter the time period, the more difficult producers find it to switch from making one product to another. So in the short term, supply is likely to be more price inelastic than in the long term. There is a number of reasons why this is the case.

- Some items take a long time to make. For example, if there is a crop failure of a product like olives, it will take until the next growing season to increase supply again whatever price the market sets for olives in the short term.
- If there is no spare capacity to make more of a product, it will be difficult to increase supply very much even if prices rise sharply. The more spare capacity, the less constraint this places on increasing supply in response to price rises.
- With some products, it is easy and relatively cheap to hold stocks to supply the market when they are demanded. With others, it is impossible to hold stocks. For example, large stocks of wheat are kept around the world that can be released if prices rise, so keeping price elasticity of supply relatively high. However, it is impossible in most cases to store electricity. So when there is a sharp rise in price of electricity in a free market, there is unlikely to be much response in terms of extra supply in the short term if the system is working at full capacity. The longer the time period, the easier it is for the market to build up appropriate stocks or to build excess capacity if stocks are not possible. So price elasticity of supply is higher in the longer term.
- Price elasticity of supply will be higher the easier it is for a firm to switch production from one product to another or for firms to enter the market to make the product.

ACTIVITY 5   SKILLS ▶ PROBLEM-SOLVING

CASE STUDY: ELASTICITY OF SUPPLY

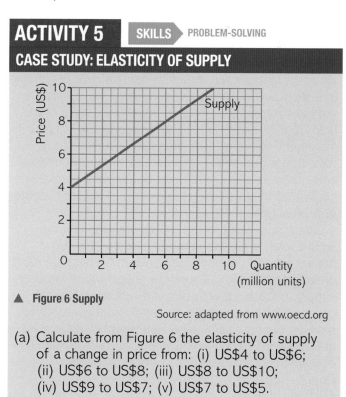

▲ Figure 6 Supply

Source: adapted from www.oecd.org

(a) Calculate from Figure 6 the elasticity of supply of a change in price from: (i) US$4 to US$6; (ii) US$6 to US$8; (iii) US$8 to US$10; (iv) US$9 to US$7; (v) US$7 to US$5.

THE SHORT RUN AND THE LONG RUN

The phrases 'short term' and 'long term' have no precise meaning in economics. For example, 'short term' might be until the next harvest, or the next delivery from China. The long term might be three months or it could be 30 years.

However, **short run** and **long run** have precise meanings in microeconomics. The long run is when all factors of production involved in making a good are variable. This means they can all be changed. The short run is defined as being a period of time when at least one factor of production is fixed. This means it cannot be changed.

For producers, price elasticity of supply is likely to be higher in the long run than in the short run. In the long run, producers can change their methods of production to increase or decrease quantity supplied in response to price changes. In the short run, there could be capacity problems. For example, a producer might not be able to increase production this week or this month because all its machines are in constant use. A coffee grower might not be able to increase supply of coffee beans because it only has a fixed number of coffee bushes.

THINKING LIKE AN ECONOMIST

ELECTRIC CAR DEMAND SPARKS LITHIUM SUPPLY FEARS

The cost of extracting vital battery material is likely to create a 'supercycle' and drive up prices. In 2016, Tesla™ Motors founder and chief executive Elon Musk joked that lithium was only the 'salt on the salad' for the batteries that are vital to the US company's electric cars.

Twelve months later, concern is growing among analysts, and some other carmakers, that the supply of what Mr Musk dismissed as 'salt' will not be able to keep pace with demand as the expansion of electric vehicles begins to reduce the world's century-long reliance on oil. 'There's a pivot', says John Kanellitsas, vice-chairman of Lithium Americas, a mining company that is developing a lithium project in Argentina. 'There's much more consensus on demand; we're no longer even debating demand. We're shifting to supply and whether, as an industry, we can deliver.'

Prices for the lithium used in batteries have more than doubled since 2015, according to CRU. Asset managers, including BlackRock and Capital Group, have bought up shares in smaller lithium producers, while there is speculation that battery and carmakers could also begin to invest in miners to secure a tighter grip on supply.

Some now point to the possibility of a 'lithium supercycle', similar to what unfolded in the iron market around the year 2000, when Chinese demand drove prices higher. 'It took many years for [iron ore] supply to catch up with demand – this will be the case in battery materials if capital is not available to develop new projects', says Reg Spencer, an analyst at Canaccord Genuity, who forecasts that US$3 billion of investment is needed to extract more lithium from the deserts of South America and hard rock in Australia. 'We saw several examples of steel mills

acquiring iron ore resources or investing in mine capacity to ensure security of supply, something we might expect in battery materials as well', Mr Spencer added.

A representative from Volkswagen recently told a lithium conference in London that supplies of lithium and cobalt, another battery metal, are of the greatest concern to the carmaker, according to people present at the event. In April BYD, the Chinese electric car and bus company part-owned by Warren Buffett, said it was talking to lithium producers in Chile about potential deals to secure lithium supply.

Swiss bank UBS has become the latest to raise its forecast for sales of electric vehicles (EVs) by more than 50 per cent. It now estimates EVs will make up 14 per cent of car sales globally by 2025 and 30 per cent in Europe as they begin to cost the same as conventional fuel vehicles in the next few years. 'While all battery materials are abundant, mining and refining capacity could represent a bottle neck when EV demand takes off, even if only temporarily', UBS analysts noted.

The growing anxiety about supply comes as the production of lithium remains dominated by a handful

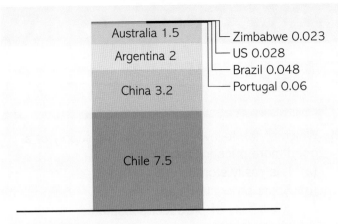

▲ **Figure 7 Lithium reserves**

Source: Roskill, Bernstein analysis

of companies: Albemarle, Sociedad Química y Minera de Chile; Chinese producers, Tianqi Lithium; and Ganfeng Lithium, which produce from Australia. Dr David Deak, chief technical officer at Lithium Americas, who formerly worked as an engineer for Tesla, says the lithium market needs to grow from its annual production of 182,000 tonnes to an average of 3.1 million tonnes for 20 years to electrify the world's fleet of vehicles.

Others remain confident that miners can meet the challenge given that lithium is widely found in the earth's crust. Analysts at consultancy CRU expect supply to increase and the market to be in a surplus from 2018 onwards. 'It will be a healthy market for producers of lithium, but there's so much lithium to be found on the earth, there's no shortage of lithium', Willem Middelkoop, founder of the Commodity Discovery Fund in the Netherlands, says.

Still, supply from new projects has been slow to come to the market. Financing is also trickier because lithium prices cannot be hedged like traded commodities, such as copper, via futures. 'Many people overestimate the simplicity of supply coming on', says Richard Seville, chief executive of Orocobre, which built the first lithium brine project in 20 years in Argentina. All of which suggests the hunt for the 'salt' may intensify further.

CHECKPOINT

1 What is meant by supply?

2 What does a supply curve show?

3 What is the difference between an extension of supply and a contraction of supply?

4 List four factors that will affect the supply of a good.

5 Create a diagram to show the impact of the following scenarios on the supply of maize:
- an increase in the wages of agricultural workers
- much better growing weather than expected
- the introduction of a more pest resistant variety of maize.

6 State the formula for price elasticity of demand.

7 If a good has a price elasticity of supply of −0.2, state whether it is price elastic or inelastic and explain why.

8 Give three determinants of price elasticity of supply.

9 Create two diagrams to show the difference between a price elastic and a price inelastic demand curve.

10 Give two examples of price elastic products and price inelastic products, for each explain why.

SUBJECT VOCABULARY

conditions of supply factors other than price, such as income or the price of other goods, that lead to changes in supply and are associated with shifts in the supply curve.

long run the period of time in which all factor inputs can be varied but the state of technology remains constant.

price elasticity of supply a measure of the responsiveness of quantity supplied to a change in price. It is measured by dividing the percentage change in quantity supplied by the percentage change in price.

producer surplus the difference between the market price that firms receive and the price at which they are prepared to supply.

short run the period of time when at least one factor input to the production process can be varied.

supply the quantity of goods that suppliers are willing to sell at any given price over a period of time.

EXAM PRACTICE

SALMON PRICES ON THE RISE   SKILLS   REASONING, PROBLEM-SOLVING, COMMUNICATION, ANALYSIS

The price of salmon is on an upward trend. Demand for the fish is growing as consumers worldwide have a greater appreciation of its health-giving properties. Supply is struggling to keep up with this trend.

Almost all salmon sold today is farmed salmon rather than wild salmon caught in the sea or rivers. Rising prices have led to increased profits for salmon farmers.

However, despite the incentive of rising profits, there are factors that are holding back the expansion of the industry. In Norway, the largest producer of farmed salmon, production by private firms is restricted by the government, which issues licences.

There is also a limit on the number of salmon that can be farmed in one place because of the risk of disease. Worldwide, the price of fish feed is rising as a result of more fish farming and limited catches of some smaller fish that are an important source of fish feed.

The weather too can impact on supply. In 2013, Norway suffered colder than usual seawater, which reduced the growth of salmon and so the total tonnage of salmon produced fell. In recent years, outbreaks of sea lice have reduced supply and in 2016, pollution in Chile killed millions of fish, cutting Chilean production by 25 per cent.

Q

1 Which of the following will make the supply of a good more price inelastic?
   (a) It is easily stored.
   (b) Spare production capacity.
   (c) Availability of producer substitutes.
   (d) Long production time.   **(1 mark)**

2 Using the data in Figure 8, analyse two significant features of the data shown.   **(6 mark)**

3 Draw supply curve diagrams to explain the effects on the supply of salmon of the following described in the article:
   (a) a change in profits by fish farmers   **(4 marks)**
   (b) licences issued by governments to salmon farmers   **(4 marks)**
   (c) a change in fish feed prices   **(4 marks)**
   (d) changes in the weather.   **(4 marks)**

4 Examine the likely price elasticity of supply for salmon.   **(8 marks)**

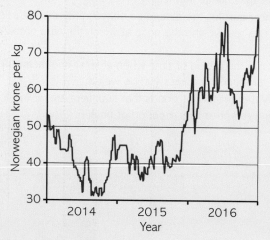

▲ **Figure 8 Salmon prices**

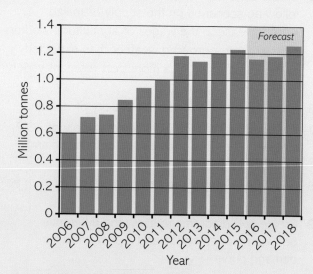

▲ **Figure 9 Total world salmon production**

PRICE DETERMINATION

The two previous sections on demand and supply are now brought together to show how a market works via the market mechanism. The unit looks at how subsequent shifts of the demand and supply curves can affect equilibrium price and quantity, and the impact this has on consumer and producer surplus. The functions of the price mechanism show the crucial role it plays in allocating scarce resources. Finally, it considers the broader area of how governments use indirect taxation and subsidies to influence the market in order to achieve their macroeconomic aims.

11 MARKET EQUILIBRIUM

LEARNING OBJECTIVES

- Understand equilibrium price and quantity, and how they are determined.
- Understand the causes of changes in the equilibrium price and quantity as a result of shifts in demand and supply curves.
- Understand the operation of market forces to eliminate excess demand and excess supply.
- Understand the distinction between consumer and producer surplus.
- Understand that changes in demand or supply might affect consumer and producer surplus.

GETTING STARTED

What is your favourite fruit? What is its price? How is this price determined? To answer that, you need to think about demand for and supply of the fruit.

EQUILIBRIUM PRICE

Buyers and sellers come together in a market. A price (sometimes called the market price) is struck and goods or services are exchanged. Consider Table 1. It shows the demand and supply schedule for a good at prices between US$2 and US$10.

- If the price is US$2, demand will be 12 million units but only 2 million units will be supplied. Demand is greater than supply and there is therefore **excess demand** (i.e. too much demand in relation to supply) in the market. There will be a *shortage* of products on the market. Some buyers will be lucky and they will quickly buy the 2 million units being sold. But supply will be 10 million units short for the rest of the unlucky buyers in the market. For instance, it is not possible to buy some luxury cars without being on a waiting list for several years because current demand is too great.
- If the price is US$10, buyers will not buy any goods. But sellers will wish to supply 10 million units. Supply is greater than demand and therefore there will be **excess supply**. There will be a surplus of products on the market: 10 million units will remain unsold. A sale in a shop is often evidence of excess supply in the past. Firms tried to sell the goods at a higher price and failed.
- There is only one price where demand equals supply. This is at a price of US$6 where demand

and supply are both 6 million units. This price is known as the **equilibrium price**. This is the only price where the demand of buyers equals the supply of sellers in the market. It is also known as the **market-clearing price** because all the products supplied to the market are bought or cleared from the market, but no buyers are left frustrated in their wishes to buy goods.

An alternative way of expressing the data in Table 1 is shown in Figure 1. The equilibrium price is where demand equals supply. This happens where the two curves cross, at a price of US$6 and a quantity of 6 million units. If the price is above US$6, supply will be greater than demand and therefore excess supply will exist. If the price is below US$6, demand is greater than supply and therefore there will be excess demand.

Price (US$)	Quantity demanded (million units per month)	Quantity supplied (million units per month)
2	12	2
4	9	4
6	6	6
8	3	8
10	0	10

▲ **Table 1 A demand and supply schedule**

FIGURE 1

Equilibrium

At US$6, the quantity demanded is equal to the quantity supplied. The market is said to be in equilibrium at this price.

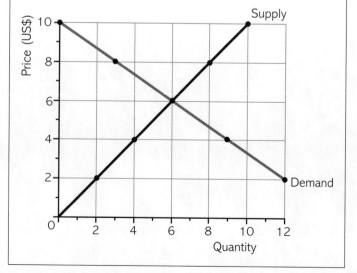

ACTIVITY 1

SKILLS   PROBLEM-SOLVING, REASONING

CASE STUDY: EQUILIBRIUM PRICE

Price (US$)	Quantity demanded (million units)	Quantity supplied (million units)
30	20	70
20	50	50
10	80	30

▲ Table 2 A demand and supply schedule

(a) Plot the demand and supply curves shown in Table 2 on a diagram.

(b) What is the equilibrium price?

(c) In what price range is there (i) excess demand and (ii) excess supply?

(d) Will there be a surplus or a shortage in the market if the price is:
(i) US$10; (ii) US$40; (iii) US$22; (iv) US$18; (v) US$20?

CHANGES IN DEMAND AND SUPPLY

It is explained in Chapters 7, 8 and 10 that a change in price would lead to a change in quantity demanded or supplied, shown by a movement along the demand or supply curve. A change in any other variable, such as income or the costs of production, would lead to an increase or decrease in demand or supply and therefore a shift in the demand or supply curve.

Demand and supply diagrams provide a powerful and simple tool for analysing the effects of changes in demand and supply on equilibrium price and quantity.

Consider the effect of a rise in consumer incomes. This will lead to an increase in the demand for a normal good. In Figure 2(a) on page 78 this will push the demand curve from D_1 to D_2. As can be seen from the diagram, the equilibrium price rises from P_1 to P_2. The quantity bought and sold in equilibrium rises from Q_1 to Q_2. The model of demand and supply predicts that an increase in incomes, all other things being equal (the ceteris paribus condition), will lead to an increase both in the price of the product and in the quantity sold. Note that the increase in income shifts the demand curve and this then leads to a movement along the supply curve.

Figure 2(b) on page 78 shows the market for televisions in the early 2000s. In the early 2000s, many manufacturers introduced flat screen televisions. As a result, there was huge increase in sales of these televisions and a dramatic fall in sales of older, more bulky sets. In economic terms, the demand for older,

bulky sets fell. This is shown by a shift to the left in the demand curve. The equilibrium level of sales in Figure 2(b) falls from OB to OA while equilibrium price falls from OF to OE. Note again that a shift in the demand curve leads to a movement along the supply curve.

Prices of television sets have fallen since the 1970s. The main reason for this was an increase in productive efficiency due to the introduction of new technology, enabling costs of production to fall. A fall in costs of production is shown by the shift to the right in the supply curve in Figure 2(c) on page 78 . At any given quantity of output, firms will be prepared to supply more television sets to the market. The result is an increase in quantity bought and sold from OA to OB and a fall in price from OF to OE. Note that there is a shift in the supply curve which leads to a movement along the demand curve.

So far we have assumed that only one variable changes and that all other variables remain constant. However, in the real world, it is likely that several factors affecting demand and supply will change at the same time. Demand and supply diagrams can be used to some extent to analyse several changes. For instance, in the 2000s the demand for flat screen and high-definition (HD) television sets increased due to rising real incomes. At the same time, supply increased too because of an increase in productive efficiency. Overall, the price of television sets fell slightly. This is shown in Figure 2(d) on page 78 . Both the demand and supply curves shift to the right. This will lead to an increase in quantity bought and sold. In theory, depending upon the extent of the shifts in the two curves, there could be an increase in price, a fall in price or no change in the price. Figure 2(d) shows the middle of these three possibilities.

FIGURE 2

Shifts in the demand and supply curves

Shifts in the demand or supply curves for a product will change the equilibrium price and the equilibrium quantity bought and sold.

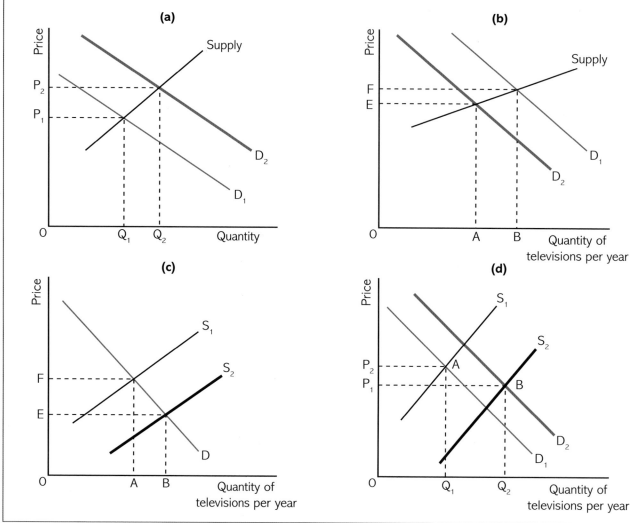

DO MARKETS CLEAR?

It is very easy to assume that the equilibrium price is either the current market price or the price towards which the market moves. Neither is correct. The market price could be at any level. There could be excess demand or excess supply at any point in time.

Nor will market prices necessarily tend to change to their equilibrium prices over time. One of the most important controversies in economics today is the extent to which markets move towards market-clearing prices.

The argument put forward by neo-classical free market economists is that markets do tend to clear. Let us take the example of the coffee market. In this market, there are many producers (farmers, manufacturers, wholesalers and retailers) that are

motivated by the desire to make as large a profit as possible. When there is excess demand for coffee (demand is greater than supply), coffee producers will be able to increase their prices and therefore their profits and still sell all they produce. If there is excess supply (supply is greater than demand), some coffee will remain unsold. Producers then have a choice. Either they can offer coffee for sale at the existing price and risk not selling it or they can lower their price to the level where they will sell everything offered. If all producers choose not to lower their prices, there is likely to be even greater pressure to reduce prices in the future because there will be unsold stocks of coffee still in the market. Therefore when there is excess demand, prices will be driven upwards while prices will fall if there is excess supply.

This can be shown in a diagram. In Figure 3, there is excess demand at a price of OE. Buyers want to purchase AC more of coffee than is being supplied. Shops, manufacturers and coffee growers will be able to increase their prices and their production and still sell everything they produce. If they wish to sell all their output, they can increase their prices to a maximum of OF and their output to a maximum OB, the market-clearing price and production levels. This they will do because at higher prices and production levels they will be able to make more profit. If there is excess supply, coffee producers will be left with unsold stocks. At a price of OG, output left unsold will be AC. Producers in a free market cannot afford to build up stocks forever. Some producers will lower prices and the rest will be forced to follow. Production and prices will go on falling until equilibrium output and price is reached. This is usually referred to as a stable equilibrium position.

FIGURE 3

The operation of market forces in the coffee market
Market pressure will tend to force down coffee prices when there is excess supply, such as at price OG, but force up coffee prices when there is excess demand, such as at price OE.

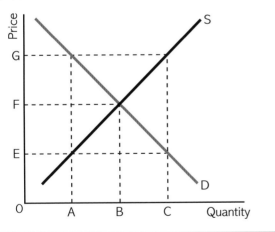

These pressures which force the market towards an equilibrium point are often called **free market forces**. However, critics of the market mechanism argue that free market forces can lead away from the equilibrium point in many cases. In other markets, it is argued that market forces are too weak to restore equilibrium. Some economists give the labour market as an example of this. In other markets, there are many forces such as government legislation, trade unions and multinational monopolies that are greater than the power of the market.

ACTIVITY 2   SKILLS ▸ REASONING, ANALYSIS, COMMUNICATION

CASE STUDY: THE 2012 LONDON OLYMPIC TORCH

The Olympic torch was carried by around 8000 people up and down the UK in the run-up to the London 2012 Olympic Games. Torch carriers were given the opportunity to buy their torch for £215. Almost immediately after the first torches were carried, a 2012 Olympic torch appeared on eBay®, the electronic auction site, with a price tag of £150,000. More appeared for auction and prices of around £10,000 were being paid. In the long term, these sorts of prices are unlikely to be maintained. By 2014, torches were being offered for sale on eBay for £2300 and the price is likely to fall further. Torches from the 2008 Beijing Olympics are selling for around £2000 on eBay, for example. A rarer torch from the 1948 London Olympics recently sold for £6250 at a Christie's auction. Only 1720 torches were made for the 1948 Olympics.

Source: adapted from © the *Financial Times* 26.5.2012, All Rights Reserved.

(a) Explain, using a demand and supply diagram, how the second-hand price of a 2012 Olympic torch is set.
(b) Why were the first few 2012 Olympic torches sold likely to have a higher price than 2012 Olympic torches sold in 2014?
(c) Explain, using a demand and supply diagram, why it is likely that, in 10 years time, a 1948 Olympic torch is likely to fetch a higher price at auction than a 2012 Olympic torch.

FIGURE 4

Consumer and producer surplus
Consumer surplus is the shaded area JGH, showing how much more consumers are prepared to pay for buying a total of OA goods. Producer surplus is FGJ, showing how much less they would have been prepared to accept in revenue for supplying OA than they actually received.

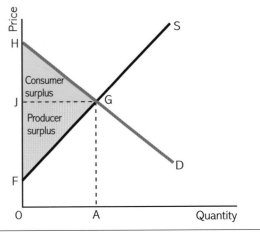

CONSUMER AND PRODUCER SURPLUS

Consumer and producer surplus can be shown on a demand and supply diagram. In Figure 4, the equilibrium price is OJ. Consumer surplus, the difference between how much buyers are prepared to pay for a good and what they actually pay, is the area JHG. Producer surplus, the difference between the market price which firms receive and the price at which they are prepared to supply, is shown by the area JGF.

The amounts of consumer and producer surplus will change if either demand or supply change. For example, in Figure 5 demand increases, shown by a shift to the right in the demand curve. For suppliers, an increase in demand results in higher equilibrium output and higher prices. Suppliers will experience an increase in producer surplus from FGJ to FKM, as shown in Figure 5(a). For consumers, the increase in demand shows that they are prepared to pay a higher price for the same quantity bought. They place a greater value on the good. So their consumer surplus also increases from JGH to MKL, as shown in Figure 5(b). In contrast, if there is a fall in demand, shown by a shift to the left in the demand curve, consumer and producer surplus will both fall.

Figure 6 shows what happens if the supply increases, shown by a shift to the right in the supply curve. For suppliers, an increase in supply results in higher equilibrium output but lower prices. Suppliers will experience an increase in producer surplus from JKH to FGM, as shown in Figure 6(a). For consumers, the increase in supply will lead to an increase in quantity bought. So their consumer surplus also increases from HKL to MGL, as shown in Figure 6(b). On the other hand, if there is a fall in supply, shown by a shift to the left in the supply curve, consumer and producer surplus will both fall.

FIGURE 5

Changing consumer and producer surplus with a rise in demand

A rise in demand from D_1 to D_2 increases producer surplus from FGJ to FKM and consumer surplus from JGH to MKL.

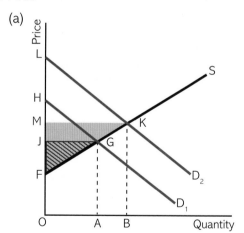

(a)

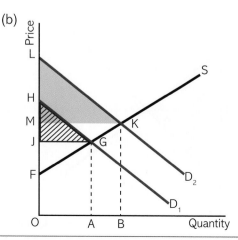

(b)

FIGURE 6

Changing consumer and producer surplus with a rise in supply

A rise in supply from S_1 to S_2 increases producer surplus from JKH to FGM and consumer surplus from HKL to MGL.

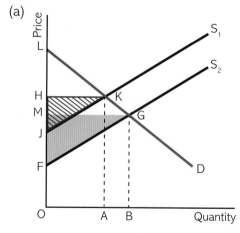

(a)

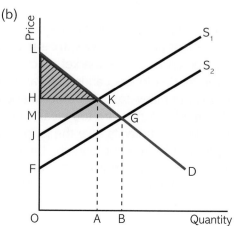

(b)

ACTIVITY 3   SKILLS   REASONING, COMMUNICATION, INTERPRETATION

CASE STUDY: METAL PRICES

Nickel

Nickel prices reached their highest levels in over two years in November 2017 as a result of growing demand for stainless steel in China.

The metal, which is used to make stainless steel, has jumped more than 10 per cent to US$12,573 a tonne. Since hitting its lowest level in a year during June 2017, nickel has appreciated by over 40 per cent.

Analysts also expect higher demand for nickel via electric vehicles as carmakers seek powerful batteries that use more of the metal.

Following years of low prices, total refined supply of nickel has remained flat over the past few years, and is likely to rise only gradually until 2020.

Cobalt

In 2018, Glencore, the world's biggest producer of cobalt, is due to bring the Katanga mine in the Democratic Republic of Congo back into production after a US$430 million modernisation of its processing system. The operation has the potential to add as much 22,000 tonnes of cobalt to a market with annual output of around 100,000 tonnes.

That could bring the price of cobalt, which has surged 135 per cent this year, back down. Goldman Sachs analysts say the restarting of production at Katanga 'will significantly change the supply situation' for cobalt and ensure the market is well supplied up to the end of 2019.

Source: Based on Sanderson, H. and Hume, N. (2017), 'Nickel prices extend blockbuster run on supply concerns and Cobalt's meteoric rise at risk from Congo's Katanga'. Financial Times, 1 November and 14 March. All Rights Reserved.

(a) Using demand and supply diagrams, explain why the prices of nickel and cobalt have changed.

POINTS TO NOTE

Equilibrium is a very powerful concept in economics but it is essential to remember that the equilibrium price is unlikely to be the most desirable price or 'right' price in the market. The most desirable price in the market will depend on how one defines 'desirable'. It may be, for instance, the one that leads to the greatest economic efficiency, or it may be the one that leads to fairest outcome. Alternatively, it may be the one that best supports the defence of the country.

Demand can also equal supply without there being equilibrium. At any point in time, what is actually bought must equal what is actually sold. There can be no sellers without buyers. So actual demand (more often referred to as realised or ex-post demand in economics) must always equal actual (or *realised* or *ex-post*) supply. Equilibrium occurs at a price where there is no tendency to change. Price will not change if, at the current price, the quantity that consumers wish to buy (called *planned* or *desired* or *ex-ante* demand) is equal to the quantity that suppliers wish to sell (called planned or desired or ex-ante supply).

Therefore only in equilibrium will planned demand equal planned supply.

THINKING LIKE AN ECONOMIST

THE PRICE OF GAS

The world price of gas has a direct impact on households in the UK. The higher the price, the higher the gas bills for households tend to be.

Most gas is sold on long-term contracts. A gas producer, like Shell or ExxonMobil, will enter into, say, a 10-year or 20-year deal to sell a customer gas at a particular price. A relatively small percentage of gas is sold in the 'spot market'. This is the market for sales of gas in the very short term.

The long-term trend has been for demand for gas to grow as Figure 7 shows. Fast growing emerging countries like China are demanding gas to fuel their economies. In developed countries, gas is being substituted for coal to produce electricity. Gas is a cleaner fuel than coal and produces fewer greenhouse gas emissions. The supply of gas has been growing too, particularly from Middle East producers, such as Saudi Arabia.

The high cost of developing gas fields and transporting gas has tended to push up world gas spot prices over time, as Figure 8 shows. However, gas prices in the USA have fallen on average over the past few years because of fracking. This is a relatively new technology that involves pushing water at high pressure into gas bearing rocks and collecting the gas released.

If there were no costs involved in the transportation of gas, gas prices in different parts of the world would be the same, assuming that other variables remained the same. However, in the USA, transportation infrastructure has not kept up with growth in gas production. There are not enough pipes or plants to convert gas into a liquid for transportation by ship to get more gas onto world markets. The gas therefore has to be sold relatively locally in the USA. This has increased supply relative to demand, pushing down gas prices in the USA at a time when gas prices in other markets, such as Japan and Europe, have been rising.

Although global consumption of gas has increased slightly since 2014, the rate of increase has declined compared to the long-term average. The biggest increase in consumption has come from the EU and China, but in Brazil and Russia consumption has fallen as the use of renewable energy has increased. At the same time, supply has increased, particularly from Australia. In 2016, proved global gas reserves rose to 186.6 trillion cubic metres, sufficient to meet more than 50 years of current production, with global supplies forecast to increase by around a further 30 per cent by 2020. Lower gas prices are likely to continue for some time.

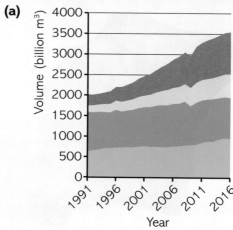

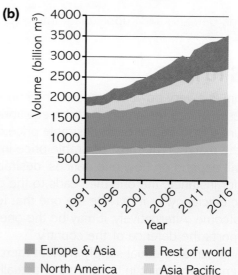

▲ **Figure 7 World (a) production and (b) consumption of gas by region, 1991–2016**

Source: adapted from *BP Statistical Review of World Energy*, 2017

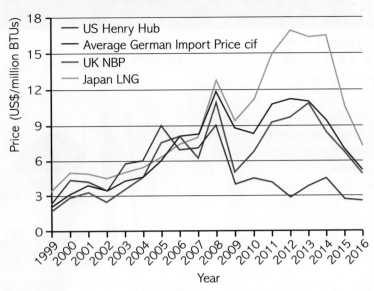

▲ **Figure 8 World gas prices, 1999–2016**

Source: adapted from *BP Statistical Review of World Energy*, 2017

CHECKPOINT

1 What is equilibrium price?

2 Create a diagram to show the impact on equilibrium price and quantity of:
- an inwards/leftwards shift of the supply curve
- an outwards/rightwards shift of the demand curve.

3 What does it mean when we say 'markets clear'?

4 Give an example of something that may prevent a market from clearing.

5 What is the difference between consumer and producer surplus?

6 What happens to consumer surplus when there is:
- a rise in demand
- a fall in supply?

SUBJECT VOCABULARY

equilibrium price the price at which there is no tendency to change because planned (or desired or ex ante) purchases (i.e. demand) are equal to planned sales (i.e. supply).

excess demand where demand is greater than supply.

excess supply where supply is greater than demand.

free market forces forces in free markets that act to reduce prices when there is excess supply and raise prices when there is excess demand.

market-clearing price the price at which there is neither excess demand nor excess supply, but where everything offered for sale is purchased.

EXAM PRACTICE

COCOA BEAN PRICES

SKILLS ▶ REASONING, ANALYSIS, COMMUNICATION, CRITICAL THINKING

The raw ingredient for the chocolate we buy in stores is cocoa beans. The world's largest producer of beans is the Ivory Coast in Africa, although the cocoa tree is native to Central and South America.

Cocoa is a commodity, and like other commodities its price is subject to variation. Cocoa beans can be stored from year to year. Rising prices will encourage those holding stocks to sell into the market. Rising prices will also encourage farmers to plant more cocoa trees but these take four to five years to grow before they will produce their first harvest. When prices fall the reverse happens. In the short term, supply is therefore very dependent on weather conditions.

After a dip in 2012, cocoa prices rose steadily, driven in part by rapidly rising demand in emerging markets, such as China and India. Between 2009 and 2014, sales in India more than doubled from 54,700 tonnes to 129,200 tonnes, while China's rose 41 per cent to 192,500 tonnes.

In 2016, a surge in cocoa prices, caused chocolate makers to use less cocoa, while the rising health consciousness among consumers has led to declining chocolate demand. On the supply side, bumper crops from the Ivory Coast and Ghana pushed cocoa prices even lower. In early 2017, cocoa prices fell to a 10-year low.

Q

1 Draw a supply and demand diagram to show:

  (a) why prices rose between 2012 and 2016   **(4 marks)**

  (b) why prices fell after 2016.   **(4 marks)**

2 Analyse why a commodity, such as cocoa, experiences price fluctuations.   **(6 marks)**

3 Discuss what might happen to cocoa prices from 2017 onwards.   **(14 marks)**

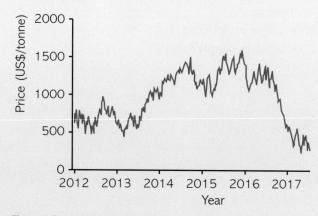

▲ Figure 9 Cocoa price, 2012–17

12 FUNCTIONS OF THE PRICE MECHANISM

LEARNING OBJECTIVES

- Understand the rationing, incentive and signalling functions of the price mechanism for allocating scarce resources.
- Understand the price mechanism in the context of different types of markets, including local, national and global markets.

GETTING STARTED

It is sales time in the stores. Prices of your favourite purchases have been cut in half. What signals does this send to you? How have your incentives to buy changed? What do low prices say about the scarcity of the product?

THE PRICE MECHANISM

The price mechanism in a market economy allocates resources between conflicting uses. In a market, there are buyers who demand goods and sellers who supply goods. The interactions of demand and supply fix the price at which exchange takes place. The forces of demand and supply also determine how much is bought and sold and by whom.

Price has three important functions in allocating resources in a market: a **rationing function**; a **signalling function**; and an **incentive function**.

RATIONING FUNCTION

Consumer wants are infinite, but we live in a world of scarce resources. Somehow, those scarce resources need to be allocated between competing uses. One function of price in a market is to allocate and ration those resources. If many consumers demand a good, but its supply is relatively scarce, then prices will be high. Limited supply will be rationed to those buyers prepared to pay a high enough price. If demand is relatively low, but supply is very high, then prices will be low. The low price ensures that high numbers of goods will be bought, reflecting the lack of scarcity of the good. This can be shown on a diagram. In Figure 1, there is a fall in supply of a good from S_1 to S_2. As a result, quantity demanded falls from OB to

OA. The movement up the demand curve shows the effect of the rationing function. Higher prices lead to a rationing of the good to buyers.

FIGURE 1

The rationing and signalling function of price
A fall in supply leads to higher equilibrium prices. This signals that buyers and sellers should change their behaviour. High prices also ration the good among buyers, shown by the movement up the demand curve to a new equilibrium.

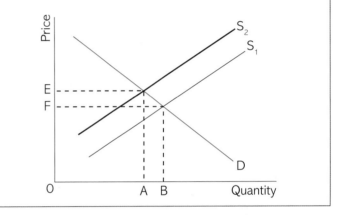

SIGNALLING FUNCTION

The price of a good is a key piece of information to both buyers and sellers in the market. Prices occur because of the transactions of buyers and sellers. They reflect market conditions and therefore act as a signal to those in the market. Decisions about buying and selling are based on those signals. In Figures 1 and 2, the change in price signals to both buyers and sellers that they should change quantity bought and sold.

INCENTIVE FUNCTION

Prices act as an incentive for buyers and sellers. Low prices encourage buyers to purchase more goods. For consumers, this is because the amount of satisfaction or utility gained per dollar spent increases relative to other goods. Higher prices discourage buying because consumers get fewer goods per dollar spent. On the supply side, higher prices encourage suppliers to sell more to the market. Firms may have to take on more workers and invest in new capital equipment to achieve this. Low prices discourage production. A prolonged fall in prices may drive some firms out of the market because it is no longer profitable for them to supply. This can be shown on a diagram. In Figure 2, there is a rise in demand for a good from D₁ to D₂. As a result, quantity supplied rises from OA to OB. The movement up the supply curve shows the effect of the incentive function. Higher prices are an incentive for firms to increase supply.

To illustrate how these functions help allocate resources, consider two examples.

- **Example 1** Assume that the demand for fur coats falls because of lobbying from animal welfare groups. The demand curve for fur coats therefore shifts to the left. At the old price, more is supplied than is now demanded, i.e. there is excess supply. The equilibrium price will then fall. The lower price is a signal to manufacturers of fur coats that market conditions have changed for the worse. The lower price reduces incentives for fur coat manufacturers. Lower prices indicate that their profits will fall. Hence, they will make fewer fur coats, shown by the movement down the supply curve.

- **Example 2** Assume that the supply of oil falls. The supply curve for oil therefore shifts to the left. At the old equilibrium price, there is excess demand. The equilibrium price will then rise with less oil

being supplied and demanded. The higher price is a signal to buyers and sellers that market conditions have changed. The new higher price also rations oil among buyers, shown by the movement up the demand curve for oil. Some consumers of oil will be priced out of the market altogether. Others will respond by purchasing less oil.

FIGURE 2

The signalling and incentive function of prices
A rise in demand leads to higher equilibrium prices. This signals that buyers and sellers should change their behaviour. Higher prices also act as an incentive for sellers to supply. They will increase the amount they supply to the market.

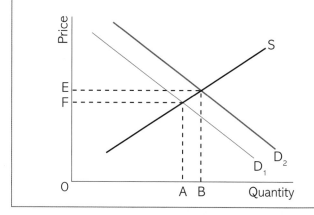

THINKING LIKE AN ECONOMIST

MOTOR CARS

The history of the UK motor car industry in recent years is a good example of how markets allocate resources. In the 1950s and 1960s, the British market was largely protected from foreign competition. The British motorist bought cars made in British factories, even if some of these factories were owned by foreign companies, such as Ford. It was largely a sellers' market, with demand restricted by the ability of consumers to obtain credit for the purchase of cars.

The 1970s and 1980s, however, were disastrous for the British car industry. British-made cars tended to be of inferior quality in both production and design to foreign made, imported cars. High costs of production, due to high wages, a lack of investment and inefficient working practices, led to low profits or losses for UK car plants. The result, as Figures 3 and 4 show, was falling production, falling exports and increased imports. The market was signalling that the UK was a poor location to make cars. Low profits and

losses provided an incentive for UK car factory owners to reduce production or close plants.

The turning point came in the mid-1980s with the arrival of Japanese manufacturers in the UK. Honda, Nissan and Toyota all set up new car plants. By using the same production methods as in Japanese factories, cars were produced at internationally competitive costs and quality. This new competition forced US and European car manufacturers in the UK market to change the way in which they designed and built cars. Today, there is no UK-owned mass manufacturer of vehicles. However, there are a number of foreign-owned car plants in the UK that are highly successful. Nissan's Sunderland car plant, for example, has one of the highest productivity (output per worker) levels in the world.

Figures 3 and 4 show both production and sales of cars in the UK fell significantly when the world economy went into recession in 2008. A shift to the left in the demand curve for cars led to both a fall in production and a fall in the average price of cars sold. The fall in demand signalled to car manufacturers that they should reduce production.

The movement down the supply curve, with falling profits, was the incentive for firms to cut production Figuboth in the UK and worldwide. Figures 5, 6 and 7 show the extent to which the UK car market has recovered from the 1970s and 1980s.

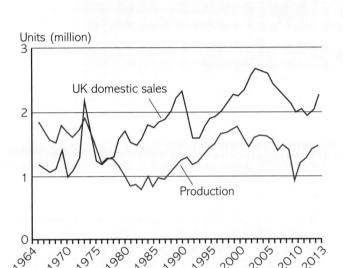

▲ **Figure 3 Annual production and sale of cars, UK, 1964–2013**

Source: adapted from *Economic & Labour Market Review*, Office for National Statistics; *Motor Industry Facts 2012*, Society of Motor Manufacturers and Traders (SMMT)

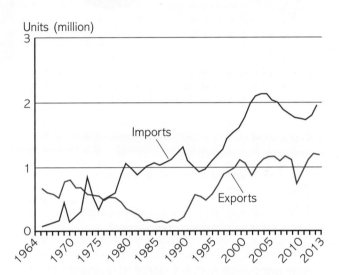

▲ **Figure 4 Annual exports and imports of cars, UK, 1964–2013**

Source: adapted from *Economic & Labour Market Review*, Office for National Statistics; *Motor Industry Facts 2012*, Society of Motor Manufacturers and Traders (SMMT)

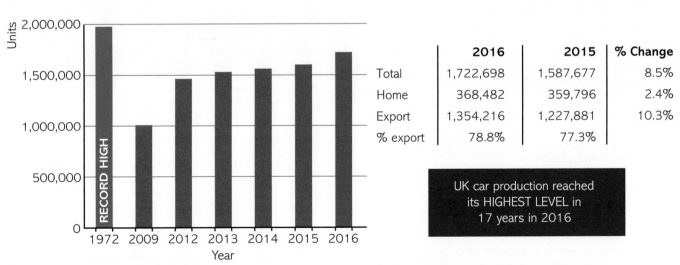

	2016	**2015**	**% Change**
Total	1,722,698	1,587,677	8.5%
Home	368,482	359,796	2.4%
Export	1,354,216	1,227,881	10.3%
% export	78.8%	77.3%	

UK car production reached its HIGHEST LEVEL in 17 years in 2016

▲ **Figure 5 UK car production, 1972–2016**

▲ **Figure 6 UK car manufacturing – 2016 vs 2015**

Source: https://www.smmt.co.uk/wp-content/uploads/sites/2/SMMT-Motor-Industry-Facts-2017_online_May.pdf

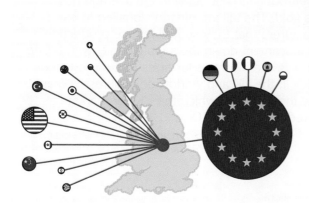

THE UK EXPORTS TO MORE THAN 160+ COUNTRIES WORLDWIDE
TOP EXPORT DESTINATIONS FOR UK CARS

Worldwide				EU	
EU	56.0%	JAPAN	1.9%	Germany	8.6%
US	14.5%	CANADA	1.8%	Italy	7.2%
CHINA	6.5%	SOUTH KOREA	1.7%	France	6.7%
TURKEY	3.1%	Other	2.2%	Belgium	6.2%
AUSTRALIA	2.5%			Spain	3.4%

1.35 million cars manufactured for export in 2016

8 out of 10 cars made in the UK are exported

The UK exports to 160 markets worldwide

▲ **Figure 7 UK car exports, 2016**

Source: https://www.smmt.co.uk/wp-content/uploads/sites/2/SMMT-Motor-Industry-Facts-2017_online_May.pdf

CHECKPOINT

1 Why do resources in a market economy have conflicting uses?

2 What are the three functions of the price mechanism in allocating resources?

3 Why do higher prices ration goods?

4 How does price act as a signal to producers?

5 Why would low prices act as an incentive to buyers but not sellers?

SUBJECT VOCABULARY

incentive function when changes in price encourage buyers and sellers to change the quantity they buy and sell. A rise in price encourages buyers to purchase less and sellers to produce more; and vice versa.

rationing function when changes in price lead to more or less being produced, so increasing or limiting the quantity demanded by buyers.

signalling function when changes in price give information to buyers and sellers that influence their decisions to buy and sell.

EXAM PRACTICE

ORGANIC FARMING IN DECLINE

SKILLS REASONING, COMMUNICATION, ANALYSIS

The amount of land used for organic products is still in decline. One-quarter of organic meat producers said prices for their products were 'definitely not' high enough to sustain organic production according to a survey carried out by the Organic Research Centre. Producers of other organic meat and dairy products too have been complaining about the prices they receive. One major problem to hit organic farmers has been the high prices they have to pay for animal feeds, which have contributed to falling profits.

The body that represents organic farmers warned that rising demand for organic dairy and meat products by consumers combined with falling output risked increasing the amount of organic food that was imported into the UK.

Source: adapted from © the *Financial Times*, 13.3.2014, All Rights Reserved.

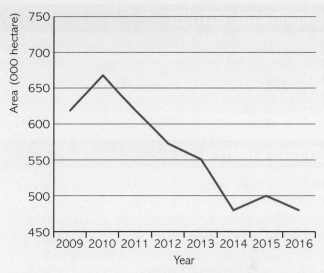

▲ Figure 8 Organically managed land in the UK, 2009–16

Source: adapted from www.gov.uk

Q

1 Using evidence from the data, explain what has happened to the amount of land used for organic farming in the UK in recent years. **(4 marks)**

2 With supply of UK-produced organic meat and dairy products falling, their prices should rise. Explain how the rationing function will then affect the allocation of resources in this market. **(4 marks)**

3 Analyse, using a diagram, how the signalling and incentive functions have acted to change the allocation of resources in the market for organic meat. **(6 marks)**

4 Discuss whether increased imports of organic produce will lead to a fall in the price of organic products in UK shops. **(14 marks)**

EXAM HINT

For Question 4, start by analysing the data using demand and supply diagrams. Are the increased imports happening with no change in UK output? Or are potentially higher UK prices for organic produce providing a signal to overseas buyers and an incentive for them to sell into the UK? Are imports the result of price changes or the cause of price changes? Weigh the different possibilities for your evaluation.

13 INDIRECT TAXES AND SUBSIDIES

LEARNING OBJECTIVES

- Understand the impact of indirect taxes on consumers, producers and the government.
- Understand the incidence of indirect taxes on consumers and producers.
- Understand the impact of subsidies on consumers, producers and the government.
- Understand the incidence of subsidies on consumers and producers.

GETTING STARTED

The government announces a new sugar and fat tax that will increase the standard rate of value added tax (VAT) on selected products from its current 20 per cent to 30 per cent. These products include lemonade, cola and chocolate bars. What is VAT and how is it calculated? By how many per cent do you think the price of these products will increase in shops? Will it have any impact on consumption of these items?

INDIRECT TAXES AND SUBSIDIES

An indirect tax is a tax on expenditure. The two major indirect taxes are value added tax (VAT) and excise duties.

VAT is an example of an **ad valorem tax**. The tax charged increases in proportion to the value of the tax base. In the case of VAT, the tax base is the price of the good. Most goods in Bangladesh now carry a 15 per cent VAT charge. Excise duties, on the other hand, are an example of a **specific or unit** tax. The amount of tax charged does not change with the value of the goods but with the amount or volume of the goods purchased. So the excise duty on a litre of petrol is the same whether the it costs US$5 or US$10, but the VAT is twice as much on the latter compared to the former. The main excise duties are on tobacco and petrol. They should not be confused with customs duties, which are charged on imports.

A **subsidy** is a grant given by government to encourage the production or consumption of a particular good or service. Subsidies, for instance, may be given on essential items such as housing or bread. Alternatively, they may be given to firms that employ disadvantaged workers, such as the long-term unemployed or people with disabilities. They may also be given to firms that manufacture domestically produced goods to help them be more competitive than imported goods.

CASE STUDY: PETROL IN INDIA

The price of a litre of petrol in India at the pumps is made up as follows:

	INR
Petrol cost before tax	28.5
Excise duty	21.5
	50.0
VAT @ 27 per cent	13.5
Price at the pumps	63.5

1. For each of the following changes, calculate the new price of petrol. For each change, assume that the price at the pumps is initially INR 63.5 (Indian rupees).

(a) An increase in the cost of crude oil pushed up the cost of petrol before tax from INR 28.5 to INR 32.

(b) The government increased excise duty from INR 21.5 to INR 23.

(c) VAT was reduced from 27 per cent to 25 per cent.

(d) The government removed both excise duties and VAT on petrol and instead introduced a subsidy of INR 2 a litre.

THE INCIDENCE OF TAX

Price theory can be used to analyse the impact of the imposition of an indirect tax on a good. Assume that a specific tax of US$1 per unit is imposed. This has the effect of reducing supply. Sellers of that particular good will now want to charge US$1 extra per unit sold. In Figure 1, this is shown by a vertical shift of US$1 in the supply curve at every level of output. However many units are produced, sellers will want to charge US$1 more per unit and therefore there is a parallel shift upwards and to the left of the whole supply curve from S_1 to S_2.

The old equilibrium price was US$7.30, at which price 60 million units were bought and sold. The introduction of the US$1 tax will raise price and reduce quantity demanded. The new equilibrium price is US$8, at which price quantity demanded falls to 40 million units.

This result might seem surprising. The imposition of a US$1 per unit tax has only raised the price of a unit by US$0.70 and not the full US$1 of the tax. This is because the **incidence of tax** is unlikely to fall totally on consumers. The incidence of tax measures the burden of tax upon the taxpayer. In this case the consumer has paid US$0.70 of the tax. Therefore the other US$0.30 which the government receives must have been paid by producers.

40 million of this, while producers will pay US$0.30 × 40 million. Consumers will therefore pay US$28 million of tax while producers will pay US$12 million. Total spending on that good will fall from US$438 million (US$7.30 × 60 million) to US$320 million (US$8 × 40 million). Revenues received by producers will fall from US$438 million (US$7.30 × 60 million) to US$280 million (US$7 × 40 million).

AD VALOREM TAXES

The above analysis can be extended to deal with ad valorem taxes. The imposition of an ad valorem tax will lead to an upwards shift in the supply curve. However, the higher the price, the greater will be the amount of the tax. Hence the shift will look as in Figure 2. Consumers will pay FG tax per unit while the incidence of tax on producers per unit will be HG.

FIGURE 1

The incidence of a specific tax
The imposition of an indirect tax of US$1 per unit will push up the supply curve from S_1 to S_2. The vertical distance between the two supply curves at any given output is US$1. As a consequence, equilibrium price will rise from US$7.30 to US$8.00. The consumer therefore pays an extra US$0.70 per unit. The other US$0.30 of the tax is paid by the producer because the price it receives per unit before tax falls from US$7.30 to US$7.00.

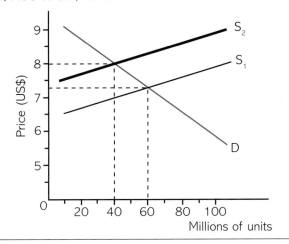

FIGURE 2

The incidence of an ad valorem tax
The imposition of an ad valorem tax will push the supply curve upwards from S_1 to S_2. The following gives the key facts about the change:
(a) original equilibrium price and quantity, OG and OB
(b) new equilibrium price and quantity, OF and OA
(c) incidence of tax per unit on consumers, GF
(d) incidence of tax per unit on producers, HG
(e) tax per unit in equilibrium, HF
(f) total tax paid by consumers, GKEF
(g) total tax paid by producers, GHJK
(h) total tax revenue of government, FHJE
(i) change in producers' revenue, OBCG – OAJH
(j) change in consumers' expenditure, OBCG – OAEF.

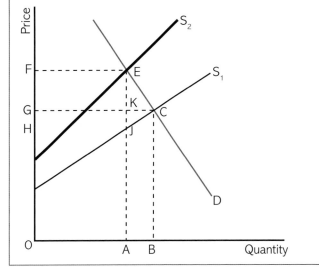

TAX REVENUES

Using Figure 1, we can also show the change in total expenditure before and after imposition of the tax as well as the amount of tax revenue gained by the government. The government will receive total tax revenue of US$1 × 40 million (the tax per unit × the quantity sold); hence tax revenues will be US$40 million. Consumers will pay US$0.70 ×

ACTIVITY 2

SKILLS   REASONING, PROBLEM-SOLVING, ANALYSIS

CASE STUDY: EFFECT OF A TAX ON DEMAND AND SUPPLY

Price (US$)	Quantity demanded	Quantity supplied
4	16	4
6	12	6
8	8	8
10	4	10
12	0	12

▲ **Table 1 A demand and supply schedule**

(a) Draw the demand and supply curves from the data in Table 1.

(b) What is the equilibrium quantity demanded and supplied?

The government now imposes a specific tax of US$3 per unit.

(c) Show the effect of this on the diagram.

(d) What is the new equilibrium quantity demanded and supplied?

(e) What is the new equilibrium price?

(f) What is the incidence of tax per unit on (i) the consumer and (ii) the producer?

(g) What is the (i) tax per unit and (ii) total government revenue from the tax?

(h) By how much will the before tax revenue of producers change?

EXAM HINT

Draw your diagram so that it is at least half a side of A4. It will help you get the right information on the diagram. It also helps examiners see that you have the right answers.

SUBSIDIES

A subsidy on a good will lead to an increase in supply. At any given quantity supplied, the price will be lower. This is because the price charged by suppliers will be higher than the price paid by consumers. The difference is the subsidy given by the government. The supply curve will therefore shift downwards and to the right, as shown in Figure 3.

The equilibrium price before the subsidy was given was OH and OA was demanded and supplied. With the subsidy, the equilibrium price is OJ and the equilibrium

output is OB. The subsidy is the vertical distance between the two supply curves. At the equilibrium output of OB, the subsidy per unit is CF (or JG). This is the difference between the cost of production to firms of BF (or OG) and the price that consumers pay, BC (or OJ).

However, as with indirect taxes, the full subsidy per unit is not passed on completely to consumers. They see a fall in price of JH, but this is less than the subsidy paid of JG. Firms receive HG of the subsidy per unit. So some of subsidy goes to consumers, but some also goes to producers.

The total cost to the government of the subsidy is the quantity bought multiplied by the subsidy per unit. It is OB × JG, which is the area JCFG.

FIGURE 3

The effect of a subsidy

The government giving a subsidy on a good will push the supply curve to the right from S1 to S2. The following gives the key facts about the change:

(a) original equilibrium price OH and equilibrium quantity OA

(b) new equilibrium price OJ and equilibrium quantity OB

(c) subsidy per unit received by consumers JH

(d) subsidy per unit received by producers HG

(e) total subsidy per unit in equilibrium JG

(f) total subsidy received by consumers JCEH

(g) total subsidy received by producers HEFG

(h) total subsidy given by government JCFG

(i) change in producers' revenue (consumers' expenditure plus government subsidy) OBFG − OAKH

(j) change in consumers' expenditure OAKH − OBCJ.

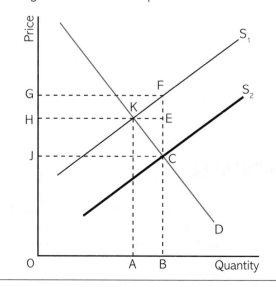

ACTIVITY 3   SKILLS   REASONING, ANALYSIS

CASE STUDY: EXCISE DUTY IN BANGLADESH

In Bangladesh, the 2017/18 budget included a new excise duty of 25 per cent to be charged on e-cigarettes and e-cigarette liquids. The budget also reduced the import duty paid on the materials and components needed to manufacture laptops and computers.

(a) Explain, using a diagram, the effect of the changes in tax in the 2017/18 budget on the quantity and price of:
  (i) e-cigarettes
  (ii) laptops and computers.

TAXES AND ELASTICITY

How much tax incidence falls on consumers rather than producers depends on the elasticities of demand and supply. Figure 4 shows situations where either the supply curve is perfectly elastic or the demand curve is perfectly inelastic. In both cases, the vertical shift in the supply curve, which shows the value of the tax per unit, is identical to the final price rise. Therefore, all of the tax will be paid by consumers.

FIGURE 4

Where the incidence of tax falls entirely on the consumer

If supply is perfectly elastic or demand perfectly inelastic, then it can be seen from the graphs that the incidence of tax will fall entirely on consumers.

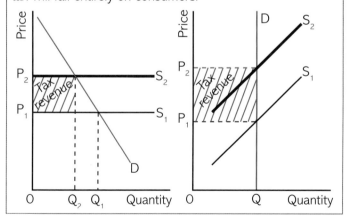

Figure 5, in contrast, shows two cases where the incidence of tax falls totally on the producer. Producers will find it impossible to shift any of the tax onto consumers if the demand curve is perfectly elastic. Consumers are not prepared to buy at any higher price than the existing price. If the supply curve is perfectly inelastic, then the supply curve after imposition of the

tax will be the same as the one before. Equilibrium price will therefore remain the same and producers will have to bear the full burden of the tax.

Examining these extreme situations, we can conclude that the more elastic the demand curve or the more inelastic the supply curve, the greater will be the incidence of tax on producers and the less will be the incidence of tax on consumers. So, for the government, taxation revenue will be greater the more inelastic the demand for the product taxed, assuming that other factors remain the same. For instance, if demand were perfectly elastic, the imposition of an indirect tax would lead to quantity demanded falling to zero and tax revenue being zero. At the opposite extreme, if demand were perfectly inelastic, consumers would buy the same quantity after imposition of the tax as before. Hence, revenue will be equal to the tax per unit multiplied by the quantity demanded before imposition. If the price elasticity of demand lies between these two extremes, the imposition of a tax will lead to a fall in quantity demanded. The higher the elasticity, the larger will be the fall in quantity demanded and hence the lower will be the tax revenue received by government. Hence, it is not a coincidence that excise duties are placed on tobacco and petrol, all of which are relatively price inelastic.

FIGURE 5

Where the incidence of tax falls entirely on the producer

If supply is perfectly inelastic or demand perfectly elastic, then it can be seen from the graphs that the incidence of tax will fall entirely on producers.

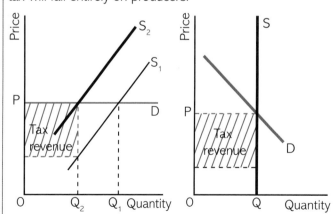

SUBSIDIES AND ELASTICITY

The same analysis can be applied to subsidies. In general, subsidies tend to be given where the policy objective is to reduce the price of the good. The largest fall in price will occur when either demand is highly inelastic or supply is highly elastic. If demand is very elastic or supply very inelastic, there will be very little, if any, change in price following the granting of a subsidy. This is because producers will not pass on the subsidy to consumers. They will absorb the subsidy, which will allow them to increase their profits.

This can be shown on a diagram. In Figure 6(a), demand is inelastic over the quantity range AB. A subsidy shifts the supply curve to the right, from S_1 to S_2. As a result, equilibrium price falls from OG to OH. Given that the subsidy is HF per unit, only FG per unit of this is absorbed by producers. Almost all of the subsidy per unit is received by consumers. The same analysis applies when supply is elastic, as in Figure 6(b).

FIGURE 6

Elasticities and subsidies

The more price inelastic is demand or price elastic is supply, the more of a subsidy will benefit consumers rather than producers. Given a subsidy of HF per unit, HG per unit is received by consumers, but only GF by producers.

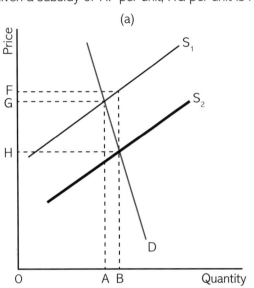

(a)

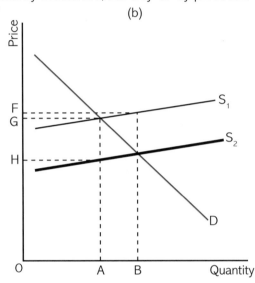

(b)

THINKING LIKE AN ECONOMIST

THE FRENCH FILM INDUSTRY

The French government has, for a long time, believed that its film industry should be protected. It believed that without aid the French film industry would die, overwhelmed by US imports of English-language films. Protecting the survival of the French film industry has mainly taken the form of a variety of subsidies to French film projects, currently around €1 billion per year. By subsidising costs of production, the French government has shifted the supply curve of French films to the right. This has resulted in considerably more films being produced compared to the free market level.

Some of the subsidies are paid for by indirect taxes on ticket sales at cinemas and on sales of DVDs. These indirect taxes shift the supply curve for cinema tickets and DVDs to the left, raising their price and lowering the quantity bought. However, demand for both products is relatively inelastic and the taxes relatively small.

Part of the tax is paid by producers rather than consumers anyway. So the fall in quantity demanded is relatively small. The gain in subsidies is much greater than any loss from fewer sales.

In 2014, a government-funded report suggested a further tax of 1 per cent on sales of Internet-connected devices such as smartphones and tablets. The report argued that the impact on sales of smartphones and tablets would be minimal. Not only is 1 per cent a small number, but sellers would probably absorb almost all the tax themselves rather than pass them on to consumers. The tax would be 'fair' because owners of digital devices can view French films without necessarily paying for them directly.

Source: adapted from © the *Financial Times*, 9.1.2014, All Rights Reserved.

CHECKPOINT

1 What is the difference between a direct and an indirect tax?

2 What is ad valorem tax?

3 What is a subsidy?

4 What does the incidence of a tax measure?

5 Which will yield more tax revenue: a price elastic or a price inelastic demand curve?

6 Which will yield more tax revenue, a price elastic or a price inelastic supply curve?

SUBJECT VOCABULARY

ad valorem tax tax charged as a percentage of the value of the good.

incidence of tax the tax burden on the taxpayer.

specific or unit tax tax charged on volume.

subsidy a grant given that lowers the price of a good, usually designed to encourage production or consumption of a good.

EXAM PRACTICE

MEXICO TAKES DRASTIC MEASURES TO HALT RISE OF 'SUPER-OBESITY'

SKILLS REASONING, ANALYSIS, INTERPRETATION

GOVERNMENT BUILDS ON ITS SUGARY DRINKS TAX TO IMPROVE HEALTH

Mexico is suffering a widespread obesity crisis that has seen obesity-related illness become the country's number one killer. One in three Mexican adults and three out of ten children are obese or overweight; one in four adults suffers from high blood pressure; and nearly one adult in ten has been diagnosed with diabetes, a condition where blood-sugar levels become too high.

According to state health insurer IMSS, which covers some 19 million Mexicans and runs more than 6000 medical centres, obesity-related conditions use up one-third of the agency's budget. IMSS estimates that the cost of treating them will increase more than 4.5 times by 2050 to MXN 344,000 billion (US$18.4 billion) a year from MXN 76 billion now. 'There's no money for that', says IMSS chief Mikel Arriola.

The government has been running a campaign encouraging Mexicans to go for check-ups, eat healthily and exercise more, while in 2014 it introduced an indirect tax of MXN 1 per litre of soda. The tax raised MXN 70.6 billion (US$3.8 billion) from January 2014 to April 2017, according to the finance ministry.

There has been some debate over how effective the tax has been, but a study by Mexico's National Institute of Public Health and the University of North Carolina at Chapel Hill, USA, in 2017 that found sales of sugary drinks were 7.6 per cent lower than would have been expected based on trends before the tax was introduced.

Efforts to double the tax have so far come to nothing, but a new study published by the Public Library of Science this month said that 10 per cent of calories in Mexico came from sugary drinks. It estimated the current tax would reduce obesity by 2.5 per cent by 2024, preventing between 86,000 and 134,000 new cases of diabetes by 2030.

Yet two-thirds of the population considered that they ate healthily and were physically active in a national health survey published last year. As Dr Castañeda put it, 'In the last four years, in spite of certain strategies…the problem is still rising.'

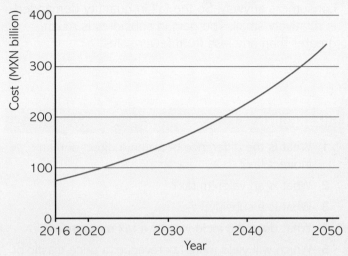

▲ **Figure 7 Growth in medical cost of the main chronic-degenerative diseases**

Q

1 Value added tax is an example of:
(a) a specific tax
(b) an ad valorem tax
(c) a direct tax
(d) a unit tax. **(1 mark)**

2 Define the term 'indirect tax'. **(2 marks)**

3 Explain one possible way of reducing obesity, apart from taxation. **(4 marks)**

4 Analyse why the Mexican government wants to reduce obesity. **(6 marks)**

5 Using suitable diagrams, discuss the impact of doubling the soda tax. **(14 marks)**

EXAM HINT

To support the case for doubling the tax you could use your knowledge of demand theory and argue that an increase in price causes a fall in demand, as the article shows a possible drop of 7.6 per cent. The effectiveness of the tax does depend on the price elasticity of demand and if it is inelastic the impact may not be as great as hoped. This is where you would use diagrams to show the differing impacts depending on whether demand is price elastic or price inelastic. By way of conclusion you may explore the idea that this policy is best used alongside others.

MARKET FAILURE

Markets do not always work or yield the anticipated results, sometimes not producing any goods at all. This section looks at some of the reasons why this happens. It also looks at the external impact that private actions can have on third parties in the form of positive and negative externalities. Diagrams are introduced to show how marginal analysis can help identify the optimum output and welfare loss and gain. The section ends with a look at how imperfect information can arise, preventing rational decision making and leading to moral hazard, speculation and market bubbles.

14 SOURCES OF MARKET FAILURE

LEARNING OBJECTIVES

- Understand what market failure means.
- Understand why market failure occurs.
- Understand sources of market failure.

GETTING STARTED

The photograph shows a nuclear power plant. What are the costs to electricity generating firms of building and operating a nuclear power plant? Are there any costs that they do not pay, but are still costs to society? Do we know all the costs of nuclear power generation and can we put a price on them? Should governments encourage the building of more nuclear power plants in the future?

MARKET FAILURE

The role of markets is to allocate scarce resources. In many cases, markets are an extremely efficient way of doing this. However, in some cases, markets fail in one of two ways:

- markets may lead to production of too many or too few goods; this is known as **partial market failure**
- much more rarely, markets may not exist (known as **missing markets**), leading to no production of a good or service; this is known as **complete market failure**.

There are a number of types of **market failure**, briefly explained in the rest of this chapter and then more completely explained in subsequent chapters.

EXTERNALITIES

Prices and profits should be accurate signals, allowing markets to allocate resources efficiently. In reality, market prices and profits can be misleading because they may not reflect the true prices and profits to society of economic activities. These differences are known as the externalities of an economic activity. For instance, in Brazil it makes commercial sense to cut down the rain forest to create land for farming cattle that are then sold as meat for hamburgers. However, this could lead to economic disaster in the long term because of global warming. The market is putting out the wrong signals, leading to a misallocation of resources.

UNDER-PROVISION OF PUBLIC GOODS

The market, for a variety of reasons, may fail to provide certain goods and services, or may underprovide them. One example of this is in the provision of public goods. These are goods such as defence, street lighting and police services. One key reason for the under-provision of public goods is that it is relatively easy to gain the benefits from the good without having to pay for it. There is then a large incentive for individuals not to pay for the good in the hope that someone else will pay for its provision. The result is that public goods are under-provided if left to free market forces.

INFORMATION GAPS

In an efficient market, both buyers and sellers have good knowledge of the product. Sometimes, though, information is imperfect. For example, a consumer buying a soft drink is likely to have tried out a variety of drinks before. The drink being bought is likely to be something the consumer likes and so the consumer has good information about the product. However, what about the purchase of a washing machine, which the consumer might only make every eight years? In this case, the consumer might have imperfect information and make the wrong choice. Other examples relate to the problem of **asymmetric information**. This is when either the buyer or seller has more information than the other party. One example is private dentists. If a dentist recommends treatments when patients are not in any pain, how do patients know that the treatments are really in their best interests? Could it be that the dentist is recommending far more work than is necessary and is more interested in gaining a fee than in treating the patients properly? Another common example given is second-hand cars. Some cars are 'lemons'. They constantly break down and require large repairs. Other cars of the same make and model are very reliable. The owner of the car for sale knows whether the car is a 'lemon' or not. However, the buyer does not have this information. Should the buyer offer a high price for the car on the assumption it is not a 'lemon' or should the buyer offer a low price, assuming it will have problems?

MORAL HAZARD

Moral hazard is a term used to describe a situation in which an individual or organisation is protected from the consequences of their actions. They know that someone else will have to deal with any problems that occur. As a result, there is no incentive to take the normal precautions and act sensibly, which may result in unnecessary risk-taking and subsequent failure.

This was the situation for many banks around the time of the financial crisis in 2008. Banks that had acted carelessly and built up massive debts were saved from collapse by the government, which intervened because, if they had not, there was a risk that the whole economy would suffer.

On an individual level, people with access to free healthcare are less likely to look after themselves than others who have to pay for any health treatment. It has been argued that welfare benefits prevent some people from not actively seeking work or retraining if they lose their jobs.

SPECULATION AND MARKET BUBBLES

Speculation means an economic agent buys or sells something in the expectation of a future price change in the hope of generating a profit. This happens all the time in financial markets as traders buy and sell stocks, shares, currencies and other financial instruments to make a small profit on the transactions. Occasionally though, the speculative motive is all one way and a market bubble can be created.

This sometimes happens in the stock market if traders expect values to keep rising. Everyone tries to buy, expecting prices to keep rising; this adds to the upwards pressure on prices and traders respond by buying more and the price keeps rising. This is a bubble and, just like real bubbles, they are at risk of sudden collapse. It may be that someone finally begins to sell, so the price rise stops and may drop. All those who bought now expect prices to fall and sell while they still can. This of course, makes things worse and

the bubble bursts with prices dropping dramatically and leaves some traders facing a huge loss.

Housing markets are also at risk of bubbles. When it is easy to get a mortgage, or interest rates are low, many people buy and house prices rise. If the economy then faces problems or interest rates go up, many house owners are forced to sell and the bubble bursts.

THINKING LIKE AN ECONOMIST

ROAD CONGESTION

Cities across Southeast Asia have struggled to cope with the rapidly increasing levels of car ownership that have accompanied a boom in Southeast Asia's middle class. Hours-long jams are the norm in big cities, as authorities fail to match economic growth with the building of new infrastructure.

Road congestion costs Asian economies an estimated 2 to 5 per cent of gross domestic product every year due to lost time and higher transport costs, according to the Asian Development Bank, which says as much as 80 per cent of the region's urban pollution – which is the worst in the world – is caused by transport.

Congestion is a direct cost to road users because it creates longer journey times. For transport firms, for example, that can be measured in terms of extra wages for lorry drivers or extra lorries needed to carry goods. For motorists, there is an opportunity cost. It could be an extra half hour in bed, more time spent with the family or more time working.

There are also indirect costs. For example, congestion influences where people live and where they work. The greater the congestion, the more likely it is that workers will take a job in their local area. This might mean taking a lower-paid job. It also reduces the number of potential workers for businesses outside of that local area.

These costs create externalities for road users. The market price of a road journey includes the fuel used as well as average maintenance costs of the vehicle and its depreciation. However, other motorists impose costs on the road user because they slow down the journey time. This cost is not reflected in the market price and so is an example of an externality.

CHECKPOINT

1 What is the difference between partial and total market failure?

2 What is a public good?

3 Give one reason why public goods are under-provided.

4 Give an example of a public good.

5 What is asymmetric information?

6 Give an example of asymmetric information.

SUBJECT VOCABULARY

asymmetric information when information is not shared equally between buyer and seller and one side has an advantage.

complete market failure when a market fails to supply any of a good that is demanded, creating a missing market.

market failure where resources are inefficiently allocated due to imperfections in the working of the market mechanism.

missing market a market where the market mechanism fails to supply any of a good.

partial market failure when a market for a good exists but there is too much or not sufficient production of the good.

EXAM PRACTICE

INDIA'S CAPITAL NEW DELHI TO REPRISE ANTI-POLLUTION CAR DRIVE

SKILLS ANALYSIS, REASONING, CRITICAL THINKING

New Delhi is one of the world's most polluted cities – its air is made filthy by diesel exhaust, construction dust, the emissions from coal-fired power plants and the burning of rubbish and other materials by those who lack clean cooking fuel. Delhi residents have only recently become aware of the health risks it poses. International companies and foreign embassies are struggling to recruit people from overseas to live and work in the city.

The city conducted a two-week experiment by imposing rules that permit each of the city's cars to be on the roads every alternate day depending on their registration numbers. Many residents were thrilled with the clearing of the city's normally jammed roads and the drop in travel times, as well as the drop in pollution. Studies showed that the level of tiny particulates – which become trapped in the lungs and cause long-term damage – was reduced by up to 13 per cent while the scheme was in force.

There are plans to repeat the exercise, but not everyone is in favour. India's car industry is already angry about existing restrictions on car use and sales imposed by India's courts. Some other groups have argued that New Delhi's pollution would be better dealt with by more aggressively enforcing pollution control rules rather than restricting car use.

Q

1 Asymmetric information exists when:
   (a) there are more buyers than sellers
   (b) buyers have more information than sellers
   (c) the government provides information
   (d) there is a shortage in the market. **(1 mark)**

2 Analyse one private cost and one external cost of New Delhi's pollution. **(6 marks)**

3 Analyse one private benefit and one external benefit of the reduction in car use. **(6 marks)**

4 Examine the likely effectiveness of the scheme to permit use of cars on alternate days. **(8 marks)**

5 Evaluate the possible impact on New Delhi of further restrictions on pollution. **(20 marks)**

15 POSITIVE AND NEGATIVE EXTERNALITIES

LEARNING OBJECTIVES

- Understand the distinction between private benefits, external benefits and social benefits.
- Understand the distinction between private costs, external costs and social costs.
- Understand the distinction between:
  - external benefits of production
  - external benefits of consumption
  - external costs of production
  - external costs of consumption.
- Understand the use of diagrams, using marginal analysis, to illustrate:
  - the external benefits from consumption
  - the external costs from production
  - the distinction between the market and social optimum positions; identification of the welfare loss or gain areas.
- Understand the impact of externalities in various contexts: transport; health; education; environment; and financial.

GETTING STARTED

Mumbai airport is working at full capacity and has no room for expansion. In 2016, it handled 35 million passengers; it is expected that by 2035 demand will increase to 100 million passengers. Plans to build a new airport involve clearing an area of lakes and jungle to the east of Mumbai. What costs do you think the nearby villagers will suffer, which will not be included in the building and operating costs? What benefits might a citizen of Mumbai gain even though they will never use the new airport?

PRIVATE AND SOCIAL COSTS AND BENEFITS

A chemical plant may dump waste into a river in order to minimise its costs. Further down the river, a water company has to treat the water to remove dangerous chemicals before supplying drinking water to its customers. Its customers have to pay higher prices because of the pollution.

This is a classic example of an **externality or spillover effect**. Externalities arise when private costs and benefits are different from social costs and benefits. A **private cost** is the cost of an activity to an individual economic unit, such as a consumer or a firm. For instance, a chemical company will have to pay for workers, raw materials and plant and machinery

when it produces chemicals. A social cost is the cost of an activity not just to the individual economic unit that creates the cost, but to the rest of society as well. It therefore includes all private costs, but may also include other costs. The chemical manufacturer may make little or no payment for the pollution it generates. The difference between private cost and social cost is the externality or spillover effect. If social cost is greater than private cost, then a **negative externality or external cost** is said to exist.

However, not all externalities are negative. A company may put up a building that is not just functional but also beautiful. The value of the pleasure that the building gives to society over its lifetime (the social benefit) may well far exceed the benefit of the building received by the company (the private benefit). Hence, if social benefit is greater than private benefit, a **positive externality or external benefit** is said to exist.

This is often the case with healthcare provision (an example of a merit good). Although one individual will benefit from having an injection that prevents an illness, the social benefit resulting from the reduced risk of other members of society catching the illness will be even greater. Positive externalities could also result from education and training. An individual may benefit in the form of a better job and a higher salary, but society may gain even more from the benefits of a better trained workforce.

Activities where social benefit exceeds private benefit are often inadequately provided by a market system. In many cases this results in either state provision or a government subsidy to encourage private provision.

ACTIVITY 1 — SKILLS ▶ REASONING, INTERPRETATION, COMMUNICATION

CASE STUDY: POSITIVE AND NEGATIVE EXTERNALITIES

(a) Why might each of the examples in the photograph and cartoon give rise to positive and negative externalities?

EXTERNALITIES OF PRODUCTION AND CONSUMPTION

Production externalities arise when the social costs of production differ from the private costs of production.

- Negative externalities of production (**or negative production externalities**) occur when social costs are greater than private costs in production. An example is when a factory pumps polluted water into a river at no cost to itself.
- Positive externalities of production (or **positive production externalities**) occur when social costs are less than private costs in production. An example would be a supermarket that redeveloped a disused industrial site for a new store, but at the same time cleaned up pollution on the site, improved the roads around the site and subsidised the construction of some social housing next to the new store. **Consumption externalities** arise when the social benefits of consumption differ from the private benefits of consumption.
- Positive externalities of consumption (or **positive consumption externalities**) occur when social benefits are greater than private benefits in consumption. For example, when a child is given an injection to prevent a disease, it makes it less likely that another unprotected child in the local area will get the illness.
- Negative externalities of consumption (or **negative consumption externalities**) occur when social benefits are less than private benefits in consumption. For example, with passive smoking, a person who smokes in their home harms the health of others in the home.

MARKET FAILURE

The price mechanism allocates resources. Output is fixed where demand equals supply at the point where private costs equal private benefits. However, a misallocation of resources will occur if market prices do not accurately reflect the costs and benefits to society of economic activities. There will only be a social optimum position if output occurs where social costs equal social benefits.

The greater the externality, the larger will be the difference between private costs and benefits and social costs and benefits. The greater the externality, the greater the market failure and the less market prices provide accurate signals for the optimal allocation of resources.

MARGINAL COSTS AND BENEFITS

The difference between social costs and social benefits changes as the level of output changes. This can be shown using **marginal analysis**. The margin is a possible point of change. So the marginal cost of production is the extra cost of producing an extra unit of output. The marginal benefit is the benefit received from consuming an extra unit of output.

The marginal cost of production is likely to change as output increases. In Figure 1, it is shown as at first falling and then rising. Marginal costs fall at first because producing more can lead to greater efficiencies. However, then they start to rise. This could be because a firm is having to pay higher prices to obtain more factors of production: to employ more workers it might have to pay higher wages, for example. Or production might be less efficient if a firm is operating beyond its optimum capacity of production.

In contrast, the marginal benefit of consumption of a product falls as consumption increases. Each extra unit of consumption brings less benefit to the consumer. The marginal benefit curve is the same as the demand curve. This is because the demand curve also shows the value of the benefit put on the consumption of the product by a buyer.

Assume that the marginal cost curve and marginal benefit curve in Figure 1 are the costs and benefits to society. Then welfare would be maximised at a quantity level of OA and a price of OB. What if production and consumption are not at OA?

If quantity produced and consumed were greater than OA, the extra cost of production would be greater than the extra benefit from consumption. Welfare would be improved by reducing production and consumption. So this would lead to an inefficient allocation of resources.

FIGURE 1

The optimal level of production and consumption
Welfare is maximised when the marginal cost of production equals the marginal benefit of consumption. This is at the output level OA and a marginal price or cost of OB.

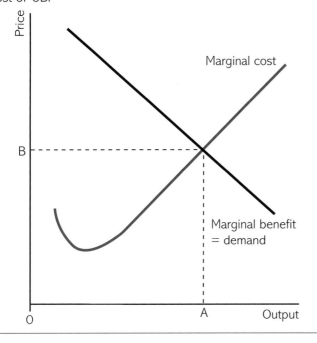

FIGURE 2

Free market and optimal levels of production
In a free market, production will take place at OB where MPC = MPB. However, the socially optimal level of production is OA where marginal social cost and marginal social benefit are the same.

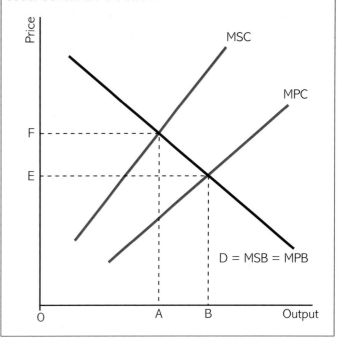

If quantity produced and consumed were less than OA, then the marginal benefit of production would be greater than the marginal cost of production. Welfare could be increased if production and consumption were increased.

Note that when this diagram is usually drawn, only the upward sloping part of the marginal cost curve is shown, as in Figure 2. This is because it is assumed that the marginal benefit curve will cut the marginal cost curve when marginal cost is increasing.

WELFARE LOSSES WITH PRODUCTION EXTERNALITIES

In many markets, social costs and private costs differ. So too do social benefits and private benefits. Figure 2 shows a situation where there are negative externalities of production. At every level of output, the **marginal social cost** of production is higher than the **marginal private cost**. So the marginal social cost curve, the MSC curve, is higher and to the left of the marginal private cost curve, the MPC curve. It is assumed here that the marginal social benefit (MSB) and marginal private benefit (MPB) are the same. So the demand curve is also the MSB and MPB curves.

The market equilibrium is where the marginal private cost equals the marginal private benefit. This is at an output level of OB and a price of OE. If the price were higher than OE, consumers would buy less than OB because the demand curve shows the value or utility placed by consumers on the product. If the price were lower than OE, producers would not be prepared to supply OB because they would make a loss on the last or marginal units produced.

However, the socially optimum level of production is lower than OB. It is OA where marginal social cost equals marginal social benefit (MSC = MSB). The price of OF is higher than the free market price of OE. This reflects the fact that the free market price does not include the production externality generated by the good.

If production and consumption take place at OB, then there is a welfare loss to society. The loss is the difference between the marginal social cost and the marginal private benefit shown in Figure 3. On the last unit produced, the OBth unit, this is JK. On the OCth unit, the welfare loss is HL. So the total welfare loss is the sum of the vertical distances between the MSC curve and MSB curve between the output levels of OA and OB. This is the triangle GJK, sometimes called the *welfare loss triangle* or the *deadweight loss triangle*.

FIGURE 4

Welfare triangle with positive consumption externalities showing potential gain from increasing output

If production takes place at the free market level of output of OA, then the triangle GHK shows the welfare gain that could be achieved if output rose to the socially optimal level of output of OB.

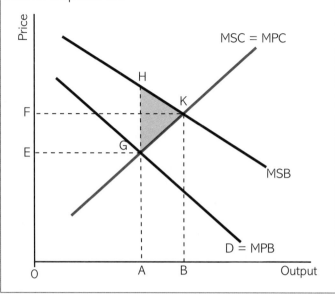

WELFARE LOSSES WITH CONSUMPTION EXTERNALITIES

The same analysis can be applied to when there are consumption externalities or externalities of consumption. Figure 4 shows a situation where the marginal social benefit is greater than the marginal private benefit. This means that there are positive externalities. For example, if some individuals pay to go to the gym to keep fit, it benefits others because they are less likely to suffer health problems later in life. In Figure 4, it is assumed that the marginal social cost and marginal private cost are the same. The free market equilibrium is at an output level of OA where MPC = MPB, the marginal private cost of production is equal to the marginal private benefit of consumption. However, the socially optimum level of output is OB where MSC = MSB, the marginal cost equals the marginal social benefit. If the output were at OB, an extra GHK of welfare could be gained. There is therefore a loss of welfare of GHK compared to the socially optimal level of production.

FIGURE 3

Welfare loss triangle from negative production externalities

If production takes place at the free market level of output of OB, then there will be a deadweight loss of welfare to society of GJK.

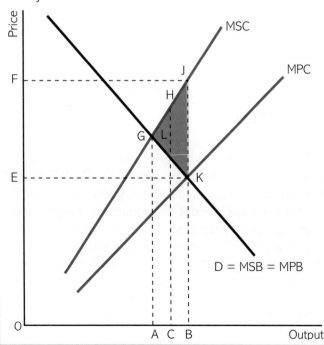

ACTIVITY 2   SKILLS   CRITICAL THINKING, ANALYSIS, REASONING

CASE STUDY: POLLUTION IN CHINA

In 2014, media sources reported that tap water was cut off for the day in the Chinese city of Jingjiang. It followed detection of an unknown pollutant in the city's water supplies. Jingjiang, a city on the River Yangtze, is a centre for shipbuilding and textiles, and it was thought that either industry could have been the source of the pollution. Photos posted online showed residents filling buckets from an emergency water source in a local public park.

China invested US$536 billion in wastewater treatment and water cleaning plants during the five years to 2015, but one-quarter of its citizens still do not have access to clean drinking water.

(a) Explain how the shipbuilding or textile industry in Jingjiang may have created an externality.

(b) Using a diagram, explain why there has been a misallocation of resources.

THINKING LIKE AN ECONOMIST

MOSQUITO NETS

The fight against malaria has had some success over the past 15 years. Sources stated that deaths from malaria fell by 42 per cent between 2000 and 2013 and occurrences of the disease have decreased by one-quarter. In large part this is due to an increase in international financial support for anti-malaria efforts, from just US$100 million in 2000 to US$1.84 billion in 2012. An estimated 3.3 million lives have been saved over the period. The hunt is still on for a drug that will cure all malaria infections quickly, a medicine that would permanently prevent infection or an effective way of completely destroying the parasite that causes malaria.

However, in the meantime, a low-technology, low-cost solution has contributed much to the reduction in malarial infections. It is a sleeping net covered with a chemical that kills the insects (mosquitoes) that carry malaria. These nets have both private benefits and positive externalities in consumption. They protect the people who sleep under the net. However, the chemical ensures that any mosquitos landing on the net will be killed. This benefits those under the net but it also reduces the number of mosquitos in a local area like a small village. The more mosquitos killed, the fewer will be alive to reproduce and bite humans. Hence people who are not sleeping under the net also benefit.

Private benefits are reduced when nets become torn through use. Positive externalities in consumption disappear when the net loses all its insecticide. Externalities also disappear when mosquitos adapt to become resistant to the chemical that covers the nets. Although resistance has been detected in 64 countries, or nearly two-thirds of countries affected by malaria, there are currently no acceptable alternatives to the chemical. For the time being, the nets remain the only way forward in the fight against malaria.

CHECKPOINT

1 What is an externality?
2 What is the difference between a private and a social cost?
3 What is the difference between a positive and a negative externality?
4 Give an example of a positive and negative externality.
5 What is the difference between an externality of production and an externality of consumption?
6 What is the social optimum position?
7 What is the difference between marginal cost and marginal benefit?
8 What is a welfare loss?

SUBJECT VOCABULARY

consumption externalities or external benefits of consumption when the social costs of consumption are different from the private costs of consumption.

externality or spillover effect the difference between social costs and benefits and private costs and benefits.

marginal analysis focuses on small or incremental changes in an economic variable such as cost or output.

marginal social and private costs and benefits the social and private costs and benefits of the last unit either produced or consumed.

negative consumption externalities when social benefits are less than private benefits.

negative externality or external cost exist if net social cost (social cost minus social benefit) is greater than net private cost (private cost minus private benefit).

negative production externalities when social costs exceed private costs.

positive consumption externalities when social benefits exceed private benefits.

positive externality or external benefit exists if net social benefit is greater than net private benefit.

positive production externalities when social costs are less than private costs.

private cost and benefit the cost or benefit of an activity to an individual economic unit such as a consumer or a firm.

production externalities or external benefits of production when the social costs of production are different from the private costs of production.

EXAM PRACTICE

GLOBAL CHILDHOOD OBESITY RISES TENFOLD IN 40 YEARS

SKILLS PROBLEM-SOLVING, REASONING, ANALYSIS

The number of obese children and teenagers across the world has increased tenfold over the past 40 years and is about to overtake the number who are underweight, according to the most extensive analysis of body weight ever undertaken.

The study, led by Imperial College London and the World Health Organization, used data on 31.5 million children and teenagers worldwide to estimate trends in body mass index (BMI) from 1975 to 2016. Over this period the number of obese girls, aged 5 to 19, rose from 5 million to 50 million, while the total for boys increased from 6 million to 74 million.

The world's highest childhood obesity levels are in the Pacific Islands of Polynesia and Micronesia. Nauru has the highest rates for girls and the Cook Islands for boys: both above 33 per cent.

Among wealthy countries, the USA has the highest obesity rates for girls and boys of about 20 per cent. Levels in most of western Europe are in the 7 per cent to 10 per cent range.

A further 213 million children are overweight but not sufficiently so to meet the WHO obesity criteria, which vary by age. Forty years ago, 0.8 per cent of the world's children were obese; now the rate is close to 7 per cent.

The study also looked at adult obesity, which increased from 100 million people in 1975 to 671 million in 2016. A further 1300 million adults were overweight (with a BMI above 25) but not defined as obese (BMI above 30).

But the authors are most concerned about the findings about childhood obesity, because of their implications for public health many years into the future. It is associated with a higher risk and earlier start of many serious diseases such as type-2 diabetes and heart disease.

Michael Bloomberg, who tried to ban the sale of large sugary drinks when he was mayor of New York and is now an ambassador for the WHO, said, 'Anti-obesity policies like sugary drinks taxes are working and the faster we spread them, the more lives we can save.'

More than 20 countries around the world have introduced sugary drink taxes, said Professor Fiona Bull of the WHO, 'and the evidence shows that they are beginning to work'.

Although the study focuses on obesity, the researchers point out that 75 million girls and 117 million boys are still moderately or severely underweight. Two-thirds of these children who do not receive enough food are in south Asia and especially in India. In south Asia, 20.3 per cent of girls and 28.6 per cent of boys are moderately or severely underweight – an improvement on 1975 when the comparable figures were 23.0 per cent and 37.8 per cent, respectively.

The nutritional world was increasingly divided between overweight and underweight, said Professor Bull, as the proportion of the world's children who were a normal healthy weight fell.

Q

1 Calculate to one decimal place the percentage increase in obesity for:
   (a) boys over the period 1975 to 2016 **(4 marks)**
   (b) girls over the period 1975 to 2016. **(4 marks)**

2 Analyse why both obesity and being underweight can be seen as examples of market failure. **(6 marks)**

3 Discuss whether sugar consumption is the main market failure resulting in a rise in global obesity. **(14 marks)**

EXAM TIP

Explain why sugar consumption might lead to market failure. Then consider other factors that might be contributing to a rise in obesity. The data suggests one factor. From your own knowledge, you should know that excessive consumption of other forms of carbohydrates, apart from sugar, and also fats contribute to obesity. Is there market failure in the markets for computer games and takeaway pizzas? Is there likely to be information gaps or asymmetric information? Conclude by weighing up whether sugar is the main market failure leading to the rise in obesity.

16 NON-PROVISION OF PUBLIC GOODS

LEARNING OBJECTIVES

- Understand the distinction between public and private goods:
  - private goods: rival and excludable
  - public goods: non-rival and non-excludable.
- Understand why public goods may not be provided by the private sector, making reference to the free-rider problem.

GETTING STARTED

An individual steals your mobile phone from your bag. Two days later, he is caught by the police. You want him to go to prison for the robbery. The police say that they will try him in court if you pay US$10,000 for the police and court costs. If you want him to go to jail for one year, that will cost you another US$50,000. Is justice something that can be sold like an online film or a can of soda? Why might people argue that everyone should pay for enforcing justice whether or not they have been a victim of crime? Why should online films or cans of soda not be provided free by the state, like the police, the courts or prisons?

PUBLIC GOODS

Nearly all goods are **private goods** (not to be confused with goods produced in the private sector of the economy). A private good is rivalrous. It is a good where consumption by one person results in the good not being available for consumption by another. For instance, if you eat a bowl of muesli, then your friend cannot eat it; if a firm builds a plant on a piece of land, that land is not available for use by local farmers. Private goods are also excludable. Once provided, it is possible to prevent others from using it. For example, football clubs can prevent fans from seeing a game at their stadium by allowing only ticket holders to enter.

A few goods, however, are **public goods or pure public goods**. These are goods that possess the opposite characteristics to private goods.

- **Non-rivalry** – consumption of the good by one person does not reduce the amount available for consumption by another person; sometimes this is also known as **non-diminishability** or **non-exhaustibility**.
- **Non-excludability** – once provided, no person can be excluded from benefiting; equally, no person can opt out of receiving the good, which is known as **non-rejectability**.

Public goods are also different from private goods because the marginal cost (the extra cost) of providing a unit of the good is zero.

There are relatively few examples of pure public goods, although many goods contain a public good element. Clean air is a public good. If you breathe clean air, it does not diminish the ability of others to breathe clean air. Moreover, others cannot prevent you from breathing clean air. Defence is another example. An increase in the population of the Philippines does not lead to a reduction in the defence protection accorded to the existing population. People in Manila cannot reject the 'benefits' of defence protection even if they were to object to current defence policy, prefer to see all defence abolished and refuse to pay to finance defence. Also, the marginal cost of providing defence for one extra citizen is zero. For example, the cost of the Philippines' navy does not increase when the Philippines population increases by 50,000.

Goods that can be argued to be public goods are:

- defence
- the judiciary and prison service
- the police service
- street lighting.

Many other goods, such as education and health, contain a small public good element.

THE FREE RIDER PROBLEM

If the provision of public goods were left to the market mechanism, there would be market failure. This is because of the **free rider** problem. A public good is one where it is impossible to prevent people from receiving the benefits of the good once it has been provided. So there is very little incentive for people to pay for consumption of the good.

A free rider is someone who receives the benefit but allows others to pay for it. For instance, citizens receive benefits from defence expenditure. But individual citizens could increase their economic welfare by not paying for it.

In a free market, national defence is unlikely to be provided. A firm attempting to provide defence services would have difficulty charging for the product since it could not be sold to benefit individual citizens. The result would be that no one would pay for defence and therefore the market would not provide it. The only way around this problem is for the state to provide defence and force everyone to contribute to its cost through taxation.

In practice, there are often ways in which providers of public goods can exclude consumers from benefiting from the public good. The problem of free riding can to some extent be solved for these **quasi-public or non-pure public goods**. For example, motorists can be made to pay a toll for using a road. Television viewers can be forced to buy subscriptions to decode television channels. Ships entering a port can be forced to pay taxes for the maintenance of safety provisions. However, quasi-public goods possess the second characteristic of pure public goods. They are non-rival. So for most roads, for example, one motorist travelling along the road does not exclude another motorist from travelling along the same road. When goods are non-rival, it is unlikely that the free market mechanism will provide enough of the good. How many country roads would private firms provide if they were tolled? The answer is very few because the tolls collected would not cover the building and maintenance of the road. Hence, there is a very strong case for government providing this quasi-public good.

CASE STUDY: STREET LIGHTING

(a) Explain why street lights might be classed as a public good.

THINKING LIKE AN ECONOMIST

THE WORLD'S HUNGER FOR PUBLIC GOODS

Public goods are the building blocks of society. Economic stability is itself a public good. So are security, science, a clean environment, trust, honest administration and free speech. The list could be far longer. The more global the public goods, the more difficult it is to secure adequate supply. Strangely, the better we have become at supplying private goods and so the richer we are, the more complex the public goods we need.

Economic stability is a public good we find quite hard to supply. A central element of the debate is how to avoid extreme financial instability. Such instability is a public bad; avoiding it is a public good. Those acting inside the market system have no incentive to supply the good or avoid the bad.

What, for those unfamiliar with the term, is a public good? In economics, a public good is 'non-excludable' and 'non-rivalrous'. Non-excludable means that one cannot prevent non-payers from enjoying benefits. Non-rivalrous means that one person's enjoyment is not at another person's expense. National defence is a classic public good. If a country is made safe from attack, everybody benefits, including residents who make no contribution. Again, enjoyment of the benefits does not reduce that of others. Similarly, if an economy is stable, everybody has the benefit and nobody can be deprived of it.

CHECKPOINT

1 Identify the two characteristics of a public good.

2 What is the marginal cost of providing one more unit of a public good?

3 Give two examples of a public good.

4 Who or what is a free rider?

5 Why are free riders regarded as a problem?

6 What is meant by a quasi-public good? Give an example.

SUBJECT VOCABULARY

free rider a person or organisation that receives benefits that others have paid for without making any contributions.

non-excludability once provided, it is impossible to prevent any economic agent from consuming the good.

non-rejectability once provided, it is impossible for any economic agent not to consume the good.

non-rivalry, non-diminishability or non-exhaustability consumption by one economic agent does not reduce the amount available for consumption by others.

private goods goods that possess the characteristics of rivalry (once consumed, it cannot be consumed by any one else) and excludability (it is possible to prevent someone else from consuming the good).

public goods or pure public goods goods that possess the characteristics of non-rivalry (or non-diminishability) and non-excludability (which includes the characteristic of non-rejectability).

quasi-public goods or non-pure public goods a good that does not perfectly possess the characteristics of non-rivalry and non-excludability and yet which also is not perfectly rival or excludable.

EXAM PRACTICE

TELEVISION VIEWING

SKILLS   REASONING, ANALYSIS, INTERPRETING, COMMUNICATION

Bangladesh Television (BTV) is the state-owned television network in Bangladesh. It first started in 1964 as Pakistan Television but was renamed after Bangladesh gained independence in 1971. Like many other Asian countries and most European countries, the majority of its funding comes from a television licence. Households need to buy a licence to legally receive broadcasts. The television signals are sent out in a way that means that anyone with an aerial and television set can receive broadcasts whether they have paid a licence fee or not.

Alongside BTV, a number of private television stations exist. Some are funded by advertising while to watch others, such as Channel i, viewers must pay for a special decoding card and box. Gazi Television broadcasts its programmes via a digital cable network that requires a monthly fee.

Q

1 Explain the difference between a public good and a private good. **(4 marks)**

2 Analyse why might Bangladesh Television be classified as a public good. **(6 marks)**

3 Examine the extent to which Channel i and Gazi Television can be classified as private goods. **(8 marks)**

EXAM TIP

In your answer to Question 3, examine Channel i and Gazi Television against the characteristics of a private good. Weigh up whether they perfectly match these characteristics. Do they have public good elements?

17 IMPERFECT MARKET

LEARNING OBJECTIVES

- Understand the distinction between symmetric and asymmetric information.
- Understand the significance of information gaps.
- Understand how imperfect market information may lead to a misallocation of resources in various contexts.

GETTING STARTED

What is your attitude to the increasing number of cars and trucks on the roads? Can you give three long-term medical problems that might be caused by exposure to pollution caused by motor vehicles? Do you know what is meant by particulate pollution? Do you know the safe limit of particulates per cubic metre? Do you suffer from information failure about traffic pollution and understand how this might lead to a welfare loss?

IMPERFECT MARKET INFORMATION

In a perfect market, buyers and sellers have potential access to the same information. There is symmetric information. However, many decisions are based on **imperfect information**. Both buyers and sellers do not find out the information they need to make the decision that maximises their welfare. There is then **information failure or an information gap**.

Information gaps also occur when either the buyer or the seller has more information than the other. There is then a situation of asymmetric information. The buyer or seller with more information can exploit that information gap to their benefit.

Information failure can be illustrated using a diagram. In Figure 1, welfare would be maximised where demand with perfect information equals supply at output OA and a price of OE. However, buyers in practice suffer information failure. They overestimate the benefits of the product and are therefore prepared to pay a higher price for a given level of output than if they enjoyed perfect information. Hence, the actual demand curve for the good is to the right of the one where buyers have imperfect information. The result is that OB is bought at a price of OF. There is a misallocation of resources because AB too much is bought compared to a situation where buyers had perfect information.

If buyers underestimate the benefits of buying a good because of information failure, then the actual

demand curve will be to the left of the demand curve with perfect information. Too little will be bought at too low a price. The same analysis applies to suppliers. If they underestimate the benefits to themselves of selling a product, then the supply curve will be to the left of the supply curve where they possess perfect information. If they overestimate the benefits, the supply curve will be to the right.

FIGURE 1

Imperfect information
Buyers possess imperfect information, overestimating the benefits of buying a good. The result is that the actual demand curve is to the right of the demand curve where they have perfect information. AB too much is bought, leading to a misallocation of resources.

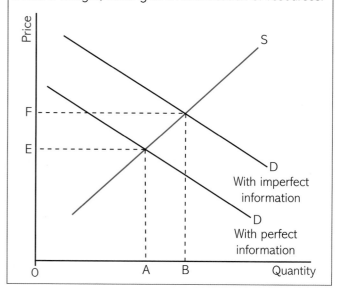

THE MARKET FOR SECOND-HAND CARS

The problem of asymmetric information was first outlined by the Nobel Prize-winning economist, George Akerlof. In 1970, he published a paper in which he used the example of second-hand cars to discuss the problem of asymmetric information. He argued that buyers of second-hand cars do not know whether any individual second-hand car is a good car or whether it is a 'lemon', a very poor quality car with significant defects. Buyers therefore have to guess whether or not a second-hand car is of good quality. Because they do not know, they are only prepared to offer to pay average prices for better than average quality cars. Owners of better than average-quality cars therefore tend not to sell them because they cannot get a high enough price.

But then second-hand cars for sale become mainly average or below-average quality. Buyers therefore are not prepared to pay average prices for a second-hand car and therefore start to offer below-average prices. Owners of average-quality cars then feel that they are not getting a high enough price for their car and so stop selling them in the market. George Akerlof argued that the final outcome was the disappearance of the market for second-hand cars. Asymmetric information has led to the collapse of the market.

In practice, second-hand car markets do exist. This is because buyers have more information that Akerlof's model assumes. For example, consumer protection laws in many countries state that car dealers must sell cars that at minimum are in a good enough condition to be driven safely. Second-hand car dealers may offer a short guarantee period of, say, three months. Consumers can make some judgements about the second-hand car dealer by the state of their premises and the number of cars they are selling. The price of the car is also determined by its age and how far it has travelled in its lifetime. Consumers can find an approximate guide to the price of the car by buying a car price guide or looking on the Internet. However, it remains true that the price of a one-day-old second-hand car is, for the most part, significantly below the price of a new car. That difference in price in part reflects the discount in the market because of asymmetric information.

ACTIVITY 1

SKILLS   REASONING, ANALYSIS

CASE STUDY: PRICE COMPARISON WEBSITES

Price comparison websites are now very common and they compete to give the consumer the best deal. These sites gather information about products and services from many suppliers. This includes prices, descriptions and features, and then shows that combined information on one page as a response to visitors' search request.

For buyers this gives them a lot more information in one place and saves them the time of having to obtain many different prices from many different suppliers. They can easily compare products they are looking for based on several criteria, like price, features and delivery options, so that they can find the best choice.

In return for directing a customer to its website, the supplier pays a commission to the price comparison website.

(a) Explain how price comparison websites can reduce asymmetric information.

(b) Will they always give the best deal to the consumer? If not, why not?

MARKET EXAMPLES

Asymmetric information can lead to a misallocation of resources and market failure, as the example of second-hand cars shows. There is a number of important markets where this occurs.

Education Education provides an example of the **principal–agent problem**. The principal is the individual or organisation that benefits or loses from a set of economic decisions. The agent is an individual or organisation that makes decisions on behalf of the principal. In education, the principal is the child or student. The agents are the parents and guardians of the child and society in general represented by government agencies, such as the school and the courts. A child suffers from asymmetric information. He or she typically does not see the long-term benefits of education. Therefore he or she may act in ways, such as missing school or failing to work to his or her potential, which act to harm its long-term interests. If allowed, he or she will devote too few resources to education and so there will be a misallocation of resources. Agents for the child, therefore, have to act in a way that will encourage the child to participate fully in the educational process.

However, the principal–agent problem occurs when parents and guardians work with the child to avoid education. In a developing country, where parents may have to pay even for primary education, there is a financial incentive not to send children to school. This incentive is increased if the child can remain at home and be put to work. There is a minority of parents for whom the emotional and financial cost of supporting their children in education is too high. They therefore could be said to be 'colluding' with their children in allowing them to be disruptive in school and in avoiding attendance. They may also not support their children if they wish to go to college or university. The state has an incentive to see all children reach their full potential. This is the reason why the state, as agent, encourages young people to stay on as long as possible in education and to perform to their potential.

Pensions Many argue that young workers today are paying too little into pensions and instead spending the money on everything from houses to cars to holidays. This is because of asymmetric information. Many 25-year-olds may not be able to imagine what it will be like to live as a 70-year-old. As a result, they may ignore the loss of welfare that will come from having a low income at 70 to boost their current spending and short-term pleasure.

Governments step in to remedy at least part of this misallocation of resources by forcing workers to save for their retirement. In some countries, workers have to save through pension schemes tied to their work.

In others, workplace pension schemes are encouraged through tax breaks. But the government forces saving through a national retirement scheme. Workers have to pay contributions and other taxes, which pay for the state retirement pension and some other benefits.

Financial services Financial institutions often have more information about the products they sell than their customers. For example, following the financial crisis that developed from 2008 onwards, it became clear that a wide range of financial institutions and their employees had mistreated their customers. In the USA, some bank employees were incentivised in the years leading up to 2008 to sell mortgages to low income households. The bank employees had enough information to know that these households would not be able to repay those mortgages after the initial discounted rates of interest had ended. Banks were then combining these mortgages and then selling them to other groups as if they were low-risk products. When it became clear in 2008 that these households were defaulting on their debts in large numbers, it led to the largest financial crisis since the 1920s. There was information failure and **moral hazard**.

Moral hazard occurs when an economic agent, like a bank or banker, makes a decision in their own best interest knowing that there are potential negative risks and that, if problems result, the cost will be partly paid by other economic agents. The bank employees who sold mortgages to risky customers knew that these were high risk loans, but they were paid on how many mortgages they sold, not on whether the mortgages were likely to be repaid. A collapse of a mortgage was a problem for their bank, not for them. Equally, senior bankers participated in risky behaviour, assuming that if the bank failed, the state would rescue it. They would keep the pay, bonuses and pensions that they had earned from the risky behaviour, while taxpayers paid the bill for the huge losses created by risky transactions that went badly wrong.

Advertising Some advertising, such as small ads in newspapers or notifications for sale on sites such as eBay®, increases information for buyers. It makes them aware of what is on offer in the marketplace. However, most advertising is persuasive advertising. It is designed to change attitudes on the part of the buyer. As such, it attempts to increase information failure on the part of the buyer to the benefit of the seller. For example, a soap powder advert might attempt to persuade buyers that a particular brand is better at cleaning clothes than another. A car advert might link owning the car with increased status for its owner.

THINKING LIKE AN ECONOMIST

THE RISE OF ANTIBIOTIC-RESISTANT INFECTIONS THREATENS ECONOMIES

Each day, an estimated 1900 people around the world die from infections that are resistant to antibiotics: that is 700,000 people every year. However, this number could rise to 10 million lives a year being lost by the middle of the century, according to the UK's 2016 Review on Anti-microbial Resistance (AMR). This would be more than the number of people who will die of cancer this year.

Life has altered dramatically since the discovery of the first antibiotic, in 1928, and its widespread introduction in the 1940s. As a result, illnesses such as pneumonia and tuberculosis no longer commonly kill the young and healthy in developed countries.

But the way infections react to antibiotics is changing. Margaret Chan, former World Health Organization director general, has said that the rise of AMR is similar to a 'slow-motion tsunami'. The danger, Dr Chan has warned, is of 'a post-antibiotic era' in which common infections regularly kill again.

Too much use of antibiotics in humans and animals has caused the pace of anti-microbial resistance to increase. A 2015 study from the Washington DC-based Center for Disease Dynamics found that global antibiotic use had risen by 30 per cent between 2000 and 2010.

It is estimated that annual global GDP could be reduced by between 2 per cent and 3.5 per cent by 2050 if nothing is done. This is equal to a total of US$60–100 trillion of economic output being lost.

Many countries have introduced or expanded campaigns to inform citizens about the risks of overusing antibiotics, but a market failure has caused problems that have slowed the development of new antibiotics.

Pharmaceutical companies have little incentive to develop antibiotics that are designed to be taken as little as possible. Only two new classes of antibiotics have reached the market in the past 50 years, as the rate of bacterial resistance has been quicker than the rate of antibiotic discovery.

CHECKPOINT

1 What is imperfect information?

2 Think of an example from you own experience where you have had imperfect information.

3 How does imperfect information lead to an information gap?

4 Why does imperfect information result in a misallocation of resources?

5 Why do governments sometimes intervene when this happens?

6 What is a moral hazard?

7 Give an example of a moral hazard.

SUBJECT VOCABULARY

imperfect information where buyers or sellers or both lack information to make an informed decision.

information failure or **information gap** where buyers or sellers or both do not have the information that is available to make a decision.

moral hazard when an economic agent makes a decision in their own best interest knowing that there are potential negative risks, and that if problems result, the cost will be partly paid by other economic agents.

principal–agent problem occurs when the goals of principals, those who would gain or lose from a decision, are different from agents, those making decisions on behalf of the principal. Examples include shareholders (principals) and managers (agents), or children (principals) and parents (agents).

EXAM PRACTICE

TOBACCO SKILLS REASONING, COMMUNICATION, ANALYSIS

Tobacco use is one of the biggest public health threats the world has ever faced, killing more than 7 million people a year. More than 6 million of those deaths are the result of direct tobacco use, while around 890,000 are the result of non-smokers being exposed to second-hand smoke.

Nearly 80 per cent of the more than 1 billion smokers worldwide live in low- and middle-income countries, where the burden of tobacco-related illness and death is heaviest. Tobacco users who die early deprive their families of income, raise the cost of healthcare and slow economic development.

In some countries, children from poor households are frequently employed in tobacco farming to provide family income. These children are especially at risk of 'green tobacco sickness', which is caused by the nicotine that is absorbed through the skin from the handling of wet tobacco leaves.

Studies show that few people understand the specific health risks of tobacco use. For example, a 2017 survey in China revealed that only 61 per cent of smokers knew that smoking causes a specific type of heart disease. In China, tobacco production and sales by the State Tobacco Monopoly Administration contributes 7–10 per cent of total annual central government revenues.

Among smokers who are aware of the dangers of tobacco, most want to quit. Specialist support and medicines can more than double the chance that a smoker who tries to quit will succeed.

National services that help smokers quit and where all or part of the cost is paid by the government are available in only 24 countries, representing 15 per cent of the world's population. There is no assistance of any kind available to help smokers quit in one-quarter of low-income countries.

Q

1 Analyse why there might be

   (a) a misallocation of resources because of tobacco use.   **(6 marks)**

   (b) asymmetric information in the tobacco market.   **(6 marks)**

2 Using suitable diagrams, discuss the effectiveness of taxation in reducing the level of tobacco consumption.   **(14 marks)**

18 MORAL HAZARD, SPECULATION AND MARKET BUBBLES

LEARNING OBJECTIVES

■ Understand how moral hazard can occur.
■ Understand the impact of moral hazard on economic agents.
■ Understand how market bubbles may arise.
■ Understand the impact of market bubbles on economic agents.

GETTING STARTED

The latest iPhone® X costs around US$1000. If you bought one knowing that if you lost it, damaged it or it was stolen you would have to pay the full price for another one, would you take great care of it? What if Apple® were to offer you a brand new replacement if anything happened to yours, would you be as careful?

IMPERFECT MARKET INFORMATION

The Getting Started above is an example of **moral hazard**, which we first came across in Chapter 14. The economist Paul Krugman described it as 'any situation in which one person makes the decision about how much risk to take, while someone else bears the cost if things go badly'.

Moral hazard is a situation where an individual or organisation is protected from the consequences of their actions. They know that someone else will have to deal with any problems that occur. As a result, there is no incentive to take the normal precautions and act sensibly, which may result in unnecessary risk-taking and subsequent failure.

It arises when both parties have incomplete information about each other. In other words, **asymmetric information**, where buyers and sellers have different amounts of information, with one group having more information than the other. In addition, this relationship affects the behaviour of the parties involved. If you know that Apple® will replace your phone, your behaviour is likely to alter and you become less careful.

This problem faces all insurance companies and other financial sectors, such as banking.

ACTIVITY 1   SKILLS   REASONING, INTERPRETATION

CASE STUDY: EXAMPLES OF MORAL HAZARD

(a) For each of the following situations, explain why they might be an example of a moral hazard and what the outcome might be for the parties involved:
  • civil servants who have secure jobs for life
  • state provision of free healthcare
  • welfare benefits for the unemployed.

One of the main causes of the 2008 financial crisis was lending by sub-prime mortgage companies. These companies granted property loans to risky clients (such as people on low incomes or the unemployed) at a time of low interest rates. These debts were sold on as assets, often together with other assets to banks and pension funds who were not aware of the true nature of the risk. The mortgage companies did not then bear the risk if people failed to repay their mortgages, so they had no incentive to be more careful to whom they offered these loans. When interest rates inevitably increased, many could no longer afford the mortgage payments and the banks and pension funds were left with large amounts of bad debt. Some collapsed and others were only able to survive because of huge bailouts by the government.

The banking system is an area where moral hazard is very real. When you deposit your wages or savings into a bank, asymmetric information applies. You trust the bank to look after your money and while you can do some research, you do not really know how safe the bank is. As we have recently seen, banks can fail.

Historically this was a major problem, as during the 1920s and before the great depression of the 1930s, around 70 banks failed each year, meaning savers and investors lost all their money. After the stock market crash during the first 10 months of 1930, 744 banks failed. In all, 9000 banks failed during the 1930s. It is estimated that 4000 banks failed during 1933 alone. By 1933, depositors had lost US$140 billion through bank failures.

When banks fail, some people lose their jobs, others lose their savings, future investors may not be able to get loans and governments may spend billions on support. All this reduces aggregate demand in the economy and can have serious effects on the whole economy. For this reason, banks are sometimes regarded as being '**too big to fail**'.

The modern banking system is heavily regulated and depositors are protected in various ways. After the 2008 financial crisis, governments in Europe and the USA intervened to stop the banks from failing by spending billions of dollars of taxpayers' money. However, the problems remain: a bank is a business like any other and businesses take risks in order to gain profit as a reward for those risks. The greater the risk, the greater the potential profit is. Banks may be tempted to take bigger risks than they would normally do if they know that the government will save them with bailouts if things go wrong.

ACTIVITY 2   SKILLS ▸ REASONING, INTERPRETATION, ANALYSIS

CASE STUDY: THE AUSTRALIAN HOUSING MARKET

In 2017, Australia's house prices rose at their fastest pace in seven years, causing fears of an emerging property bubble. Recent figures show that residential property prices have increased 12.9 per cent in the past 12 months, with prices in Sydney surging up by 18.9 per cent – the fastest rate of growth in almost 15 years. Four of Australia's eight state capital cities are now showing an annual growth rate in house values higher than 10 per cent.

The steep rise in house prices was magnified by the Reserve Bank of Australia's decision to cut interest rates twice in 2016 to a record low of 1.5 per cent and an increase in buy-to-let investor activity during the second half of 2016.

Australia does not have the same housing oversupply or unemployment levels that caused house price crashes in Spain and Ireland.

(a) Explain what has caused the property bubble in Australia.

(b) Explain why an oversupply of houses and unemployment might cause a property bubble to burst.

SPECULATION AND MARKET BUBBLES

Speculation means an economic agent buys or sells something in the expectation of a future price change in the hope of generating a profit. This happens all the time in financial markets as traders buy and sell stocks, shares, currencies and other financial instruments to make a small profit on the transactions. Occasionally though, the speculative motive is all one way and a **market bubble** can be created.

A market bubble occurs when rising demand, for whatever reason, drives prices beyond the level that might normally be expected. Emotion and peer pressure appear to overcome rational analysis. As more buyers join in, the value of what they are buying increases; this in turn encourages more buyers, which forces the price even higher and it becomes an upward cycle. However, this is a bubble and just like real bubbles they can suddenly collapse. It may be that someone finally begins to sell or panic and the price stops increasing and may even drop. Panic can spread among investors and all those who bought now expect prices to fall and sell while they still can. This of course, makes things worse and the bubble bursts with prices collapsing, leaving some traders facing disastrous losses.

Market bubbles are not new and have been around for a long time. The first in history is generally thought to have been the tulip bubble in 1637 (see 'Thinking like an economist' at the end of the chapter). The South Sea bubble happened in the UK in 1721, bankrupting thousands of investors, including Sir Isaac Newton. More recently the stock market bubble of the 1920s led to the Wall Street Crash and the Great Depression in the USA.

Even more recently, the dot.com bubble of the late 1990s, centred around the many newly formed Internet start-up firms, their names usually ending in '.com'. The inevitable crash came when many of these companies proved to be unprofitable or just founded on business plans that were not realistic. Once again, many people and financial institutions lost large amounts of money. Not all the dot.com start-ups were failures though; Amazon.com® was part of that same dot.com boom.

What all these market bubbles had in common, apart from investors hoping to get rich, was that they were centred on something new that the market had not seen before. Whether it was the exotic arrival of tulip bulbs, the automation and technology of the 1920s or the promise of the Internet, these all caught the imagination of investors and set off a speculative bubble. At the time of writing there is much speculation over the rise of the bitcoin and whether it is another bubble about to burst.

The trading of stocks and shares create the spectacular bubbles described above. The housing market is also at risk of such phenomena. Housing bubbles usually start with two events: an increase in demand and a relatively limited supply. Speculators buy property as an investment, often as a safe bet,

which increases the normal demand for housing. Supply is limited in the short run and tends to increase more slowly than demand and so prices rise further. As property prices rise, more people rush in to buy and the bubble takes off.

The US housing bubble burst dramatically in the mid-2000s as the sub-prime sector of the market collapsed. Houses that cost tens of thousands of dollars were being sold for just a few hundred by 2010. In the UK, the housing market is still rising with many first-time buyers unable to afford even a small property. In China, there is the strange sight of 'ghost cities', vast modern urban developments left empty when the mass migration of people from country to town began to reduce. Many developers have gone bankrupt, leaving entire housing developments and infrastructure empty.

THINKING LIKE AN ECONOMIST

TULIP BULBS VERSUS BITCOIN: A BUBBLE COMPARISON

Is **cryptocurrency** like 1990s-era dot. com stocks, South Sea Company or Dutch flowers?

Bitcoin recently nearly broke the US$10,000 barrier, having only broken US$2000 for the first time earlier in 2017. However, claims that the bitcoin boom of the past year is in some way a repeat of the dot. com bubble, which finally popped in March 2000, are well wide of the mark.

Going further back in history, however, there do seem to have been some investment manias that went even further, such as the Netherlands' tulip 'mania' of 1637. Records are not precise enough for us to create daily price charts to match bitcoin. Also, not all tulip bulbs were comparable — the rarer and, to a lesser extent, the more beautiful, the more you would pay. The maximum price reliably recorded for a tulip bulb during the mania was 5200 guilders (the Dutch currency before the euro was introduced). As this was more than triple the 1600 guilders that Rembrandt charged for his painting, *The Night Watch*, at about the same time, this sounds excessive. For a better comparison, a 5 kg loaf would at the time have cost 0.4 guilders. So at the very top, you could have exchanged one tulip bulb for approximately 71 tonnes of bread or 400 tonnes of Dutch herring.

Nowadays, a packet of 100 tulip bulbs can be bought for around US$33, while a 500 g loaf of white bread costs around US$2, so you can get roughly 10 bulbs per kilogram of bread. As the ratio at the top was 71 tonnes of bread per bulb, it does look as though the Dutch tulip mania deserves its historical status as the most absurd example of overvaluation in history. But note that a bulb physically exists, and that its price can be compared with other physical objects. It is not clear that any such fundamental valuation is possible for bitcoin, which is at risk of action by governments.

Was the acceleration in tulip prices comparable to the recent increase in bitcoin prices? From August to November 2017, bitcoin only gained 253 per cent. So cryptocurrencies are still not as overbought as tulip bulbs used to be. A broader lesson is that bitcoin as an investment or speculation phenomenon is unlike anything that has been seen in a long time. It is behaving even more dramatically than most previously recorded bubbles, although it has not yet reached the excesses of the tulip bubble.

CHECKPOINT

1 How does moral hazard occur?

2 Why does the government protect some banks?

3 What does the phrase 'too big to fail' mean?

4 What is a market bubble?

5 Give a common characteristic of market bubbles.

6 What two conditions can start a housing bubble?

SUBJECT VOCABULARY

asymmetric information where buyers and sellers have different amounts of information, with one group having more information than the other.

cryptocurrency a digital or virtual currency that uses cryptography as security, thereby making it secure.

market bubble occurs when rising demand drives prices beyond the level that might normally be expected.

moral hazard when an economic agent makes a decision in their own best interest knowing that there are potential adverse risks, and that if problems result, the cost will be partly borne by other economic agents.

speculation means buying or selling something in the expectation of a future price change and a profit.

too big to fail occurs when the cost to the economy is so great that the government cannot allow it to happen.

EXAM PRACTICE

CHINA'S HOUSING BOOM ENDS AS PRICES FALL IN TOP CITIES

SKILLS REASONING, ANALYSIS, CRITICAL THINKING

DECLINE MARKS END TO HUGE GROWTH THAT SAW VALUES RISE AS MUCH AS 40 PER CENT LAST YEAR (2016)

House prices have fallen across most of China's hottest property markets for the first time in almost two years, marking an end to the enormous growth that saw prices rise as much as 40 per cent in 2016. The end of the housing boom will also mean the end to an important source of economic growth that could have helped China hit its economic growth targets this year.

'We are seeing a peak in the property market… Last year was an incredible surge', said Shen Jianguang, chief economist at Mizuho Securities Asia.

Prices of newly built residential properties dropped between 0.1 and 0.4 per cent in December from the previous month in 12 out of 15 cities that had previously seen the largest price increases, according to data released by the National Bureau of Statistics.

Price rises in cities such as Shanghai and Beijing reached 5 per cent a month in August 2016. Investors rushed into the housing market, especially after a dramatic stock collapse in 2015, seeing property as one of a few options left for high returns on the mainland.

However, their hopes were dashed when the government decided to deal with potential market bubbles last autumn. More than 20 city governments passed restrictions on house purchases and increased the minimum deposit required for a mortgage.

Financial regulators also stopped property developers from borrowing to finance land purchases in an attempt to keep land prices down. Last month, Beijing's mayor promised that house prices would not rise this year. Although many analysts expect property prices to fall at most 5 per cent year on year in the current downturn, local governments are ready to move to avoid sharper crashes.

'Local governments do not want prices to decrease too much', said Mr Shen, explaining that governments sometimes restrict land supply to stop property prices from falling too quickly. 'The local government cannot endure less construction because then they will have no revenue', he added. Many Chinese local governments are dependent on land sales to meet their budget requirements.

▲ Housing in Qinhuangdao, Hebei province, China

'If prices go too far one way, the government will introduce new policies', said James MacDonald, head of China research at Savills, an international property consultancy with an office in Shanghai.

China's real estate and construction sectors made up one-fifth of GDP growth in the first half of 2016, according to Liang Hong, chief economist at China International Capital Corporation. GDP data to be released on Friday will show how reliant China's economy was on property and related sectors in 2016.

Q

1 Using the extract, explain why China's property markets could be described as bubbles. **(4 marks)**

2 Analyse why investors are attracted to property markets. **(6 marks)**

3 Discuss the possible impact of further regulation by the government in property markets.

(14 marks)

EXAM TIP

In your answer to Question 3, you need to look at the extract and analyse the extent to which the regulation has had an impact so far. This has been to reduce the demand for housing by making it more difficult for purchasers of houses and of land. Support this with figures and then discuss the impact of further regulation, which might burst the bubble and damage a valuable part of China's economy, again using evidence and figures. The government needs to carefully balance the need to regulate the market and at the same time protect economic growth.

GOVERNMENT INTERVENTION IN MARKETS

When market failure occurs, the government intervenes to correct it with a range of policies and methods, including financial measures, legislation, regulation and the direct provision of goods and services. The areas where the government intervenes are considered; these include social contexts, such as housing and education, and areas of infrastructure, such as transport and energy. The concluding part examines the causes of government failure. This occurs because government intervention does not always work and may result in making the problem worse or lead to other unintended consequences.

19 PURPOSE AND METHODS OF GOVERNMENT INTERVENTION

LEARNING OBJECTIVES

- Understand the purpose of government intervention, including reference to market failure.
- Understand methods of intervention.
- Understand contexts in which governments may intervene.

GETTING STARTED

Litter in the streets is always a problem. People drop finished cigarettes or soft drink bottles, or throw away the wrapping from their chips or hamburgers. What might be the best way to deal with this? Introducing laws or regulations banning littering, subject to a fine? Taxing cigarette and soft drink manufacturers and using the money to clean up the litter? Running information campaigns about litter? Accepting that it will always be a problem and getting local authorities and taxpayers to pay to clean up the streets?

GOVERNMENT INTERVENTION TO CORRECT MARKET FAILURE

There is a variety of types of market failure that include externalities, provision of public goods and information failure. Governments can intervene in a number of different ways to correct market failure. Total welfare will be increased if the cost of an intervention is less than the benefits gained from the intervention.

INDIRECT TAXES

One way in which governments can correct market failure is through imposing indirect taxes. For example, assume that there is environmental market failure. Firms are releasing too much pollution into the atmosphere. This results in negative externalities. The government could impose a tax on production. Firms would respond by producing less because their costs of production have now risen due to the tax.

FIGURE 1

Imposition of an ad valorem tax
With an optimal level of output of OB, a tax of EG per unit needs to be imposed to maximise welfare.

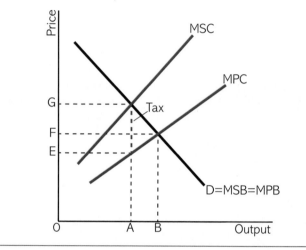

The level of the tax needs to be set so that negative externalities are eliminated and the marginal social cost of production equals the marginal social benefit.

This is shown in Figure 1. The free market level of output is OB where the marginal cost to firms, the marginal private cost, is equal to their marginal private benefit. The free market price is OF. However, the optimal level of output is OA where the marginal social cost is equal to the marginal social benefit. To achieve this level of output, a government could impose a tax of EG per unit. This would shift the marginal private cost curve up to equal the marginal social cost curve at output OB.

In Figure 1, the MPC and MSC lines move further apart as output increases. This shows that the negative externality per unit increases as output increases. It is then appropriate to impose an ad valorem indirect tax where the amount of tax paid in money terms rises as price rises. In Figure 2, the MPC and MSC lines are parallel. It is appropriate here to impose a specific tax, like duty on petrol in the UK. The amount of tax per unit stays the same as the price of the good increases. As in Figure 1, the socially optimal level of output is OB and a specific tax of EG should be imposed to correct the market failure.

FIGURE 2

Imposition of a specific tax
With an optimal level of output of OB, a tax of EG per unit needs to be imposed to maximise welfare.

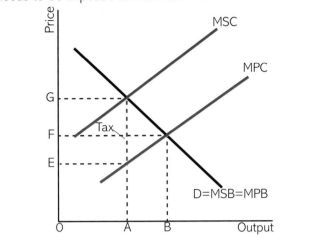

Indirect taxes can have disadvantages.

- They may be difficult to target. So the tax may be too large or too small to correct the market failure exactly. Partly, this may be down to information failure on the part of government: it does not know the exact size of the market failure or it may not know the impact a tax will have on the market.
- Governments may use indirect taxes to raise revenues as well as reduce market failure. The two objectives can then conflict when decisions are made about the size of the tax.
- Taxes are unpopular. In 2017, the state of Louisiana in the USA abandoned a plan to raise tax on fuel because of political opposition. It claimed that the increase in tax revenue was needed to repair the road system.

FIGURE 3

Impact of a subsidy to correct market failure
With an optimal level of output of OB, a subsidy of EG per unit is needed to maximise welfare.

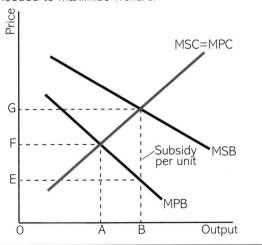

ACTIVITY 1　SKILLS　REASONING, COMMUNICATION, CRITICAL THINKING

CASE STUDY: IMPOSITION OF A CARBON TAX

Singapore is home to some of the world's biggest oil processing plants, with total capacity of about 1.5 million barrels of oil per day. It plans to introduce a carbon tax, from 2019, of between SGD 10 (Singapore dollar) (US$7) and SGD 20 (US$14) per tonne of greenhouse gas emissions. Operating costs for Singapore refiners could rise by US$3.50–US$7 per barrel as a result of the tax, the government estimates.

The proposed tax is the latest indication that countries in Asia, the world's biggest oil market, are moving to limit greenhouse gas emissions. China, the world's biggest emitter of greenhouse gases, was preparing to introduce a national emissions trading system in 2017. South Korea launched an emissions trading scheme in 2015, overcoming strong industry opposition.

Explain, using a diagram, how:
(a) a carbon tax could help correct an environmental market failure
(b) the imposition of a carbon tax could increase market failure.

SUBSIDIES

Another way in which governments can correct market failure is through the provision of subsidies. For example, there are positive externalities in consumption from electric vehicles. The private benefit to the owner of the electric vehicle is less than the benefit to society of more environmentally friendly electric vehicles on the road. Then a government could provide subsidies, for example, for the purchase of more such cars.

This can be shown in Figure 3. If left to the market mechanism, there would be OA electric vehicles because this is where MPB = MPC. However, the marginal social benefit is higher than the marginal private benefit. The optimal level of electric vehicles is therefore OB where MSB = MSC. To achieve this, the government has to give a subsidy of EG per unit to owners of electric vehicles.

Subsidies can be used where there are positive externalities. They can also be used to correct information failure. The government could subsidise the provision of information to those suffering from a lack of information.

Subsidies can have disadvantages.

- They may be difficult to target. As with taxes, the subsidy may be too large or too small to correct the market failure exactly. Partly, this may be down to information failure on the part of government: it does not know the exact size of the market failure or it may not know the impact a subsidy will have on the market.

- There can be conflict with other policy objectives. Someone must pay the subsidies. If it is government, this can conflict with objectives about low taxes or reducing government deficits. Subsidies can also be provided by firms. In the case of the UK electricity industry, government regulations force electricity producers to buy a certain percentage of their power from renewable sources. The prices paid are above the prices for conventional coal or gas electricity. To make a profit, electricity producers then charge their customers a higher price. So customers are subsidising renewable energy by paying higher prices than they would otherwise have done.

This can increase inflation. It can also impact on fuel poverty and the ability of low income households to heat their houses.

- Subsidies can be difficult to remove. Those who receive the subsidies effectively receive an increase in their income. If the subsidy is lowered or removed, they can lobby government to delay or abandon plans to change the subsidy. Attempts to remove subsidies on basic foods or fuel in countries like Iran, Venezuela or India have caused major riots in the past. In some cases, governments have even been toppled as a result.

ACTIVITY 2 SKILLS REASONING, ANALYSIS, CRITICAL THINKING

CASE STUDY: KEROSENE SUBSIDY

India is one of the world's biggest consumers of the fuel kerosene, which has associated health hazards and environmental consequences. In the absence of any alternatives, many poorer households in rural areas rely on it as a source of heating and lighting.

The Indian government is reducing the level of subsidies given to the Indian states for kerosene to reduce the total amount of subsidy paid by the government.

(a) Explain, using a diagram and kerosene as an example, how a subsidy increases output of a product.

(b) Analyse, using a diagram, how the subsidy before it was reduced, could 'cost too much' for the government.

MAXIMUM PRICES

Market failure can arise if consumers cannot afford to buy basic necessities such as food and housing. These

goods can have positive externalities in consumption. For example, if poor parents in Indonesia cannot afford to buy sufficient food for their children, those children may suffer from ill-health. This may permanently affect their physical health and ability to function in society in future. Poor housing can also cause ill health. Children brought up in poor housing may suffer physically. It could affect their schooling and limit their ability to gain qualifications.

Imposing maximum prices for these goods will make them more affordable. In Figure 4, the free market rent for housing is OG and OB is demanded and supplied in equilibrium. The socially optimal level of housing is OC. If the government imposes a maximum rent or price of OF, then housing becomes more affordable and OC is demanded.

A problem with this policy is that if prices are forced down to make goods more affordable, then the quantity supplied falls. In Figure 4, at a price of OF, quantity supplied falls to OA. There is then excess demand of AC. Those able to buy OA are better off than before, but some of the consumers who want to buy AC are worse off because the good is not available.

Maximum prices often lead to black markets. For example, some of the goods bought at price OF by consumers are resold on the black market at a higher price. Equally, producers may sell directly onto the black market to get higher prices.

Note that if the maximum price is set above the free market price, at more than OG in Figure 4, there will be no effect on the market. The equilibrium price in the market will remain where the quantity demanded equals the quantity supplied and equilibrium output will remain at OB.

FIGURE 4

Maximum prices
OG is the free market price. If the government sets a maximum price of OF, quantity demanded will increase to OC, while quantity supplied will fall to OA. The result will be excess demand of AC.

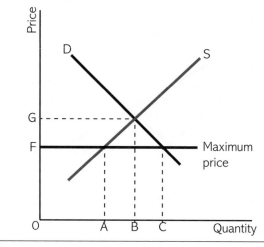

ACTIVITY 3

SKILLS REASONING, ANALYSIS, INTERPRETATION, CRITICAL THINKING

CASE STUDY: CAPPING MEDICINE PRICES

In recent years, the Indian government has capped the prices of hundreds of life-saving drugs and devices to make them more affordable. In February 2017, it imposed a 75 per cent price cut for certain heart stents – wire tubes used to treat some heart conditions.

The government justified its action by referring to 'huge unethical markups'. But global medical device makers have protested the new maximum price, with some saying it would force them to sell below cost.

Before the pricing order, Boston Scientific was selling its high-end Synergy stent for about US$3000 in India, well above its US$750 cost. The new cap reduces the price to US$450, and the company says it would result in losses of at least US$7 million a year.

The US government warned that people would be denied access to the latest medical advances if companies stopped supplying India's US$5 billion medical-technology market.

(a) Explain, using a diagram, why the Indian government's reduction of the price of stents might lead to shortages.

(b) (i) Explain why the government might originally have decided to intervene in the healthcare market.

   (ii) Do you think the latest intervention is likely to be successful? Explain your reasons.

MINIMUM PRICES

Some goods, such as cigarettes, have significant negative externalities in consumption. Governments may attempt to correct the resulting market failure by raising their price to a level where marginal social cost and marginal social benefit are equal. One way of doing this is to set a minimum price for the good.

In Figure 5, the free market equilibrium price is OF and output is OB. The government can then set a minimum price of OG above the free market price. This reduces the quantity demanded from OB to OA. However, it also increases the quantity supplied from OB to OC. The result is excess supply of AC.

Excess supply becomes a problem if it is able to return to the market. In the case of cigarettes, minimum prices tend to create black markets where cigarettes are sold at less than the minimum price.

Note that if the minimum price is set below the free market price at less than OF in Figure 5, there will be no effect on the market. The equilibrium price in the market will remain where the quantity demanded equals the quantity supplied and equilibrium output will remain at OB.

FIGURE 5

Minimum prices

OF is the free market price. If the government sets a minimum price of OG, supply will increase from OB to OC, while demand will fall to OA. The result will be excess supply of AC.

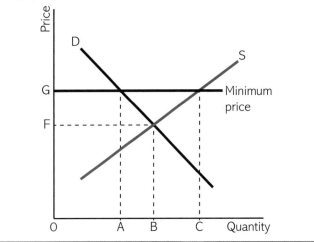

REGULATION

Regulation is widely used to correct market failure. For example, regulation could be used to close information gaps. Airlines could be forced to reveal all the charges for an airline ticket at the start of the booking process rather than the end. Banks are forced to tell customers the rate of interest on a loan. Regulation is also widely used to control externalities. The government could lay down maximum pollution levels or might even ban pollution-creating activities altogether. Santiago, the capital of Chile, has been suffering from serious pollution problems. In recent years, thousands of buses and trucks with inadequate pollution controls have been removed from the roads; regulations have been implemented to control harmful industry emissions and burning has been restricted. From 2020, the Chilean government will introduce a regulation requiring all vehicles to comply with the equivalent of the EU's tough Euro 6 emissions standard.

Regulation is easy to understand and relatively cheap to enforce. However, there are problems with this approach to market failure. First, it is often difficult for government to fix the right level of regulation to ensure efficiency. Regulations might be too loose or too tight. The correct level would be where the economic benefit arising from a reduction in externality was the same as the economic cost imposed by the regulation. For instance, if firms had to spend US$30 million fitting anti-pollution devices to plant and machinery, but the fall in pollution was only worth US$20 million, then the regulation would have been too tight. If the fall in pollution was worth US$40 million, it implies that it would be worth industry spending even more on anti-pollution measures to further reduce pollution and thus further increase the US$40 million worth of benefits.

Moreover, regulations tend not to discriminate between different costs of reducing externalities. For instance, two firms might have to reduce pollution emissions by the same amount. Firm A could reduce its emissions at a cost of US$3 million, while it might cost firm B US$10 million to do the same. However, firm A could double the reduction in its pollution levels at a cost of US$7 million. Regulations that set equal limits for all firms will mean that the cost to society of reducing pollution in this case is US$13 million (US$3 million for firm A and US$10 million for firm B). However, it would be cheaper for society if the reduction could be achieved by firm A alone at a cost of US$7 million.

ACTIVITY 4

SKILLS ▸ REASONING, ANALYSIS, INTERPRETATION, CRITICAL THINKING

CASE STUDY: ASBESTOS

In Dunedin, New Zealand, a roof repair company has been fined NZD 30,000 (New Zealand dollars) after its contractor worked on an old roof in a way that spread polluting asbestos dust over nearby surroundings. Sealtec Otago Ltd employed the contractor to work on the roof of an engineering business. The engineering business reported the suspected asbestos dust to the Department of Labour after it was found on floors, machinery and cars.

Sealtec admitted two charges under the Health and Safety in Employment Act 1992, and was fined NZD 15,000 on each charge in Dunedin District Court. The charges were of failing to take all possible steps to ensure the safety of the contractor, and of failing to take all possible steps to ensure that a hazard (asbestos dust) did not harm people near their place of work.

On average, 170 people die each year in New Zealand from asbestos-related diseases, typically from working with the material in the past. Asbestos was widely used in the 1950s and 1960s in the building industry.

(a) Explain why the use and removal of asbestos might lead to market failure.
(b) Explain how regulation might prevent market failure linked to the removal of asbestos.

TRADE POLLUTION PERMITS

Externalities caused by pollution can be reduced through the use of **trade pollution permits**, a key element of **cap and trade schemes**. To understand

how they work, assume that the government wishes to control emissions of carbon, a greenhouse gas responsible for global warming. It has set a limit or cap on the amount of carbon to be emitted over a period of time, for example, a year. This cap acts as the target for carbon emissions and is likely to be lower than current levels of carbon emission. The government then allocates permits to emit carbon, the total of which equals the cap. It could issue these, for example, by giving them to firms that currently emit carbon. The permits are then tradable for money between polluters. Firms that succeed in reducing their carbon emissions below their permit levels can sell their permits to other producers who are exceeding their limits. The higher the price of the permits, the greater the incentive for carbon-emitting firms to reduce their carbon emissions.

The main advantage of trade pollution permits over simple regulation is that costs in the industry and therefore to society should be lower than with regulation. Each firm in the industry will consider whether it is possible to reduce emissions and at what cost. Assume that firm A, with just enough permits to meet its emissions, can reduce emissions by 500 tonnes at a cost of US$10 million. Firm B is a high polluter and needs 500 tonnes worth of permits to meet regulations. It calculates that it would need to spend US$25 million to cut emissions by this amount.

If there was simple regulation, the anti-pollution costs to the industry, and therefore to society, would be US$25 million. Firm B would have to meet its pollution limit while there would be no incentive for firm A to cut pollution.

With permits, firm A could sell 500 tonnes of permits to firm B. The cost to society of then reducing pollution would only be US$10 million, the cost that firm A would incur. It might cost firm B more than $10 million to buy the permits. It would be prepared to spend anything up to US$25 million to acquire them. Say firm A drove a hard bargain and sold the permits to firm B for US$22 million. Society would save US$15 million, distributed between a paper profit of US$12 million for firm A and a fall in costs from what otherwise would have been the case for firm B of US$3 million.

STATE PROVISION OF PUBLIC GOODS

Public goods are goods such as defence, the judiciary and prison service, the police service and street lighting. Because of their characteristics of non-rivalry and non-excludability, they will either not be provided by the market mechanism or will only be provided in small quantities. The result is market failure. In Figure 6, the socially optimal level of output of a public good is OA. However, the maximum amount that is demanded in a free market is OB and this is when the price is zero. Governments tend to respond to this by providing these goods directly and paying for them via taxes. In Figure 6, state provision is shown by the vertical supply curve (Supply).

FIGURE 6

Direct provision of a public good
Assume this is the market for defence. To prevent market failure, OA should be produced. However, there is no price on the demand curve at which OA would be demanded. The government therefore steps in and provides OA whatever the price of defence.

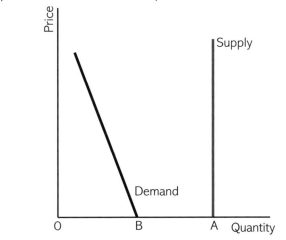

Direct provision can have disadvantages. It may lead to inefficient production, particularly if the government produces the good itself. This is because employees of the state, whether providing the good or buying it in, may have no incentive to cut costs to a minimum. It may also be inefficient because the wrong mix of goods is produced, especially if the goods are provided free of charge to taxpayers. The government may provide too many soldiers and too few hospital beds, for example. Markets, in contrast, give consumers the opportunity to buy those goods that give the greatest satisfaction. In a market, if producers supplied too many soldiers, they would be left unsold. Firms would then move resources out of the production of defence and into the production of a good that consumers were prepared to buy.

There are a variety of ways in which the government could deal with the provision of street lighting.
1. Discuss the relative merits of each of the following options.
(a) It could leave it completely to market forces. Households and firms would pay the full cost for any street lights they wanted, including providing the land on which the street lights would be built.
(b) It could subsidise households and firms wishing to provide street lighting on their land but not provide any street lighting itself.
(c) It could provide street lighting directly and pay for it through taxation.

PROVISION OF INFORMATION

Information failure occurs because one party to a transaction does not have the information that is available to make a decision. A government can step in to provide the information itself. For example, it might run advertising campaigns to deliver messages about not smoking. Or it might force parties to a transaction to release information. Forcing cigarette manufacturers to put messages about the dangers of smoking on cigarette packets is an example.

THINKING LIKE AN ECONOMIST

POLLUTION PROBLEMS

Country A's economy has been growing rapidly for the last 30 years. Its national income has more than quadrupled in this time. However, this rapid growth has caused a number of unintended changes. Many inhabitants live and work in highly polluted environments. Growth of manufacturing and heavy industries has led to massively increased air, soil and water pollution.

Local authorities and the government have found this challenging to deal with. They know that pollution is a side effect of increasing output, jobs and prosperity. They also know that tackling the complex issues will be costly and may affect this growth. However, citizens are increasingly concerned about the effects of pollution on their health.

The most common way to control pollution is government regulation. For example, in recent years, Country A has banned single-use plastics. Before this, they phased out older and less efficient steel and aluminum production processes. Some smaller and less-efficient factories in urban areas have been closed down altogether. There are numerous regulations in place now about the amount of allowable pollution a plant can release; however, these are often ignored by companies or local authorities in charge of enforcing the regulations.

Subsidies have been used to reward polluters that reduce emissions. Subsidies have also been given for the installation of cleaner technology and to fit pollution-controlling equipment to some power stations.

Country A has also been experimenting with pollution permits for carbon emissions. Permits are given out to companies creating carbon emissions. Companies that do not use their whole allocation can sell these permits to other companies, hopefully creating a net reduction in emissions across the economy as a whole.

Balancing the needs of a rapidly growing and maturing economy against the environmental concerns this has created is proving to be a challenging task, but Country A hopes that through these actions a real impact on pollution levels will be seen within a generation.

CHECKPOINT

1 Give two problems of using indirect taxes to correct market failure.

2 Give examples of two problems of using subsidies to correct market failure.

3 Give an example of when a government might introduce maximum prices.

4 Give an example of one problem that might arise from using maximum prices.

5 Give an example of when a government might introduce minimum prices.

6 Give an example of one problem that might arise from using minimum prices.

7 Name one problem that might arise from using regulation.

8 Name two key features of a pollution permits scheme.

SUBJECT VOCABULARY

cap and trade schemes schemes that set a limit on a particular type of pollution, and then issue pollution permits to the total of that limit, which can be bought and sold between firms that pollute.

trade pollution permit or pollution permit or pollution credit a permission issued, usually by a government, to allow a fixed amount of pollution to be created; this permit can be used by the owner or sold to another firm.

EXAM PRACTICE

CARBON DIOXIDE EMISSIONS FROM MOTOR VEHICLES

SKILLS REASONING, COMMUNICATION, INTERPRETATION, CRITICAL THINKING

Motor vehicles are a significant source of carbon dioxide (CO_2) emissions, which contribute to the growth of greenhouse gases in the atmosphere and global warming.

Governments in the European Union (EU) are committed to reducing CO_2 emissions. For example, high levels of VAT (an ad valorem tax) and excise duties (a specific tax) on fuel raise the cost of motoring and so reduce the number of miles travelled. In Germany, the Motor Vehicle tax is an annual tax on all vehicles based on engine size measured in cubic centimetres (cc). It ranges from €5 to €25 per 100 cc for petrol engines and €13 to €37 per 100 cc for diesel engines.

At a European level, the EU has set emission targets for motor vehicles. Between 2011 and 2021, car manufacturers must cut emissions from the cars they sell by approximately 50 per cent. If they fail to do so, they will be fined €295 per gram of CO_2 that their vehicles release over the 95 gram limit, multiplied by the number of cars they sold that year. According to the 2014 annual report by Transport & Environment, four of Europe's largest car manufacturers are predicted to miss these targets: General Motors, BMW, Fiat and Hyundai. All four companies denied they would fail to meet the 2021 deadline. They said that future engines and vehicle designs would speed up their rate of emissions reduction in the coming years.

Q

1 Setting a maximum price is most likely to:
(a) reduce demand
(b) increase supply
(c) increase price
(d) reduce supply.   **(1 mark)**

2 Explain the difference between ad valorem taxes and specific taxes, using motor fuel as an example.   **(4 marks)**

3 Draw a diagram to show how taxes on fuel reduce CO_2 emissions.   **(4 marks)**

4 Using your own knowledge and the data, evaluate whether regulations are always the best way to correct market failure.   **(20 marks)**

EXAM HINT

Analyse the different ways in which regulations and other forms of government intervention work to reduce market failure. What are their advantages and disadvantages? Weigh these up, taking the issue of CO_2 emissions from motor vehicles as an example.

20 GOVERNMENT FAILURE

LEARNING OBJECTIVES

- Understand 'government failure' as intervention that results in a net welfare loss.
- Understand causes of government failure.

GETTING STARTED

In 2017, Hong Kong (PRC) lowered the cap on guaranteed earnings for Hong Kong's two power companies from 9.99 per cent to 8 per cent. Would that result in a net benefit to society or a loss? For example, would households in Hong Kong be better off in the short term and in the long term? Would it encourage the power companies to invest in new equipment and power plants? Are power companies simply making too much profit?

GOVERNMENT FAILURE

Markets may fail. They may underprovide public goods. They may overprovide private goods that have negative externalities. They may cause prices to be too high because of asymmetric information. One response is for governments to intervene to correct these market failures. However, if markets can fail, so too can governments. **Government failure** occurs when it intervenes in the market, but this intervention leads to a net loss of economic welfare rather than a gain. So government failure arises when the total social costs arising from intervention are greater than the total social benefits that are created by that intervention. There are a number of reasons why government failure may occur.

DISTORTION OF PRICE SIGNALS

Some types of government intervention change price signals in the market. For example, many governments intervene in their domestic agricultural markets to support farmers. One way is to impose tariffs (taxes) on a product like wheat or rice being imported into the country. This allows farmers with high costs, who would otherwise be forced out of production by cheaper imports, to stay in business and make a profit. However, it means that domestic consumers have to pay higher prices for the product. It also means that farmers are growing a crop on land that could be more

efficiently used for something else if there were no price distortions. If the losses to consumers and to efficiency are greater than the gains to farmers, then there is government failure.

There are many examples of changes in price signals in the labour market that can potentially lead to government failure. For example, the government may want to raise income levels for the poor by setting a high minimum wage. However, this may be so high that companies stop employing low-paid workers, putting large numbers of people whom the government wanted to protect out of work. Similarly, the government may sharply raise unemployment benefit to help the unemployed. This may discourage them from looking for work if they are now better off on benefits than working. This increases the numbers of unemployed.

UNINTENDED CONSEQUENCES

Some interventions by government create unintended consequences. For example, when member countries of the EU first implemented a Common Agricultural Policy (CAP) in 1962, they did not predict what a boost it would give to agricultural production. The result was that in the 1970s and 1980s, most of the EU budget was spent on CAP and EU consumers paid much higher prices for food than if CAP had not existed. Another unintended consequence of CAP was that it depressed world prices of certain agricultural products. Under CAP, the EU bought up certain agricultural products at a minimum price. It then disposed of the produce by selling it below that price onto world markets. Farmers in rich countries like the USA and New Zealand suffered lower prices for their produce as a result. But so too did some farmers in developing countries round the world who could not compete with the low EU prices.

EXCESSIVE ADMINISTRATIVE COSTS

Sometimes, the administrative cost of correcting market failure is so large that it outweighs the welfare benefit from the correction of market failure. For instance, the government may put into place a scheme to help the unemployed back into work. During a year, 100,000 people pass through the scheme. Of those, 50,000 would have found jobs anyway but simply use the scheme because it provides advantages to them or their employer to do so. A further 10,000 find a job who would otherwise not have done so and 40,000 remain unemployed. It may cost US$6000 per person per year on the scheme, giving a total cost of US$600 million. This means that the cost per worker who would otherwise not have got a job is US$600 million ÷ 10,000 or US$60,000 per worker. This is an enormous cost for the benefit likely to be gained by the 10,000 workers. Indeed, they almost certainly would have preferred to have been given the US$60,000 rather than gain a job. Another example would be the payment of welfare benefits. If it costs US$1 to pay out a US$3 benefit, is this likely to improve economic welfare?

INFORMATION GAPS

Governments, like any economic agents, rarely possess complete information on which to base a decision. In some cases, the information available is positively misleading. It is not surprising, then, that governments may make the wrong policy response to a problem. For example, a government may decide to spend millions of pounds building a new road bridge between the mainland and a small island with a population of 10,000. It may justify the cost by predicting a number of benefits such as more jobs, more tourism to the island and lower cost of travel to and from the island. However, projections of costs and benefits like these are often wrong. Costs, such as the cost of building the bridge, may be underestimated while benefits, such as the number of extra tourists, may be overestimated. The result can be government failure.

CONFLICTING OBJECTIVES

Governments often face conflicting objectives. For instance, they may want to cut taxes but increase spending on defence. Every decision made by the government has an opportunity cost. Sometimes, a decision is made where the welfare gain from an alternative would have been even higher. In the case of education, contrast two systems. In one, there are selective schools and state schools for everyone who failed to pass an entrance test. In the other, every child, whatever their ability, goes to the same state school. Assume that those receiving their education in selective schools receive a better education than if they were in a state school. In contrast, assume that those who fail to get into a selective school achieve less than they would have done if all children, whatever their abilities, had gone to the same state school. There is now a conflict of objectives about

which system to implement. Are the needs of those who would be selected for selective schools more important than those of the rest of the school population, or vice versa? Governments may make the wrong policy decision when there are such conflicts of objective, choosing the option that gives lower economic welfare rather than higher economic welfare. They may do this because of lack of information, or they may act on their own political beliefs, ignoring information that is contrary to these beliefs.

POLITICIANS MAXIMISING THEIR OWN WELFARE

Much of economics assumes that governments will act in a way that maximises the welfare of their citizens. Public choice theory suggests that politicians act in a way that maximises their own utility whether or not this leads to improved welfare for the citizens they are supposed to represent. For example, politicians in office who are fighting to get re-elected may implement policies that benefit their own voters at the expense of the welfare of all other citizens. Or they adopt policies that will produce benefits shortly before an election but that in the long term will lead to a net loss of economic welfare. Politicians may also display rent-seeking behaviour. This is where those in power influence the distribution of resources to benefit themselves without creating any extra wealth for society. For example, politicians may receive bribes from companies to make sure they win a government contract, or a politician may be bribed to vote in a certain way on an issue.

MARKET VERSUS GOVERNMENT FAILURE

In economic theory, it is often assumed that market failure should be corrected by governments. If markets fail to provide public goods, then the government should ensure their provision. If a monopolist is exploiting the consumer, then the government should regulate or abolish the monopoly. If a polluter is damaging the environment, then the government should act to limit the actions of those responsible. However, government intervention may lead to a loss of economic welfare rather than a gain in economic welfare and so government failure will exist. At one extreme, there are those who argue that government failure is so large and frequent that governments should only rarely intervene in markets. This tends to be associated with right-wing political viewpoints. At the other extreme, there are those who argue that market failures are so large and frequent that the government must intervene in all the key parts of a market economy, either by regulating markets or by abolishing them completely and having state provision of goods. This tends to be associated with left-wing political viewpoints.

The evidence would suggest that the truth lies somewhere in between these two positions. Market failure is widespread and markets do need controlling by governments to some extent. However, markets often perform a better job of allocating resources than government, even when market failure is present.

ACTIVITY 1

SKILLS ⟩ REASONING, ANALYSIS, INTERPRETATION, COMMUNICATION, CRITICAL THINKING

CASE STUDY: RED TAPE

In the 19th century, cookery books recommended that readers should always make their own vinegar. This was because shop-bought vinegar of the day was usually made from sulphuric acid mixed with water.

Today, food manufacturers and retailers in most countries are so controlled by government regulations that this could not happen. Some argue, though, that such regulations are excessive. They suggest that government red tape restricts the opening and running of new businesses and that consumers have to pay higher prices for their food because it costs firms money to obey government regulations. For

example, a report commissioned by the EUWEP, the EU trade association for egg packers, traders and processors, found that egg production in the EU was among the most expensive in the world in 2012. Fifteen per cent of the costs of producing eggs in the EU were the result of meeting EU legislation, including higher animal welfare legislation. Major world egg producers such as Argentina, India and Ukraine had no specific animal welfare legislation, while in the USA, there were only voluntary guidelines.

(a) Explain why markets fail according to the data.

(b) Discuss whether there is government failure in the market for food in the EU.

THINKING LIKE AN ECONOMIST

VENEZUELA IN CRISIS

Commentators argue that Venezuela should be a rich and prosperous country. It has some of the world's largest oil reserves, an educated workforce, a modern industrialised economy and is well located for foreign trade. However, figures suggest that it has had economic problems for many years, arguably caused by poor governance. Between 1999 and 2013, the country was run by President Hugo Chavez, a socialist who was determined to redistribute income in favour of the poor. Economists would argue that his policies led to significant distortions and inefficiencies in the economy.

One example of government failure was a policy that saw large subsidies on petrol and gas. In 2013, Venezuela was earning US$100 billion in oil revenues and selling petrol at approximately US¢2 per litre to Venezuelan motorists. The subsidy was costing the government US$12 billion a year. In most countries, petrol is taxed, not subsidised. This subsidy had two negative effects. One was that large amounts of subsidised petrol were being smuggled illegally

across the border to Colombia where it could be sold for profit. In 2014, this was estimated at 140,000 barrels of oil per day. Venezuelan citizens were effectively subsidising Colombian motorists. The other negative effect was high inflation of over 50 per cent a year. The government depended for almost all its revenues on oil rather than taxes on citizens and non-oil businesses. By 2013, it was running a large government deficit, including the US$12 billion in fuel subsidies, and financing that through printing money. The result was high inflation.

Another example of government failure occurred in 2013. The government fixed the exchange rate of the currency, the bolivar, at VEF 6.3 to US$1. Purchases of foreign currency at banks was strictly regulated. This was necessary because the black market exchange rate was seven times that amount. One way to avoid this was that anyone buying an airline ticket to fly abroad could get up to US$3000 at the official exchange rate. Venezuelans exploited this by buying an airline ticket, exchanging bolívars at the official exchange rate of VEF 6.3 to US$1 and then exchanging the dollars back into bolivars on the black market. The airline ticket would be thrown away, unused. So long as the airline ticket was less than the profit made on the currency, people using the trick would make a profit at the expense of everyone else. Airlines flying out of Venezuela were also doing good business at the government's expense.

Government subsidies cover all basic items, from food to toilet paper. However, shortages were widespread because the government placed maximum prices on goods. The maximum price was too low for importers to make a profit on goods bought abroad. It was also too low to prevent domestic producers from refusing to supply and closing down. One response of government was to nationalise companies. In response to shortages of toilet paper, for example, the government took over the largest manufacturer of toilet paper in September 2013. However, Venezuelans have to queue at shops, often for hours, to get basic goods. In 2014, the government introduced fingerprint checks at supermarkets to stop Venezuelans from buying too many cheap items. At the same time, 27,000 government inspectors were checking shop prices to ensure that they were 'fair' and that shops were not making illegal profits.

Shortages, queues and refusal to supply goods impose heavy costs on an economy. If the Venezuelan government wanted to help the poorest people in the country, it would be far more efficient simply to pay a welfare benefit to those on low incomes and allow them to buy what they want.

In 2017, Venezula still faces many problems. President Maduro's government is facing political challenges and frequent violent demonstrations. Maduro is accused of governing by force and of reducing civil and democratic rights. The economy has also suffered; oil makes up 95 per cent of Venezuela's exports and falling oil prices have meant falling revenues. Inflation is high, with some economists warning of hyperinflation in the near future and the currency, the bolivar, has plunged in value.

CHECKPOINT

1 What is government failure?
2 Give an example of unintended consequences.
3 Give an example of an information gap.
4 Give an example of conflicting objectives.
5 What is public choice theory?
6 What is rent-seeking behaviour?

SUBJECT VOCABULARY

government failure occurs when government intervention leads to a net welfare loss compared to the free market solution.

public choice theory theories about how and why public spending and taxation decisions are made.

rent-seeking the use of political power by an economic agent to influence the distribution of resources for their own benefit at the expense of others without creating any extra wealth for society.

EXAM PRACTICE

GOVERNMENT FAILURE

SKILLS REASONING, ANALYSIS, INTERPRETATION, COMMUNICATION, CRITICAL THINKING

In 2009, the European Union set a target for 10 per cent of transport fuel to be met from biofuels (fuels made from plants). It also set a target for member countries to generate one-fifth of their energy from renewable sources by 2020. Governments have spent large amounts of money in subsidies to create a market for biofuels.

However, there was widespread criticism when farmers both in Europe and the USA began to plant large amounts of crops to be made into biofuels. It was argued that it was a waste of good-quality farmland that should be used to grow food. This could potentially drive up world food prices because of the fall in supply, making it more difficult for the poor to feed themselves.

There was also criticism of the use of wood products to generate electricity. For example, the EU demand for wood pellets has risen to 19 million tonnes per year. It is argued that burning wood pellets is better than burning coal because wood is a renewable resource and that carbon emissions from burning wood are absorbed by newly planted trees. The USA exports 4.5 million tonnes of wood pellets (96.6 per cent of its total output) to just two European countries, Belgium and the UK. They are meant to come from sawdust, offcuts or trees cut down during forest management rather than healthy trees. However, critics say that regulation in the USA is very weak and that too much of the wood comes from whole trees specifically cut down to create wood pellets. They also say that it is difficult to monitor that trees are being replaced.

In January 2014, the media reported that the Australian government gave approval for a group to create the world's largest seaport for the export of coal, at Abbot Point. Its investors argued that it would allow tens of billions of dollars of coal reserves in Queensland to be used and provide a boost for the Australian economy. However, the plans were fiercely opposed by environmentalists because they involved the dumping of 3 million cubic metres of mud near the Great Barrier Reef, which already faces threats from environmental factors such as global warming. Two million tourists a year visit the Great Barrier Reef. UNESCO had already warned that it may place the reef on its list of sites in danger this year before the announcement of the Abbot Point development was made.

Q

1 The government intervenes to correct a market failure. Government failure is the result if:
   (a) total social benefits are greater than total social costs
   (b) the administrative cost is greater than the social benefits
   (c) there is a net gain in economic welfare
   (d) total social benefits increase and total social costs decrease. **(1 mark)**

2 Explain the difference between market failure and government failure. **(4 marks)**

3 Analyse how increasing the output of biofuels could:
   (a) help solve the problem of market failure in the market for fuels **(6 marks)**
   (b) create an example of government failure. **(6 marks)**

4 Using the data and your own economic knowledge, evaluate whether the main source of government failure arises from information gaps on the part of government. **(20 marks)**

EXAM HINT

In your answer to Question 3, you need to analyse the different sources of government failure, applying economic theory to the examples in the data and other examples you may have. Each source of market failure should be given a separate paragraph. Alongside the analysis, evaluate whether or not this is an important source of government failure with particular reference to the examples you have included. In a concluding paragraph, weigh up the evidence to come to a conclusion.

MEASURES OF ECONOMIC PERFORMANCE

This first section in Unit 2 looks at measures of economic performance. These are economic growth, inflation, the balance of payments and employment/unemployment. The unit explains how each of these performance measures are defined and calculated, and how to interpret this data. The section discusses in depth using national income to compare living standards over time, and between countries. It explores the concept of well-being and how this might be measured. This section also looks at the causes and effects of inflation and unemployment.

21 INTRODUCTION TO THE MEASURES OF ECONOMIC PERFORMANCE

LEARNING OBJECTIVES

■ Understand the measures of economic performance:
  ● economic growth
  ● inflation
  ● employment and unemployment
  ● balance of payments.

GETTING STARTED

Find out the current rate of economic growth, the rate of unemployment, the **inflation** rate and the level of the **current account** deficit on the balance of payments for Japan, the USA, Brazil and Greece (the OECD website is a useful source of data as well as general searches on the Internet). Which economy do you think is currently performing best?

MICROECONOMICS AND MACROECONOMICS

Microeconomics is the study of individual markets within an economy. For instance, microeconomics is concerned with individual markets for goods or the market for labour. Housing, transport, sport and leisure are all mainly microeconomic topics because they concern the study of individual markets.

In contrast, macroeconomics is concerned with the study of the economy as a whole. For instance, macroeconomics considers the total value produced of goods and services in an economy. The price level of the whole economy is studied. Total levels of employment and unemployment are examined. Housing becomes a macroeconomic issue when, for instance, rises in house prices significantly affect the average level of all prices in the economy.

NATIONAL ECONOMIC PERFORMANCE

One of the reasons why macroeconomics is useful is because it tells us something about the performance of an economy. In particular, it allows economists to compare the economy today with the past. Is the economy doing better or worse than it was, say, 10 years ago? It also allows economists to compare different economies. Is the Japanese economy doing better than the US economy? How does the UK compare with the average in Europe?

An economy is a system that attempts to resolve the basic economic problem of scarce resources in a world of infinite wants. An economic system is a mechanism for deciding what is to be produced, how production is to take place and who is to receive the benefit of that production. When judging the performance of an economy, one of the criteria is to consider how much is being produced. The more that is produced, the better is usually considered the economic performance. Another criterion is whether resources are being used fully. If there are high levels of unemployment, for instance, the economy cannot be producing at its potential level of output. Unemployment also brings poverty to those out of work and therefore affects the living standards of individuals. The rate at which prices rise is important too. High rates of price rises disrupt the performance of an economy. A national economy must also avoid spending more than it can afford. So over a long period of time, the value of what it buys from other economies must roughly equal what it sells. In this, it is no different from a household that cannot overspend and build up debts in the long term.

ECONOMIC GROWTH

One of the key measures of national economic performance is the rate of change of output. This is known as **economic growth**. If an economy grows by 2.5 per cent per year, output will double roughly every 30 years. If it grows by 7 per cent per year, output will approximately double every 10 years. At growth rates of 10 per cent per year, output will double every seven years.

There is a standard definition of output based on a United Nations measure that is used by countries around the world to calculate their output. Using a standard definition allows output to be compared between countries and over time. This measure of output is called **gross domestic product** or GDP. So growth of 3 per cent in GDP (adjusted for inflation) in one year means that the output of the economy has increased by 3 per cent over a 12-month period. If GDP has been adjusted for inflation, then it is called real GDP or GDP at constant prices. An increase in real GDP (or GDP at constant prices) means output in the economy has risen. The economic growth rate is the rate of change in real GDP. The economic growth rate measures how much output is changing, typically over the course of a year, and is expressed as a percentage. For example, Ireland's economic growth rate was 26.29 per cent in 2015. This means its output grew by 26.29 per cent over the course of 2015. In contrast, Brazil's economic growth rate was −a3.85 per cent in 2015. This means the output in Brazil was 3.85 per cent lower in 2015 than 2014. Its output contracted. The term **recession** means an economy has experienced negative economic growth over at least two consecutive quarters.

Economic growth is generally considered to be desirable because individuals prefer to consume more rather than fewer goods and services. This is based on the assumption that wants are infinite. Higher economic growth is therefore better than lower economic growth. Periods when the economy fails to grow at all, or output shrinks as in a recession or depression, are periods when the economy is performing poorly. The depression years of the 1930s in Europe and the Americas, for instance, were years when poverty increased and unemployment brought misery to millions of households. In contrast, a boom is a period when the economy is doing particularly well with economic growth above its long-run average.

UNEMPLOYMENT

Unemployment is a major problem in society because it represents a waste of scarce resources. Output could be higher if the unemployed were in work. It also leads to poverty for those who are out of work. So high unemployment indicates poor national economic performance. Similarly, low unemployment indicates good national economic performance.

Economic growth and unemployment tend to be linked. Fast-growing economies tend to have low unemployment. This is because more workers are needed to produce more goods and services. Low levels of economic growth tend to be associated with rising levels of unemployment. Over time, technological change allows an economy to produce more with fewer workers. If there is little or no economic growth, workers are made redundant through technological progress but fail to find new jobs in expanding industries. If growth is negative and the economy goes into recession, firms will lay off workers and unemployment will rise.

Fast economic growth, then, will tend to lead to net job creation. More jobs will be created than are lost through the changing structure of the economy. So another way of judging the performance of an economy is to consider its rate of job creation.

INFLATION

Inflation is the increase in average prices in an economy. The inflation rate shows how much prices have changed, compared to the same time the previous year. A positive inflation rate means prices have risen over the year. A negative inflation rate means prices have fallen over the year. Low, but positive, inflation is generally considered to be better than high inflation. This is because inflation has a number of negative effects. For instance, rising prices mean that the value of what savings can buy falls. If a French citizen had €50 in savings and the price of a T-shirt went up from €10 to €25, then they would be worse off because their savings could only now buy two T-shirts compared to five before. Another problem with inflation is that it disrupts knowledge of prices in a market. If there is very high inflation, with prices changing by the month, consumers often don't know what is a reasonable price for an item when they come to buy it.

Today, inflation of a few per cent is considered to be acceptable. When inflation starts to climb through the 5 per cent barrier, economists begin to worry that inflation is too high. Inflation was a major problem for many countries including the UK in the 1970s and 1980s. In the UK, inflation reached 24.1 per cent in 1975, for instance. Today, some countries in the industrialised world are faced with the opposite problem: **deflation**, or falling prices. Japan, for example, has experienced periods of deflation during the past 20 years. Deflation makes it more difficult for a country to grow its GDP. Hence deflation and recessions are linked.

BALANCE OF PAYMENTS

A household must pay its way in the world. If it spends more than it earns and takes on debt, then at some point in the future it must repay that debt. Failure to repay debt can lead to debt collectors taking a household's assets and the household not being able to borrow in the future. The same is true of a national economy. A nation's spending on foreign goods and services is called the value of its imports. It earns money to pay for those imports by selling goods and services, known as **exports**, to foreigners. If the value of its **imports** is greater than the value of its exports then this must be financed, either through borrowing or reducing savings held abroad. The economic performance of a country is healthy if, over a period of time, its exports are either greater than or approximately equal to its imports. However, if its imports are significantly greater than exports, then it could face difficulties.

The **balance of trade** is a major part of the current account of the balance of payments. The balance of trade records the value of goods and services sold abroad (exports) and the value of goods and services bought from abroad (imports). Where exports of goods and services are greater than imports, there is said to be a **balance of trade surplus**. Where imports exceed exports, there is a **balance of trade deficit**. Deficits become a problem when foreign banks and other lenders refuse to lend any more money. This occurred, for instance, in Mexico in 1982 and Thailand in 1998. Countries have to respond to restore confidence. This is likely to involve cutting domestic spending, which leads to less demand for imports. Cutting domestic spending, though, also leads to reduced economic growth and rising unemployment. So the current account position of a country is an important indicator of performance.

ACTIVITY 1   SKILLS   INTERPRETATION, REASONING, CRITICAL THINKING

CASE STUDY: BRAZIL'S ECONOMIC PERFORMANCE

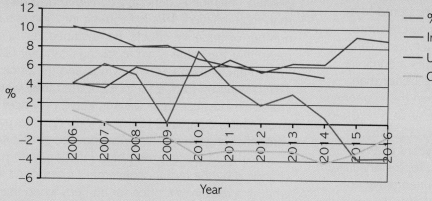

▲ Figure 1 Measures of Economic performance for Brazil

(a) If the current account as a percentage of GDP is negative, what does this mean?

(b) What is happening to Brazil's economic growth over the period shown? Are there any time periods when economic growth fell sharply or rose quickly? What is particularly significant about economic growth in 2015 and 2016?

(c) What is happening to unemployment for the period shown?

(d) Which year saw the sharpest rise in the level of prices?

THINKING LIKE AN ECONOMIST

THE IRISH ECONOMY

In the 1990s and early 2000s, Ireland was nicknamed a 'tiger economy'. The rate of growth of GDP averaged 4–5 per cent and unemployment was low. By 2007, income per head in Ireland was higher than in the UK. That all changed in 2008.

High economic growth in the Irish economy had been funded by a booming property market. Irish banks had lent carelessly to property developers, builders and households. The worldwide financial crash of 2008 led to the failure of the two main Irish banks, Allied Irish Bank and Bank of Ireland, as well as a number of smaller banks. They were rescued by the Irish government at a cost of €62.8 billion.

The crisis had a direct impact on Ireland's main economic indicators, as Figures 2 and 3 show. The economy shrank in size, led by the construction industry. Unemployment increased dramatically. It would have been even worse had many younger Irish workers not gone overseas to work. Prices fell due to lack of demand for goods and services. The current account on the balance of payments improved because falling incomes hit the ability of households and firms to spend on imports. In 2014, the economy showed signs that a long-term recovery was taking place, six years after the disastrous events of 2008. In fact, in 2015 economic growth surged to 26.3 per cent after foreign companies, who had moved their base to Ireland, were included. In 2016 economic growth had fallen to 4.3 per cent, with forecasts of 3.2 per cent for 2017 and 2.3 per cent for 2018. Although the economic growth rate had fallen lower than its 2014 rate, output is still growing in Ireland. However, the rate at which it is growing has slowed down.

Source: with information from www.oecd.org

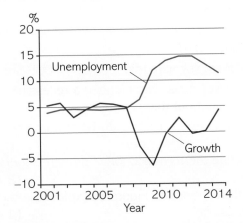

▲ Figure 2 Ireland, rate of growth of real GDP (%), unemployment rate (%), 2001–14

Source: adapted from www.oecd.org

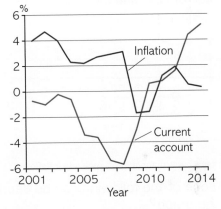

▲ Figure 3 Ireland, inflation (%), current account on the balance of payments as % of GDP, 2001–14

Source: adapted from www.oecd.org

CHECKPOINT

1 What is used as a standard measure of output for an economy?

2 What does economic growth measure?

3 State one advantage of high economic growth.

4 If an economy has a negative economic growth rate, what has happened to total output, compared to the previous year?

5 What is a recession?

6 State one reason why unemployment is a problem for society.

7 What happens to unemployment in a recession?

8 State one reason why high inflation might be a problem.

9 What is deflation?

10 What is meant by the term 'balance of trade deficit'?

SUBJECT VOCABULARY

balance of trade part of the current account. The balance of trade records the value of goods and services sold abroad (exports) and the value of goods and services bought from abroad (imports). A positive value shows a surplus, a negative value shows a deficit.

balance of trade deficit when the value of imports is greater than exports.

balance of trade surplus when the value of exports is greater than the value of imports.

current account part of the balance of payments account. A major component of the current account is the balance of trade.

economic growth a measure of how much output has increased by over a 12-month period. It is expressed as a percentage.

exports goods and services sold abroad.

gross domestic product (GDP) a standard measure of the output of an economy, used by countries around the world.

imports goods and services bought from abroad.

inflation a continuing and general rise in prices across an economy.

recession two quarters of negative economic growth in a row.

unemployment occurs when individuals are without a job but are actively seeking work.

EXAM PRACTICE

SKILLS REASONING, INTERPRETATION

Q

1 Figure 4 shows Turkey's current account balance as a percentage of GDP and the inflation rate.

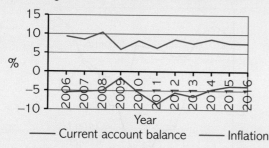

▲ **Figure 4 Turkey's current account balance and inflation rate, 2006–16**

(a) Which one of the following can be deduced from the graph?

A The current account balance was in deficit throughout this period.

B Prices were falling between 2010 and 2011.

C There was deflation throughout this period.

D Prices did not change between 2015 and 2016. **(1 mark)**

2 Figure 5 shows economic growth and unemployment in Turkey.

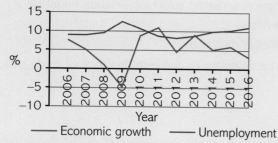

▲ **Figure 5 Turkey's rate of growth and unemployment rate, 2006–16**

(a) Which one of the following can be deduced from Figure 5?

A Output in the economy fell between 2013 and 2014.

B Unemployment rose between 2009 and 2011.

C Turkey never experienced a recession throughout this period.

D Between 2011 and 2012 output increased, but at a slower rate. **(1 mark)**

(b) Define the term economic growth (Figure 5). **(2 marks)**

(c) With reference to Figure 5, explain the term 'recession'. **(4 marks)**

(d) Between 2013 and 2016, economic growth in Turkey fell from 8.9 per cent to 3.1 per cent. Explain the likely impact of this fall in economic growth on the level of unemployment in Turkey. **(4 marks)**

3 In 2010, Cambodia's GDP, measured in US dollars, was US$11.2 billion. In 2016, it had increased to US$17 billion (at constant 2010 prices). With reference to the information above, explain how output has changed in Cambodia between 2010 and 2016. **(4 marks)**

22 ECONOMIC GROWTH AND GDP/GNI

LEARNING OBJECTIVES

- Know that the most commonly used measure of national income is gross domestic product (GDP).
- Know that gross national income (GNI) is an alternative measure of national income.
- Understand that national income can be measured in real or nominal terms and as a total or per capita.
- Know that the rate of change in real GDP is a measure of economic growth.
- Understand that economic growth rates are often compared between countries and over time.
- Understand the distinction between positive and negative economic growth rates.
- Understand the concept 'recession'.
- Understand that national income statistics can be inaccurate because of statistical errors, the existence of the hidden economy, of non-traded sectors and difficulties with valuing public sector output.

- Understand how GDP/GNI can be used to compare living standards between countries and over time.
- Understand that problems occur when comparing national income over time as a measure of living standards because of factors such as the hidden economy, changes in the quality of goods and services and changes in income distribution.
- Understand that further problems occur when comparing national income between countries. In particular, an exchange rate has to be constructed that accurately reflects different purchasing power parities.
- Understand that there is only a partial correlation between levels of national income and levels of national happiness.
- Understand that there are a range of indicators of national happiness and well-being.

GETTING STARTED

If you are studying in Sri Lanka, think about a student in China who is of the same age and intelligence as you studying for the equivalent of an A level. What do you think the student in China might be earning in 10 years' time in comparison with you? Twice as much? Half as much? One-tenth as much? How would you compare your incomes given that Sri Lanka uses rupees and China uses the yuan? Would your standard of living be greater or lower than that of a student in China? What might that depend on? Would you be happier than the student in China? What might that depend on?

MEASURES OF NATIONAL INCOME

One of the most important economic statistics is national income, which measures the size of an economy. Calculating national income is difficult and no measure of national income exactly captures the size of an economy and how it is changing.

The accounting standard used by most countries is based on the United Nations' System of National Accounts 2008. Most countries today either have

introduced this accounting standard or are in the process of revising their national income statistics to meet these accounting standards.

The key measure of national income used is **gross domestic product (GDP)**. This is the total market value of all goods and services produced over a period of time. GDP is measured at market prices, which means it is a measure of national income that includes the value of indirect taxes (taxes on expenditure) like VAT (known as a goods and services tax in some countries). Indirect taxes are not part of the output of the economy, so this measure makes the actual value of national income appear higher. There are other measures of national income.

Gross value added (GVA) at basic prices This is GDP minus indirect taxes plus subsidies on goods. Indirect taxes minus subsidies is called the basic price adjustment.

Gross national product (GNP) and gross national income (GNI) at market prices These are very similar measures of the domestic output of the country (as measured by GDP) plus earnings from overseas. More precisely, **gross national income (GNI)** is the value of the goods and services produced by a country over a period of time (GDP) plus net overseas interest payments and dividends (factor incomes). **Gross national product (GNP)** is the market value of goods and services produced over a period of time through the labour or property supplied by the citizens of a country, both domestically (GDP) and overseas.

Net national income at market prices Each year, the existing capital stock or physical wealth of the country depreciates in, or loses, value because of use. This is like depreciation on a car as it gets older. If individuals run down their savings to finance spending, their actual income must be their spending minus how much they have used from their savings. Similarly with a country, its true value of income is gross (i.e. before depreciation has been taken into account) national income minus depreciation. This is **net national income**.

GDP at market prices is the main headline figure used for national income because the data to calculate it is most quickly available. When comparing over time and between countries, movements in GDP at market prices are broadly similar to movements in other measures of national income. So it is a good guide to what is happening in the economy and can be used to judge the performance of the economy. In particular, the rate of growth of real GDP is the main indicator of the economic growth of an economy.

ACTIVITY 1 **SKILLS** ANALYSIS, INTERPRETATION, REASONING

CASE STUDY: MEASURES OF NATIONAL INCOME

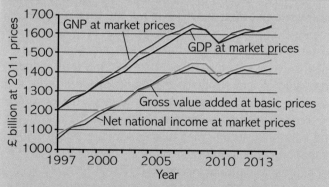

▲ Figure 1 Different measures of national income for the UK, 1997–2013

Source: adapted from www.ons.gov.uk

(a) Briefly explain the difference between each measure of national income shown on the graph.

(b) 'Changes in GDP at market prices broadly reflect changes in other measures of national income over time.' To what extent does the data support this?

REAL OR VOLUME VERSUS NOMINAL OR VALUE

Data such as national income statistics can be measured either in real values or nominal values. Using nominal values means measuring data at the prices of the day, not taking into account the effect that inflation might have on the data. For example, according to the Trading Corporation of Bangladesh, the price of 1 litre of diesel of was BDT 44 (Bangladeshi taka) in 2009. In 2015 this was BDT 68. In nominal terms, this is approximately 1.5 times higher. However, between 2009 and 2015, prices in general rose. To make a comparison in real terms, the data must be adjusted for inflation over the period. If prices in general increased one and a half times between 2009 and 2015, then at today's prices the diesel price is the same. If prices in general had tripled in value, then at today's prices the price of diesel would have halved!

When measuring national income, the real value of national income can also be described as measuring the **volume of national income**. It is the basket of goods and services that can be bought with a given amount of money. When comparing national income in a previous year with that of today in real terms, what is being measured is the relative size of that basket of goods and services. In contrast, the **value of national income** measures the cost of the basket of goods and services at a given level of prices. The value is equal to the volume times the current price level.

ECONOMIC GROWTH

If GDP has been adjusted for inflation, then it is called real GDP or GDP at constant prices. An increase in real GDP (or GDP at constant prices) means output in the economy has risen. This is because changes in real GDP represent changes in the *volume* of national income. The economic growth rate is the rate of change of real GDP (GDP at constant prices). The economic growth rate is the annual percentage change in real GDP. For example, Indonesia's economic growth rate was 4.9 per cent in 2015. This means the output in Indonesia's economy increased by 4.9 per cent in 2015, compared to 2014. In contrast, Russia's economic growth rate was -2.8 per cent, in 2015. This means output in Russia was 2.8 per cent lower in 2015 than 2014. Its output contracted. The term recession means an economy has experienced *negative economic growth* over at least two consecutive quarters.

Economists often compare rates of growth between countries and over time. In the above example, Russia's economic growth rate is significantly weaker than Indonesia's economic growth rate in 2015.

In 2010, Indonesia's output grew by 6.4 per cent. Between 2010 and 2015 its economic growth rate fell from 6.4 per cent to 4.9 per cent. A fall in economic growth, provided the growth rate remains positive, means output is still increasing, but at a slower rate. The fall in Indonesia's economic growth rate between 2010 and 2015 shows a slight deterioration in economic performance over this period.

Annual percentage changes in nominal GDP or GNI can also be used by economists. However, these are not used as a measure of economic growth because they do not show changes in the volume of national income.

ACTIVITY 2   SKILLS   PROBLEM-SOLVING

CASE STUDY: CALCULATING GDP

Year	GDP (€ billion)	Population (millions)	Price index Year 1 = 100
1	100	1.00	100
2	120	1.20	100
3	150	1.25	200
4	200	1.25	250

▲ Table 1 GDP (€ billion), population (millions) and prices (Year 1 = 100)

The table gives data for GDP (at nominal prices), population and prices for four years. Calculate:

(a) GDP per capita at nominal prices

(b) total GDP at real Year 1 prices

(c) GDP per head at Year 1 prices.

MATHS TIP

To calculate numbers at Year 1 prices, divide nominal GDP by the ratio of the change in prices over the period. For example, prices increased 2.5 times (250 ÷ 100) between Year 1 and Year 4. So real GDP in Year 4 at Year 1 prices was €200 billion euros ÷ 2.5.

TOTAL AND PER CAPITA

The national income of the USA is approximately the same as that of China today and seven times that of the UK (at PPPs). However, this measure compares total national income of those economies. To compare the living standards it is better to compare national income **per person or per head or per capita**. This means dividing national income by the size of the population.

Measuring national income per capita considerably alters the comparison between these three countries.

The USA has a population of approximately 320 million, China 1.4 billion and the UK 64 million. As a result, national income per capita of the USA is approximately 4.5 times that of China and 1.4 times that of the UK.

TRANSFER PAYMENTS

Not all types of income are included in the final calculation of national income. Some incomes are received without there being any corresponding output in the economy. For instance:

- most developed economies have a system of welfare payments (payments are given to individuals by the government if their income falls below a minimum level, for example, if they are unemployed; these payments are given without those who receive them producing anything in return)
- children receive pocket money and allowances from their parents
- an individual selling a second hand car receives money, but no new car is created.

These incomes, called **transfer payments**, are excluded from final calculations of national income.

For instance, government spending in national income is **public expenditure** minus spending on benefits and grants.

WHY IS NATIONAL INCOME MEASURED?

National income is a measure of the output, expenditure and income of an economy. National income statistics provide not only figures for these totals but also a breakdown of the totals. They are used in a number of different ways.

- Academic economists use them to test hypotheses and build models of the economy. This increases our understanding of how an economy works.
- Government, firms and economists use the figures to forecast changes in the economy. These forecasts are then used to plan for the future. Government may attempt to direct the economy, making changes in its spending or its taxes at budget time. Groups, such as trade unions, will make their own recommendations about what policies they think the government should pursue.
- They are used to make comparisons over time and between countries. For instance, national income statistics can be used to compare the income of Cyprus in 1990 and 2017, or they can be used to compare Cyprus' income with that of Malta. Of particular importance when making comparisons over time is the rate of change of real national income (i.e. the rate of economic growth).

- They are used to make judgements about economic welfare. Growth in real national income per capita, for instance, is usually understood to mean a rising **standard of living**. A rise in real GDP per capita indicates the economy is producing more goods and services per person in the population.

THE ACCURACY OF NATIONAL INCOME STATISTICS

National income statistics are inaccurate for a number of reasons.

Statistical inaccuracies National income statistics are calculated from millions of different returns to the government. Inevitably mistakes are made: returns are inaccurate or simply not completed. The statistics are constantly being revised in the light of fresh evidence. Although revisions tend to become smaller over time, national income statistics are still being revised many years after first publication.

ACTIVITY 3

SKILLS ANALYSIS, INTERPRETATION, REASONING

CASE STUDY: GREECE'S HIDDEN ECONOMY

In 2013, it was estimated that 24 per cent of all economic activity in Greece went undeclared to evade tax and regulation, well above the European average of 19 per cent. With around one-quarter of individuals recorded as unemployed, the hidden economy can offer a way of survival. Greece also has high levels of self-employment, which make it easier for those individuals to declare less income than they earn. In 2015, the EU said that governments were missing out on €168 billion of VAT revenues. There is a substantial amount of undeclared work, ranging from cleaning to construction, which means official GDP data is an inaccurate indication of income and output created by an economy over a year. According to the OECD, the scale of the informal economy is even higher in developing countries. The International Monetary Fund puts the blame on corruption and excessive regulation by governments. For example, satisfaction with Greece's public services is extremely low and people feel taxes are wasted due to corruption.

(a) Suggest reasons individuals might work in the hidden economy.

(b) Explain how the size of the hidden economy affects the accuracy of official GDP data.

(c) Explain what problems the hidden economy creates for governments.

The hidden economy Taxes such as goods and services taxes, and government regulations such as health and safety laws, impose a burden on workers and businesses. Some are tempted to evade taxes and they are then said to work in the **hidden, black or informal economy**. In the building industry, for instance, it is common for workers to be self-employed and to under-declare or not declare their income at all to the tax authorities. Transactions in the black economy are in the form of cash. Cheques, credit cards, etc. could all be traced by the tax authorities. Tax evasion is the dominant motive for working in the hidden economy but a few, particularly in developed economies, also claim welfare benefits to which they are not entitled. The size of the hidden economy is difficult to estimate. An IMF working paper in 2017 estimated the size of the informal economies in sub-Saharan Africa. The researchers concluded that the informal economy in sub-Saharan Africa remains among the largest in the world, although there is a wide difference between these countries. The size of the informal economy ranged from a low of 20 to 25 per cent in Mauritius, South Africa and Namibia to a high of 50 to 60 per cent in Benin, Tanzania and Nigeria.

Home-produced services In the poorest developing countries in the world, GDP per person is valued at less than US$130 per year. It would be impossible to survive on this amount if this were the true value of output in the economy. However, a large part of the production of farming is not traded and therefore does not appear in national income statistics. People work in subsistence farming, consuming what they produce. Hence the value of national output is in reality much higher. In many countries the output of the services of housewives and househusbands is equally not recorded. Nor is the large number of home improvement jobs completed each year. The more home improvement activity, the greater will be the under-recording of national output by national income statistics.

The public sector Valuing the output of much of the public sector is difficult because it is not bought and sold. This problem is avoided by valuing non-traded output at its cost of production. For instance, the value of the output of a state school is the cost of running the school. This method of valuation can lead to some surprising results. Assume that through more efficient staffing the number of nurses on a hospital ward is reduced from ten to eight and the service is improved. National income accounts will still show a fall in output (measured by a drop in the two nurses' incomes).

In general, increased productivity in the public sector is shown by a fall in the value of output. It looks as though less is being produced when in fact output remains unchanged.

THE LIMITATIONS OF USING GDP/GNI TO COMPARE LIVING STANDARDS OVER TIME

Comparing national income for an economy over time requires care if meaningful conclusions are to be drawn. Economists will want to judge whether the output of the economy has increased and to what extent (the rate of economic growth). They will also want to assess how much living standards have improved over time for the citizens of an economy. This means there may be limitations in using GDP/GNI to compare living standards over time unless adjustments are made and further information is available. Consideration must be made for the following.

Prices Prices tend to increase over time. So an increase in national income over the period does not necessarily indicate that there has been an increase in the number of goods and services produced in the economy. Only if the rate of increase of national income measured in money terms (the nominal rate of economic growth) has been greater than the increase in prices (the inflation rate) can there be said to have been an increase in output. So when comparing over time, it is essential to consider real and not nominal changes in income.

The accuracy and presentation of statistics National income statistics are inaccurate and therefore it is impossible to give a precise figure for the change in income over time. Moreover, the change in real income over time will also be affected by the inflation rate. The inevitable errors made in the calculation of the inflation rate increase the problems of inaccuracy. The method of calculating national income and the rate of inflation can also change over time. It is important to attempt to eliminate the effect of changes in definitions.

Changes in population National income statistics are often used to compare living standards over time. If they are to be used in this way, it is essential to compare real national income per capita (i.e. per person). For instance, if the population doubles while real national income increases by four times, people are likely to be nearer twice as well off than four times.

Quality of goods and services The quality of goods may improve over time due to advances in technology but they may also fall in price. For instance, cars today are far better than cars 80 years ago and yet are far cheaper. National income would show this fall in price by a fall in national income, wrongly indicating that living standards had fallen.

Defence and related expenditures The GDP of the UK was higher during the Second World War than in the 1930s, but much of GDP between 1940 and 1945 was devoted to defence expenditure. It would be difficult to argue that people enjoyed a higher standard of living during the war years than in the pre-war years. So the proportion of national income devoted to defence, or for instance to the police, must be taken into account when considering the standard of living of the population.

Consumption and investment It is possible to increase standards of living today by reducing investment and increasing consumption. However, reducing investment is likely to reduce standards of living from what they might otherwise have been in the future. As with defence, the proportion of national income being devoted to investment will affect the standard of living of the population both now and in the future.

Externalities National income statistics take no account of externalities such as pollution produced by the economy. For example, the World Health Organization (WHO), has said that air pollution across the world's cities is particularly high in a number of Asian cities (Karachi, Pakistan, New Delhi, India, Kathmundu, Nepal, Bejing, China), in Latin America (Lima and Arequipa, both Peru) and in Cairo, Egypt, in Africa. A rise in national income for many developing countries often comes with a rapid rise in pollution. This negatively affects the standard of living for many of its citizens, particularly the health problems that this creates. This means a rise in national income may give a misleading impression of how much living standards have actually risen. Living standards will have risen at a lower rate than national income.

There has been some work on developing a measure called **green GDP**, which takes away the environmental costs of production from GDP. Environmental costs include loss of biodiversity, pollution and the use of non-renewable resources.

Income distribution When comparing national income over time, it is important to remember that an increased national income for the economy as a whole may not mean that individuals have seen their income increase. Income distribution is likely to change over time, which may or may not lead to a more desirable state of affairs.

ACTIVITY 4

SKILLS PROBLEM-SOLVING, COMMUNICATION

CASE STUDY: THE HUNGARIAN ECONOMY

Year	GDP at current prices HUF billion	GDP deflator (a price index) 2010=100	GDP at constant 2010 prices	Population (millions)	GDP, at constant 2010 prices, per capita
2013	30,127.3	108.8		9.893	
2014	32,400.1	112.5		9.866	
2015	33,999.0	114.4		9.843	
2016	35,005.4	115.5		9.821	

▲ Table 2 Hungary's economy, 2013–16

Source: OECD *Main economic indicators* Volume 2017/4 April and World Bank.

Note: HUF = Hungarian forints.

(a) Using examples from Table 2, explain what 'GDP at current prices' means.

(b) Calculate GDP per capita at current prices (current prices is the same as nominal prices).

(c) Calculate 'GDP at constant 2010 prices' for each of the years. Explain what this data means and then calculate the economic growth rate for Hungary for 2014, 2015 and 2016. Over which year did total output increase by the greatest percentage?

(d) Calculate the GDP per capita at constant 2010 prices for each of the years. To what extent is it possible to judge from the data whether living standards increased between 2013 and 2016?

MATHS TIP

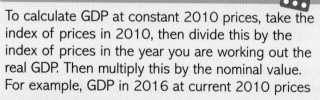

To calculate GDP at constant 2010 prices, take the index of prices in 2010, then divide this by the index of prices in the year you are working out the real GDP. Then multiply this by the nominal value. For example, GDP in 2016 at current 2010 prices

$$= \frac{100}{115.5} \times 35005.4.$$

(We know real GDP in 2016 at constant 2010 prices must be less than the nominal value, since prices were lower in 2010 than 2016.)

THE LIMITATIONS OF USING GDP/GNI TO COMPARE LIVING STANDARDS BETWEEN COUNTRIES

Economists often compare national income between countries. This is either to compare economic growth rates between countries over a period of time, or to compare living standards between countries. Comparing national income between economies is fraught with difficulties too for many of the same reasons that it is difficult to compare national income over time.

- Countries may use different accounting conventions to calculate national income.
- The quality of national income data gathered varies greatly. For example, a poor country like Tanzania spends far less on gathering data than a rich country like the UK.
- The size of the unrecorded part of the economy differs between countries. Italy and Greece, for example, have much larger hidden economies than Sweden or the UK.
- National income figures must be adjusted for the size of the population. So GDP per capita rather than GDP itself is the variable that must be used to make comparisons.
- The quality of goods and services differs. For example, countries differ significantly in the speed and coverage of broadband and yet national income statistics will only record how much is being spent on broadband.
- Countries spend different proportions of their GDP on defence and related expenditures but these expenditures do not necessarily contribute to the standard of living of citizens.
- National income statistics take no account of externalities created by different economies.
- Income distributions differ between economies and so, for example, low income earners are likely to be better off in Denmark or Sweden than in the USA, which has a much higher GDP per capita.
- Geography distorts comparisons. For example. Mexicans are likely to have lower heating bills than Russians. So the fact that more is spent, per capita, on domestic fuel in Russia does not indicate they have better standard of living.
- Market exchange rates do not reflect purchasing power. So simple comparisons using market exchange rates may give a distorted picture of living standards between countries. A way round this is to use purchasing power parities.

ACTIVITY 5   SKILLS ▷ COMMUNICATION, ANALYSIS

CASE STUDY: GNI AMD PPPs

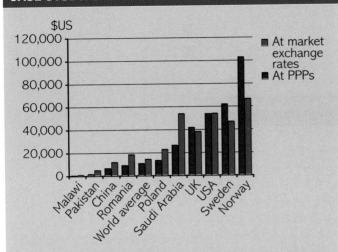

▲ Figure 2 Gross national income per head at market exchange rates and PPPs, 2013, US$

Source: adapted from www.worldbank.org

(a) Explain the difference between income per head measured at market exchange rates and at purchasing power parities. Illustrate your answer with examples from the data.

(b) With reference to Norway and China, explain why using market exchange rates would give a very misleading impression of comparative living standards between these two countries.

(c) Explain what Figure 2 suggests about comparative living standards in the countries shown.

PURCHASING POWER PARITIES

The day-to-day market exchange rate can bear little relation to relative prices in different countries. So prices in some countries like Sweden or Germany can be much higher at official exchange rates than in the USA, China or India. Therefore if national income statistics are to be used to compare living standards

between countries, it is important to use an exchange rate that compares the cost of living in each country. These exchange rates are known as **purchasing power parities**. For example, if a typical basket costs CYP 1 (Cypriot pounds) in Cyprus and LKR 290 (Sri Lankan rupees) in Sri Lanka, then national income should be converted at an exchange rate of CYP 1 to LKR 290, even if the market exchange rate gives a different figure.

Purchasing power parities often differ significantly from market exchange rates when comparisons are made between rich and poor countries. For example, it might be possible to survive on £2 a day in Kenya or Vietnam when £2 is converted at the market exchange rate into the local currency. In contrast, it is not possible to survive on £2 a day in the UK, as £2 buys far more in Kenya or Vietnam than it would buy in the UK. The market exchange rate undervalues the value of the local currency in Kenya or Vietnam when it comes to buying a basket of goods on which people can survive.

So, to compare living standards between economies, it is vital that purchasing power parity exchange rates have been used to convert the data into one currency. A comparison of national income per capita at PPP (purchasing power parity) between countries will show how much purchasing power differs between the countries for the 'average' citizen. This means a judgement can be made on the comparative living standards between countries. However, it should be remembered that the use of GDP per capita, as a measure of living standards, is only a proxy measure. This is because of the many limitations that have been discussed.

INDICATORS OF NATIONAL HAPPINESS AND WELL-BEING

National income is often used as a substitute measure for economic welfare or the standard of living. This measure tends to focus on standard of living as a measurement of material welfare. Even with this focus, GDP per capita may only be a useful guide combined with other indicators such as average household real disposable income or quality of housing. Income is also often used as a measure of 'happiness': the higher the income, the happier the individual. However, there are many other factors apart from income and GDP that contribute to the standard of living of an individual.

Here, the term 'standard of living' can be interpreted more widely as reflecting quality of life and well-being (these three are often used with the same meaning). A measure of well-being or happiness

ACTIVITY 6   SKILLS   PROBLEM-SOLVING, ANALYSIS, REASONING

CASE STUDY: COMPARING LIVING STANDARDS

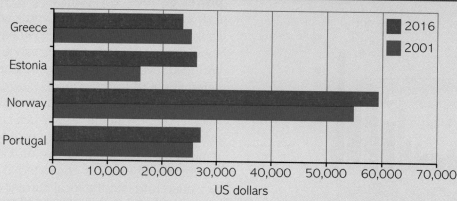

▲ Figure 3 GDP per head, constant PPPs, US$, 2001 and 2016

OECD: note Greece's 2016 data is a provisional figure

(a) Explain why GDP per capita at purchasing power parity may provide a useful measure for comparing living standards between countries for a given year. How do living standards seem to compare between Norway and Portugal in 2016?

(b) Explain why 'GDP per capita at constant prices' is a useful measure for comparing changes in living standards over time for an economy. Which country has experienced the most significant change in living standards between 2001 and 2016? Explain your answer.

(c) Which country seems to have experienced a fall in living standards between 2001 and 2016? Explain your answer.

(d) Explain reasons why the data above might provide a misleading impression of how living standards compare between countries and over time.

would include material welfare, but it would also include a wider range of dimensions that matter to most individuals in their lives. These include quality of jobs (which links to job satisfaction), high quality education (which not only gives individuals the power to earn a decent wage but helps people to fully enjoy their lives), quality of the environment, security, feeling part of a community, leisure time etc. A measure of well-being or happiness needs to include these wider dimensions too. Indicators to measure these wider dimensions include pollution levels, access to education, crime statistics, feelings of safety, long term unemployment levels, healthy life expectancy etc. Some of these measures are objective, but some are subjective if they involve individuals giving their opinion or feelings about something. Studies to measure well-being might also include an individual's evaluation of their subjective happiness. However, critics will argue that attempting to measure subjective happiness and comparing it, over time or between countries, is meaningless since there is no objective measurement unit for happiness. Asking people how they feel about something also has similar problems. In general, using a range of indicators to measure

well being makes it complicated to combine into a simple statistic. So, while economists argue that GDP per capita is an imperfect measure of living standards, it is likely to remain an important indicator of living standards and national well-being. The 'Thinking Like an Economist' section looks at the World Happiness Report and the OECD's Better Life Index, which use a broad range of indicators to compare well-being between different countries.

REAL INCOMES AND SUBJECTIVE HAPPINESS

Economists have been interested in the concept of 'happiness' for nearly 200 years. Jeremy Bentham, a philosopher working in the first half of the 19th century, famously said that human beings should act in a way that would cause 'the greatest happiness of the greatest number'. One of the key problems with this as a moral philosophy was how individuals could measure happiness both for themselves and for others.

Psychologists have long conducted surveys on happiness, by simply asking respondents how happy they felt. These surveys, when compared, produce similar responses. Respondents do seem to be able to say whether or not they are happy on a particular day. This has been backed up by more recent experiments in brain science. During the 1990s, it was discovered that happiness was associated with measurable electrical activity in the brain. This could be picked up by MRI scans. So it is possible to physically assess whether or not someone is telling the truth when they say they are happy.

One key finding dates back to the 1970s. Using surveys from across the world (cross-sectional surveys), it was found that happiness and income are positively related at low levels of income but higher levels of income are not associated with increases in happiness. This is called the Easterlin Paradox, after Richard Easterlin, an economist, identified this problem in a 1974 research paper. The conclusion from his research is that an increase in consumption of material goods will improve well-being when basic needs are not being met, such as adequate food and shelter. But once these are being met, then increasing the quantity of goods consumed makes no difference to well-being. Having a new high-definition (HD) television, or a new car when you already have a reasonable functioning television and car does not increase your well-being in the long term. What this means is that average levels of happiness in developed countries, which already enjoy a high standard of living, will not increase if GDP doubles.

Some economists have questioned this finding. Reworking survey evidence, they suggest there is a correlation between income and happiness. Even if they are correct, the idea that happiness is caused by a wide variety of factors and not just income would suggest that GDP and happiness are likely to be only weakly correlated.

There is, however, one other important factor to consider in this debate about changes in absolute incomes. Survey evidence suggests that within a population, there is a positive correlation between relative income and happiness. Surveys across countries regularly show that those with above average incomes tend to have higher levels of happiness than those with below average incomes. So if incomes for every individual in, for example, South Africa doubled, there would be no increase in happiness. But if an individual worker had their pay doubled, they would be happier because their income relative to everyone else has increased. Equally, the top 10 per cent of income earners in Bolivia might have half the income of the top 10 per cent of income earners in France. But they both have the same level of happiness because their income is higher than the other 90 per cent in their populations. Alternatively, if everyone owns a HD television, there is no increase in happiness compared to a situation where no one owns a HD television. But if you buy a HD television and 80 per cent of the population do not own one, then your happiness increases.

There are two suggested explanations for the correlation between relative income and happiness. One is that income is a symbol of social status. Psychologically, we are happier if we feel we have more status. This competitive behaviour probably comes from our biological roots. The second explanation is that above average incomes are correlated with a number of other factors that are associated with happiness. For example, those on above average incomes tend to enjoy better health and live longer. They have more control over their environment and are less likely to perform short, repetitive tasks. They are less likely to be unemployed.

THINKING LIKE AN ECONOMIST

INDICATORS OF NATIONAL HAPPINESS AND WELL-BEING

Comparing happiness and well-being between countries is hard, but attempts are made. The results are often interesting, since countries rankings will often come out very differently to those based only on real GDP per capita.

The World Happiness Report

In 2011, the UN General Assembly invited member countries to measure the happiness of their citizens and to use this to help guide their public policies. The first World Happiness Report was published in 2012, in support of the UN High Level Meeting on happiness and well-being.

The World Happiness Report is a survey of global happiness and, in 2017, ranked 155 countries by their happiness levels. This ranking is done by asking a sample of individuals (Gallup World poll), in the different countries, to evaluate their life and rate it on a scale of 0–10 (subjective happiness). In general, research has found six key factors (indicators) that affect happiness levels reported between countries. These are real GDP per capita(PPP), health life expectancy at birth (the average years of healthy life that a person may expect to have), freedom to make choices about your life, social support (having a friend or relative you can rely on), trust in government, and generosity. Analysts will look at these indicators within each country and work out how much each of them contribute to the happiness levels reported.

The findings are interesting. In 2007, the USA was third out of the OECD members in a happiness survey. However, in the 2017 report, which took the average of 2014–16 happiness scores, it had fallen to 14th place. Despite real GDP per capita and healthy life expectancy at birth rising, happiness levels were falling. What was pushing happiness levels down was a decline in the other key indicators. The USA showed less social support, less sense of personal freedom, lower donations to charity and more perceived corruption of government and business. In contrast, Costa Rica stands out as being 12th in the rankings, despite having a much lower GDP per capita than most in the top 20.

GDP per capita among the top 10 were 25 times higher than in the bottom 10. Income differences were found to be more than one-third of the total explanation for differences in happiness levels between countries. However, this also means that there are other important factors that affect happiness and well-being. Reports such as these highlight to policy makers that there is not a clear link between economic growth and happiness.

Source: adapted from World Happiness Report 2017

The OECD Better Life Index

The OECD produces 'The OECD Better Life Index' in an attempt to compare material living conditions and quality of life between countries. It looks at 11 dimensions of life that contribute to the well-being of individuals. These include income, housing, jobs, community, education, environment, civic engagement, health, safety, work–life balance and life satisfaction (this is when individuals are asked to rate their life satisfaction; subjective happiness). Some of these dimensions are positively related. For example, countries with higher levels of GDP and incomes tend to have more resources invested in health and education.

Some of the types of data collected are in Table 3. If all these dimensions are given equal importance to well-being, then of the countries in Figure 4, in 2017, Norway came top, with South Africa the country with the lowest well-being in the group. It is interesting to see that New Zealand, with a relatively low real GDP per capita, comes second. Analysis of the OECD data shows that countries ranked in the top third of GDP per capita seem to do well on most of the dimensions, especially the ones more directly connected to material well-being, such as household income. However, countries can have weaker performing dimensions on areas such as job security, air quality, housing affordability and work life balance at any level of GDP per capita. This shows that 'GDP per capita' may give a misleading impression. Overall well-being in high income countries may be lower than the GDP per capita (PPP) data suggests.

Comparing happiness levels within a country is just as tricky. Are individuals necessarily happier if their income goes up? Would you be?

Source: OECD Better Life Index in 2017 website and 'How's life? 2015 Measuring Well-being' OECD

How's Life? 2016	South Africa	Brazil	Italy	New Zealand	OECD average
Average household net adjusted disposable income per capita (US$)	8712	11,487	25,004	23,213	29,016
People aged 15–64 with paid job	43%	67%	57%	74%	66%
Adults aged 25–64 with secondary education completed	65%	46%	59%	74%	76%
Life expectancy at birth	57 years	75 years	83 years	81 years	80 years
People satisfied with water quality	69%	73%	70%	92%	81%
People who say they know someone they could rely on in times of need	90%	90%	91%	99%	88%
People who live in dwellings with private access to indoor flushing toilet	79.5%	93.3%	99.2%	(no estimate available)	97.9%
Labour force unemployed for a year or longer	14.4%	0.8%	7.8%	0.8%	2.6%
People who say they feel safe walking alone at night	40%	40%	59%	64%	68%
Subjective well-being score (0–10)*	4.9	6.5	5.8	7.4	6.5

▲ **Table 3 Selected Better Life Index data and countries**

Source: OECD 2016 Better Life Index   Note: *The higher the score, the higher the well-being of individuals.

Figure 4 shows a ranking of countries by the OECD Better Life index, from highest well-being to lowest well-being, assuming all dimensions are given equal importance.

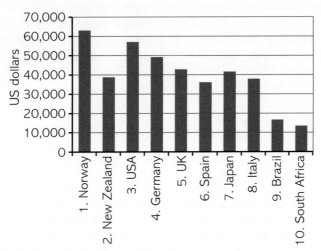

▲ **Table 4 GDP per capita, in 2016, at current prices and PPP's**

CHECKPOINT

1 What is the difference between real and nominal GDP?

2 What does 'GDP per capita' mean?

3 Why should GDP per capita, at purchasing power parities, be used to compare living standards between countries?

4 State two limitations of using GDP/GNI to compare living standards over time.

5 State two limitations of using GDP per capita, at PPP, to compare living standards between countries.

6 State five indicators that might be used to measure happiness or well-being.

7 Is it likely that happiness will increase if incomes rise in a developing country?

SUBJECT VOCABULARY

economic growth a measure of how much output has increased by, over a 12-month period. It is expressed as a percentage.

green GDP a measure of GDP that takes account of the environmental costs of production such as pollution and the use of non-renewable resources.

gross domestic product (GDP) a measure of the output or value added of an economy that does not include output or income from investments abroad or an allowance for the depreciation of the nation's capital stock.

gross national income (GNI) the value of the goods and services produced by a country over a period of time (GDP) plus net overseas interest payments and dividends (factor incomes).

gross national product (GNP) the market value of goods and services produced over a period of time through the labour or property supplied by citizens of a country both domestically (GDP) and overseas.

hidden, black or informal economy economic activity where trade and exchange take place but which goes unreported to the tax authorities and those collecting national income statistics.

national happiness and well-being the terms well-being, standard of living and quality of life are often used with the same meaning. However, the term 'living standards' tends to have a slightly narrower focus on material welfare. The term well-being covers every dimension of a person's life.

net national income a measure of national income that includes both net income from investments abroad and an allowance for depreciation of the nation's capital stock.

per person or per head or per capita per individual in a population.

public expenditure another name for government expenditure. Public spending is the amount of money spent by the government.

purchasing power parities an exchange rate of one currency for another which compares how much a typical basket of goods in one country costs compared to that of another country.

recession two consecutive quarters of negative economic growth.

standard of living how well off is an individual, household or economy, measured by a complex mix of variables such as income, health, and the environment.

subjective happiness this term is used when an individual rate their happiness by giving it a score, based on their self-evaluation of happiness. This can be problematic, since there is no measurement unit for happiness. This means objective indicators of happiness and well-being are also often used in studies to provide a clearer picture. Objective measures are things that affect our happiness or well-being, such as income, health, education, safety, etc.

transfer payments income for which there is no corresponding output, such as unemployment benefits or pension payments.

value/volume of national income the value of national income is its money value at the prices of the day; the volume is national income adjusted for inflation and is expressed either as an index number or in money terms at the prices in a selected base year.

EXAM PRACTICE

Q

1 Table 4 shows GDP data for four countries.

GDP, 2016, PPP	US$ (millions)	Population 2016	GDP per capita
China	21,417,150	1.4 billion	
Bangladesh	583,480	163.0 million	
Sri Lanka		21.2 million	12,318
Cyprus		1.2 million	23,050

▲ **Table 4 GDP, PPP (purchasing power parity), for 2016**

Source: World Bank, Cyprus noted as estimate

(a) Define the term 'purchasing power parity'.
(2 marks)

(b) Using the information in Table 4, calculate the ratio of Bangladesh's GDP per capita to China's GDP per capita. **(4 marks)**

(c) Using the information in Table 4, calculate the ratio of Sri Lanka's GDP in 2016 to Cyprus's GDP in 2016. **(4 marks)**

2 South Korea's GDP at market prices in 2013 was KRW 1429.4 trillion (Korean won). In contrast, Australia's GDP at market prices in 2013 was AUD 1559.7 billion (Australian dollar).

With reference to the information above, explain the term 'GDP at market prices'. **(4 marks)**

3 In 1995, Costa Rica's GDP, at constant 2007 prices, was CRC 11,372,750 million (Costa Rican colón). By 2015 its GDP, at constant 2007 prices, had risen to CRC 25,945,973 million. With reference to the information above, explain the term 'GDP at constant prices'. **(4 marks)**

4 Extract

Comparing living standards between countries is difficult. GDP per capita, at purchasing power parity, is a useful starting point. However, there are limitations with this approach. One reason is the size of the hidden economy. A recent IMF working paper suggested the size of Namibia's hidden economy fell in the range 20–25 per cent of GDP; whereas Tanzania's was estimated to be between 50 and 60 per cent of GDP. The size of the hidden economy, in advanced economies such as the USA, is likely to be significantly smaller.

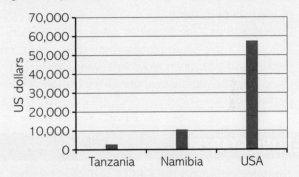

▲ **Figure 5 GDP per capita, 2016, PPP (current US$) for Tanzania, Namibia and the USA**

With reference to Figure 5 and the extract, analyse one reason why using GDP per capita, at PPP, to compare living standards between countries has limitations. **(6 marks)**

5 In 2016, according to GDP per capita at purchasing power parity, Sri Lanka was ranked 85th in the world and Bolivia 112th. However, the World Happiness Report, which includes a range of well-being measures to rank countries, ranked Bolivia 58th out of 155 countries and Sri Lanka 120th.

Source: World Bank and World Happiness Report 2017

Evaluate the use of GDP per capita, at PPP, as a measure of comparing well-being between countries. **(20 marks)**

EXAM TIP

Begin by explaining what GDP per capita, at PPP, means and why it provides a useful starting point for comparing living standards. Expand by discussing what well-being means and why a range of indicators are useful to measure this. Think about why higher income countries are likely to have higher well-being for some of these indicators. Evaluate by discussing why some countries may have high GDP per capita, at PPP, but low well-being overall. However, why are some rankings, which use a broad range of well-being measures, often criticised?

23 MEASURING INFLATION AND UNEMPLOYMENT

LEARNING OBJECTIVES

- Understand that inflation is a general sustained rise in the price level.
- Understand the concepts of inflation, deflation and disinflation.
- Understand that inflation is measured by calculating the change in a weighted price index over time, using the consumer price index (CPI).
- Understand the limitations of the CPI as a measure of the rate of inflation.
- Understand that the producer price index (PPI) is an indicator of the future trends in the rate of inflation.
- Understand how unemployment is measured, using the International Labour Organisation (ILO) definition.

GETTING STARTED

On the Internet, using the OECD and World Bank data links, collect inflation and unemployment rates, over time, for a range of economies. How do these rates compare between economies and over time?

INFLATION, DEFLATION AND DISINFLATION

Inflation is defined as a continuous general rise in prices across an economy. The opposite of inflation is **deflation**. This is defined as a continuous general fall in prices across an economy. **Disinflation** is defined as a fall in the rate of inflation.

For example, if prices in general are rising by 3 per cent per annum, there is inflation. If prices in general are falling by 1 per cent per annum, there is deflation. If the rate of inflation falls from 4 per cent to 2 per cent, there is disinflation. Note that if there is disinflation, it means there is inflation in the economy, but the rate of inflation is falling.

A general rise in prices may be quite moderate. Creeping (slow) inflation would describe a situation where prices rose a few per cent on average each year. **Hyperinflation**, in contrast, describes a situation where inflation levels are very high. There is no exact figure at which inflation becomes hyperinflation.

However, annual inflation rates of 50 per cent or more would be classified as hyperinflation by most economists.

The term **reflation** is used to describe the rise in GDP, which occurs following a recession. **Stagflation** is the term used to describe a period when inflation is rising or is very high at a time when the economy is in recession. The economy is stagnating (not growing) but there is also inflation.

ACTIVITY 1  SKILLS COMMUNICATION, REASONING

CASE STUDY: INFLATION IN ANGOLA

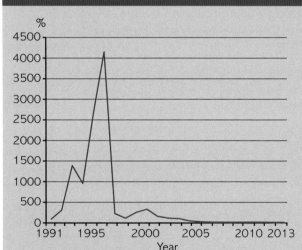

▲ Figure 1 Angola: annual inflation, 1991–2013

Source: adapted from www.oecd.org

(a) Describe the changes in prices in the African country of Angola shown in the data.

(b) To what extent could Angola be said to have experienced hyperinflation during the period shown?

MEASURING INFLATION USING THE CPI

The **Consumer Price Index (CPI)** is a measure of the price level and inflation. It is produced to international standards, which means comparisons can be made between countries. The price level is measured in the form of an index. So, if the price index were 100 today and 110 in one year's time, then the rate of inflation would be 10 per cent.

The CPI attempts to measure how much more money a typical household needs to buy the same 'basket of goods' at the same time the previous year. To calculate the CPI, information must be collected to identify what a typical household spends its money on. A sample of households are asked to keep a record of what items they buy and how much they spend on these. From this, a 'typical household' spending pattern is identified. For example, a typical UK household may spend £8 a week on lamb mince. Surveyors are then sent out each month to record the prices of these goods. Clearly the price of lamb, per kilogram, will differ between shops and regions of the country. So, the price of lamb per kilogram is recorded from a large and varied sample. This is then combined to record the price of lamb, per kilogram, over time. It is then possible to calculate how much the price of lamb, per kilogram, has risen in percentage terms over the year. This figure is then converted into an index number form.

Commodity	Proportion of total spending	Weight	Increase in price	Contribution to increase in CPI
Food	75%	750	8%	6%
Cars	25%	250	4%	1%
Total	100	1000		7%

▲ Table 1 Weights and inflation

Changes in the price of food are more important than changes in the price of, say, petrol. This is because a larger proportion of total household income is spent on food than on petrol. Therefore the figures have to be weighted before the final index can be calculated. For instance, assume that there are only two goods in the economy, food and cars, as shown in Table 1. Households spend 75 per cent of their income on food and 25 per cent on cars. There is an increase in the price of food of 8 per cent and of cars of 4 per cent over one year. In a normal average calculation, the 8 per cent and the 4 per cent would be added together and the total divided by two to arrive at an average price increase of 6 per cent. However, this provides an inaccurate figure because spending on food is more important in the household budget than spending on cars. The figures have to be weighted. Food is given a weight of $\frac{3}{4}$ (or 0.75 or 750 out of 1000) and cars a weight of $\frac{1}{4}$ (or 0.25 or 250 out of 1000). The average increase in prices is 8 per cent multiplied by $\frac{3}{4}$ added to 4 per cent multiplied by $\frac{1}{4}$ (i.e. 6 per cent + 1 per cent). The weighted average is therefore 7 per cent. If the CPI were 100 at the start of the year, it would be 107 at the end of the year.

Over time, the basket of goods will change as consumers change their spending behaviour. For example, smart phones have been added to the basket in recent years for many economies. The weights will also have to be updated over time. This is because the proportion of total spending, on different items, by the typical household, will change as income rises and fashions change etc. For example, leisure travel is likely to be given a greater weighting over time as incomes rise.

ACTIVITY 2　　SKILLS　PROBLEM-SOLVING

CASE STUDY: PRICE INDEX WEIGHTS

Year	Weights			Percentage annual increase in prices	
	Food	All other items	Total	Food	All other items
1	300	700	1000	10	10
2	250	750	1000	5	10
3	200	800	1000	4	6
4	150	850	1000	3	2
5	125	875	1000	4	4
6	120	880	1000	6	4
7	120	880	1000	5	7
8	110	890	1000	8	10

▲ Table 2 Price index weights

Table 2 shows the price index weights given to food and to all other items in each of eight years. It also shows the percentage annual increase in prices of those items.

(a) Calculate the rate of inflation (i.e. the percentage increase in prices) in each year 1 to 8.

(b) What would the price index in years 2–8 be if the price index were 100 in year 1?

LIMITATIONS OF THE CPI

There are some limitations of the CPI as a measure of inflation. The CPI only provides information for how much more money a typical household needs to buy the same basket of goods as the same time the previous year. The weights will be adjusted annually to reflect any changes in the typical consumer's spending pattern over time. However, for many households, their basket of goods will differ substantially.

So, in theory, each individual household will have their own inflation rate, which will depend upon their own spending behaviour. For example, a married couple with no children who both own cars will have a very different spending pattern compared to a household with two children but no car. Households made up by older people will have spending patterns that differ significantly from younger age households, and households on high incomes will also devote very different proportions of their spending to food and other items. In general, a high income household devotes a smaller proportion of their spending on food.

The index cannot indicate changes in the quality of goods. Cars might increase in price because specifications improve rather than because there has been an inflationary price rise. Statisticians must make suitable adjustments to compare like with like.

For new products, it can be hard to know how to include them, since the price level for that good did not exist the previous year.

The CPI also excludes a number of items relating to housing, including mortgage interest repayments. In many countries housing costs have increased faster than other items, so the CPI gives a misleading idea of how much more money a typical household needs to spend over time to maintain their purchasing patterns as well as afford their housing costs.

THE PRODUCER (WHOLESALE) PRICE INDEX (PPI)

The **producer price index** is used to measure the change in the price of a typical basket of goods bought and sold by the manufacturers of an economy. Like the CPI it is a weighted index to reflect the relative importance of different types of products to manufacturers. The PPI includes price indices of materials and fuels purchased by manufacturers (input prices) and price indices of finished goods or intermediate goods as they leave the factory gate (factory gate prices). Factory gate prices are also called output prices.

The input price measures the price of materials and fuel bought by the manufacturers in an economy for processing, for example, prices of metals, chemicals and oil. Some of these will be imported, so the price paid by manufacturers will be affected by the value of the currency on foreign exchange markets. For example, if the value of the euro falls, a Eurozone manufacturer will have to use more euros to buy the Chinese currency, called the yuan. This means commodities bought from China will cost more euros. This will push up these input prices in the Eurozone. *Input price indices* will measure the changes in the prices of materials and fuels bought by manufacturers for processing into goods.

The factory gate price (output price) is the price of goods sold by the manufacturers in an economy to the domestic market. The factory gate price (output price) will reflect the cost of labour, raw materials and energy as well as other costs for a manufacturer, such as renting a factory and so on. Manufacturers include firms who produce semi-processed goods and other intermediate goods, as well as firms who produce the final product. Semi-processed goods and intermediate goods are sold on to other manufacturers to produce the finished good. Manufacturers who produce the finished goods will sell these to retailers. *Output price indices* will measure the changes in prices of goods sold as they leave the producer.

If data does not distinguish between input prices or output prices, then the producer price index will be the output producer price index.

USE OF THE PRODUCER PRICE INDEX

The producer (wholesale) price index is used as an indicator of future trends in the rate of inflation (CPI). If retailers have to pay more for the products they buy from manufacturers, then retailers will try to pass on these higher costs to consumers. They will want to raise the price they charge to consumers. So, a rise in the producer price index is likely to cause a rise in inflation, as measured by the consumer price index. However, the relationship will not be perfect. There is also likely to be a time lag effect, so the impact on the CPI inflation rate may take a few months.

MEASURING UNEMPLOYMENT

Governments need to measure unemployment. It is an important measure of economic performance for an economy. The International Labour Organisation (ILO) has set an international standard for measuring unemployment. This measure of unemployment is used by the OECD, the statistical office of the EU and many other countries. This means unemployment can be compared between countries, since the same method of calculation unemployment is used.

SOME DEFINITIONS

The population of working age is all people within a certain age range, typically the statutory age for leaving school and the state retirement age. This could be 16–65.

The unemployed, according to the ILO measure, are those without a job, who want a job, have actively looked for work in the last four weeks and are available to start work in the next two weeks. (It also includes those who have just found a job and are waiting to start in the next two weeks.)

ACTIVITY 3   SKILLS   INTERPRETATION, REASONING

CASE STUDY: THE PRODUCER INDEX

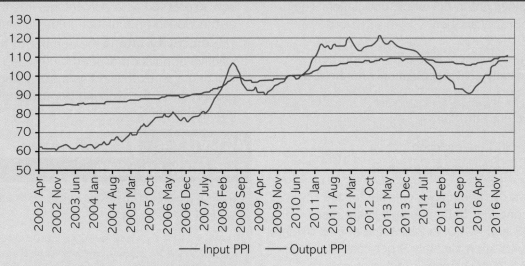

▲ Figure 2 UK input and output PPI, 2010 = 100, April 2002–November 2016

Source: Office for National Statistics

(a) Comment on how input prices have changed, compared to output prices, over the period shown.

(b) Explain why the governor of the Bank of England, whose job it is to keep the CPI inflation rate at a target level of 2 per cent, would be interested in monitoring the producer price index.

The employed are those who have work. The majority of workers are employees, which means they are employed by another individual or a firm. A minority are self-employed, working for themselves and not part of a company structure. Most are in full-time work, meaning they work the hours and the days that are the norm for a job. A minority are **part-time workers** who work for a proportion of the hours of full-time workers.

As far as the ILO definition of employment is concerned, anyone who carries out at least one hour's paid work in a week is employed. Also counted as in employment, according to this measure, are people on government-supported training schemes and people who work unpaid in their family business.

The labour force is made up of those in employment and those unemployed according to the definitions above. The labour force is also known as the economically **active population**.

Those who are out of work, but do not meet the criteria of ILO unemployment are economically **inactive**. This includes people such as students, parents who stay at home to look after children, people who have taken early retirement, and those who are unable to work due to sickness or disability.

The term 'hidden unemployment' is sometimes used for those people who want to work, but are not seeking work. Even though these people want to work, they are not included as unemployed. They do not meet the definition of unemployed as set out by the ILO. They include people who may have become so discouraged with job searching that they no longer look, those who grudgingly stay on in education since they think they couldn't get a job and the underemployed. The **underemployed** are those who work, but want to work more hours. For example, they might be part-time workers who really want a full-time job, self-employed workers who want to work more hours or those who want a job that makes full use of their skills and abilities. In the last global recession, many individuals were underemployed as a means of avoiding unemployment.

To summarise:
- the population of working age (16–65) = economically active population + economically inactive population
- the labour force (economically active population) = those in employment + ILO unemployed.

THE LABOUR FORCE SURVEY AND THE ILO UNEMPLOYMENT RATE

The ILO **unemployment rate** is calculated using Labour Force Survey (LFS) statistics. The LFS is a sample survey of households. The survey asks questions about individual's personal circumstances and their activity in the labour market. Questions are asked so an individual in the survey can be classified as either in employment, ILO unemployed or economically inactive. From the results of this survey, a statistical judgement can be made on the size of unemployment in the whole population. The unemployment rate can then be calculated.

The ILO unemployment rate is the proportion of the economically active population who are ILO unemployed.

ILO unemployment rate (%) =

$$\frac{\text{ILO unemployed}}{\text{economically active population}} \times 100$$

Figure 3 shows the unemployment rate for the USA and the eurozone. For both, unemployment rose between 2008 and 2010. In 2009, the unemployment rate for both was approximately 9 per cent. However, the period from 2010 showed a different pattern. For the eurozone, the unemployment rate continued to rise, reaching a peak in 2013. In contrast, the US unemployment rate was on a downward trend between 2010 and 2015. Throughout the period, the USA's unemployment rate, with the exception of 2009, was consistently lower than the eurozone's. In terms of unemployment, the US economy performed better than the eurozone.

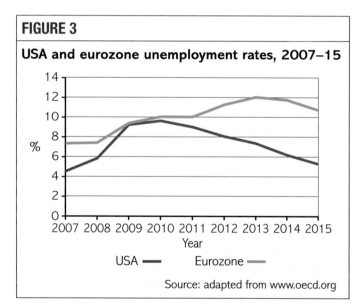

FIGURE 3

USA and eurozone unemployment rates, 2007–15

Source: adapted from www.oecd.org

There are four important statistics that are often quoted by economists and governments.

1 The **employment rate** is the number of those in work divided by the population of working age, expressed as a percentage.

2 The **ILO unemployment rate** is the number of ILO unemployed divided by the labour force (active population), expressed as a percentage.

3 The **activity rate or participation rate** is the number of those in work or unemployed (active population) divided by the population of working age, expressed as a percentage. It is the proportion of the working population in the labour force.

4 The **inactivity rate** is the number of those in the inactive population divided by the population of working age, expressed as a percentage. It is the proportion of the working population that is not in the labour force.

ACTIVITY 4 — SKILLS PROBLEM-SOLVING, REASONING

CASE STUDY: EMPLOYED

(a) Pedro worked 36 hours last week as an electrician.

(b) Sarah lost her job as a part-time secretary two months ago. Every week she visits a job centre to try to find a new job. She would be able to start within a week if she found one.

(c) Alex is out of work, he would like a job but stopped looking three months ago since he became so discouraged. No jobs seemed to be available.

(d) Ideally, Joanne would like to work. She is not seeking work at the moment because she is caring for an elderly relative at home. In any case, she would not be able to start a job within two weeks.

(e) John works less hours than he would like. He became self-employed in the last recession when he lost his previous job. Although he works, he does look at job adverts in case something better comes up.

For each of the above, decide whether those people are employed, unemployed or part of the economically inactive population.

THE UNDERUTILISATION OF LABOUR

The ILO measure of unemployment is an internationally recognised standard. However, a wider definition may be useful for measuring the degree of labour market slack in an economy. In the global financial crisis, many job seekers became so discouraged that they stopped 'actively seeking work', they no longer believed it was possible to get a job. Another group were forced into 'underemployment' (working fewer hours than they would like) by taking on part-time jobs, when they actually wanted a full-time job as an employee. This included some people who, unable to find employment, became self-employed with very few hours of paid work. The European Central Bank estimated, in 2017, that there were around seven million underemployed part-time workers across the eurozone. The official unemployment rate in the eurozone stood at 9.5 per cent, the lowest in seven years, since the global financial crisis. However, a measure of labour slack, which includes the unemployed, according to the ILO definition, part-time employees who would like to work more hours, and those individuals who are without work and want a job but do not meet one of the other two criteria set out by the ILO, suggests that 18 per cent of the eurozone are currently underutilised. A similar measure records a rate of 9.2 per cent for US. In the USA, this measure peaked at 17 per cent in 2010, caused by the effects of the global financial crisis.

Source: ECB *Economic Bulletin*, issue 3/2017, 'Assessing labour market slack' and 'Plight of eurozone jobless found to be worse than data shows', *Financial Times*, 10 May 2017

ACTIVITY 5   SKILLS   PROBLEM SOLVING, ANALYSIS

CASE STUDY: EMPLOYMENT IN ITALY

Part-time employment is defined as people in employment (whether employees or self-employed) who usually work less than 30 hours per week in their main job. The part-time employment rate shows the proportion of persons employed part-time, compared to all employed persons. However, the employment rate is expressed as a percentage of the working age population. Employment includes full-time and part-time employees.

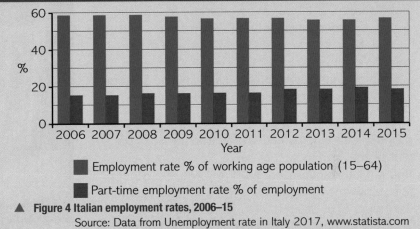

■ Employment rate % of working age population (15–64)

■ Part-time employment rate % of employment

▲ **Figure 4 Italian employment rates, 2006–15**

Source: Data from Unemployment rate in Italy 2017, www.statista.com

(a) Compare the trend in the employment rate with the part-time employment rate over the period shown.

(b) Explain how the data might suggest that the number of unemployed, underemployed and discouraged individuals who would like a job but have stopped looking, has increased during this period.

THINKING LIKE AN ECONOMIST

LOOK BEHIND THE HEADLINES

In May 2017, newspapers reported that unemployment in France had fallen by 115,000 in the first quarter of 2017, to 2.7 million. Similarly, in March 2017, UK headlines were celebrating a fall in the UK's unemployment rate to 4.7 per cent, its lowest level since 1975. For both economies, these headlines suggest things are improving for both French and UK citizens. However, it is important to look at the detail behind the statistics.

In France, unemployment fell by 115,000 to 2.7 million, but the employment rate remained unchanged at 64.7 per cent. This might suggest that some individuals, who originally met the ILO classification for unemployed, no longer do so, even though they still want a job. They would now be part of the inactive population and would no longer be classified as 'unemployed', according to the ILO definition. In this case, levels of unemployment could fall despite employment levels remaining constant.

The newspapers also said that the unemployment rate in France had fallen to a five-year low of 9.6 per cent. However, it would still be unclear to what extent the fall in unemployment levels is due to individuals gaining employment, rather than moving to the 'inactive' part of the population. The unemployment rate only tells us what proportion of the active population are unemployed. Whatever the case, if employment rates remain unchanged, there is still the same proportion of the population of working age who are not working.

Similarly, the UK's low unemployment rate might not mean individuals of working age are as well off as it seems. The quality of jobs created may be questioned. There has been a rapid growth in self-employment in the UK since 2007–08.

MATHS TIP

For example, in a simple economy there may be 10 people who are classified as unemployed, out of a labour force of 20. The unemployment rate would be 50 per cent. If unemployment levels fall by 5 people, it could be 1 of these is now in employment, but 4 of them are now no longer actively looking for a job. The ILO level of unemployment would be 5 people. At the same time, the 4 people no longer actively seeking work are now not included in the economically active population. The labour force now falls to 16. The measured unemployment rate would fall to $\frac{5}{16} \times 100 = 31$ per cent. This might give a misleading impression of job creation, since the unemployment rate has fallen significantly, despite only 10 per cent of the original unemployed people getting a job!

In 2017, self-employment accounted for 15.1 per cent of the workforce. For some, this might mean high job satisfaction and good rewards. For others, self-employment can mean low wages and working less hours than desired. Also, according to the ONS, the number of people employed on zero hours contracts in their main job, during October to December 2016 was 905,000. This is an increase of 101,000 compared to the same time the previous year. These are not the high-quality jobs most workers are looking for. Underemployment is still clearly an issue. It means labour is significantly underutilised, with the economy operating well inside its production possibility frontier. So, a fall in the number of people unemployed or a fall in the unemployment rate does not necessarily reflect a better outlook for an economy.

Source: ONS and Insee

SUBJECT VOCABULARY

active population those in work or actively seeking work; also known as the labour force.

activity rate or participation rate the number of those in work or unemployed divided by the population of working age, expressed as a percentage.

anticipated inflation increases in prices that economic actors are able to predict with accuracy.

consumer price index (CPI) a measure of the price level used to measure inflation. It is produced to international standards.

deflation a fall in the price level.

disinflation a fall in the rate of inflation.

employed the number of people in paid work.

employees workers employed by another individual or firm.

employment those in paid work.

employment rate the number of those in work divided by the population of working age, expressed as a percentage.

full-time workers workers who work the hours and days that are the norm for a particular job.

hidden unemployed partly those in the population who would take a job if offered, but are not in work and are not currently seeking work; and partly those who are underemployed.

hyperinflation large increases in the price level.

inactive the number of those not in work and not unemployed.

inactivity rate the number of those not in work and not unemployed divided by the population of working age, expressed as a percentage.

indexation adjusting the value of economic variables such as wages or the rate of interest in line with inflation.

inflation a general and continued rise in prices.

labour force those in work or actively seeking work; also known as the active population.

part-time workers workers who only work a fraction of the hours and days that are the norm for a particular job.

population of working age total number of people aged between the state school leaving age and the state retirement age.

price level average price of goods/services in the economy.

producer price index used to measure the change in the price of a typical basket of goods bought and sold by the manufacturers of an economy.

reflation the process of increasing the amount of money being used in a country in order to increase trade.

self-employed workers who work on their own account and are not employees.

stagflation an economic situation in which there is inflation but many people do not have jobs and businesses are not doing well.

underemployed those who would work more hours if available or are in jobs that are below their skill level.

unemployed those not in work but seeking work.

unemployment occurs when individuals are without a job but who are actively seeking work.

unemployment rate the number of those not in work, but seeking work, divided by the labour force, expressed as a percentage.

CHECKPOINT

1 What is inflation?
2 What is happening to the price level if the inflation rate is negative?
3 What is meant by 'weighting' the basket of goods and services as part of the process of calculating the rate of inflation?
4 State two limitations of the CPI as a measure of the rate of inflation.
5 What is the producer price index?
6 State one use of the producer price index.
7 What is unemployment, according to the ILO definition?
8 State which people would be classified as underemployed.
9 What is the 'unemployment rate'?
10 What is 'labour force'?

EXAM PRACTICE

EMPLOYMENT IN SPAIN

SKILLS ▶ PROBLEM SOLVING, REASONING, INTERPRETATION, ANALYSIS

Q

1 Figure 5 shows Spain's employment and unemployment rate (ILO) from 2010 to 2016.

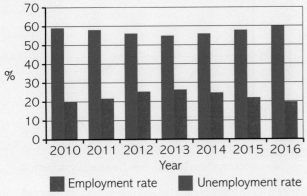

Figure 5 Spanish employment and unemployment rates, 2010–16

OECD

Which one of the following can be deduced from the chart?

(a) The number of unemployed, as a proportion of the labour force, rose between 2010 and 2013.

(b) The number of unemployed, as a proportion of the total population, fell between 2013 and 2016.

(c) The data for each year is inaccurate because the percentages do not add up to 100.

(d) The number of people employed must have fallen between 2010 and 2013. **(1 mark)**

2 In 2016, among the OECD member countries, Greece's unemployment rate was the highest at 26.7 per cent. Iceland's unemployment rate, the lowest, was 3.0 per cent. The OECD average, in 2016, was 6.3 per cent. The OECD uses the ILO measure of unemployment.

With reference to the information above, explain the term 'ILO measure of unemployment'. **(4 marks)**

3 China's inflation

Extract A: China's producer price inflation

In November 2016, China's producer price inflation was 3.3 per cent. This was the highest it had been since late 2011. This was the third consecutive month of rising producer prices; this had been preceded by four years of factory gate deflation. The Chinese statistics bureau said industrial prices had risen for a wider variety of goods; particularly those tied to coal and metals production. Along with price rises in fuel processing and chemicals, these sectors contributed 1.6 per cent to the producer price inflation rate.

Extract B: China's consumer price inflation

Consumer price inflation also continued to rise to an annual rate of 2.3 per cent. Food prices, which carry a heavy weighting in the basket of goods used to calculate the consumer price index, grew 3.2 per cent year on year. This accounts for almost 1 per cent of the total rise in the CPI inflation rate. Price pressure also rose in transport and communications costs.

Source: adapted from 'Chinese producer price inflation hits five year high', *Financial Times*, 9 December 2016

Year	Consumer price index (CPI) 2010 = 100	Producer price index (wholesale) 2010 = 100
2012	94.2	98.3
2013	96.7	96.4
2014	98.6	94.6
2015	100	89.6

▲ **Table 3 China's CPI and PPI, 2012–15**

Source: World Bank

(a) Define the term 'producer price index' (Table 3). **(2 marks)**

(b) With reference to extract A and Table 3, explain the term 'deflation'. **(4 marks)**

(c) Using the information in Table 3, explain how the producer price index is an indicator of future trends in the CPI inflation rate. **(4 marks)**

(d) Using the information in extract B, calculate the weight (out of a total of 1000), which would be given to food. **(4 marks)**

(e) With reference to extract B, explain how the CPI inflation rate is measured. **(4 marks)**

MATHS TIP

To do this you need to look at Table 1 in the 'Measuring inflation' part of the chapter, and work backwards!

4 Unemployment in the USA

MATHS TIP

One quantitative skill you need to understand is the meaning of seasonally adjusted figures. For example, The Bureau of Labour Statistics, in the USA, publishes both seasonally adjusted and non-seasonally adjusted unemployment rates.

As stated, 'Total employment and unemployment are higher in some parts of the year than in others. For example, unemployment is higher in January and February, when it is cold in many parts of the country and work in agriculture, construction, and other seasonal industries is reduced. Also, both employment and unemployment rise every June, when students enter the labor force in search of summer jobs. Because these seasonal events follow a more or less regular pattern each year, their influence on statistical trends can be eliminated by **seasonally adjusting** the statistics from month to month'. Seasonally adjusted data makes it easier to identify any **underlying trends** in unemployment data.

(a) With reference to Figure 6, explain the term 'the seasonally adjusted unemployment rate'. **(4 marks)**

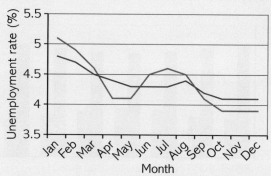

▲ **Figure 6 US seasonally adjusted and non-seasonally adjusted unemployment rates, 2017**

Source: Bureau of Labor Statistics: The Current Population Survey (CPS) is a monthly survey of households conducted by the Bureau of Census for the Bureau of Labor Statistics

24 BALANCE OF PAYMENTS

LEARNING OBJECTIVES

- Understand components of the balance of payments, with particular reference to the current account.
- Understand the distinction between deficits and surpluses in the trade in goods and services balance.
- Understand the distinction between balance of payments deficits and surpluses on the current account.

GETTING STARTED

Do you own a mobile phone? Where has it and its components been manufactured? To find out something about this, do an Internet search. If world trade stopped tonight, list ten things you would not be able to buy in the future.

THE INTERCONNECTEDNESS OF ECONOMIES

Over time, the world economy has been growing more interconnected. There are four key ways in which this process of globalisation has been taking place.

- The proportion of output of an individual nation economy that is traded internationally is growing.
- There is ever-increasing ownership of physical and financial assets, such as companies or shares or loans, in one country by economic actors in another country.
- Individuals are moving in increasing numbers from one country to another.
- Technology is being shared between countries on a faster basis.

Vietnam, for example, attracted US$36.7 billion of greenfield foreign direct investment (FDI) in 2016. Greenfield is a form of FDI where a foreign company sets up its operations in a foreign country without having any previous involvement there. This means it builds factories and infrastructure. Vietnam has been particularly successful in attracting investment to its manufacturing industry. Another example is net migration between Mexico and the USA. In 2010, the net migration of Mexicans to the USA was 8.5 per

10,000 people. This had risen to 29 per 10,000 by 2014. A final example is Russia, where around one-quarter of its output was exported in 2016.

THE BALANCE OF PAYMENTS ACCOUNT

Governments keep records of the numerous ways in which economies are interconnected. One important record is the **balance of payments account**. This is a record of all financial deals over a period of time between economic agents of one country and all other countries. Balance of payments accounts can be split into two components:

- the **current account** where payments for the purchase and sale of goods and services are recorded
- the **capital and financial accounts** where flows of money associated with saving, investment, speculation and currency stabilisation are recorded.

Flows of money into the country are given a positive (+) sign on the accounts. These inflows are recorded as a credit item. Flows of money out of the country are given a negative (−) sign. These outflows are recorded as a debit item.

THE CURRENT ACCOUNT

The current account on the balance of payments is itself split into several components.

Trade in goods Trade in goods is sometimes called trade in visibles. This is trade in raw materials such as copper and oil, semi-manufactured goods such as car components and finished manufactured goods such as cars, tablets or mobile phones. Visible exports are goods that are sold to foreigners. Goods leave the country while payment for these goods goes in the opposite direction. Hence visible exports of, say, cars result in an inward flow of money and are recorded with a positive sign on the balance of payments account. Visible imports are goods that are bought by domestic residents from foreigners. Goods come into the country while money flows out. Hence visible imports of, say, wheat are given a minus sign on the balance of payments. The difference between the value of visible exports and visible imports is known as the **balance of trade** in goods.

ACTIVITY 1

SKILLS ▶ INTERPRETATION, PROBLEM-SOLVING, REASONING

CASE STUDY: DIFFERENT TYPES OF INTERNATIONAL TRANSACTIONS

A country has the following international transactions on current account: exports of manufactured goods US$20 billion; imports of food US$10 billion; earnings from foreign tourists US$5 billion; interest, profits and dividends paid to foreigners US$4 billion; purchase of oil from abroad US$8 billion; earnings of nationals working overseas that are sent home US$7 billion; sale of coal to foreign countries US$2 billion; payments by foreigners to domestic financial institutions for services rendered US$1 billlion.

(a) Which of these items are: (i) visible exports; (ii) exports of services; (iii) primary income and secondary income credits; (iv) visible imports; (v) imports of services; (vi) income and current transfer debits?

(b) Calculate: (i) the balance of trade on goods (ii) the balance of trade on services (iii) the current balance.

(c) How would your answers to (b) be different if it cost the country US$3 billion to transport its exports (i) in its own ships and (ii) in the ships of other countries?

Trade in services A wide variety of services are traded internationally, including financial services such as banking and insurance, transport services such as shipping and air travel, and tourism. Trade in services is an example of trade in invisibles. Unlike physical goods, services are often intangible or unable to be touched. Exports of invisibles are bought by foreigners. So an American tourist paying for a stay in a London hotel is an invisible export. So too is a Chinese company buying insurance in the City of London or a Saudi Arabian company hiring a UK-owned ship. With invisibles, money flows into the UK as it would if a French company bought a machine manufactured in the UK, a visible export for the UK. Hence, on the official UK balance of payments accounts, invisible service exports are called export credits in services. Imports of services for the UK are services that are bought from other countries. A holiday taken by a UK national in Spain would be an invisible import for the UK. So too would be a UK firm hiring a private jet from a German company. With invisible imports, money flows abroad. Hence they are called debits on the official UK balance of payments accounts. The difference between the value of invisible exports and invisible imports is known as the balance of trade in services.

Primary and secondary income Not all flows of money result from trade in goods and services. Primary income results from the loan of factors of production abroad. For an economy, income is generated from interest, profits and dividends on assets owned abroad. Equally, interest, profits and dividends on an economy's assets owned by foreigners have to be paid out. For example, Samsung, a South Korean company, entered Vietnam in 2009. By 2017, it had invested US$16.7 billion in 15 separate projects in Vietnam. This investment will lead to investment income flows back to South Korea in the form of dividends and profit flows. This will show up as a debit on Vietnam's primary account.

Secondary income is when income is transfered between countries. Money is received without a corresponding output. Examples include personal transfers and government transfers between countries for international assistance.

THE DISTINCTION BETWEEN BALANCE OF TRADE DEFICITS AND SURPLUSES

The balance of trade (sometimes called net exports or net trade balance) is the value of exports minus the value of imports. The balance of trade in goods will be recorded separately from the balance of trade in services. These two balances will then make up the balance of trade in goods and services. When the value of exports is greater than the value of imports, there is a **trade surplus** on that component of the current account. When the value of imports is greater than the value of exports, there is a trade deficit. Economists often use the term 'widening or narrowing' of the trade deficit or surplus. This means the difference between the value of exports and the value of imports is getting bigger or becoming smaller.

THE DISTINCTION BETWEEN BALANCE OF PAYMENTS DEFICIT AND SURPLUS ON THE CURRENT ACCOUNT

The current account is made up of the trade in goods, trade in services account (together forming the balance of trade in goods and services), the primary income account and the secondary income account. The overall balance on these accounts is called the **current account balance**. If overall credits are greater than overall debits, then there is a **current account surplus** (also called a balance of payments surplus on the current account). If overall debits are greater than credits, then there is a **current account deficit**. The terms 'widening or narrowing' can also be applied to the current account balance.

The term deficit or surplus can also be applied to the primary income balance or secondary income balance.

GOVERNMENT DEFICITS AND BALANCE OF PAYMENTS DEFICITS

One common mistake is to assume that any current account deficit is paid for by the government. Another common mistake is to assume that government borrowing is the same as the current account deficit. The current account is made up of billions of individual transactions. Each one is financed in a different way. So a US firm importing machinery will use different finance from a family taking a holiday in France. A Chinese firm buying specialist car parts from a South Korean company will finance this in a different way from a German firm buying insurance from Lloyds of London. If a current account deficit has been caused mainly by excessive government spending, then the government is likely to have borrowed at least some of the money from abroad. However, a current account deficit may be caused mainly by private consumers and firms buying too many imports and borrowing the money from abroad to pay for them. The relationship between the current account deficit, private sector borrowing and government borrowing is therefore complex and depends upon individual circumstances.

Governments may choose to attempt to correct current account deficits or surpluses. They have a variety of ways in which they could attempt this, which have various advantages and disadvantages. However, governments may choose to do nothing and allow free market forces to correct any deficit or surplus.

THINKING LIKE AN ECONOMIST

MEXICO'S CURRENT ACCOUNT

According to the IMF, Mexico features in their 'Current account deficit, top 10 economies'. Other countries on this list include, among others, the USA, the UK, Brazil, Australia, Saudi Arabia and Turkey.

Figure 1 shows that between 2006 and 2016, Mexico had a current account deficit in every year. Since 2010, there was a sharp increase in the size of the current account deficit. It increased from approximately US$5 billion, in 2010, to approximately US$31 billion in 2013. In 2014, the current account deficit narrowed slightly and then widened again in 2015. The significance of the size of the deficit, over time, can be seen in Figure 2. In 2010, the current account deficit was approximately 0.5 per cent of its GDP, but by 2015 this had risen to 2.5 per cent of GDP.

The current account itself is split into four parts. Figure 7 shows these parts and whether a deficit or surplus has been recorded on the individual accounts. For each of the years shown, only the secondary account has recorded more money inflows than money outflows. The balance on the current account is shown by the line graph. This will be the addition of all the balances on the individual accounts.

- **Trade in goods**. This is the value of goods exported minus the value of goods imported. Some of Mexico's main exports include manufactured goods (such as vehicles and machinery) and oil. Figure 3 shows exports and imports of goods. Between 2012 and 2014, both exports and imports rose. Imports rose at a slightly faster rate. The deficit on the balance of trade on goods rose slightly. However, between 2014 and 2015 exports of goods fell at a much sharper rate than imports. As a result, the deficit on this account rose from approximately US$2.8 billion to US$14.6 billion (Figure 4). This was largely because of the collapse in oil prices over this period and the fall in oil production; both reducing the value of oil exports.

- **Trade in services**. This is the value of exports on services minus the value of imports on services. For Mexico an important source of foreign exchange is tourism. Figure 5 shows the balance of trade in services over the same period. Between 2012 and 2016, the deficit on the balance of trade in services narrowed. In 2012, the deficit was approximately US$15 billion, by 2016, this had fallen to approximately US$9 billion. This shows an improvement on the balance of trade in services over this period.

The balance of trade in goods and services is the combined balance of the trade in goods and trade in services. This is shown in Figure 6.

- **Primary income**. This shows income flows between countries, associated with production or with ownership of financial assets, such as property. This section includes 'compensation of employees'. This is income flows of border, seasonal and other short-term workers who are employed in an economy where they are not resident, for example, Mexicans who work in the USA, but are resident in Mexico. Other examples of primary income include investment income flows, for example, dividends, profits and interest flows. Figure 7 shows the primary account balance is a significant cause of the deficit on the current account. This is partly explained by foreign direct investment in Mexico. If foreign firms invest in business activities in Mexico, then dividends and profits will flow back to these countries.

- **Secondary income**. This shows income transfers, when flows of income occur without anything of economic value being supplied as a direct return. Examples include personal transfers and current international assistance. Personal transfers include workers remittances. Worker remittances are transfers made by employees who are residents of one economy, to residents of another country. Mexico heavily depends on

income sent by workers living in the USA back to Mexico. In 2010, personal transfer flows into Mexico, were US$21.3 billion. By 2016, this had risen to US$27 billion. This was partly because of the recovery in the US economy, making the job market more favourable for employment. Table 1 shows that, in 2016, the secondary income account is the only one that had a positive balance. The balance of US$27 billion, for secondary income, comes mainly from personal transfers. This shows how significant remittance payments are for Mexico and how these minimise the overall deficit on the current account.

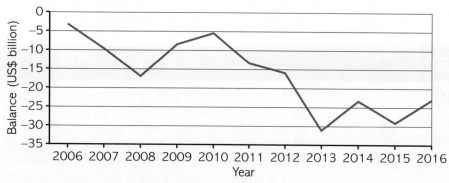

▲ Figure 1 Mexico's current account balance, 2006–16

Source: OECD

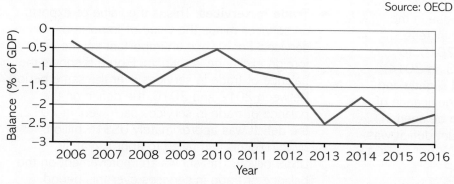

▲ Figure 2 Mexico's current account balance as percentage of GDP, 2006–16

Source: OECD

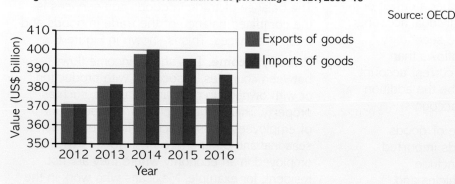

▲ Figure 3 Mexico's exports and imports, 2012–16

Source: IMF data portal

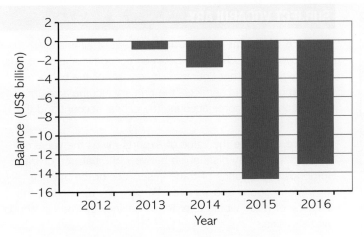

▲ Figure 4 Mexico's balance of trade on goods, 2012–16

Source: IMF data portal

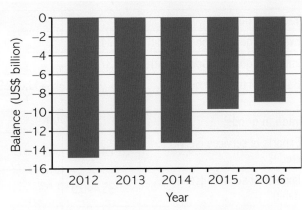

▲ Figure 5 Mexico's balance of trade on services, 2012–16

Source: IMF data portal

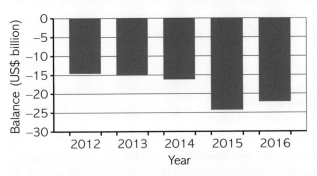

▲ Figure 6 Mexico's balance of trade on goods and services, 2012–16

Source: IMF data porta

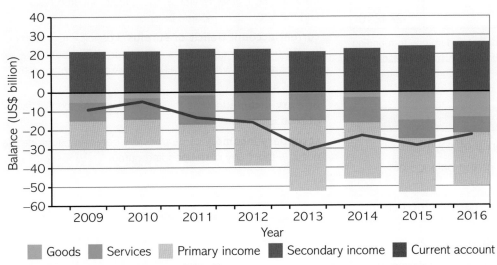

▲ Figure 7 Mexico's current account, 2009–16

Source: IMF (exported from data portal)

Trade in goods		
Export of goods (goods, credit)	1,374,296.1	
Import of goods (goods, debit)	387,369.0	
Balance of trade on goods		−13,072.9
Trade in goods		
Exports of services (services, credit)	24,499.6	
Imports of services (services, debit)	33,440.9	
Balance of trade on services		−8941.3
Balance of trade on goods and services		−22,014.1
Primary income		
Credits	8075.8	
Debits	34,987.0	
Primary income balance		−26,911.2
Secondary income		
Credits	27,235.8	
Debits	730.4	
Secondary income balance		26,505.4
Current balance		−22,420.0

Note: balances do not add up due to rounding.

▲ Table 1 Mexican current account balance, 2016 (US$ millions)

Source: IMF data portal

CHECKPOINT

1 What is meant by the balance of payments?

2 What are the components of the balance of payments?

3 State the four accounts that make up the current account.

4 What is the balance of trade in goods?

5 What is meant by a widening of the balance of trade in goods and services deficit?

6 What is a current account surplus?

7 What is meant by the current account's surplus narrowing?

8 Give an example of a flow of income that is recorded on the primary income account.

9 Give an example of a flow of income that is recorded on the secondary income account.

SUBJECT VOCABULARY

balance of payments account a record of all financial deals over a period of time between economic agents of one country and all other countries. It consists of the balance of trade in goods and services, the primary income account, the secondary income account, the capital account and the financial account.

balance of trade the value of exports minus the value of imports. Data may distinguish between the balance of trade in goods, the balance of trade in services or the balance of trade in goods and services. Without any distinction, the balance of trade would refer to the balance of trade in goods and services.

balance of trade deficit or surplus a deficit exists when the value of imports is greater than the value of exports. A surplus exists when the value of exports is greater than the value of imports.

capital and financial accounts that part of the balance of payments account where flows of savings, investment and currency are recorded.

current account part of the balance of payments. The current account has four components: the trade in goods, trade in services, primary income and secondary income accounts.

current account balance records the overall difference between the credits and debits on each separate part of the current account – the balance of trade in goods, the balance of trade in services (these two then form the balance of trade in goods and services), the primary income balance and the secondary income balance.

current account deficit or surplus a deficit exists when overall debits exceed credits on the current account. A surplus exists when overall credits exceed debits on the current account.

primary income income that results from the loan of factors of production abroad.

secondary income income transfers between countries that occur without any corresponding output.

EXAM PRACTICE

CURRENT ACCOUNT BALANCES

SKILLS ▶ PROBLEM SOLVING, REASONING, INTERPRETATION, ANALYSIS

Q

1 Figure 8 shows Thailand's current account balance between 2009 and 2016.

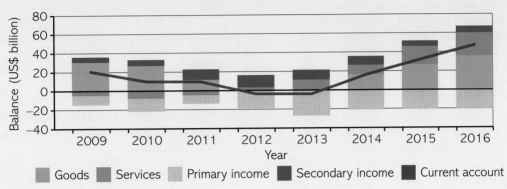

▲ **Figure 8 Thai current account balance, 2009–16**

Source: IMF data portal

Which of the following can be deduced from the chart?

(a) The current account deficit increased between 2013 and and 2016.

(b) The balance of trade in services was in deficit between 2009–11, from 2012–16 it was in surplus.

(c) The balance of trade on goods improved each year between 2009 and 2016.

(d) In 2011, the current account balance was approximately US$20 billion. **(1 mark)**

2 In the Philippines remittance payments received from Filipinos working overseas and sending money back home reached US$25 billion in 2014. The USA is the largest single source of remittances to the Philippines. These are recorded on the secondary account, which is part of the current account. Without these, the current account surplus of 4.4 per cent of GDP for the Philippines would have been a deficit.

Source: *Financial Times*, 'US recovery drives jump in remittances', 2.10.2015

With reference to the information above, explain the term 'current account surplus'. **(4 marks)**

3 Table 2 shows a breakdown of Indonesia's current account on the balance of payments for 2016. In 2016. Indonesia's GDP was US$932.3 billion.

	US$ (billion)
Goods, credit (exports)	144.4
Goods, debit (imports)	129.0
Services, credit (exports)	23.5
Services, debit (imports)	30.5
Primary income balance	−29.7
Secondary income balance	4.4
Current account balance	

▲ **Table 2 Breakdown of Indonesian current account balance of payments, 2016**

Source: IMF

Calculate Indonesia's current account balance as a percentage of GDP for 2016. **(4 marks)**

4 The Caribbean

Extract A:

The Caribbean region is heavily dependent on tourism. For example, tourism makes up approximately 12 per cent of the GDP of Barbados. It is a significant source of export earnings, along with finance and information services, which brings in valuable foreign exchange. Some of its main imports include fuel, food, consumer goods and materials for construction. Barbados has a very open economy with significant trade flows occurring between Barbados and the USA, other Caribbean nations, China and the UK.

Extract B:

During the global financial crisis, the number of tourists visiting many regions of the Caribbean fell sharply. It was inevitable that the fall in GDP per capita and reduced consumer confidence in economies such as those of the USA, Canada and the UK would hit most of the Caribbean tourism sector hard. The impact was different in different countries, but most were harmed by the external shock caused by the crisis. For example, in Barbados, international tourism receipts as a percentage of total exports were 59.6 per cent in 2009, but had fallen to 45.6 per cent by 2011.

	2012	2013
Balance of trade in goods and services	−99.0	−67.6

▲ **Table 3 Barbados current account (US$ million), 2012 and 2014**

Source: IMF (latest data available)

Year	International tourism receipts (current US$ billion)
2008	1.244
2009	1.122
2010	1.074
2011	0.983

▲ **Table 4 Barbados international tourism receipts, 2008–11**

Source: World Bank

(a) With reference to Table 3 and extract A, explain the term 'balance of trade in goods and services'. **(4 marks)**

(b) With reference to Table 4 and extract B, analyse one reason why the balance of trade in services surplus for Barbados is likely to have fallen between 2008 and 2011. **(6 marks)**

25 EMPLOYMENT AND UNEMPLOYMENT (CAUSES AND EFFECTS)

UNIT 2
2.3.1

GETTING STARTED

Find out the unemployment rate in your country. Think of two reasons why people might be unemployed. What effect does that unemployment have on those individuals, the local community and the wider economy?

INTRODUCTION

The measurement of employment and unemployment was covered in Chapter 23. Chapter 23 also discussed the distinction between unemployment and underemployment and how it is important to interpret data with care. This chapter focuses on the causes of unemployment, the effects of unemployment, the impact of net migration and the significance to the economy of changes in employment and unemployment rates.

CAUSES OF UNEMPLOYMENT

Unemployment occurs for a variety of reasons. A number of different types of, or reasons for, unemployment can be distinguished.

Frictional unemployment Most workers who lose their jobs move quickly into new ones. This short-term unemployment is called **frictional unemployment**.

There will always be frictional unemployment in a free market economy and it is not regarded by most economists as a serious problem. The amount of time spent unemployed varies. The higher the level of unemployment benefits or redundancy pay, the longer workers will be able to afford to search for a good job without being forced into total poverty. Equally, the better the job information available to unemployed workers through newspapers, employment centres and websites, the shorter the time workers should need to spend searching for jobs.

Seasonal unemployment Some workers, such as construction workers or workers in the tourist industry, tend to work on a seasonal basis. **Seasonal unemployment** tends to rise in winter when some of these workers will be laid off, while unemployment falls in summer when they are taken on again. There is little that can be done to prevent this pattern occurring in a market economy where the demand for labour varies through the year.

Structural unemployment Far more serious is the problem of **structural unemployment**. This occurs when the demand for labour is less than its supply in an individual labour market in the economy. One example of structural unemployment is regional unemployment. For example, in 2009, Ethiopia's unemployment rate for urban areas was estimated to be at 20.6 per cent, which was ten times higher than in rural areas (2.6 per cent). (The average urban unemployment rate in Ethiopia, between 2006 and 2016, was 17.8 per cent.) This is likely to be explained by the increase in migration from rural to urban areas. For the city Addis Ababa, there were not enough job opportunities for those with primary and secondary education levels, relative to the supply of labour. In many economies, unemployment differences between regions occurs because factors of production are geographically immobile. For example, workers might be geographically immobile because of family ties or cost of living differences between regions, which makes it hard to move.

Another example is sectoral unemployment. The steel and shipbuilding industries in the UK declined sharply in the late 1970s and early 1980s, leaving a considerable number of skilled workers unemployed. Unfortunately, their skills were no longer needed in the economy and without retraining and possibly moving, they were unable to adapt to the changing demand.

Technological unemployment is another example of structural unemployment. Groups of workers across industries may be put out of work by new technology. Again, without retraining and geographical mobility, these workers may remain unemployed. For any economy to maintain its employment levels in a competitive global market, it must invest in the skills of its workforce over time. In competitive environments it is likely that mismatches will arise between the types of skills demanded by firms and the skills offered by job seekers. This creates structural unemployment. For example, as reported in the Malaysia Central Bank's 2016 annual report, firms in Malaysia have said there are significant skills gaps among new graduates. Firms wanted more industrial training and better communication skills among graduates. The tertiary youth unemployment rate in 2015 was 15.3 per cent. This was despite a national unemployment rate of only 3.1 per cent and an overall youth unemployment rate of 10.7 per cent. If firms cannot provide the training needed to meet the skills gap, then governments, if they have the resources, must step in to correct this type of market failure. Often governments will change the types of education provided by the state to reduce this type of structural unemployment. However, all governments face the problem of limited resources. As a result, many job seekers may become long-term unemployed because their skills are not relevant or good enough to take the jobs on offer.

Cyclical or demand-deficient unemployment

Cyclical or demand-deficient unemployment is unemployment that occurs when there is insufficient aggregate demand in the economy for all workers to get a job. Cyclical unemployment will be higher when an economy is in a recession. In a recession, it is not just workers who are unemployed. Capital too is underutilised. So factories and offices can remain empty. Machinery and equipment can remain unused.

Real wage unemployment

Real wage unemployment or classical unemployment exists when real wage rates are stuck at a level above that needed to reduce unemployment further. Real wage rates are inflexible downwards. One cause of real wage unemployment is minimum wages. Unemployed workers might be prepared to work for less than the minimum wage. Employers might be prepared to take on more workers, but only if they could pay workers less than the minimum wage. However, the fact that employers are legally not allowed to pay workers less than the minimum wage means that those unemployed workers cannot get a job. Another cause of real wage unemployment is unemployed workers refusing to take low paid jobs because they can receive more in welfare payments than working.

Cyclical unemployment is caused by a lack of demand in the economy. Frictional, seasonal, structural and real wage unemployment are caused by supply-side factors. For example, if labour markets were more efficient, workers would move from job to job more quickly. So the time taken to get a new job would be shorter. In the case of frictional unemployment, an increase in the amount of information of jobs available to jobseekers would reduce the time they spent searching for a job. In the case of structural unemployment, making it easier to get cheap rented accommodation in areas of low unemployment would help workers in areas of higher unemployment to move. Better retraining of workers would also help to reduce structural unemployment.

ACTIVITY 1   SKILLS   REASONING

CASE STUDY: TYPES OF UNEMPLOYMENT

The following workers are unemployed. Explain under which type of unemployment their circumstances might be classified.

(a) Katie Morris is a 30-year-old with a husband and two children. She works in the local hotel trade in the summer months on a casual basis but would like to work all the year round.

(b) John Penny, aged 22, was made redundant a couple of weeks ago from a furniture store that closed down. He is currently seeking work in the retail sector but, since the economy is in recession, job vacancies across most sectors have fallen sharply.

(c) Manus O'Brien lives in Belfast in Northern Ireland. Aged 56, he last had a job 12 years ago working in a local factory.

(d) Nayara Jimenez, aged 21, has recently graduated from university. She is spending a few months researching all the job options available to her.

(e) Seo-yun Kim used to work in manufacturing, but when her company invested in new automation she was made redundant.

ACTIVITY 2   SKILLS ▷ REASONING, INTERPRETATION, CRITICAL THINKING

CASE STUDY: US MANUFACTURING JOBS

Between 2000 and 2010, 5.6 million manufacturing jobs were lost in the USA. Many believe international trade is to blame, as cheap imports threaten US manufacturing jobs. However, according to a study by the Center for Business and Economic Research Ball State University, 85 per cent of these job losses are largely caused by automation. Although many low-skilled jobs have been lost, productivity has increased and manufacturing output has grown.

(a) Explain why the use of technology might benefit manufacturing firms in the USA.

(b) To what extent will workers, who have lost their jobs through automation, remain unemployed?

USING DIAGRAMS TO ILLUSTRATE UNEMPLOYMENT

Unemployment can be illustrated using a variety of diagrams. Figure 1 shows a production possibility diagram. The economy is operating at its productive potential when it is somewhere on the production possibility frontier, such as at point A. There are unemployed resources when the economy is operating within the frontier, such as at point B.

FIGURE 1

The production possibility frontier
At any point on the production possibility frontier there is no unemployment due to a lack of demand. At point B, there is cyclical unemployment.

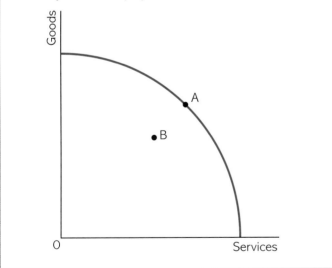

Aggregate demand and supply analysis can be used to distinguish between demand-side and supply-side causes of unemployment. In Figure 2, the economy is in short-run equilibrium at an output level of Y1. However, what if the long-run aggregate supply curve (LRAS) curve is to the right of this point? Then there

must be cyclical or demand-deficient unemployment. The economy is in recession. Output at OY_1 does not represent the productive potential of the economy, which is higher at OY_2. However, if there is an increase in aggregate demand, shown in Figure 3 by the shift in the aggregate demand curve from AD_1 to AD_2, full employment can be restored.

FIGURE 2

Cyclical unemployment
The economy is in equilibrium in the short run at an output level of OY_1. This is below the level of OY_2, shown by the long-run aggregate supply curve, where there would be no demand-deficient unemployment.

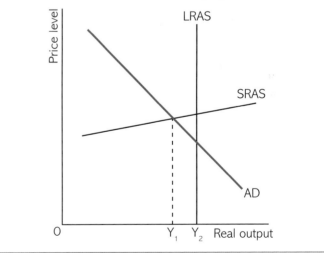

The same point can be illustrated using the concept of the output gap. The trend growth of the economy is shown by the upward sloping straight line in Figure 4. At point A, there is a negative output gap and the economy is in recession. So there is cyclical unemployment. An increase in demand will move the economy to B and eliminate demand-deficient unemployment.

FIGURE 3

Cyclical unemployment

Cyclical unemployment in the economy at the short-run equilibrium of OY_1 can be eliminated by raising aggregate demand, shown by the shift in the aggregate demand curve from AD_1 to AD_2.

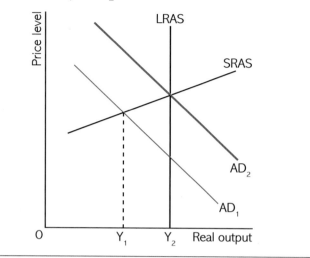

FIGURE 4

Unemployment and the output gap

Cyclical unemployment occurs if the actual level of income is below its long-run trend level, for example at A.

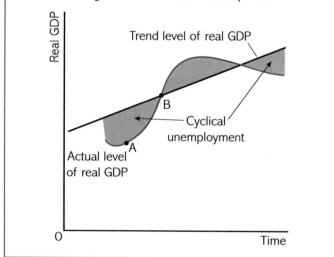

Supply-side causes of unemployment include frictional, seasonal and structural unemployment. In Figure 3, there is likely to be some frictional, seasonal and structural unemployment at an output level of OY_2. This is because the LRAS curve is drawn on the assumption that there are limited resources and markets may work imperfectly. For example, some workers may be structurally unemployed because they do not have the right skills for the jobs on offer in the market. This lack of skills is taken into account when drawing the LRAS curve. If through training

they acquire new skills and then get jobs, this leads to a rightward shift of the long-run aggregate supply curve. A fall in frictional, seasonal and structural unemployment is shown by a rightward shift of the long-run aggregate supply curve.

In Figure 4, the long-run trend line of growth is drawn assuming the gradual shift to the right in the long-run aggregate supply curve shown in Figure 3. If the long-run trend rate of growth is 2.5 per cent, then in Figure 3, the LRAS curve is shifting to the right by 2.5 per cent per year on average. So the trend rate of growth assumes there will be supply-side improvements to the economy over time. This may or may not include supply-side improvements that reduce frictional, seasonal or structural unemployment. However, past evidence would suggest that existing structural unemployment tends to fall over time. Of course, there may be new supply-side shocks that lead to new structural unemployment. If the long-run trend rate of growth could be raised, say from 2.5 per cent to 3 per cent, there is a greater probability that structural unemployment will fall. A rise in the long-run trend rate of growth would be shown by a shift upwards in the trend growth line in Figure 4.

ACTIVITY 3 SKILLS REASONING, INTERPRETATION, CRITICAL THINKING

CASE STUDY: BRAZILIAN EXPORTS AND UNEMPLOYMENT

In some emerging economies, such as Russia and Brazil, falling commodity prices since 2014 have caused recessions. Economic growth in Brazil fell from 3 per cent in 2013, to −3.4 per cent in 2016. Some of Brazil's major exports include iron ore, soya beans and raw sugar. When commodity prices fall, export revenues decline. Unemployment in Brazil increased from 6.8 per cent in 2014 to 11.45 per cent in 2016.

(a) With reference to the passage, explain how a fall in commodity prices from 2014 caused unemployment to rise in Brazil (make the link with aggregate demand and use an AD/AS diagram).

EMPLOYMENT, UNEMPLOYMENT AND ACTIVITY RATES

Governments attempt to achieve full employment in their economies. Unemployment represents a significant cost and so reducing unemployment rates is seen as economically desirable.

Some governments are also committed to increasing employment rates and reducing inactivity rates. Two main groups tend to be targeted.

- Women tend to have lower activity rates. This is mainly caused by a lack of educational opportunities for women in some countries, cultural views on role of women in society, lack of job opportunities for women and women being far more likely to give up jobs to look after children. For example, employment rates in the developing world tend to be low because many women, in particular, do not participate in the labour market. Participation rates are the lowest in countries in the North African regions. However, many governments are adopting policies to increase female participation rates. Bringing more women into the labour force increases recorded GDP and so increases growth rates, a goal for most governments. For example, in 2015, the Japanese government introduced new legislation to encourage companies to hire and promote women. The size of Japan's working age population is currently declining, so increasing the female participation rate will help to increase economic growth.

- Older workers, particularly over the age of 60, have lower activity rates. In developed economies, there is often a state retirement age. This means individuals receive a state pension (form of welfare payment) from the government to support them in old age. Governments in Europe have been raising the retirement age in order to reduce the amount of government spending on pensions. At the same time, they have been encouraging workers to stay in work or get a new job rather than retire. They want to prevent individuals from claiming benefits because they have little or no income. So raising activity rates is part of the same policy of raising retirement ages in order to reduce the welfare benefit bill.

MIGRATION

Significant levels of migration can have an important impact on employment and unemployment. For example, Russia has experienced net inward migration ever since the fall of communism. The immigrants are primarily lower skilled workers from the poorer parts of the former Soviet Union (e.g. the Ukraine and Kazakhstan). This is likely to drive down wages in lower skilled jobs. The ability of Russian firms to recruit foreign workers means the supply of labour is increased, reducing the equilibrium price of labour, the wage rate. Russian workers with low skills will be most affected. They will also have to compete with more potential workers for jobs. If there are insufficient jobs available, this will increase unemployment. However, for any economy, net immigration may bring benefits. Owing to the circular flow of income, the spending of these workers creates further jobs. It is possible for

total employment to increase without an increase in unemployment. There would be a greater impact on an economy if the immigrants were skilled workers. These workers would transfer knowledge that promotes innovation and adoption of new technologies. In turn this can increase potential growth in an economy. In Russia, the working age population had been shrinking since 2007, due to relatively low birth rates in the 1980s and 1990s, so the net immigration has helped to fill labour shortages in some sectors. The overall impact of migration on an economy will depend on many factors, such as the skills of migrants compared to existing workers and the state of the economy. For developing countries, remittance payments sent back home to relatives are a significant source of income and source of foreign exchange. However, if most emigrants are relatively skilled, then this human capital flight will have a significant impact on long-run growth.

ACTIVITY 4  SKILLS REASONING, ANALYSIS

CASE STUDY: EU IMMIGRATION TO THE UK

Immigrants from the EU made a net contribution to government finances of £2732 per year in the 10 years to 2011. In total, EU inward migration added £22 billion to tax revenues over the whole 10-year period. These figures come from a report published by the Migration Advisory Committee. It found that the employment rate of UK-born workers has been 'practically unchanged' despite the entry of 500,000 migrants from central and eastern Europe after EU expansion in 2004. In contrast, non-European migrants only contributed a net £162 per person per year to public finances in the decade to 2011. One in six of Britain's 13 million low-skilled jobs are now held by migrants. Some migrants are exploited by their employers and are paid less than the minimum wage. In a separate study, the OECD found that immigration leads to higher pay for native workers. Immigrants are in general more educated than native workers. Immigration is 'likely to create more opportunities for the receiving economy', wrote the researchers.

Source: adapted from © the *Financial Times*, 9.7.2014, 30.9.2014 All Rights Reserved.

(a) Explain two advantages to the UK of inward migration of workers.

(b) Analyse what impact the fact that migrants are generally 'more educated than native workers' might have on (i) native UK workers and (ii) UK firms.

THE COSTS OF UNEMPLOYMENT

Long-term unemployment is generally considered to be a great social evil. This is perhaps not surprising in view of the following costs of unemployment.

Costs to the unemployed and their dependants

The people who are likely to lose the most from unemployment are the unemployed themselves. One obvious cost is the loss of income that could have been earned had the person been in a job. Subtract from this the value of any welfare payments that the worker might receive and any value placed on the extra leisure time that an unemployed person has at his or her disposal. For most unemployed people, it is likely that they will be net financial losers.

The costs to the unemployed, however, do not finish there. Evidence suggests that unemployed people and their families suffer in a number of other ways. One simple but very important problem for them is the negative view of being unemployed. Unemployment is often seem as failure both by the unemployed themselves and by society in general. Many feel embarrassed by receiving welfare payments and not being able to support themselves or their families. In many economies, except for the most advanced, there is unlikely to be any form of income support provided by the government in times of unemployment. In this case, unemployment may mean extreme poverty, unless there is family support. Studies suggest that the unemployed suffer from a wide range of social problems including above average rates of stress, divorce, suicide, physical and mental illness, and that they have higher death rates compared with those in employment.

For the short-term unemployed, the costs are relatively low. Many will lose some earnings, although a few who receive large redundancy payments may benefit financially from having lost their job. The social and psychological costs are likely to be limited too.

However, the long-term unemployed are likely to be major losers on all counts. The long-term unemployed suffer one more cost. Evidence suggests that the longer the period out of work, the less likely it is that the unemployed person will find a job. There are two reasons for this. First, being out of work reduces the human capital of workers. They lose work skills and are not being trained in the latest developments in their occupation. Second, employers use length of time out of work as a quick way of sorting through applicants for a job. For an employer, unemployment is likely to mean that the applicant has, to some extent, lost or forgotten their skills. There is a fear that the unemployed worker will not be capable of doing the job after a period of unemployment. It could show that the worker has personality problems and might be an undisciplined employee. It could also be an indication that other employers have turned down the applicant for previous jobs and hence it would be rational to save time and not consider the applicant for this job. The long-term unemployed are then in an impossible situation. They cannot get a job unless they have recent employment experience. However, they cannot get recent employment experience until they get a job.

Costs to society: the impact on local communities

Costs of unemployment to local communities are more difficult to establish. Some have suggested that unemployment, particularly among the young, leads to increased crime, violence on the streets and vandalism. Areas of high unemployment tend to become run down. Shops go out of business. Households have no spare money to look after their properties and their gardens. Increased vandalism further destroys the environment. The social costs of unemployment include the private costs to the unemployed themselves and the external costs that impact the local communities in which they live.

Costs to the government The cost of unemployment to the taxpayer could be a heavy one. On the one hand, governments in many economies, particularly high income ones, have to pay out increased welfare payments. On the other hand, governments lose revenue because these workers would have paid taxes if they had been employed. For instance, they would have paid income tax on their earnings. They would also have paid more in indirect taxes, such as a sales tax, because they would have been able to spend more. So taxpayers not only pay more taxes to cover for increased government spending but they also have to pay more because they have to make up the taxes that the unemployed would have paid if they had been in work. Many governments also provide help to the unemployed to get a job. They might provide information about available jobs, such as through job centres. They may provide training schemes or subsidise employers who take on unemployed workers.

The impact of unemployment on resource utilisation Taxpayers paying money to the unemployed is not a loss for the economy as a whole. It is a transfer payment that redistributes existing resources within the economy. However, unemployment does create a cost to the economy as a whole. Unemployment means labour is underutilised in the economy. This means not all factors of production are being employed. As a result, the economy will be operating inside the production possibility frontier. The loss to the economy is the loss of output that those workers now unemployed could have produced had they been in work. The economy could have produced more goods and services, which would have been available for consumption. This would satisfy more needs and wants. A fall in unemployment, by moving the economy closer to the production possibility frontier, is desirable. Full employment means the economy is operating at maximum potential output.

Costs to consumers The unemployed as consumers lose out because they have to spend less. Consumers in areas of high unemployment also lose out because local shopping centres tend to be run down and don't offer the range of shops available to those in areas of low unemployment.

Costs to firms Firms suffer because unemployment represents a loss of demand in the economy. If there were full employment, the economy would be more healthy and there would be more spending. Long-term unemployment also reduces the pool of skilled workers that a firm could hire.

ACTIVITY 5　　SKILLS　REASONING, INTERPRETATION

CASE STUDY: YOUTH UNEMPLOYMENT

The ILO estimated that the global youth unemployment rate was 13.1 per cent in 2016 and likely to remain at that level in 2017. The global number of unemployed youths is expected to be 71 million in 2016. But this figure excludes many youths who do not participate in the labour market at all. Among the 34 members of the OECD, a club of advanced economies, it was estimated in 2013 that there are 26 million youths not in education, employment or training (so called NEETs). Similarly, across the developing countries, the World Bank estimated there are 262 million such youths. Some of these youths choose not to work. About one-quarter of the world's NEETs are south Asian women who do not work for cultural reasons. And the under 24s who are working are more likely to be working in informal or temporary employment. In advanced economies, it is estimated that one-third of under 24s are on temporary contracts: in developing countries one-fifth are unpaid labourers or work in the informal sector. In total, nearly one-half of the world's young are contributing to the labour market less effectively than they could be.

(a) Explain how the passage above shows evidence of 'under employment'.

(b) Explain the likely costs of high unemployment, under employment and high inactivity rates on the individuals themselves, local communities, the government and the economy.

THINKING LIKE AN ECONOMIST

INTELLIGENT MACHINES THREATEN JOBS

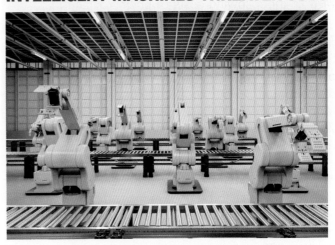

There is currently great debate about the impact of the 'Fourth Industrial Revolution' on unemployment. Artificial intelligence, the use of computer systems to perform tasks normally associated with human intelligence, is about to have a significant impact on labour markets.

An example of the use of artificial intelligence can be found in healthcare. CT scans of patient's organs can be processed by 'deep learning systems'. This means malignant tumours can be identified more accurately, compared to humans. The system will also highlight any feature that needs further investigation – thus reducing the need for an expert radiology human. It is believed the use of artificial intelligence will make healthcare more accurate and efficient.

However, the downside is that many jobs may become automated. Those individuals vulnerable to this threat, experts say, are the ones whose work is 'routine'. This will affect both white-collar and manual workers. Even if the job requires high-level skills, such as a radiographer, if the work itself can be broken down into routine steps, then that job has the potential to be replaced by automation.

A study published in 2013 examined the probability of computerisation for 702 occupations. It found that 47 per cent of Americans had jobs at high risk of automation (e.g. taxi drivers, delivery drivers, security guards, accountants). It concluded that recent developments in machine learning will put a substantial share of employment, across a wide range of occupations, at risk soon. Other studies have put the figure at 35 per cent of the workforce of the UK and 49 per cent for Japan. In 2017, the Institute for Public Policy Research Scotland said 46 per cent of jobs in Scotland are at high risk of automation.

A study published in 2013 examined the probability of computerisation for 702 occupations. It found that 47 per cent of Americans had jobs at high risk of automation (e.g. taxi drivers, delivery drivers, security guards, accountants). It concluded that recent developments in machine learning will put a substantial share of employment, across a wide range of occupations, at risk soon. Other studies have put the figure at 35 per cent of the workforce of the UK and 49 per cent for Japan. In 2017, the Institute for Public Policy Research Scotland said 46 per cent of jobs in Scotland are at high risk of automation.

The cost of artificial intelligence will be technological unemployment. Artificial intelligence has the potential to be used in many different labour markets ranging from banking through to traditional manufacturing; so the impact on unemployment could be huge. The jobs to survive will be those that are non-routine cognitive (thinking processing) and non-routine manual.

However, will the effect on unemployment be so huge? There are some good reasons not to be too worried. First, jobs in industries using automation may increase. For example, the automation of shopping through e-commerce, along with accurate personal recommendations, encourages consumers to spend more. This means overall employment in retailing will rise. Second, jobs in new industries will be created. For example, jobs for video-game designers are 'new' jobs that did not exist 50 years ago. Third, jobs dependent on human traits such as creativity, emotional intelligence and social skills (such as teaching, nursing, social care) are unlikely to be replaced by robots yet.

Although technology will destroy some jobs, it is hoped that new jobs will be created. Companies and governments must make sure that workers continue to acquire new skills and can switch jobs quickly, when the need arises. If workers can be occupationally and geographically mobile, the impact of the 'rise of the robot' may produce more benefits than costs.

CHECKPOINT

1 State the meaning of frictional unemployment.
2 State one way to reduce frictional unemployment.
3 Why is demand-deficient or cyclical unemployment high in a recession?
4 State why technological advances are likely to cause some structural unemployment.
5 What sort of unemployment is caused by a mis-match in skills required by employers, but not offered by job seekers?
6 How is cyclical unemployment reduced?
7 State two ways of reducing structural unemployment.
8 Create an AD/AS diagram to illustrate cyclical unemployment.
9 State two possible benefits of immigration for an economy's employment levels.
10 State how unemployment might affect consumers, firms and the economy as a whole.

SUBJECT VOCABULARY

cyclical or demand-deficient unemployment when there is insufficient demand in the economy for all workers who wish to work at current wage rates to obtain a job.
frictional unemployment when workers are unemployed for short lengths of time between jobs.
long-term unemployed in the UK, those unemployed for more than one year.
real wage or classical unemployment when workers are unemployed because real wages are too high and inflexible downwards, leading to insufficient demand for workers from employers.
seasonal unemployment when workers are unemployed at certain times of the year, such as building workers or farm workers in winter.
short-term unemployed in the UK, those unemployed for less than a year.
structural unemployment when the pattern of demand and production changes, leaving workers unemployed in labour markets where demand has shrunk. Examples of structural unemployment are regional unemployment, sectoral unemployment or technological unemployment.
technological unemployment when developments in technology cause roles to become redundant.

EXAM PRACTICE

Q

1 The impact of technology for Ethopia

Extract A

A recent report by the World Bank, in 2016, highlighted that the high cost of job searching is one key factor that explains Ethiopia's high urban unemployment rate. For example, job advertisements appear on physical job boards at specific points in the city of Addis Ababa. This means the unemployed have to spend large sums on transport costs, which amounts to almost 25 per cent of their monthly expenditure. The report recommends greater use of technology to increase access to information on job vacancies. This would help to reduce the cost of job searching and improve the quality of matching individuals to the right job.

Source: 'Why so idle? Wages and employment in a crowded labour market', World Bank, December 2016

Extract B

Recent analysis by the Oxford Martin School in 2013 concluded that 47 per cent of US jobs were at risk of automation over the coming 20 years. However, its follow up analysis suggested the impact would be greater still in the developing world. Ethiopia was the most exposed of the countries analysed. The study suggests that 85 per cent of all jobs in Ethiopia are in danger of being lost to technological advances.

At the moment, lower income countries have a competitive cost advantage, over higher wage ones, in trade sectors such as agriculture and manufacturing. However, as robots start to replace workers in many sectors, this cost advantage will be lost. Companies, in higher income countries, might be encouraged to bring manufacturing production back home. Also, an economy such as Ethiopia's is likely to have a greater number of easily automatable jobs where technology can replace human workers. The impact of automation may be potentially more disruptive for countries, such as Ethiopia, with little consumer demand and limited social safety nets.

Source: 'Rise of the robots threatens the poor', *Financial Times*, 26.1.2016

(a) With reference to extract A, explain the term 'frictional unemployment'. **(4 marks)**

(b) With reference to the information provided, discuss the likely impact of technological advances on Ethiopia's unemployment rate. **(14 marks)**

EXAM HINT

Use the 'Thinking like an economist' section for some ideas. Use extract A to identify what sort of unemployment might fall in Ethiopia as a result of technology. For extract B, explain clearly what sort of unemployment might be caused by advances in technology in Ethiopia. What effect will advances in technology in higher income countries have on Ethiopia's unemployment rate? Use the extract to help you analyse whether any impact on unemployment for Ethiopia will be significant. What will it depend upon?

2 High unemployment in Spain

European economies have been affected by the problems of high unemployment. Some of the worst hit European countries include Spain, Greece and Italy. For Spain, the rapid growth of the property sector in the 10 years before the financial crisis 2007/08 created huge demand for casual labour on building sites. In 2007, 2.7 million Spanish workers were active in the construction sector. This represented 13 per cent of the workforce and the construction sector accounted for more than 10 per cent of GDP.

When the property bubble burst, construction stopped on many sites and many low-skilled jobs vanished. These workers, many of whom had left school early, had limited employable skills useful to other industries. Since construction was a key industry in Spain, unemployment rose significantly and became a wider problem as the economy dropped into a recession lasting five years. Positive economic growth followed, but it was only in 2017 that GDP started to exceed its pre-crisis level. However, despite the sharp fall in unemployment, it was still high at 18.8 per cent in the first quarter of 2017. This is far above the pre-crisis level and almost double the eurozone average.

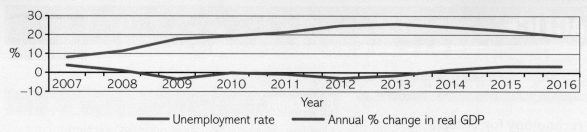

▲ Figure 5 Spanish annual real GDP percentage change rate and unemployment rate, 2007–16

Source: OECD

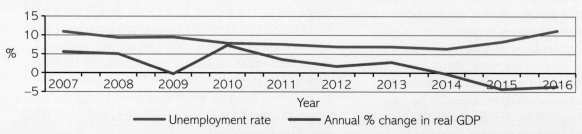

▲ Figure 6 Brazilian annual real GDP percentage change rate and unemployment rate, 2007–16

Source: OECD

(a) With reference to Figure 5 and the extract, analyse one possible cause of the rise in the rate of unemployment, between 2007 and 2013, in Spain. **(6 marks)**

(b) With reference to the information available, discuss the likely causes of Spain's higher unemployment, over the period shown, compared to Brazil. **(14 marks)**

EXAM HINT

The extract mentions that Spain was in a recession during this period, use Figure 5 to support this. Use Figure 6 to identify if Brazil experienced a recession too. Analyse how a fall in aggregate demand will affect unemployment. To evaluate, use Figures 5 and 6 to compare how the unemployment rate changes for both countries, over the period shown. Does the scale of the fall in aggregate demand for Spain seem consistent with such a dramatic increase in unemployment between 2007 and 2013? What other causes of unemployment for Spain are mentioned in the extract? Analyse these. To what extent are these likely to be significant causes?

3 Evaluate the likely costs of a sustained high level of unemployment on the Spanish economy. **(20 marks)**

EXAM HINT

Analyse the likely costs of unemployment. Evaluate the costs by considering what factors might affect the size of these costs. Can any of these costs be minimised, even if unemployment remains high? Are there any offsetting benefits? Does the scale of the costs depend on how long high unemployment lasts?

26 INFLATION (CAUSES AND EFFECTS)

LEARNING OBJECTIVES

- Understand the concepts of inflation, deflation and disinflation.
- Understand the causes of inflation.
- Understand the causes of deflation.
- Understand the effects of inflation and deflation.

GETTING STARTED

In 1923, Germany suffered a disastrous period of hyperinflation. Find out what caused it and what effect it had on German citizens and firms. Contrast this with Japan in the 1990s and 2000s. It suffered deflation. Find out what caused this and what effect it has had on the Japanese economy.

INFLATION, DEFLATION AND DISINFLATION

Inflation is defined as a sustained general rise in prices across an economy. The opposite of inflation is **deflation**. This is defined as a sustained general fall in prices across an economy. **Disinflation** is defined as a fall in the rate of inflation.

Hyperinflation, on the other hand, describes a situation where inflation levels are very high. There is no exact figure at which inflation becomes hyperinflation. However, annual inflation rates of 50 per cent or more would be classified as hyperinflation by most economists.

THE CAUSES OF INFLATION

Inflation can be caused by two main factors: too much demand in the economy or rising costs.

Demand-pull inflation In the market for oil, a significant rise in demand for oil with no increase in supply will lead to a rise in the price of oil. The same occurs at a macroeconomic level. If aggregate or total demand rises and there is no increase in aggregate supply, then **demand-pull inflation** is likely to occur. Demand-pull inflation is caused by excess demand in the economy. When there is too much demand, the **price**

level (or average level of prices in the economy) will rise. Excessive increases in aggregate demand in any economy can occur for a variety of reasons.

- Consumer spending may rise excessively. Interest rates could be low and consumers are spending large amounts on their credit cards, or consumer confidence could be rising because house prices are rising.

- Firms may substantially increase their spending on investment. Perhaps they are responding to large increases in demand from consumers and need extra capacity to satisfy that demand.

- The government might be increasing its spending substantially, or it could be cutting taxes.

- World demand for that country's exports may be rising because of a boom in the world economy.

Demand-pull inflation may also be caused by growth of the money supply. Both central banks and the banking system can influence the amount of borrowing and lending in the economy. If banks increase their lending to customers, the money supply will grow. Customers are likely to spend the money they have borrowed. The result will be increased aggregate demand. This can cause inflation. The most famous inflation caused by an increase in the money supply was Germany in 1923 when there was hyperinflation. Most examples of hyperinflation occur because the central bank lends money to the government, which uses it to pay its bills rather than raise taxes.

Figure 1 shows how an increase in aggregate demand in the short run leads to inflation. Aggregate demand increases from AD_1 to AD_2. The price level increases from P_1 to P_2, showing the inflationary impact of this increase in aggregate demand.

FIGURE 1

A rise in aggregate demand leads to demand-pull inflation

A rise in aggregate demand from AD_1 to AD_2 leads to an increase in prices of P_1P_2.

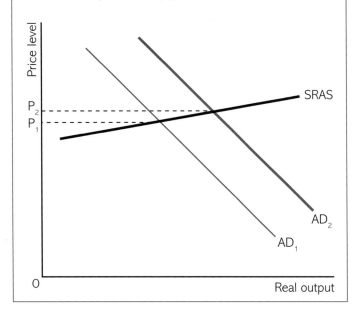

Cost-push inflation Inflation may also occur because of changes in the supply side of the economy. **Cost-push inflation** occurs because of rising costs. There are four major sources of increased costs.

- Wages and salaries are generally a high proportion of national income. An increase in wages will have a significant impact on costs of production.

- Imports can cause a rise in price. A boom in the world economy, for example, may push up commodity prices such as oil, copper and wheat. It will also push up the price of finished goods. This will lead to higher import prices for an economy.

- Profits can be increased by firms when they raise prices to improve profit margins. The more price inelastic the demand for their goods, the less will such behaviour result in a fall in demand for their products.

- Government can raise indirect tax rates or reduce subsidies, thus increasing prices.

Firms will try to pass on increases in their costs to customers. For example, if a firm gives a 5 per cent pay rise to its workers, and wages account for 80 per cent of its costs, then it will need to increase prices by 4 per cent (80 per cent of 5 per cent) to maintain its profit margins. Competition in the market may mean that it finds it difficult to pass on these price rises and maintain sales. However, if costs are rising over time, firms will have to increase their prices and this leads to inflation.

Figure 2 shows how a fall in short-run aggregate supply (SRAS) will lead to inflation. The SRAS curve is pushed up from $SRAS_1$ to $SRAS_2$, for example, by a rise in wage rates or a rise in import prices. The price level increases from P_1 to P_2, showing the inflation impact of this increase in SRAS.

Sometimes, inflation may be primarily demand-pull in nature. In other time periods, it may be mainly cost-push. In a stable but growing economy with no demand-side or supply-side shocks, inflation is likely to be caused by a mix of the two factors.

FIGURE 2

A fall in short-run aggregate supply leads to cost-push inflation

A shift upwards in short-run aggregate supply curve from $SRAS_1$ to $SRAS_2$ leads to an increase in prices of P_1P_2.

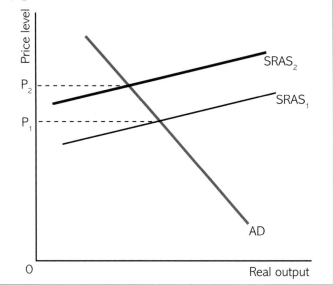

The effect of a fall in aggregate demand or an increase in aggregate supply (a downward shift in the SRAS caused by costs falling) will show the price level falling in an economy. For example, a fall in government spending, because it is a component of aggregate demand, will shift the AD curve to the left (see Figure 4). The price level will fall from P_1 to P_2. If the value of a currency rises on foreign exchange markets, this will make domestic goods more expensive for foreigners, so exports should fall. Again, the AD curve will shift to the left and the price level will fall from P_1 to P_2. However, in the real world, it is unlikely that the price level will actually fall. The diagram in this case will illustrate that demand-pull inflationary pressures have eased. So prices will still be rising, but at a slower rate. In the same way, a fall in some costs (shifting the SRAS curve to the right – see

Figure 3) will reduce cost push inflationary pressures as shown by the fall in the price level in the diagram.

For most economies, it is very rare to experience deflation. Deflation is when the price level is actually falling. Deflation is caused by falling aggregate demand (caused by a fall in any of the components of aggregate demand or a fall in the money supply) or falling costs (an increase in aggregate supply). A single factor, such as weaker exports, would have to have an effect that was greater than the other components of aggregate demand which would be rising, to cause deflation. This is why deflation is more likely if there is a significant negative output gap (there is significant unused productive potential in the economy so the economy is operating below full employment). In the same way, a fall in oil prices would have to be very significant to offset the other cost rises that normally occur in the economy, for example, positive wage growth, for deflation to occur. In this case the diagram, showing a fall in the price level, would show deflation.

FIGURE 4

A fall in aggregate demand, from AD$_1$ to AD$_2$, leads to a fall in the price level from P$_1$ to P$_2$.

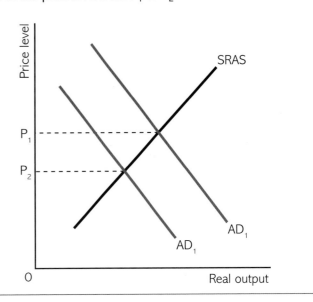

FIGURE 3

An increase in short-run aggregate supply, from SRAS$_1$ to SRAS$_2$, leads to a fall in the price level from P$_1$ to P$_2$.

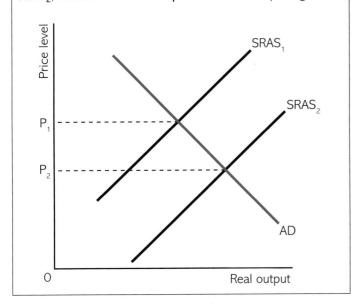

ACTIVITY 1   SKILLS ▷ COMMUNICATION, REASONING

CASE STUDY: HEADLINE INFLATION

In March 2017, the OECD reported that headline inflation was rising in most countries because of higher energy prices. OPEC had cut oil production as part of an agreement in November. Headline inflation includes price changes in food and energy. However, price changes in energy and food are very volatile. Excluding these price changes helps economists spot the overall trend in inflation over time (the underlying inflation rate). The OECD reported that the underlying rate in advanced economies was still low, but would increase slowly as global growth picked up.

(a) Using an AD/AS diagram, explain the effect of a rise in energy prices on headline inflation.

(b) Using an AD/AS diagram, explain the likely effect of an increase in global growth on the inflation rate for advanced economies.

Make sure your explanations clearly distinguish between demand-pull and cost-push inflation.

ACTIVITY 2

SKILLS COMMUNICATION, REASONING

CASE STUDY: UNEMPLOYMENT IN THE EUROZONE

In May 2017, the official eurozone unemployment rate was 9.5 per cent. However, a measure of labour market slack indicated that between 15 and 18 per cent of the eurozone workforce were without jobs or would like to work longer hours. With so many people unemployed or under employed, it makes it very difficult for workers to bargain for higher wages. With wage growth so low, it is not surprising that the eurozone is still experiencing very low inflation.

(a) Explain why eurozone inflation remains low (make sure you link the two causes of inflation to the context of the passage).

THE COSTS OF HIGH INFLATION

A sustained rise in the price level is generally considered to be a problem. The higher the rate of inflation the greater the economic cost. There is a number of reasons why this is the case.

Growth and unemployment High inflation is typically unpredictable. Both consumers and firms find it hard to predict what will be the rate of inflation next month or next year. This **unanticipated inflation** makes it difficult, if not impossible, for consumers and firms to plan for the future. Firms, for example, may reduce their investment because they are less willing to take risks in an unstable macroeconomic climate. Consumers may bring forward or reduce their purchases depending on what they think might be in their best interests. But this then disrupts patterns of spending in the whole economy, making it difficult for firms to supply goods. Economic disruption is likely to lead to lower levels of output and spending than would otherwise be the case. Lower economic growth or falling GDP then leads to higher unemployment.

Competitiveness High inflation can lead to a balance of payment effect. If inflation rises faster in one economy compared to others, and the value of the currency does not change on foreign currency markets, then exports will become less competitive and imports more competitive. This will cause a deficit on the balance of trade in goods and services on the current account to widen, or a surplus to narrow or move into a deficit. The result will be a loss of jobs in the domestic economy and lower growth.

Redistributional costs Inflation can redistribute income and wealth between households, firms and the state. This redistribution can occur in a variety of ways. For instance, anybody on a fixed income will suffer. In the UK, for example, many pensioners have received fixed pensions from private company pension schemes that are not adjusted for inflation. If prices double over a five-year period, their real income will be halved. Any group of workers that fails to be able to negotiate pay increases at least in line with inflation will suffer falls in its real income too.

If real interest rates are negative as a result of inflation, there will be a transfer of resources from lenders to borrowers. With interest rates at 10 per cent and inflation rates at 20 per cent, a saver will lose 10 per cent of the real value of saving each year while a borrower will see a 10 per cent real reduction in the value of debt per annum.

Taxes and government spending may not change in line with inflation. For instance, if the government's finance minster fails to increase tax on cigarettes each year in line with inflation, real government revenue will fall while smokers will be better off in real terms, assuming their incomes have risen at least by as much as inflation. Similarly, if the finance minister fails to increase personal income tax allowances (the amount that a worker can earn 'tax free') in line with inflation, then the burden of tax will increase, transferring resources from the taxpayer to the government.

Psychological and political costs Price increases are deeply unpopular. People feel that they are worse off, even if their incomes rise by more than the rate of inflation. High rates of inflation, particularly if they are unexpected, disturb the distribution of income and wealth as we shall discuss below, and therefore affect the existing social order greatly. Change and political upheaval in the past have often accompanied periods of high inflation.

Shoe-leather costs If prices are stable, consumers and firms come to have some knowledge of what is a fair price for a product and which suppliers are likely to charge less than others. At times of rising prices, consumers and firms will be less clear about what is a reasonable price. This will lead to more 'shopping around' (wearing out your shoes), which in itself is a cost.

High rates of inflation are also likely to lead to households and firms holding less cash and more interest-bearing deposits. Inflation decreases the value of cash, but since nominal interest rates tend to be higher than with stable prices, the opportunity cost of holding cash tends to be larger, the higher the rate of inflation. Households and firms are then forced to spend more time transferring money from one type of account to another or putting cash into an account to maximise the interest paid. This time is a cost.

Menu costs If there is inflation, restaurants have to change their menus to show increased prices. Similarly, shops have to change their price labels and firms have to calculate and issue new price lists. Even more costly are changes to fixed capital, such as automatic drinks machines and parking meters, to take account of price increases.

Some of these costs can be reduced if inflation can be predicted. **Anticipated inflation** allows economic actors to plan for the future and adjust their decision to take inflation into account. One way of doing this is through **indexation**. This is where economic variables like wages or taxes are increased in line with inflation. For instance, a union might negotiate a wage agreement with an employer for stepped increases over one year of 2 per cent plus the change in the consumer price index. The annual changes in welfare payments in an economy might be linked to the consumer price index.

Economists are divided about whether indexation provides a solution to the problem of inflation. On the one hand, it reduces many of the costs of inflation, although some costs such as shoe-leather costs and menu costs remain. On the other hand, it reduces pressure on government to tackle the problem of inflation directly. Indexation eases the pain of inflation but is not a cure for it.

Moreover, indexation may obstruct government attempts to reduce inflation because indexation builds in further cost increases, such as wage increases, which reflect past changes in prices. If a government wants to get inflation down to 2 per cent a year, and inflation has just been 10 per cent, it will not be helped in achieving its target if workers are all awarded at least 10 per cent wage increases because of indexation agreements.

ACTIVITY 3   SKILLS   COMMUNICATION, REASONING, ANALYSIS

CASE STUDY: INDIAN CPI

In March 2016, the IMF published a survey on India's economy. It stated that India's consumer price inflation had declined from an average of 10 per cent during the period 2009–13, to 5.6 per cent in December 2015. This reflected 'economic slack, an appropriately tight monetary policy stance by the Reserve Bank of India (this means money supply growth was restricted, which pushes up interest rates) and lower global commodity prices'.

(a) Using AD/AS diagrams, explain the causes of the fall in India's consumer price inflation over this period.

(b) Explain two likely problems for the Indian economy of a high inflation rate over the period 2009–13.

ACTIVITY 4   SKILLS   COMMUNICATION, REASONING, ANALYSIS

CASE STUDY: EFFECTS OF RISE IN THE CPI

In 2012, the UK's consumer price index rose by 2.8 per cent and in 2013 by 2.6 per cent.

1. How might the following have been affected in real terms by the change?

(a) A pensioner on a fixed income.

(b) A bank deposit saver, given that the rate of interest on a bank deposit saving account was 0.5 per cent in both 2012 and 2013.

(c) A worker whose personal income tax allowance was £8105 between April 2012 and March 2013 and £9440 between April 2013 and April 2014.

(d) A parent with one child who received £20.30 per week in child benefit in both 2012 and 2013.

THE COSTS OF DEFLATION

Over the past 50 years, the main problem that countries have faced is high rates of inflation. However, there can also be problems associated with deflation of falling price levels. For example, between 1995 and 2014, Japan experienced nine years of falling prices. This might seem insignificant, but it had a serious impact on the Japanese economy. Falling prices were caused mainly by a lack of demand in the economy. However, they also caused demand to be depressed.

With falling prices, consumer confidence tends to be low. Consumers are concerned about the future and know that if they do not buy today, they might be able to buy at a cheaper price tomorrow. They will therefore reduce consumption, causing aggregate demand to fall. A lack of consumer confidence and falling sales then feeds into a lack of business confidence and lower investment. This sets off a negative multiplier effect. Although interest rates tend to be very low with deflation, the real cost of borrowing is higher. If prices fall by, say, 1 per cent, then the real cost of borrowing is the actual or nominal interest rate plus 1 per cent.

The other major problem with deflation is the effect on asset values. Savers can see the real value of their savings grow even if they only receive 1 or 2 per cent interest. If prices fall by 2 per cent and they receive 1 per cent interest, then the real rate of return on their savings is 3 per cent. Deflation encourages households to save rather than spend and this leads to low or negative rates of economic growth. For borrowers, deflation leads to the real value of their debt increasing. This will discourage households and firms from borrowing and spending and so reduce aggregate demand.

The fall in aggregate demand is likely to cause cyclical unemployment, particularly as workers are reluctant to accept a nominal wage cut.

Some groups in society may benefit from deflation, particularly those on fixed incomes, because their real income will rise when prices fall. Savers will also gain as mentioned above. Firms who target export markets may also gain as their goods become more price competitive on international markets. However, firms will experience a fall in domestic demand that is likely to affect most domestic firms in an economy. Although consumers may initially benefit from a fall in prices (their real incomes rise so their purchasing power increases), the long-run impact will not be beneficial if the fall in aggregate demand causes significant job losses. Overall, the costs of deflation are likely to be high and is a situation governments seek to avoid.

THE BENEFITS OF LOW INFLATION

Many central banks today set a target for inflation of around 2 per cent. This is a very low rate of inflation but it is still a positive increase in prices.

The reason why 2 per cent is considered desirable is because this is not deflation but nor is it a significant rate of inflation. An inflation rate of 2 per cent avoids the problems associated with high inflation and deflation. It gives policymakers, such as central banks and governments, room to adjust the economy if inflation goes higher or lower. If annual inflation is 0.5 per cent, it is a signal that the rate of growth of aggregate demand needs to increase to avoid the risk of price growth becoming negative. If inflation is 4 per cent, it is a signal that growth in aggregate demand needs to decrease to avoid the risk of the inflation rate increasing even further.

Another reason why 2 per cent is considered desirable is because of its effect on assets prices. At 2 per cent, the real value of borrowing falls gradually over time. This is seen as desirable because it makes it easier for those who borrow to finance consumption or investment to repay their borrowings. It also does not impact much on the incentive to save because it is argued that savers do not take the real erosion of their savings into account. They suffer from money illusion, thinking that inflation is 0.

THINKING LIKE AN ECONOMIST

DEFLATION FEARS FOR THE EUROZONE

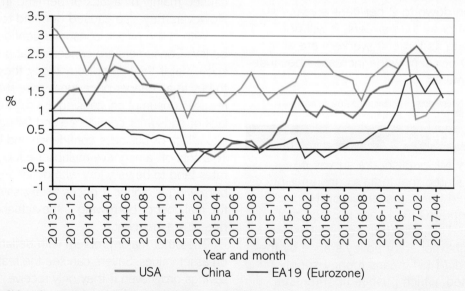

▲ Figure 5 Inflation in China, the eurozone and USA, October 2013–April 2017

In 2014, there were fears that the eurozone was heading for deflation. By October 2014, prices were falling in eight European countries. The eurozone's overall inflation rate had fallen to 0.3 per cent. There was also concern that China and the USA's inflation was falling to dangerously low levels.

One of the causes of the fall in inflationary pressures over this period came from the fall in the price of oil. Between the middle of 2014 to January 2016, oil prices fell by 70 per cent. Such a fall in energy costs, which affect most business costs, will reduce cost-push inflationary pressures in most economies. Another cause of the fall in inflationary pressures across most of the OECD member countries was relatively weak demand. This will reduce demand-pull inflationary pressures.

However, the eurozone is more exposed to the risk of deflation than others. Figure 5 shows the eurozone's inflation rate was around 0 per cent, both positive and negative, for nearly two years. Even when eurozone member economies are contracting, there is still a policy of budget deficit reduction. This means governments are forced to commit to reducing government spending and raising taxation (to keep budget deficits as a percentage of GDP within 3 per cent), even when economic growth is low or negative. This commitment will further reduce aggregate demand and makes deflation more likely.

The problem with deflation is that it can stick. If prices start to fall, people and firms will start to believe that prices will continue to fall, so they will stop spending. It is better to spend later when prices are lower than today. This means aggregate demand will start to fall, further causing deflation. There is no easy way out of the cycle. A fall in prices means a fall in revenues for businesses. This makes it harder for businesses to pay off old debts. If aggregate demand falls as spending is delayed, national income falls and the government will raise less tax revenue. This puts more strain on public finances.

The good news was that by January 2017, after two years of unusually low price pressures, inflation is set to return to target levels.

After 54 months of declining producer prices in China, prices at the factory gate rose by 5.5 per cent in the year to December 2016. This is a signal that CPI inflation in China will rise in the future (there is a time delay between a rise in producer price index and the consumer price index). Higher prices for goods and services imported from China will cause imported inflation to rise among the advanced economies. Economic growth rates in China were also picking up in early 2017. Since China is such a large economy, this will significantly increase demand for global commodities. Commodity prices will rise. This will cause cost-push inflation for most economies. Combined with this, oil prices have risen steadily since January 2016, further increasing cost-push inflation.

Across Asia and in the 'rich' world, aggregate demand is also picking up. Many economies are working with less spare capacity and moving towards full employment. So this combination puts more upward pressure on prices and removes the fear of deflation. However, some countries, such as Italy, Spain and Greece, still have ample spare capacity. Unemployment rates were, respectively, 11.5, 18.2 and 22.5 per cent in quarter 1 of 2017. This means the threat of deflation in the eurozone may not be over yet.

CHECKPOINT

1 What are deflation and disinflation?

2 Create an AD/AS diagram to show demand-pull inflation.

3 Create an AD/AS diagram to show cost-push inflation.

4 State what is likely to happen to inflation if the money supply increases.

5 State two causes of deflation.

6 State how inflation might affect the government.

7 State how inflation might affect income distribution.

8 How might deflation affect levels of investment?

9 How might inflation affect the current account on the balance of payments?

10 Why do many central banks set an inflation target around 2 per cent?

SUBJECT VOCABULARY

anticipated inflation increases in prices that economic actors are able to predict with accuracy.

cost-push inflation inflation caused by increases in the costs of production in the economy.

deflation a fall in the price level.

demand-pull inflation inflation that is caused by excess demand in the economy.

disinflation a fall in the rate of inflation.

hyperinflation large increases in the price level.

indexation adjusting the value of economic variables such as wages or the rate of interest in line with inflation.

inflation a general rise in prices.

price level the average price of goods and services in the economy.

unanticipated inflation increases in prices that economic actors like consumers and firms fail to predict accurately and so their decisions are based on poor information.

EXAM PRACTICE

INFLATION

SKILLS REASONING, INTERPRETATION, ANALYSIS, CRITICAL THINKING

Q

1 Figure 6 shows Japan's consumer price inflation between 2011 and 2017.

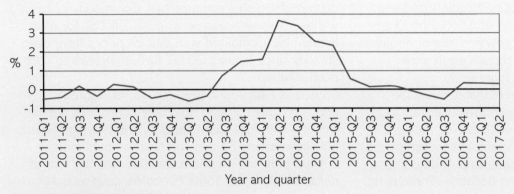

▲ Figure 6 Japanese CPI, 2011–17

Source: OECD

(a) Which one of the following is most likely to explain the data.

   A Oil prices rose between 2014 and 2016.

   B Aggregate demand was falling from 2016 onwards.

   C In April 2014 Japan raised its sales tax from 5 to 8 per cent.

   D Unemployment was falling from 2014 onwards.
                                           (1 mark)

(b) With reference to Figure 6, explain the term 'deflation'.   **(4 marks)**

2 By September 2017, inflation across emerging markets had fallen to its lowest level on record. Since 1996, emerging market-wide inflation had fallen from 20 per cent to a record low of 2.5 per cent in July 2017. However, while no one was expecting a return to very high inflation rates, except for a limited number of countries, there was a belief that the disinflationary trend may be at an end. For example, consumer price inflation in Turkey jumped to 10.7 per cent in the year to August 2017, up from 9.8 per cent a month earlier. In Mexico, inflation went from 6.4 to 6.7 per cent, an 18-year high.

(a) With reference to the information above, explain the term 'disinflation'.   **(4 marks)**

3 Singapore's inflation

In September 2017, the Monetary Authority of Singapore (MAS) expected that economic growth in 2017 would be stronger than 2016. Economic growth in 2016 was 2 per cent. Real GDP growth in 2017 was expected to be between 2 and 3 per cent. However, the MAS reported that demand-pull inflationary pressures would be weak, as excess supply remained in the labour market. It was also expected that any change in price pressures, due to slightly improved economic conditions, would only come only after a time delay.

(a) With reference to the extract, examine the likely impact on Singapore's inflation rate of the expected rise in aggregate demand in 2017.
                                          (8 marks)

EXAM HINT

Use a short-run AD/AS diagram – consider which AS curve to use. Is the economy close to full employment? If there is excess supply in the labour market, what does this suggest about wage bargaining powers? For evaluation, use the last sentence in the extract to give you an idea what to discuss.

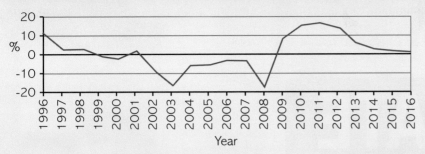

▲ Figure 7 Zimbabwean real GDP growth, 1996–2016

Source: World Bank

4 Swapping hyperinflation for deflation with the use of the US dollar: Zimbabwe

From the late 1990s, Zimbabwe's inflation rate was out of control. By 2008, annual inflation in Zimbabwe had peaked at 89.7 sextillion per cent – that's roughly 9 followed by 22 zeros. A single egg could cost well over ZWD 1 billion (Zimbabwean dollar), assuming one could be found. Zimbabwe was so deeply damaged by its years of severe hyperinflation, even the central bank could no longer afford the paper to print practically worthless trillion-dollar notes.

As a result, authorities stopped printing the Zimbabwe dollar in 2009 and moved to a hard currency system, dominated by the US dollar. Having swapped the world's weakest currency for its strongest, Zimbabwe began to import deflation. According to best estimates, consumer prices fell between 2 and 4 per cent in 2015. The prices of goods coming from South Africa, across the border, where the rand (South Africa's currency, ZAR) had fallen by nearly one-third against the dollar in 2015, have dropped enormously.

There is concern that this will send the country into a cycle of shrinking demand and falling production. Use of industrial capacity had already fallen from 57 per cent in 2011, to just 34 per cent in 2015, according to the Confederation of Zimbabwe industries. It was likely that companies would be forced to lay off staff or stop paying wages due to cash shortages. It was unclear how long deflation would last. The government does not have the tools to increase economic activity. For example, the government, which spends nearly 90 per cent of its revenue on salaries, would find it difficult to finance more government spending to inject money into the circular flow of income.

(a) Explain the likely impact on Zimbabwe's inflation rate of the fall in the value of the South African rand (ZAR) against the US dollar. **(4 marks)**

(b) With reference to the extract and Figure 7, examine the likely impact of deflation on Zimbabwe's economy. **(8 marks)**

EXAM HINT

Make sure you use the extract and Figure 7. Integrate economic terms, such as 'circular flow of income' and aggregate demand. Use Figure 7 to show the effect on the economy so far. What will be the impact on unemployment? You need to include some evaluation for 2 marks. Is it possible to reverse the trend? Will the impact be as bad as the previous hyperinflation period?

5 Annual consumer prices were rising fast in Turkey over the first four months of 2017. Turkey's economy was battling with a sharply falling lira and rising energy prices. The rise in costs was pushing up prices.

Source: *Financial Times*, 'Turkish inflation accelerated to 11% in March', 3.4.2017

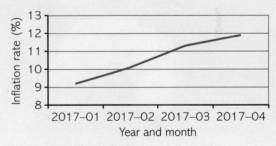

▲ Figure 8 Turkey's CPI inflation rate

(a) With reference to the extract and Figure 8, analyse one cause of rising inflation in Turkey, over this period. **(6 marks)**

EXAM HINT

Use a short-run AD/AS diagram to support your answer. Explain clearly why a fall in the value of the lira and rising energy prices will cause cost-push inflation. Make reference to Figure 8.

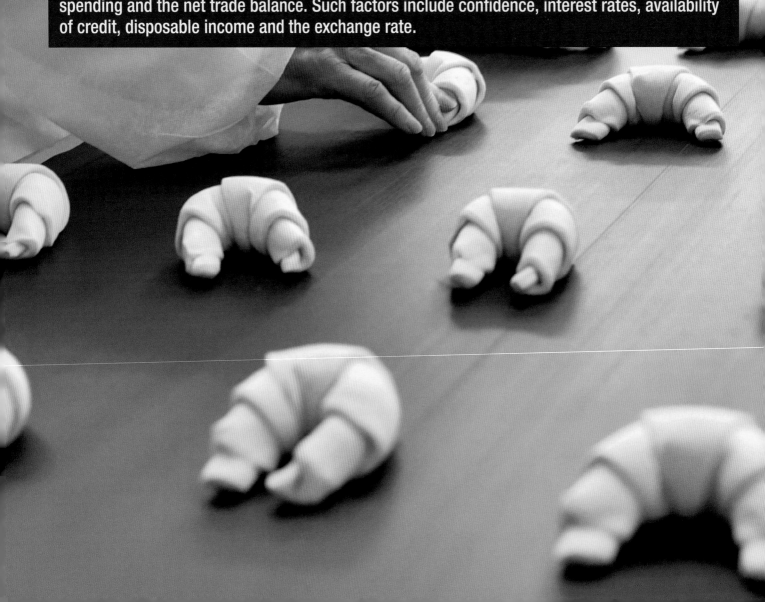

AGGREGATE DEMAND

Understanding what affects total spending in an economy is crucial for economists and policymakers. The section starts by introducing aggregate demand and its components. It explains the concept of the aggregate demand curve and why the aggregate demand curve may shift. It fully explores factors that influence consumer spending, investment, government spending and the net trade balance. Such factors include confidence, interest rates, availability of credit, disposable income and the exchange rate.

27 CHARACTERISTICS OF AGGREGATE DEMAND

UNIT 2
2.3.2

LEARNING OBJECTIVES

■ Know that the aggregate demand curve is downward sloping. It shows the relationship between the price level and equilibrium output in the economy.

■ Understand that a movement along the aggregate demand curve shows how real output will change if there is a change in the price level.

■ Understand that a shift in the aggregate demand curve is caused by a change in variables, such as consumption and exports at any given price level.

GETTING STARTED

GDP records total spending in an economy. Search the Internet to find out what is happening to GDP for an economy of your choice. Pick newspaper articles to read. Is total spending (GDP) increasing? If so, how much has it been increasing? What is household spending called? Is investment increasing? How much are foreigners spending on goods and services produced in that economy?

AGGREGATE DEMAND

Demand for an individual good is defined as the quantity that is bought at any given price. In this chapter, we will consider what determines **aggregate** demand. 'Aggregate' in economics means a 'total' or 'added up' amount. **Aggregate demand** is the total of all demands or expenditures in the economy at any given price. National expenditure is one of the three ways of calculating national income, usually measured as GDP. National expenditure is made up of four components.

- **Consumption (C)** This is spending by households on goods and services.
- **Investment (I)** This is spending by firms on investment goods.
- **Government spending (G)** This includes current spending, for instance on wages and salaries. It also includes spending by government on investment goods like new roads or new schools.
- **Exports minus imports (X – M)** Foreigners spend money on goods produced in the **domestic economy**. Hence it is part of national expenditure. However, households, firms and governments

also spend money on goods produced abroad. For instance, a Taiwanese household might buy a car produced in Japan, or an Indian firm might use components imported from East Asia in a computer that is sold to Germany. These imported goods do not form part of national output and do not contribute to national income. So, because C, I, G and X all include spending on imported goods, imports (M) must be taken away from $C + I + G + X$ to calculate a figure for national expenditure.

National expenditure or aggregate demand (AD) can therefore be calculated using the formula:
$$AD = C + I + G + X - M$$

ACTIVITY 1   SKILLS   REASONING, COMMUNICATION

CASE STUDY: COMPONENTS OF AGGREGATE DEMAND

In 2014, consumption, as a percentage of GDP, was 34 per cent in China and 57 per cent in France. In the same year, exports minus imports represented –2 per cent in France and 3 per cent in China.

(a) What formula is used to calculate aggregate demand?

(b) What is the relationship between exports and imports for France? How does this compare to China?

(c) Why is it likely that China's investment spending, as a percentage of GDP, is higher than France's?

THE AGGREGATE DEMAND CURVE

The **aggregate demand curve** shows the relationship between the price level and the level of real expenditure in the economy. Figure 1 shows an aggregate demand (AD) curve. The price level is put on the vertical axis while real output is put on the horizontal axis.

The price level is the average level of prices in the economy. Governments calculate a number of different measures of the price level.

The consumer price index (CPI) is used as a key indicator of how much prices are changing in an economy. It is produced to international standards, so comparisons can be made between countries. A change in the price level is inflation.

Real output on the horizontal axis must equal real expenditure and real income. This is because, in the circular flow model of the economy, these are three different ways of measuring the same flow. The aggregate demand curve plots the level of expenditure where the economy would be in an equilibrium position at each price level, all other things being equal.

Demand curves are nearly always downward sloping. Why is the aggregate demand curve the same shape? One simple answer is to consider what happens to a household budget if prices rise. If a household is on a fixed income, then a rise in average prices will mean that they can buy fewer goods and services than before. The higher the price level in the economy, the less they can afford to buy. So it is with the national economy. The higher the price, the fewer goods and services will be demanded in the whole economy.

A more sophisticated explanation considers what happens to the different components of expenditure when prices rise.

Consumption Consumption expenditure is influenced by the rate of interest in the economy. When prices increase, consumers (and firms) need more money to buy the same number of goods and services as before. One way of getting more money is to borrow it and so the demand for borrowed funds will rise. However, if there is a fixed supply of money available for borrowing from banks and building societies, the price of borrowed funds will rise. This price is the rate of interest. A rise in interest rates leads to a fall in consumption, particularly of durable goods, such as cars, which are commonly bought on credit.

Another way a rise in the price level affects consumption is through the **wealth effect**. A rise in the price level leads to the real value of an individual consumer's wealth being lower. For instance, €100,000 at today's prices will be worth less in real terms in a year's time if average prices have increased 20 per cent over the 12 months. A fall in real wealth will result in a fall in consumer spending.

Investment As has just been explained, a rise in prices, assuming that other factors remain the same, leads to a rise in interest rates in the economy. Investment is affected by changes in the rate of interest. The higher the rate of interest, the less profitable new investment projects become and therefore the fewer projects will be undertaken by firms. So, the higher the rate of interest, the lower will be the level of investment.

Government spending Government spending in this model of the economy is assumed to be independent of economic variables. It is exogenously determined, fixed by variables outside the model. In this case, it is assumed to be determined by the political decisions of the government of the day. Note that government spending (G) here does not include transfer payments. These are payments by the government for which there is no corresponding output in the economy, like welfare payments.

Exports and imports A higher price level an economy means that foreign firms will be able to compete more successfully. For instance, if South African shoe manufacturers put up their prices by 20 per cent, while foreign shoe manufacturers keep their prices the same, then South African shoe manufacturers will become less competitive and more foreign shoes will be imported. Equally, South African shoe manufacturers will find it more difficult to export charging higher prices. So a higher South African price level, with price levels in other economies staying the same, will lead to a fall in South African exports.

Hence, aggregate demand falls as prices rise, first, because increases in interest rates reduce

---

FIGURE 1

The aggregate demand curve
A rise in the price level will lead to a fall in the equilibrium level of national income and therefore of national output. Hence the aggregate demand curve is downward sloping.

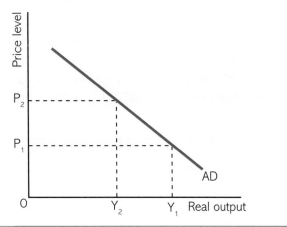

consumption and investment and, second, because a loss of international competitiveness at the new higher prices will reduce exports and increase imports.

SHIFTS IN THE AD CURVE

The aggregate demand (AD) curve shows the relationship between the price level and the equilibrium level of real income and output. A change in the price level results in a movement along the AD curve. Higher prices lead to falls in aggregate demand.

Shifts in the aggregate demand curve will occur if there is a change in any other relevant variable apart from the price level. When the AD curve shifts, it shows that there is a change in real output at any given price level. In Figure 2, the shift in the AD curve from AD_1 to AD_2 shows that at a price level of P, real output increases from Y_1 to Y_2. A number of variables can lead to a shift of the AD curve. Some of these variables are real variables, such as changes in the willingness of consumers to spend. Others are changes in monetary variables such as the rate of interest.

Consumption A number of factors might increase consumption spending at any given level of prices, shifting the AD curve from AD_1 to AD_2 in Figure 2. For instance, unemployment may fall, making consumers less afraid that they will lose their jobs and more willing to borrow money to spend on consumer durables. The government or central bank might reduce interest rates, again encouraging borrowing for durables. A substantial rise in stock market prices will increase consumer wealth, which in turn may lead to an increase in spending.

A reduction in the relative numbers of high saving 45–60-year-olds in the population will increase the **average propensity to consume** (the proportion of total income that is spent) of the whole economy. New technology, which creates new consumer products, can lead to an increase in consumer spending as households want to buy these new products. A fall in income tax would increase consumers' disposable income, leading to a rise in consumption.

Investment One factor that would increase investment spending at any given level of prices, pushing the AD curve from AD_1 to AD_2 in Figure 2, would be an increase in business confidence – an increase in 'animal spirits', as the economist John Maynard Keynes put it. This increase in business confidence could occur, for instance, because the economy was starting to grow rapidly. A fall in interest rates ordered by the government would lead to a rise in investment. An increase in company profitability would give firms more retained profit to use for investment. A fall in taxes on profits would lead to the rate of return on investment projects rising, leading to a rise in investment.

Government spending Government spending can change automatically because of previous government spending commitments, or the government can announce changes to its spending. A rise in government spending with no change in taxation will lead to a fall in its budget surplus or a rise in its deficit. This will increase aggregate demand, pushing the AD curve to the right from AD_1 to AD_2 in Figure 2. A fall in government spending with no change in taxation will lead to a shift to the left in the aggregate demand curve.

Exports and imports A number of factors can affect the balance between exports and imports. For example, a rise in the exchange rate is likely to lead to lower exports but higher imports. Exports minus imports will therefore fall, reducing aggregate demand. This is shown by a shift in the aggregate demand curve to the left. In contrast, an improvement in innovation and quality of manufactured goods is likely to lead to a rise in exports. This will increase aggregate demand and shift the aggregate demand curve to the right from AD_1 to AD_2 in Figure 2.

FIGURE 2

A shift in the aggregate demand curve
An increase in consumption, investment, government spending or net exports, given a constant price level, will lead to a shift in the aggregate demand curve from AD_1 to AD_2.

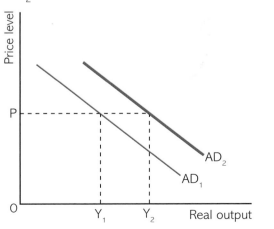

ACTIVITY 2

SKILLS ▶ PROBLEM-SOLVING, REASONING, INTERPRETATION

CASE STUDY: AGGREGATE DEMAND CURVE

1. Explain, using a diagram, the likely effect of the following on the aggregate demand curve for the individual economies mentioned. Assume a factor other than price has caused the change.

(a) The increase in real household consumption by 3.7 per cent in Chile in 2013.

(b) Real investment, by the private and the public sector, in the Netherlands is forecast to rise by 4.2 per cent in 2018.

(c) The fall in long-term interest rates for the USA of approximately 2.8 per cent to 1.5 per cent between 2014 and 2016 (long-term interest rates affect borrowing costs for firms).

(d) The value of the British pound falling by 17.1 per cent against the US dollar between 23 June 2016 and January 2017 after the Brexit announcement (UK).

(e) Housing market crashes in countries such as the UK and the USA during the financial crisis of 2007/08.

(f) An improvement in the current account surplus for Slovenia in 2016 to record levels.

IMPORTANT NOTES

Changes and shifts in AD Aggregate demand and aggregate supply analysis is more complex than demand and supply analysis in an individual market. You may already have noticed, for instance, that a change in interest rates could lead to a movement along the aggregate demand curve or lead to a shift in the curve. Similarly, an increase in consumption could lead to a movement along or a shift in the curve. To distinguish between movements along and shifts in the curve it is important to consider what has caused the change in aggregate demand.

If the change has occurred because the price level has changed, then there is a movement along the AD curve. For instance, a rise in the price level causes a rise in interest rates. This leads to a fall in consumption. This is shown by a movement up the curve.

If, however, interest rates or consumer spending have changed for a different reason than because prices have changed, then there will be a shift in the AD curve. A government or central bank putting up interest rates at a given price level would lead to a shift in the curve.

Levels and changes As with any economic analysis, it is important to distinguish between absolute changes and rates of change. For example, a fall in the level of investment will lead to a fall in aggregate demand, assuming that other factors remain the same. However, a fall in the rate of change of investment, when this rate of change is positive, means that investment is still rising. If growth in investment has fallen from 5 per cent to 3 per cent, investment is still increasing. So a fall in the rate of growth of investment will lead to an increase in aggregate demand and a shift of the AD curve to the right.

THINKING LIKE AN ECONOMIST

UK AGGREGATE DEMAND

Aggregate demand (AD) is made up of private sector consumption (C), private sector investment (I), government spending (G) and exports (X) minus imports (M). Figure 3 shows the composition of UK aggregate demand in 2013. In that year, 65 per cent of GDP was made up of private consumption expenditure, the largest single component of aggregate demand. Private sector investment was the smallest component at 15 per cent of GDP. 23 per cent was government spending on current spending, such as teachers' salaries, and investment, such as new road building. Exports were 30 per cent of GDP but the overall balance of X − M was negative because imports were even higher at 32 per cent of GDP. The contribution of net exports (exports minus imports) to aggregate demand is extremely small. Between 1997 and 2013, net exports varied from +0.7 per cent to −4.2 per cent of aggregate demand.

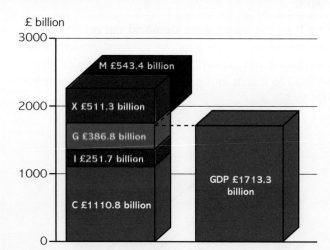

▲ **Figure 3 GDP and its components, 2013**

Source: adapted from www.ons.gov.uk

Figure 4 shows how aggregate demand and its components have changed over time at constant prices. The period 1997 to 2007 saw a significant rise in aggregate demand. However, the financial crisis of 2008 ended this growth. Between 2008 and 2013 the UK suffered the longest period without economic growth since the 19th century, longer even than the Great Depression of the 1930s.

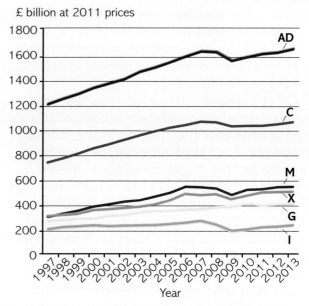

£ billion at 2011 prices

▲ Figure 4 Aggregate demand and its components, 1997–2013

Source: adapted from www.ons.gov.uk

Slovenia

SLOVENIA'S AGGREGATE DEMAND (GDP)

Slovenia is located between the Balkans and Western Europe. Slovenia's aggregate demand (GDP) is shown in Table 1.

National expenditure GDP or aggregate demand is published 'at current prices' or 'at constant prices'. For example, in Table 1, GDP at 'current prices' records the value of total spending in Slovenia, using the actual prices that existed that year. Between 2013 and 2014, GDP at current prices increased by €1415 million.

	2008	2009	2010	2011	2012	2013	2014	2015
GDP at current prices	37,951	36,166	36,252	36,896	36,002	35,917	37,332	38,570
GDP at constant 2010 prices	38,837	35,809	36,252	36,488	35,507	35,121	36,212	37,050

▲ Table 1 Slovenian aggregate demand, 2008–15 (€ million)

Source: OECD

Actual expenditure has risen by 3.9 per cent. However, actual spending is likely to have increased partly because prices rise over time. Economists will want to know to what extent the change in spending is real (reflects an increase in volume or quantity of good and services bought).

GDP at 'constant 2010 prices,' has taken the volume of spending in each year, but valued it using the prices that exist in 2010. This means GDP at constant prices will show how real spending has changed over time. The data has been adjusted for the effects of inflation. For example, real spending in Slovenia increased by 3.1 per cent in 2014. [(36,212 − 35,121) / 35,121 × 100]. Figure 5 shows the economic growth rates for Slovenia for the years 2009–18.

In 2013, the economic growth rate was −1 per cent. Real spending was 1 per cent lower in 2013 than 2012. Figure 6 shows how each of the components of aggregate demand contributed to this decrease. The fall in real household consumption was the main factor driving down aggregate demand in 2013. There was export led growth and investment acting to increase aggregate demand. However, the overall effect of the changes in the components of aggregate demand meant real GDP fell by 1 per cent.

The financial crisis of 2008/09 resulted in Slovenia's real GDP shrinking by a severe 7.8 per cent in 2009 and negative growth also for 2012 and 2013 (−2.3 per cent and −1 per cent). However, the outlook for 2017 and 2018 is positive. In 2018, real

GDP should rise by 2.3 per cent. This will be driven largely by an increase in consumption and investment.

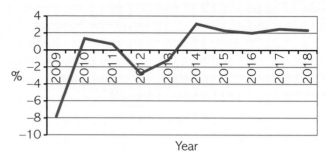

▲ **Figure 5 Slovenian economic growth, 2009–18**
Source: OECD, 'Economic Outlook', 2016, Issue 2 (2016, 2017, 2018 are forecast years)

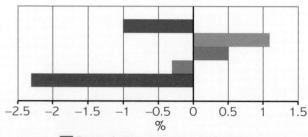

■ Rate of growth in real GDP 2013
■ Net exports (exports − imports)
■ Investment by private sector and government
■ Government spending on day to day items (known as government construction)
■ Consumption (household consumption)

▲ **Figure 6 Slovenian components of aggregate demand, 2013**
Sources: OECD: 'National accounts at a glance' 2015; other sources; CIA Factbook

CHECKPOINT

1 What does aggregate demand mean?

2 State the components of aggregate demand.

3 What can cause consumption to rise at each and every price level?

4 State how business confidence affects investment.

5 What might happen to the exchange rate to cause exports to rise?

6 What happens to aggregate demand if government spending rises?

7 Create an aggregate demand curve.

8 List reasons why the aggregate demand curve may shift to the left.

SUBJECT VOCABULARY

aggregate the sum or total.

aggregate demand the total of all demand or expenditure in the economy at any given price.

aggregate demand curve shows the relationship between the price level and equilibrium national income. As the price level rises, the equilibrium level of national income falls.

average propensity to consume the proportion of total income spent. It is calculated by C ÷ Y.

domestic economy the economy of a single country.

wealth effect the change in consumption following a change in wealth.

EXAM PRACTICE

AGGREGATE DEMAND

SKILLS PROBLEM SOLVING, REASONING, INTERPRETATION, ANALYSIS

Q

1 Table 2 shows the components of aggregate demand for Indonesia, 2013.

		Expenditure (market prices), 2013, IDR trillion
Total domestic demand	$C + I + G$	9622
Exports	X	2284
Imports	M	2359

▲ **Table 2 Indonesian components of aggregate demand, 2013**
IDR = Indonesian rupiah   Source: OECD

(a) Calculate exports as a percentage of Indonesia's GDP in 2013. **(4 marks)**

EXAM HINT

First calculate GDP at market prices, using the data in the table, by using the formula for aggregate demand. Then calculate exports as a percentage of GDP.

2 Which one of the following is most likely to cause a shift to the left of the aggregate demand curve.

(a) A rise in the price level.

(b) An increase in business confidence.

(c) A fall in government spending, with no change in taxation.

(d) A fall in imports, caused by a switch in spending to higher quality domestic goods. **(1 mark)**

3 Spain has been through difficult times since the world financial crisis of 2008. Aggregate demand in 2014 had still not reached its 2007 levels. However, in 2013 there was a significant rise in exports and, in 2014, consumption and investment began to increase after several years of negative growth.

(a) With reference to the information above, explain the term 'aggregate demand'. **(4 marks)**

4 Japan's total expenditure

In 2017, Japan recorded its longest run of sustained growth in real GDP in more than a decade. By March 2017, there had been five quarters of continuous expansion in GDP. The increase in aggregate demand was well balanced across the components of aggregate demand, with consumption and exports the biggest driving forces. Weakness in consumer spending had been one of Japan's biggest problems in recent years. The increase in consumption suggests consumers may finally be gaining confidence that higher wages will last.

(a) With reference to the extract, explain the term 'components of aggregate demand'. **(4 marks)**

EXAM HINT

Explain the term 'components of aggregate demand'. Make sure you use the information in the extract to comment on how the components of aggregate demand have changed for Japan over the recent period.

28 CONSUMPTION

LEARNING OBJECTIVES

- Know that consumption can be divided into spending on durable goods and non-durable goods.
- Understand that the consumption function shows the relationship between consumption and its determinants, the main one being disposable income.
- Understand that consumption is also affected by changes in interest rates, consumer confidence, level of welfare payments, wealth, the availability of credit, inflation and the composition of households.
- Know that the factors that influence consumption also influence savings.
- Understand that the relationship between total household savings in an economy and total disposable income is called the savings ratio.
- Understand that the savings ratio can change over time. You should know different reasons why the savings ratio might change.
- Know that changes in the savings ratio will have an impact on an economy.

GETTING STARTED

What is the most important factor in determining how much you spend? An allowance or pocket money given to you by parents? Wages from a paid job? Access to borrowed money? Your wealth in the form of savings? Confidence about your future income and wealth? The prices of goods you buy? Taking advantage of a discount?

DEFINING CONSUMPTION AND SAVING

Consumption in economics is spending on consumer goods and services over a period of time. Examples are spending on chocolate, tablets or mobile phones, or buying a car. Consumption can be broken down into a number of different categories. One way of classifying consumption is to distinguish between spending on goods and spending on services. Another way is to distinguish between spending on **durable goods** and **non-durable goods**. Durable goods are goods that, although bought at a point in time, continue to provide a stream of services over a period of time. A car, for instance, should last at least

six years. A television set might last 10 years. Non-durable goods are goods and services that are used up immediately or over a short period of time, like an ice cream or a packet of soap powder.

Saving is what is not spent out of income. For instance, if a Malaysian takes home MYR 1000 (Malaysian ringgit) in her wage packet at the end of the month, but only spends MYR 850, then MYR 150 must have been saved. The saving might take the form of increasing the stock of cash, or an increase in money in a bank or building society account, or it might take the form of stocks or shares. Income in this case is **disposable income**. Disposable income is income after any taxes on income have been deducted (taken away). All income is included, for example, any welfare payments received by individuals from the government.

CONSUMPTION AND DISPOSABLE INCOME

There is a number of factors that determine how much a household consumes. The relationship between consumption and these factors is called the **consumption function**. The most important determinant of, or influence on, consumption is disposable income. Other factors, discussed in sections below, are far less important but can bring about small but significant changes in the relationship between consumption and income.

Assume that one year a Malaysian household has an income of MYR 1000 per month. The next year, due to salary increases, this rises to MYR 1200 per month. Economic theory predicts that the consumption of the household will rise.

How much it will rise can be measured by the **marginal propensity to consume** (MPC), the proportion of a change in income that is spent:

$$\text{MPC} = \frac{\text{Change in consumption}}{\text{Change in income}} = \frac{\Delta C}{\Delta Y}$$

where Y is income, C is consumption and Δ is 'change in'.

If the MYR 200 rise in income leads to a MYR 150 rise in consumption, then the marginal propensity to consume would be 0.75 (MYR 150 ÷ MYR 200).

For the economy as a whole, the marginal propensity to consume is likely to be positive (i.e. greater than 0) but less than 1. Any rise in income will lead to more spending but also some saving too. For individuals, the marginal propensity to consume could be more than 1 if money was borrowed to finance spending higher than income. In 2013, a working paper published by the Central Bank of Malaysia investigated how household spending responded to changes in disposable income for different household income levels. Using data from a household expenditure survey in 2009/10, the researchers found that households with a disposable income of less than MYR 1000 per month will consume an average of MYR 0.81 from MYR 1 in extra income, whereas households with disposable income of above MYR 10,000 per month were estimated to have a marginal propensity to consume of only 0.25. Although this research represents the views of the authors only, and cannot be taken to represent the views of the Bank, it does illustrate the general principal that the MPC is higher for those on low incomes in any economy.

The **average propensity to consume** (or APC) measures the average amount spent on consumption out of total income. For instance, if total disposable income in an economy were US$100 billion and consumption were US$90 billion then the average propensity to consume would be 0.9. The formula for the APC is:

$$APC = \frac{Consumption}{Income} = \frac{C}{Y}$$

In a rich industrialised economy, the APC is likely to be less than 1 because consumers will also save part of their earnings.

The theory that income is the most important determinant of consumption is called the Keynesian theory of consumption. John Maynard Keynes was one of the greatest economists working in the first half of the twentieth century. He was the creator of modern macroeconomics. 'Keynesian' means that an idea is linked to an idea first put forward by Keynes. Keynesians suggested that as incomes rose, households would prefer to save more and so the average propensity to consume would decline. Also, higher income households would save a larger proportion of their income than poorer households. Redistributing (giving) income from high income earners to those on low incomes would therefore increase total consumption in the economy. This explains why governments may choose to raise income tax rates for high earners and redistribute this income to those on low incomes through welfare payments. This policy should increase the average propensity to consume in an economy.

ACTIVITY 1

SKILLS ▷ COMMUNICATION, REASONING, PROBLEM-SOLVING

CASE STUDY: CONSUMPTION AND DISPOSABLE INCOME

	£ billion at 2011 prices	
	Consumption	Disposable income
1997	703.7	786.2
1998	734.8	809.3
2001	842.9	934.0
2002	876.5	959.0
2005	973.1	1018.6
2006	994.2	1037.4
2009	982.5	1079.3
2010	987.0	1088.6
2012	1000.9	1084.6
2013	1017.3	1082.1

▲ Table 1 Real consumption and household disposable income for the UK

Source: adapted from www.ons.gov.uk

(a) Using the data, explain the relationship between consumption and disposable income.

(b) (i) Calculate the MPC and APC for 1998, 2002, 2006, 2010 and 2013.

(ii) What happened to saving during these years?

OTHER INFLUENCES ON CONSUMPTION

There are a number of other determinants of consumption apart from disposable income.

Interest rates Households rarely finance expenditure on non-durables, such as food or entertainment, by borrowing money. However, much of the money to buy durables such as cars, furniture, kitchen equipment and hi-fi equipment comes from credit finance. An increase in the rate of interest increases the monthly repayments on these goods. This means that, effectively, the price of the goods has increased. Households react to this by reducing their demand for durables and thus cutting their consumption.

Many households have also borrowed money to buy their houses. Increased interest rates lead to increased mortgage repayments. Again, this will directly cut spending on other items and perhaps, more importantly, discourage households from borrowing more money to finance purchases of consumer durables.

Furthermore, a rise in the rate of interest reduces the value of stocks on stock markets and thus reduces the value investments and in turn of household wealth. This in turn leads to a fall in consumption.

Consumer confidence Purchases of consumer durables and non-essential items like holidays are affected by consumer confidence. If consumers expect their situation to be the same or better in the future, they will tend to maintain or increase their spending. If they expect it to get worse, they are likely to hold back on purchases of non-essential items. Consumer confidence deteriorates during a recession. Some workers worry that they might lose their jobs. Others worry that their take-home pay will fall because they will work less overtime or their bonuses will be cut. They might also worry that banks will refuse to lend them money and so they do not apply for loans. In a boom, consumer confidence increases, boosting spending.

ACTIVITY 2 — SKILLS COMMUNICATION, REASONING

CASE STUDY: CHINA'S YOUNG PEOPLE ARE FEELING GOOD

The *Financial Times* conducts surveys to judge the mood of consumers. The sudden improvement in Chinese consumer sentiment (attitude), in 2017, was led by 18–24-year-olds, who make up the youngest survey group. This group are thought to be particularly positive, since they became adults during China's most rapid growth phase, and during the period of fastest growth in household income. The feel-good factor also comes from rising asset prices. The *Financial Times* household survey found 85 per cent of 18–24-year-olds said their household owned at least one property, and 26.6 per cent said it owned more than one.

(a) Explain how consumer confidence can influence consumption.

(b) Explain why rising house prices is likely to cause consumption to rise.

Wealth effects The wealth of a household is made up of two parts. Physical wealth is made up of items such as houses, cars and furniture. Monetary wealth is comprised of items such as cash, money financial institutions, such as bank, stocks and shares, life assurance policies and pension rights.

If the wealth of a household increases, consumption will increase. This is known as the **wealth effect**. There are two important ways in which the wealth of households can change over a short time period.

- A change in the price of houses. According to the IMF Global Housing Watch, real house prices increased over the year 2016 to 2017 for most countries. For example, real house prices in Malaysia increased by 3.9 per cent and for China 9.2 per cent. If the real price of houses increases over an extended period of time, then households feel able to increase their spending. They do this mainly by borrowing more money secured against the value of their house.

- A change in the value of stocks and shares. Households react to an increase in the real value of a household's portfolio of securities by selling part of the portfolio and spending the proceeds. The value of stocks and shares is determined by many factors. One of these is the rate of interest. If the rate of interest falls, then the value of stocks will rise. So consumption should be stimulated through the wealth effect by a fall in the rate of interest.

ACTIVITY 3 — SKILLS COMMUNICATION, REASONING, ANALYSIS

CASE STUDY: CHINA'S CONSUMER LOANS INCREASE

Since regulators opened up the consumer finance market in 2014, availability of credit has hugely increased for the Chinese consumer. Lenders use salespeople in shops and car parks to hand out on-the-spot loans for phones, electronic gadgets and cars. Often younger people, who have struggled to obtain loans from traditional lenders, have obtained the finance from these lenders. This lending market is expected to be worth CNY 3.4 trillion (Chinese yuan) by 2019. This consumption-led growth will help the Chinese economy be less dependent on investment spending and exports as a means of increasing aggregate demand. However, although these lenders may offer 0 per cent interest deals for the loans in the shopping centre, these companies then go on to offer online loans with interest rates averaging in the mid-20s. In the past only banks were allowed to lend. There is concern that the rapidly climbing household debt, combined with high interest repayments, will mean some borrowers will be unable to repay.

(a) Identify examples of consumer durables in the passage.

(b) Explain why consumption is increasing more rapidly in China.

(c) Identify the advantages and disadvantages of the greater availability of credit for China's economy.

The availability of credit The rate of interest determines the price of credit. However, the price of credit is not the only determinant of how much households borrow. Governments in the past have often imposed restrictions on the availability of credit. For instance, they have imposed maximum repayment periods and minimum deposits. In Malaysia, in 2011, the central bank began imposing strict lending requirements on consumers because of concern over rising household debt. This, combined with the 2015–16 economic slowdown, reduced Malaysia's ratio of household debt to GDP. However, in 2016, Malaysian and Thai households were still the most indebted among the Asean (Association of Southeast Asian Nations) countries. Reducing the availability of credit will reduce consumption.

Inflation Inflation, a rise in the general level of prices, has two effects on consumption. First, if households expect prices to be higher in the future they will be tempted to bring forward their purchases. For instance, if households know that the price of cars will go up by 10 per cent the next month, they will attempt to buy their cars now. So expectations of inflation increase consumption and reduce saving.

However, this can be outweighed by the effect of inflation on wealth. Rising inflation tends to reduce the real value of money wealth. Households react to this by attempting to restore the real value of their wealth (i.e. they save more). This reduces consumption.

The composition of households Young people and old people tend to spend a higher proportion of their income than those in middle age. Young people tend to spend all their income and move into debt to finance the setting up of their homes and the bringing up of children. In middle age, the cost of homemaking declines as a proportion of income. With more income available, households often choose to build up their stock of savings in preparation for retirement. When they retire, they will run down their stock of savings to increase their pensions. So if there is a change in the age composition of households in the economy, there could well be a change in consumption and savings. The more young and old the households, the greater will tend to be the level of consumption.

THE DETERMINANTS OF SAVING

Factors that affect consumption also by definition must affect saving (remember, saving is defined as the part of disposable income that is not consumed). The **savings function** therefore links income, wealth, inflation, the rate of interest, expectations and the age profile of the population with the level of saving. However, because a typical **average propensity to save** (the APS – the ratio of total saving to total income calculated by Saving ÷ Income) is 0.05 to 0.2 in Western European countries, income is far less important in determining saving than it is in determining consumption. Factors other than income are therefore relatively more important. The **marginal propensity to save** (the proportion that is saved out of a change in income calculated by Change in saving ÷ Change in income) is equally unstable for these reasons.

Confusion sometimes arises between 'saving' and 'savings'. Saving is a flow concept that takes place over a period of time. Saving is added to a stock of savings fixed at a point in time. A household's stock of savings is the accumulation (result) of past savings. For instance, a UK citizen might have £100 in the bank. This is their stock of savings. They might then get a job over a public holiday and save £20 from that. Their saving over the holiday is £20. Their stock of savings before the holiday was £100 but afterwards it was £120. The savings function explains the relationship between the flow of savings and its determinants. It attempts to explain why they saved £20 over the holiday. It does not explain why they have £100 in the bank already.

ACTIVITY 4   SKILLS ▶ PROBLEM-SOLVING

CASE STUDY: CALCULATING PROPENSITY TO SAVE

Year	Saving US$ billion	Disposable income US$ billion	Average propensity to save	Marginal propensity to save
1	7.5	100		
2	7.9	102		
3	8.0	103		
4	8.3	106		
5	8.9	111		
6	9.0	112		

▲ Table 2 Saving and disposable income, US$ billion

(a) Calculate, to three decimal places, the average propensity to save and the marginal propensity to save for each year shown in the table.

THE SAVINGS RATIO

Savings is the difference between household disposable income and their spending on consumer goods and services. The **savings ratio** for an economy associates the total level of savings to the total level of household disposable income in nominal terms (i.e. at current prices). It is the proportion of income that is saved. It is usually expressed for household savings as a percentage of total household disposable income. For example, the savings ratio in Mexico in 2015 was 6.6 per cent. This means that for every MXN 1000 of household disposable income, MXN 66 are saved and MXN 934 are spent.

For Greece in 2015 the savings ratio was −19.3 per cent. This means there is **dis-saving**. This is when individuals in total were spending an amount of money that was greater than their disposable income. This is financed either by running down existing stocks of savings, or by borrowing. Dis-saving can occur when disposable income levels are very low, relative to prices of goods and services, so households are forced to run down their savings or borrow to finance consumption. Dis-saving can also occur when the economy is strong. If households are confident that incomes will rise over time, they will be more prepared to run down existing savings or borrow to finance consumer spending today. They assume they can repay their debt, or increase their savings stock in the future.

Factors that influence consumption and savings decisions will obviously affect the savings ratio (the 'Thinking like an economist' section looks at some of the causes of changes in the savings ratio).

THE POTENTIAL CONSEQUENCES OF CHANGES IN THE SAVINGS RATIO

For an economy, a rising savings ratio may reduce aggregate demand by reducing consumption. However, it is possible that investment will increase to counteract (compensate for) this. Household saving is the main domestic source of funds to finance investment. For example, when individuals save in pension funds or other savings, these savings flow into stock markets. This raises share capital for companies and provides the funds needed to finance investment. This is beneficial, since investment is a key driver of long-run economic growth. So, provided the economy is strong

and firms want to invest, a rising savings ratio may provide the funds to do this.

A falling savings ratio over time does not *necessarily* mean *real* consumption levels are rising in an economy. If disposable income levels are increasing more slowly than the prices of consumer goods and services are rising, then households will need to spend a greater fraction of their income to buy the same quantity of goods as before. They cannot afford to save as much, so the savings ratio falls. However, for a given level of disposable income and price level in the economy, a fall in the savings ratio will increase consumption. This will generate economic growth.

A fall in the savings ratio means consumer spending is increasing as a proportion of disposable income. An increase in consumption should raise current living standards. Consumers tend to save less if they are confident about future incomes. However, some will be funding consumer spending by borrowing. This build-up of personal debt may create a long-term problem if it is impossible to maintain. Consumers may be becoming over-dependent on credit. At some point consumers will have to limit their spending to repay debt; particularly if their incomes grow slower than expected. Also, an over dependence on consumer spending may create an unbalanced economy. Investment may be too low and imports too high. Imports are likely to be high because some spending by consumers will inevitably be on imported consumer goods. This could cause a deficit on the balance of trade in goods and services, on the current account of the balance of payments.

It is useful to remember that a rising saving ratio, or falling saving ratio, is not necessarily problematic. It will depend on the current state of the economy. For example, if economic growth is low or negative, a rising savings ratio would make this problem worse. However, if aggregate demand is growing *too* quickly, then a rising saving ratio would be beneficial.

THINKING LIKE AN ECONOMIST

CONSUMPTION AND SAVINGS

The influence of disposable income on consumption

Keynesian theory suggests that income is the main determinant of consumption. For example, the relationship between real household consumption and real disposable household income for the UK, between 1997 and 2013, is shown in Figure 1. It shows a close correlation (connection) between consumption and income. However, the correlation is not perfect. If disposable income were the only determinant of consumption then the APC would be constant. (The APC shows the proportion of income which is spent – in this data it is shown as a proportion of total disposable income.) However, as shown in Figure 2, the APC rose over the period 1997 to 2008, then fell sharply in 2009 before rising again. This means that factors other than income affected consumption over this period, for example, levels of consumer confidence, availability of credit and wealth effects.

EXAM HINT

Calculating the APC and the APS from Figure 1. The relationship between savings and consumption:

Total real disposable income in the UK in 2010 was approximately £1070 billion (Figure 1). If the APC in the UK in 2010 is approximately 0.91 (Figure 2), then consumption can be calculated as 0.91 × £1070 billion = £974 billion. This figure does tie in with the data shown in Figure 1 for real consumption expenditure in 2010.

If the APC = 0.91 then APS = 0.09. APC + APS = 1 (savings = £1070 billion − £974 billion = £96 billion: So 96/1070 = 0.09).

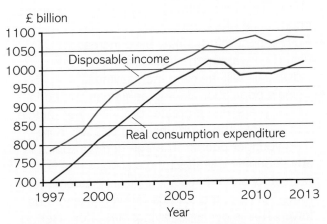

▲ Figure 1 Real consumption expenditure and disposable income, 1997–2013

Source: adapted from www.ons.gov.uk

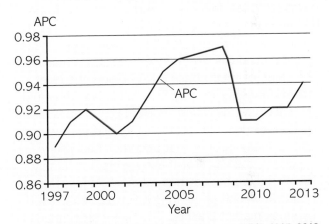

▲ Figure 2 The average propensity to consume (APC), 1997–2013

Source: adapted from www.ons.gov.uk

Changes in the savings ratio over time and differences between countries

Factors that affect consumption also, by definition, affect savings (since saving is defined as that part of disposable income which is not consumed). Figure 3 shows a comparison of savings ratios between countries between 2009 (the height of the global financial crisis) and 2014.

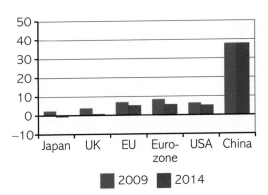

▲ Figure 3 Household savings as a % of household disposable income, 2009 and 2014

Significant points of comparison:

The savings ratios in 2009 were higher than 2014 for all the countries shown, except for China, where savings ratios have remained broadly constant since 2009. At the height of the impact of the global financial crisis, this is to be expected. Some reasons for the higher savings ratios in 2009 include the following.

- Globally, consumer confidence was low (there was job insecurity (uncertainty) as unemployment rose). In these circumstances, households try to save a greater proportion of disposable income 'just in case'. They limit any unnecessary consumer spending. By 2014, confidence was largely restored.

- Central banks in the UK, Europe, Japan and the USA reduced interest rates to historically low levels in 2008/09 and these have been maintained since. The incentive (motivation) to save fell dramatically over this period.

- As the financial crisis hit, the value of houses, pension funds and stocks and shares fell. In the UK and USA, many individuals own houses as their main store of wealth. A fall in house prices meant some individuals experienced negative equity, the value of their house falling below the level of mortgage still to pay. This fall in wealth would increase savings ratios. Individuals will save more of their disposable income to rebuild their wealth and to repay debt, if that becomes necessary. By 2014, the value of these assets had largely recovered, so the savings ratio would fall. The negative wealth effect in 2009 was also caused by stock market crashes. The major stock market indices in the USA and UK halved between a peak in autumn/summer 2007 and a low in March 2009. Other countries suffered too, for example, Italy's FTSE MIB fell by 70 per cent between May 2007 and March 2009.

- In 2009, the availability of credit in global financial markets was scarce and borrowing costs for individuals remained high, despite central bank's attempts to lower interest rates for consumers. Consumers would be reluctant to borrow to finance spending. Hence, consumption is a lower fraction of total household disposable income,

which means savings represent a higher fraction. After the global financial crisis, access to credit increased. This meant consumers could increase spending by financing it through borrowing. This reduced the savings ratio.

China's savings ratio is significantly higher than the other countries shown and all the member countries of the OECD. The savings ratio in China is expected to be higher than developed economies for the following reasons.

- The nature of China's financial and banking system means it is often hard for individuals to get access to credit. Consumers will need to save more of their disposable income to fund the purchase of durable consumer goods.

- Individuals need to build up their stock of savings to fund housing, education and health because state provision of these is limited.

- There is a lack of a state welfare system or private pensions to support old age. People rely heavily on their stock of savings to fund this period.

- There are strong cultural views that promote the importance of saving.

- Government reforms may have increased uncertainty about the future for individuals. Individuals will increase their savings.

- China's population demographic has shifted in recent years with a greater proportion of middle age groups. These groups tend to save more than younger people. The age demographics in any economy will affect the savings ratio. For populations that have a significant percentage of retired people, the savings ration is likely to be lower. This is because savings are often used to help fund retirement.

A consequence of such a high savings ratio is that it depresses consumption. Consumption in China is only approximately 40 per cent of GDP. However, high savings enables more private sector investment. Economic growth in China has been led by high exports and high investment pushing up aggregate demand.

Source: lfs.org.uk for reference to stock market data

CHECKPOINT

1 Which concept links how much is spent of each additional amount of income?

2 What is the average propensity to consume?

3 What happens to consumption as disposable income rises?

4 State one reason consumption falls if interest rates rise.

5 If consumer confidence rises, what happens to consumption when disposable income remains the same?

6 If the value of an individual's wealth rises, why is consumer spending likely to rise?

7 State three factors that influence how much an individual is likely to save.

8 What is meant by the term 'savings ratio'?

9 State one cause of a fall in the savings ratio.

10 State one advantage of a high savings ratio for an economy.

SUBJECT VOCABULARY

average propensity to consume the proportion of total income spent. It is calculated by $C \div Y$.

average propensity to save the proportion of a total income that is saved. It is calculated by $S \div Y$.

consumption total expenditure by households on goods and services over a period of time.

consumption function the relationship between the consumption of households and the factors that determine it.

disposable income household income over a period of time including state benefits, less direct taxes.

dis-saving when individuals spend an amount of money that was greater than their disposable income. This is financed either by running down existing stocks of savings, or by borrowing.

durable goods goods that are consumed over a long period of time, such as a television set or a car.

marginal propensity to consume the proportion of a change in income that is spent. It is calculated by $\Delta C \div \Delta Y$.

marginal propensity to save the proportion of a change in income that is saved. It is calculated by $\Delta S \div \Delta Y$.

non-durable goods goods that are consumed almost immediately, like an ice cream or a packet of washing powder.

savings function the relationship between the saving of households and the factors that determine it.

saving (personal) the portion of households' disposable income that is not spent over a period of time.

savings ratio usually expressed for household savings as a percentage of total household disposable income.

wealth effect the change in consumption following a change in wealth.

EXAM PRACTICE

 SKILLS   PROBLEM SOLVING, REASONING, INTERPRETATION, ANALYSIS, CRITICAL THINKING

Q

1 Malaysian consumers happier to spend

Extract A

By 2017, consumer spending was starting to rise more rapidly. Between the second quarter of 2016 and the same time in 2017, consumer spending had increased by 7.1 per cent. This followed two years of slower consumption growth. The fall in inflation, combined with continuing income increases, meant consumers were now able to afford more non-essential purchases.

Extract B

By 2017, there was also a greater demand for borrowing. This was a sign that consumers had become more confident, so loan applications to buy big ticket items, such as cars, had risen. In response, the banks had approved more loans. Malaysians generally use bank loans to buy cars, unlike in Indonesia and the Philippines, where consumers normally use cash. Data from the Malaysian Automotive Association showed that car sales had increased January–June by 4.7 per cent, compared to the same period the previous year.

(a) With reference to extract A, explain the likely effect of a rise in incomes on consumption.
(4 marks)

(b) With reference to extract B, examine the likely impact on consumer spending of the rise in consumer confidence in Malaysia. **(8 marks)**

EXAM HINT

Consider the link between consumer confidence and attitude towards borrowing. To evaluate, consider what might restrict how much consumers are able to increase their debt by.

2 Japan's consumption a cause for concern

Extract A

During 2016, the growth in consumer spending was low. This was surprising, since income had increased in 2016 as the number of people in work grew. Between 2014 and 2016 the average propensity to consume had fallen. It was likely that consumer anxiety about the future was keeping consumption low.

However, the Bank of Japan's outlook in 2017 was more positive. 'Consumption is expected to increase moderately, supported by a steady improvement in employee income, as well as the wealth effects stemming from a rise in stock prices.' Consumer confidence was also picking up. The average propensity to consume, calculated on disposable income, was now expected to rise.

Components of national expenditure (aggregate demand)	2015 current prices (yen trillion)
Consumption	293
Investment	85
Government spending	125
Exports	89
Imports	94

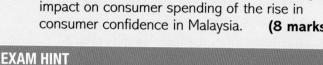
Table 3 Components of Japanese aggregate demand, 2015
Source: adapted from OECD Japan's economic forecast summary November 2016: public corporations investment added to government consumption for government spending. Investment adjusted for deduction of public corporation investment

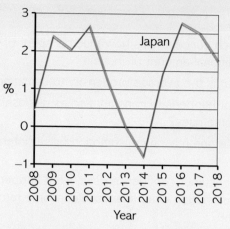
Figure 4 Japanese household savings ratio, 2008–18
Source: OECD: Household savings forecast 2017

(a) Using Table 3, calculate consumption as a percentage of aggregate demand for Japan in 2015. **(2 marks)**

(b) Define the term 'average propensity to consume' (extract A). **(2 marks)**

(c) With reference to Figure 4 and extract A, analyse one reason, apart from a rise in income, why consumption was expected to rise from 2017. **(6 marks)**

Historically, Japan used to have a very high savings ratio. At its peak in the mid-1970s, it was 20 per cent; it has fallen dramatically since then: in 2016 it was 2.7 per cent. This is partly because Japan now has one of the most ageing populations in the world. Older individuals who no longer work tend to take out their savings to fund consumption.

(d) Evaluate the view that the age distribution of the population is the most important factor likely to influence the savings ratio of an economy. **(20 marks)**

EXAM HINT

If you know the factors that influence consumption, then you also know what factors influence savings. You need to think about what affects the fraction of total disposable income which is saved. Why might the age distribution of a population affect savings? What other factors also affect the savings ratio between economies and over time? Use the 'Thinking like an economist' section to help you. To evaluate, consider whether the age distribution differences between economies, and over time, would be sufficient to explain the differences in the savings ratio.

29 INVESTMENT

UNIT 2
2.3.2

LEARNING OBJECTIVES

- Understand that investment is the purchase of capital goods that are then used to create other goods and services.
- Understand the distinction between gross investment and net investment.
- Understand that the level of investment is determined by a number of variables, including the rate of interest, the rate of economic growth, costs, business confidence and expectations, the state of the world economy, availability of credit, retained profit, government policy and regulation.

GETTING STARTED

An international chain of coffee shops is investigating opening a coffee shop in your local area. It will borrow the money to finance the deal. What do you think might be the factors that will influence whether or not it goes ahead with the investment?

A DEFINITION OF INVESTMENT

Economists use the word **investment** in a very precise way. Investment is the addition to the capital stock of the economy – factories, machines, offices and stocks of materials used to produce other goods and services.

In everyday language, 'investment' and 'saving' are often used to mean the same thing. For instance, we talk about 'investing in the building society' or 'investing in shares'. For an economist, these two would be examples of saving. For an economist, investment only takes place if real products are created. To give two more examples:

- putting money into a bank account would be saving; the bank buying a computer to handle your account would be investment
- buying shares in a new company would be saving; buying new machinery to set up a company would be investment.

A distinction can be made between **gross investment** and **net investment**. The value of the capital stock depreciates over time as it wears out and is used up. This is called **depreciation or capital consumption**. Gross investment measures investment before depreciation, while net investment is gross investment

less the value of depreciation. Depreciation in recent years in the UK has accounted for about three-quarters of gross investment. So only about one-quarter of gross investment represents an addition to the capital stock of the economy.

Another distinction made is between investment in physical capital and in human capital. Investment in human capital is investment in the education and training of workers. Investment in physical capital is investment in factories etc. and is the subject of this unit. It is physical investment that is the investment component, I, in aggregate demand.

Investment is made both by the public sector and the private sector. Public sector investment is limited by complex political considerations. In the rest of this unit, we will consider how private sector investment in physical capital is determined.

ACTIVITY 1   SKILLS ANALYSIS

CASE STUDY: INVESTMENT IN A BANK

Using the photograph showing the interior of a bank, give examples of:

(a) past investment in physical capital

(b) past investment in human capital

(c) saving

(d) capital consumption.

THE RATE OF INTEREST

One variable that affects the level of investment is the rate of interest. This works in two ways.

- Some investment is financed by firms borrowing money from banks or the money markets. Interest paid on a loan is then part of the cost of an investment project. The higher the rate of interest, the lower will be the profit that can be made from any investment, all other things being equal. At some point, the rate of interest will be so high that an investment project will become unprofitable. A rise in interest rates will therefore reduce the number of profitable investment projects and so firms will invest less. The lower the rate of interest, the more investment projects will be profitable and so there will more investment.

- Some investment is financed by **retained profit**. This is the savings that firms keep and do not distribute to their owners. The higher the rate of interest that banks and money markets offer on savings, the more attractive it is for firms to save money rather than invest it in physical capital. The lower the rate of interest, the greater the incentive for firms to use their savings to buy investment goods.

THE RATE OF ECONOMIC GROWTH

If the same products and the same amount is being produced in an economy year after year, the level of investment will remain the same. Firms will invest to replace physical capital, such as machines that have worn out and can no longer be used profitably. But there will be no need to increase investment beyond this replacement level.

In contrast, if the economy is expanding, firms will need to increase their investment to have the capital equipment to produce more goods and services.

If the economy is shrinking in size, as in a recession, firms will not need to replace all their investment goods that have become worn out. With lower output, they will need less capital equipment. So investment will fall when the rate of economic growth is negative.

The idea that investment is linked to changes in output or income in the economy is called the **accelerator theory**. The simplest form of the accelerator theory can be expressed by the equation:

$$I_t = a (Y_t - Y_{t-1})$$

where:

- I_t is investment in time period t
- $Y_t - Y_{t-1}$ is the change in real income during year t
- a is called the **accelerator coefficient** and is the **capital–output ratio**.

The capital–output ratio is the amount of capital needed in the economy to produce a given quantity of goods. So if €10 of capital is needed to produce €2 of goods, then the capital–output ratio is 5. With a capital–output ratio of 5, an increase in income or output in the economy of €1 billion will lead to an increase in investment of €5 billion (5 × €1 billion).

COSTS

Private sector firms need to make a profit. They have to be able to sell the products made from an investment. They also have to keep their costs per unit below the selling price. Increases in costs, such as increases in wages or raw materials, will reduce the profitability or rate of return on an investment, all other things being equal. Costs and predictions about what will happen to costs over the lifetime of the investment are therefore important to firms considering whether or not to invest.

BUSINESS EXPECTATIONS AND CONFIDENCE

If firms expect their sales to increase, they are more likely to invest in new capital equipment. When the economy is growing rapidly, for example, investment is likely to rise. If firms lose confidence and expect sales to fall in the future, they are likely reduce their plans for investment.

John Maynard Keynes, writing in the 1930s, used the phrase **animal spirits** to describe the mood of managers and owners of firms. Keynes argued that animal spirits, or confidence, was not something that could easily be measured. It was a feeling on the part of those who made decisions about investment as to whether the future was going to be better or worse. Moods can change. If enough firms feel confident in the future, investment will increase sufficiently to raise income and output in the whole economy. Equally, if decision makers are pessimistic about future output, that in itself can lead to economy-wide falls in output and income.

THE WORLD ECONOMY

If the world economy is growing rapidly, demand for exports is likely to increase. This in turn should lead to a rise in domestic investment. However, a worldwide recession will reduce the demand for exports. So exporting firms are likely to reduce their investment. This will have a knock-on effect on other firms in the economy, reducing their sales and reducing their willingness to invest.

AVAILABILITY OF CREDIT

Some investment is financed through borrowing. The amount of money that is available for borrowing within the financial system varies. For example, in the years before the financial crisis of 2008, it was relatively easy for firms in many advanced economies to borrow money from banks. After the financial crisis, banks became less willing to take risks. This meant they were less willing to give loans because they feared that firms would not be able to pay the money back with interest. So firms may want to borrow money to buy capital equipment but they may be turned down by banks as being too risky a customer.

According to the World Bank Enterprise Survey, the percentage of investments in the world financed by bank loans was around 15 per cent. In India, in 2014, 18.1 per cent of investments were financed by bank loans and around 30 per cent of firms were using banks to finance investment.

RETAINED PROFIT

About 70 per cent of investment, in all countries in total, are financed from **retained profit**. However, this differs between countries. According to the World Bank Enterprise Survey in India 2014, 71.8 per cent of investments were financed from retained profit. This compares with 96.3 per cent for Cambodia (2016), but only 58.6 per cent for Bolivia (2017). Retained profit is profit that is kept back by firms and not distributed to shareholders. Some economists argue that firms, particularly small firms, tend not to consider the opportunity cost of investment – the interest lost from lending it out. Firms can also be unwilling to take risks, not wanting to borrow money in case the investment fails to make a profit. If the money is available, firms will invest. If retained profit is low, firms will tend not to invest. So retained profit helps determine the level of investment in the economy.

A company has to pay a tax on company profits. This is usually called corporate tax or corporation tax. The corporate tax rate will affect how much profit the company makes after tax. The profit after tax is then either distributed to shareholders or retained by the business. This means corporate tax rates will influence levels of investment in an economy. A fall in corporate tax rate would be expected to increase investment.

THE INFLUENCE OF GOVERNMENT AND REGULATIONS

Governments can influence investment across the economy and in particular sectors. For example, some economists argue that cutting the tax on company profits, known as corporation tax or corporate tax, will increase investment. This is because cutting the rate of tax on profits effectively cuts costs for a firm on its investments. This raises the rate of return or profitability. Governments can target the cut in profits tax better by allowing any investment made by firms to be offset against the profits tax they pay. This is called tax relief. Alternatively, the government could directly give financial assistance to firms to fund investment. This is called a subsidy. Another way that governments can encourage investment is by guaranteeing loans made by banks to firms for investment. If the firm fails to pay back the money, the government pays the bank instead.

This encourages banks to lend money on higher risk projects. Regulations can also affect investment. Some economists argue that highly regulated economies discourage investment. This is because regulation tends to increase costs for firms and so reduces their profitability. Regulation can also directly prevent a firm from investing in a project because it is not permitted by regulations. For example, a firm may want to build a new factory on a site that it owns but is not allowed to because of planning regulations.

THINKING LIKE AN ECONOMIST

INVESTMENT IN ITALY

In 2014, Janssen, a medium-sized pharmaceutical manufacturing plant in Italy, invested €500,000 in a machine capable of producing up to 70,000 capsules per hour, compared with older machinery that could only produce 17,000 capsules per hour. The equipment is used to produce a new hepititis C medicine.

It is hoped that this is symbolic of a wider change. Since 2008, Italy has experienced two periods of negative economic growth and investment has plummeted as a result over the period 2008–14. For example, in 2012, investment spending (gross fixed capital formation – GFCF) fell by 9.3 per compared to the previous year. Between 2010 to a Eurostat analysis. On international comparisons this is weak. Over the same period, France, Germany, the UK and USA maintained their investment level.

▲ Borsa Italiana, the Italian stock exchange

The data in Figure 1 suggests that there is a stong correlation between the annual rate of growth in real GDP and the annual percentage change in investment (GFCF). A rising rate of growth in real GDP coexists with a rising rate of growth in investment. The data supports the theory that the rate of economic growth influences investment. Since company profits are also likely to be affected by how well the economy is performing, it seems likely that a link between retained profits and investment would also be found.

Long-term interest rates are also a main determinant of business investment. This is shown in Figure 2. For example, a fall in interest rates from 2012 onwards corresponds with investment picking up. Although investment still falls between 2012 and 2014, it is falling at a slower rate. By 2015, the annual percentage change in investment was 1.6 per cent. Investment spending had now increased from the previous year. Figure 2 suggests a relatively clear link between the level of interest rates and investment.

For Italy it is hoped that lower borrowing costs and improved confidence can kick-start investment growth again. However, in 2016, credit to firms had been shrinking for some time as banks struggled to cope with previous bad loans. This made access to credit difficult for firms and might constrain how much investment spending can rise.

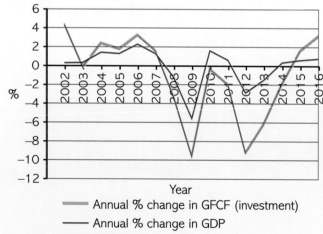

▲ Figure 1 Italian annual percentage change in GFCF and rate of ecomonic growth, 2002–16

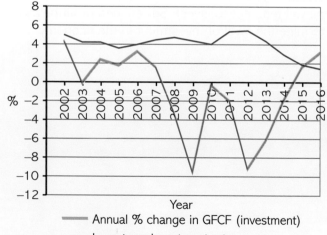

▲ Figure 2 Italian annual percentage change in GFCF and long-term interest rate, 2002–16

The composition of gross fixed capital formation includes:
- investment in housing
- investment in 'other new buildings and structures', for example, factories and offices
- investment in vehicles, ships and aircraft
- investment in other machinery and equipment, for example, factory machinery and computers
- intangible fixed assets, such as patents, copyright and goodwill
- costs associated with the transfer of ownership of non-produced assets, for example, taxes and legal costs associated with the buying and selling of assets.

CHECKPOINT

1 What is investment?

2 What is the difference between gross investment and net investment?

3 What happens to the amount of capital equipment needed if output falls?

4 If the interest rate on loans increases, what happens to the level of investment?

5 What should happen to investment if business confidence improves?

6 Why is availability of credit an influence on investment?

7 What should happen to investment if corporate tax rates fall?

8 What is tax relief?

SUBJECT VOCABULARY

accelerator coefficient the capital–output ratio.

accelerator theory the theory that the level of investment is related to past changes in income.

animal spirits business confidence: the mood of managers and owners of firms about the future of their industry and the wider economy.

capital–output ratio the ratio between the amount of capital needed to produce a given quantity of goods and the level of output.

depreciation (of the capital stock) or capital consumption the value of the capital stock that has been used up or worn out.

gross investment the addition to capital stock, both to replace the existing capital stock, which has been used up (depreciation), and the creation of additional capital.

investment the addition to the capital stock of the economy.

net investment gross investment minus depreciation.

retained profit profit kept back by a firm for its own use that is not distributed to shareholders or used to pay taxation.

EXAM PRACTICE

INDIA'S FIRMS SHOW LITTLE APPETITE FOR INVESTMENT

SKILLS PROBLEM SOLVING, DECISION MAKING, REASONING, INTERPRETATION, ANALYSIS, CRITICAL THINKING

Extract A

Firms in India are still reluctant to invest. Despite a favourable economic growth outlook, with real GDP predicted to increase from 7.4 per cent in 2016 to 7.6 per cent in 2017, private sector investment in 2016 seemed unlikely to increase. Past delayed investment projects have failed to make the profits expected, leaving firms with too much debt. There is little appetite to start new investment projects and there is no need while firms have spare capacity.

Extract B

In October 2015, total capital expenditure had dropped dramatically and was set to hit its lowest level since 2010. Mr Modi, India's prime minister elected in 2014, had made encouraging the private sector to invest again one of his key objectives.

In October 2015, the central bank governor cut interest rates by 0.5 per cent in a bid to increase business investment. It is thought that high interest rates in India have played a part in causing weak levels of investment. However, this may not increase private sector investment if business confidence remains low. With global growth weaker, firms will want to be confident that domestic demand is strong enough before they start investing again. They may even wait until the global outlook is more positive.

Many banks are struggling too. India's banking system is weighed down by bad loans, which means they are reluctant to lend. However, the Reserve Bank of India has recently made steps to free up credit.

Sources: *Financial Times*, 'Modi struggles to unleash investment from uneasy private sector' 12.10.2015 and IMF Survey, 2.3.2016 'India can lock in good fortune with private investment'; OECD Economic forecast summary, Nov 2016

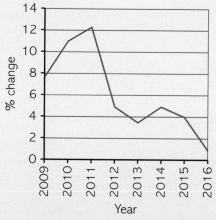

▲ **Figure 3 Indian annual percentage GFCF growth, 2009–16**
Source: OECD 'Economic Outlook: Statistics and Projections'. Gross fixed capital formation includes both private and public sector investment.2016 forecast data

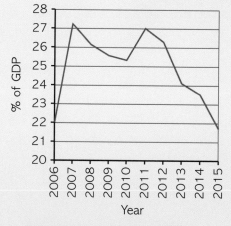

▲ **Figure 4 Indian private sector GFCF as percentage of GDP, 2006–15**
Source: World Bank

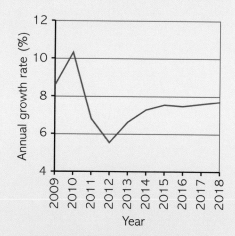

▲ **Figure 5 Indian percentage change in real GDP, 2009–18**
Source: real GDP forecast, OECD 'Economic Outlook: Statistics and Projections'

The business confidence index (BCI) is based on enterprises' assessment of production, orders and stocks, as well as its current position and expectations for the immediate future. Opinions compared to a 'normal' state are collected and the difference between positive and negative answers provides a qualitative index on economic conditions.

Q

1 (a) Define investment (extract A).   **(2 marks)**

   (b) With reference to extract B and Figures 3 and 4, analyse one cause of India's low level of business investment in recent years.   **(6 marks)**

   (c) With reference to the information provided, discuss the likely impact of the 'favourable economic growth outlook' on the level of business investment in India.   **(14 marks)**

EXAM HINT

'Discuss' requires knowledge, application, analysis and evaluation. You need to explain why economic growth should promote investment, then consider whether any of the other influences on investment might be affected by the rise in economic growth. Under what circumstances might firms not increase investment, despite economic growth? In your conclusion, weigh up whether the projected growth for India would overcome all the other negative influences on investment in India. Use the extracts and data to support your arguments. Careful use of the extracts also helps to identify themes of discussion.

2 'The cost of credit has a significant influence over the level of investment'.

   Evaluate the view that the rate of interest on loans is the most important factor influencing investment.   **(20 marks)**

EXAM HINT

For KAA (knowledge, application and analysis), consider a range of influences on investment that may be important. To evaluate, consider whether a fall in interest rates would necessarily increase investment. To what extent is investment financed by borrowing? Are other factors influencing investment more likely to be significant? Even if interest rates fall, will firms increase investment? Evaluation can also include what assumptions must be made for any influence on investment to be important.

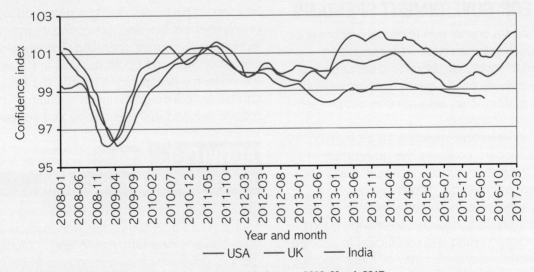

▲ Figure 6 Indian business confidence index, long-term average = 100, January 2008–March 2017

Source: OECD

30 GOVERNMENT EXPENDITURE AND NET TRADE

LEARNING OBJECTIVES

■ Understand influences on government expenditure:
  - fiscal policy
  - the level of economic activity
  - correction of market failures
  - political priorities.
■ Understand the impact on the net trade balance of changes in:
  - real income
  - the exchange rate
  - the state of the global economy
  - degree of protectionism
  - non-price factors.

GETTING STARTED

What does government spend money on in your local community? Why does it spend this money? What do you buy that is made abroad? Why do you buy these goods rather than goods made in your own country?

REASONS FOR GOVERNMENT SPENDING

Government plays a crucial role in modern economies. One way in which they intervene is by spending money on a wide variety of goods and services. For example, they provide public goods such as defence and the court system. They also provide goods such as education and healthcare.

The size of government spending varies from country to country. In a modern economy, the government will fund defence, the police and court system, roads and education. There are then big differences between economies. In a free market economy like that of the USA, the private sector is expected to provide goods such as healthcare, housing and social care. In a mixed economy, the state will provide many of these goods. Some mixed economies, like Sweden, have much higher state involvement than countries like the UK.

Much of government spending is fixed from year to year. Schools must be funded. Fuel for army vehicles

must be bought. Pensions must be paid. However, governments vary what they spend their money on and how much they spend from year to year. Government announcements about changes in spending are made in budgets. Decisions about government spending, together with taxes and government borrowing, are called the **fiscal policy** of the government.

Typically, changes in government spending reflect changing priorities about how to spend money. A government might choose to spend more on education and less on defence next year, for example. These decisions will depend partly on the political priorities of the government in charge. Governments will also have different views on the role of government spending to correct market failures. For example, subsidies on public transport or solar panels might be used where there are positive externalities.

However, changes in government spending can also be made deliberately to affect total spending in the economy. The government may want the level of economic activity to increase or decrease. Higher government spending can boost total spending and so affect variables such as unemployment and inflation. In particular, during a recession when unemployment is rising, governments may choose to increase government spending. This should reduce unemployment and boost demand in the economy. If the economy is expanding rapidly, the government may choose to reduce government spending. This should reduce demand in the economy and so reduce inflation.

ACTIVITY 1   SKILLS   REASONING, ANALYSIS AND COMMUNICATING.

CASE STUDY: BRUNEI'S RECESSION

By 2017, Brunei had seen its economy contract every year since 2013, and was expected to remain in recession for a fifth year in 2017. During this period, government spending rose from 29.7 per cent of GDP in 2011 to 39.8 per cent in 2016.

(a) Explain how a recession will likely affect the level of government expenditure.

The current level of economic activity, or total spending in an economy, will also automatically affect the level of government spending. This is without any deliberate intervention by the government. For example, government spending will rise automatically during a recession. In a recession, unemployment rises and some workers will earn less. There will then be a rise in government spending on unemployment benefits and benefits to support those on low or no income.

The impact of changes in government spending on total spending in the economy depends on levels of taxation. If the government raises taxes by the same amount as a rise in its spending, then there might be little impact on total spending in the economy. In contrast, a rise in total spending with no change in taxation will have more impact.

Government spending can be greater than government receipts such as taxation. When this happens, there will be a **budget deficit** (the term **fiscal deficit** is also used). When government spending is less than government receipts such as taxation, there will be a **budget surplus** (the term **fiscal surplus** is also used). A rise in government spending with no change in taxation will either reduce a budget surplus or increase a budget deficit.

EXPORTS AND IMPORTS

Exports are goods and services sold to foreign countries. Imports are goods and services bought from foreign counties. **Net exports or the net trade balance** are exports minus imports. Exports are an important part of total demand in an economy. The demand for exports and imports is influenced by a number of factors.

Price Buyers make decisions partly on the price of a good. The higher the price, the lower the quantity demanded. The price itself depends on a variety of supply factors including costs. Over the past 15 years, production of low- and medium-technology manufactured goods has gone from high wage economies like the UK to low wage economies like China. So imports into the UK from China have increased because UK domestic producers can no longer compete.

Real income in the domestic economy If the economy is doing well and real incomes of households are rising, they spend more. Part of this spending will be on imported goods and services. So rising real incomes lead to more imports. However, if the economy is doing badly and is in recession, real incomes will fall and so too will imports.

The exchange rate The **exchange rate** is the price at which one currency is sold for another. For example,

a rise in the value of the Japanese yen means that it costs foreigners more to buy yen with their local currency. This makes exports from Japan less price-competitive and hence Japanese exports are likely to fall. Equally, a rise in the value of the yen means that Japanese buyers can buy foreign currency more cheaply with yen. So imports become more price-competitive to Japanese buyers. A fall in the value of the yen leads to the opposite result. Japanese exports become more price-competitive to foreign buyers. In contrast, Japanese buyers find that imports become less price-competitive.

State of the world economy If Japan's main trading partners are doing well economically, then Japanese exports are likely to rise. The largest export markets for Japan are the USA and China. Recession in the USA or China could lead to a fall in Japanese exports, whereas fast economic growth in China or the USA will boost Japanese exports.

Degree of protectionism Almost all countries limit goods and services coming into their economies in various ways. For example, they may put quotas on goods, which are physical limits on the amount that can be imported. Or they may put tariffs on imports. A tariff is a tax on imports. The greater the degree of **protectionism** internationally, the more difficult it will be for firms to export. For example, the great advantage for a country, such as Germany, being part of the EU is that barriers to trade are very low for exports to other countries within the EU. Equally, though, other EU countries will be able to export their goods to Germany without facing protectionist barriers.

Non-price factors Exports and imports may be bought solely on price. This is particularly true where goods are of standard quality. Copper, steel or wheat, for example, are standard commodities that tend to be traded on price. However, many products are unique in quality. They may have a unique design protected by patents. It may be a unique service, such as next day delivery. So a whole range of **non-price factors** affects the competitiveness of exports and imports.

ACTIVITY 2   SKILLS   REASONING, ANALYSIS AND COMMUNICATING

CASE STUDY: SOUTH AFRICA'S NET TRADE BALANCE

South Africa's economic growth rate of 0.3 per cent in 2016 was the lowest it had been for the previous 16 years, except for the 2009 recession. The recent slow growth of real incomes was having an impact on the net trade balance.

(a) Explain the likely impact on South Africa's net trade balance of the slow growth in real incomes.

THINKING LIKE AN ECONOMIST

FRENCH CUTS IN GOVERNMENT SPENDING

In 2014, various sources in the media reported that the French government, led by Francois Hollande from the Socialist Party, was caught in a dilemma. On the one hand, the French economy was not growing. Increasing government spending would be one way to increase demand in the economy and stimulate economic growth.

On the other hand, government spending was already very high as a percentage of the output of the French economy measured by GDP. France was spending over 10 per cent more of its GDP on government compared to the largest economy in Europe, Germany, as can be seen from Figure 1.

Moreover, the difference between government spending and tax revenues in France was more than 3 per cent, the maximum level set by the European Union for countries using the euro as their currency. There was therefore strong pressure on the French government to cut its spending.

The government was, in fact, committed to cutting public spending by €50 billion between 2015 and 2017 following a €15 billion cut in 2014. However, making cuts is always difficult. Economists pointed out that the government could maintain services but save large amounts of money by making public spending more efficient. For example, an estimated €5 billion could be saved if French hospitals increased the proportion of same day surgery from current 40 per cent levels to the European norm of 80 per cent. The savings would come from not having patients staying overnight in hospitals when they had a minor operation.

However, making the French state more efficient will not help boost total spending in the economy. French businesses need to invest more to create both jobs and output. More private sector spending is needed to make up for the cuts in public sector spending.

With the election of Emmanuel Macron as French president in 2017, there was continued commitment to cut public spending. With public spending at 55 per cent of GDP in 2017, he plans to cut public sector jobs by 120,000 and, with other cost savings, bring this down to 52 per cent of GDP. His supporters hope other policies, such as his planned reduction in corporation tax rates, will help increase aggregate demand. A fall in corporation tax should increase business investment and create more private sector jobs. There were also plans to increase government spending in some targeted areas; for example, extra spending worth €50 billiion over five years to be spent on training schemes for the unemployed youth.

Source: adapted from © the *Financial Times* 18.3.2014
All Rights Reserved

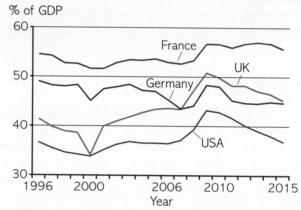

▲ Figure 1 Government spending as a percentage of GDP, selected countries, 1996–2015

Source: adapted from www.oecd.org

SUBJECT VOCABULARY

budget deficit (or fiscal deficit) when government spending is greater than tax revenue.
budget surplus (or fiscal surplus) when government spending is less than the amount of money received in taxation or other income during a particular period. Income received by the government is sometimes called government receipts.
exchange rate the price at which one currency is sold for another.
fiscal policy decisions about government spending, together with taxes and government borrowing, are called fiscal policy.
net exports or the net trade balance exports minus imports.
non-price factors factors, other than price, that affect the demand for a good or service.
protectionism government actions or polices that restrict international trade.

EXAM PRACTICE

GOVERNMENT EXPENDITURE AND TRADE

SKILLS REASONING, ANALYSIS, COMMUNICATING, PROBLEM-SOLVING, INTERPRETING

Q

1 In November 2016, the value of Egypt's currency, the Egyptian pound (EGP), fell. Within a few weeks it had fallen to around half its value. Explain the likely impact on Egypt's net trade balance of this change in the exchange rate.

(4 marks)

2 Figure 2 shows the forecast for Japan's balance of trade between 2016 and 2018. Which one of the following can be deduced from Figure 2?

(a) Japan's trade deficit is forecast to be US$46 billion in 2018.

(b) Japan's net trade balance is forecast to improve each year between 2016 and 2018.

(c) Japan's net trade balance is forecast to be −US$30 billion in 2017.

(d) Japan's balance of trade surplus is forecast to narrow over the period 2016–18.　　**(1 mark)**

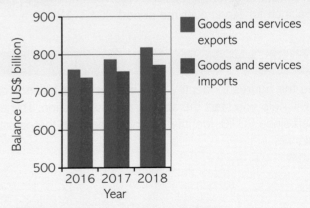

▲ **Figure 2 Japanese balance of trade, 2016–18**

Source : OECD, 'Economic outlook', 2016, Issue 2, preliminary version

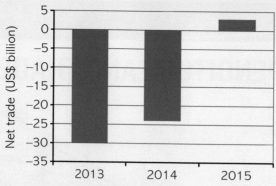

▲ Figure 3 Japan's trade in goods and services, net trade (US$ billion)

Source: OECD

3 With reference to Figure 3, explain the term 'net trade balance'. **(4 marks)**

4 Japan's net trade balance

Extract A

According to the Bank of Japan 2017, Japan's exports have picked up recently, as overseas economies have continued to grow at a moderate rate. The rise in exports has mainly been led by automobile-related exports to advanced economies and IT related exports to emerging economies in Asia. Exports are likely to continue their upward trend. It is expected that advanced economies, such as the US and European economies, will continue to grow steadily and the recovery in emerging economies will take hold.

The election of Donald Trump in the USA, in November 2016, also caused the yen to weaken sharply against the dollar. A US dollar exchanged for 100–105 Japanese yen before the election, and afterwards, a US dollar exchanged for 110–115 Japanese yen. This has helped to boost export competitiveness. Provided the yen remains weak and Mr Trump's trade polices do not cause a rise in protectionism, export growth should remain strong for Japan.

Source: adapted from 'Outlook for Economic Activity and Prices January 2017', Bank of Japan; 'Weak yen helps push Japanese growth back on track', February 13 2017 by Robin Harding @ *Financial Times*.

With reference to the extract, Figure 2 and Figure 3, analyse **one** cause of the improvement in the net trade balance for Japan over the period 2013–18.

(6 marks)

AGGREGATE SUPPLY

Both aggregate demand and aggregate supply are important concepts in economics and, together, they explain changes in economic performance. This section explains the concept of aggregate supply as well as the aggregate supply curve. It fully develops factors that affect both the short-run and long-run aggregate supply curves. Economists have different views on the shape of the aggregate supply curve. This section discusses the issue, as well as the impact this may have on views about how the economy reacts to different events.

31 AGGREGATE SUPPLY

LEARNING OBJECTIVES

- Understand the concept of aggregate supply (AS) and the AS curve.
- Understand the distinction between a movement along and a shift of the AS curve.
- Understand the factors influencing SRAS, such as changes in costs of raw materials and energy, exchange rates and tax rates.
- Understand Keynesian and classical AS curves.
- Understand factors influencing LRAS: changes in: the state of technology; productivity education and skills; government regulations and tax; demography and net migration; and competition policy.

GETTING STARTED

For an economy of your choice, research how costs for firms might have changed over the last five years. For example, think about how movements in exchange rates might have affected the cost of imports. Have wage costs risen? What has happened to the price of oil?

THE SHORT-RUN AGGREGATE SUPPLY CURVE

In Chapter 10, it was argued that the supply curve for an industry was upward sloping. If the price of a product increases, firms in the industry are likely to increase their profits by producing and selling more. So the higher the price, the higher the level of output. The supply curve discussed here is a microeconomic supply curve. Is the macroeconomic supply curve (i.e. the supply curve for the whole economy) the same?

The macroeconomic supply curve is called the **aggregate supply curve**, because it is the sum of all the industry supply curves in the economy. It shows how much output firms wish to supply at each level of prices.

In the short run, the aggregate supply curve is upward sloping. The short run is defined here as the period when money wage rates and the prices of all other factor inputs in the economy are fixed. Assume that firms wish to increase their level of output. In the short run, they are unlikely to take on extra workers. Taking on extra staff is an expensive process. Sacking them if they are no longer needed is likely to be even more costly, not just because of the money needed, but also in terms of industrial relations within the company. So firms tend to respond to increases in demand in the

short run by working their existing labour force more intensively, for instance through overtime.

Firms will need to provide incentives for workers to work harder or longer hours. Overtime, for instance, may be paid at one and a half times the basic rate of pay. While basic pay rates remain constant, earnings will rise and this will tend to put up both the average and marginal costs per unit of output. In many sectors of the economy, where competition is imperfect and where firms have the power to increase their prices, the rise in labour costs will lead to a rise in prices. It only needs prices to rise in some sectors of the economy for the average price level in the economy to rise. So in the short term, an increase in output by firms is likely to lead to an increase in their costs, which in turn will result in some firms raising prices. However, the increase in prices is likely to be small because, given constant prices (e.g. wage rates) for factor inputs, the increases in costs (e.g. wage earnings) are likely to be fairly small too. Therefore the **short-run aggregate supply curve** is relatively price elastic. This is shown in Figure 1. A movement along the curve, caused by an increase in real output, from Y_1 to Y_2, leads to a small rise in the average price level from P_1 to P_2.

FIGURE 1

The short-run aggregate supply curve

A change in real output, for example from Y_1 to Y_2, will lead to a movement along the short-run aggregate supply curve. The slope of the SRAS line is very shallow because, while it is assumed that in the short-run wage rates are constant, firms will face some increased costs, such as overtime payments, when they increase output.

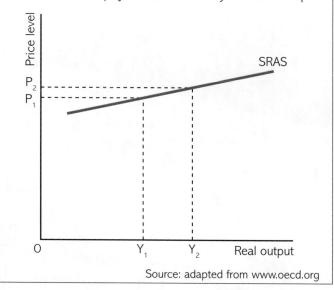

Source: adapted from www.oecd.org

If demand and real output fall in the short run, some firms in the economy will react by cutting their prices to try to stimulate extra orders. However, the opportunities to cut prices will be limited. Firms will be reluctant to sack workers and their fixed costs will remain the same, so their average cost and marginal cost will barely be altered. Again, the aggregate supply curve is relatively price elastic. The movement along the curve, caused by a fall in real output from Y_2 to Y_1, leads to a small fall in the average price level from P_2 to P_1.

ACTIVITY 1
SKILLS ▶ REASONING, PROBLEM-SOLVING

CASE STUDY: SHORT-RUN AGGREGATE SUPPLY CURVE

Using a short-run aggregate supply (SRAS) curve, explain the likely effect on the price level, for each economy, of the following. Assume that the prices of all factor inputs are fixed.

(a) In 2016, there was a recession in Brazil. Brazil's real GDP contracted by 3.6 per cent.

(b) In 2017, the OECD forecast strong growth for the Indian economy. Real GDP was forecast to rise by 7.3 per cent in 2017.

SHIFTS IN THE SHORT-RUN AGGREGATE SUPPLY CURVE

The SRAS curve shows the relationship between aggregate output and the average price level, assuming that money wage rates in the economy are constant. A change in real output will lead to a movement along the SRAS curve and a change in the price level. But what if wage rates do change, or some other variable that affects aggregate supply changes? Then, just as in the microeconomic theory of the supply curve, the aggregate supply curve will shift.

Wage rates An increase in wage rates will result in firms facing increased costs of production. Some firms will respond by increasing prices. So at any given level of output, a rise in wage rates will lead to a rise in the average price level. This is shown in Figure 2 by a shift in the SRAS curve from $SRAS_1$ to $SRAS_2$.

Raw material prices A general fall in the prices of raw materials may occur. Perhaps world demand for commodities falls, or perhaps the value of the pound rises, making the price of imports cheaper. A fall in the price of raw materials will lower industrial costs and will lead to some firms reducing the prices of their products. Hence there will be a shift in the SRAS curve downwards. This is shown in Figure 2 by the shift from $SRAS_1$ to $SRAS_3$.

Taxation An increase in the tax burden on industry will increase costs. Hence the SRAS schedule will be pushed upwards, for instance from $SRAS_1$ to $SRAS_2$ in Figure 2.

Exchange rates If the exchange rate falls, the price of imported goods is likely to rise. This will lead to an increase in prices throughout the economy. So a fall in the exchange rate will shift the short-run aggregate supply curve up from $SRAS_1$ to $SRAS_2$ in Figure 2. However, a rise in the exchange will lead to a fall in the price of imported goods. This will lead to a fall in prices throughout the economy. So a rise in the exchange rate will shift the short-run aggregate supply curve downwards, from $SRAS_1$ to $SRAS_3$ in Figure 2.

FIGURE 2

Shifts in the short-run aggregate supply curve
The SRAS curve is drawn on the assumption that costs, in particular the wage rate, remain constant. A change in costs is shown by a shift in the curve. For instance, an increase in wage rates would push $SRAS_1$ up to $SRAS_2$ while a fall in wages rates would push the curve down to $SRAS_3$.

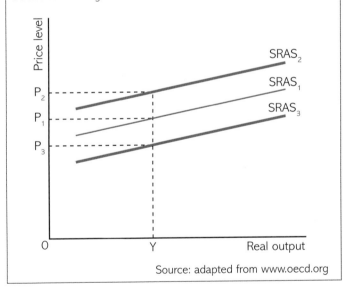

Source: adapted from www.oecd.org

Productivity Productivity is output per unit of input employed. So labour productivity is output per worker. Labour productivity is often measured as GDP per hour worked. Capital productivity is output per unit of capital employed. Increases in productivity over time, for example because of a better-educated workforce or improved technology, will lead to an increase in long-run supply. However, it will also reduce costs of production in the short run, so shifting the SRAS curve downwards.

This is because a rise in productivity reduces unit costs (the cost per unit of output produced). 'Unit labour costs' is also a term widely used by economists.

Unit labour costs measures the average cost of labour per unit of output. So, if labour productivity rises and wages remain the same, unit labour costs will fall, so shifting the SRAS curve downwards.

When there is a large change in wage rates, raw material prices or taxation, a **supply-side shock** is said to occur. A supply-side shock, like a doubling of the price of oil, can have a significant impact on aggregate supply, pushing the SRAS curve upwards.

ACTIVITY 2 SKILLS PROBLEM-SOLVING, REASONING, INTERPRETATION

CASE STUDY: SOUTH KOREA

Using a diagram, show the likely effect on the SRAS curve for South Korea in the following situations.

(a) Labour productivity (output per worker) increased by around 1 per cent between 2011 and 2015.

(b) A sharp fall in oil prices from a peak of US$115 per barrel in June 2014 to US$27 per barrel in January 2016. South Korea is a big oil importer.

THE LONG-RUN AGGREGATE SUPPLY CURVE

In the short run, changes in wage rates or the price of raw materials have an effect on the aggregate supply curve, shifting the SRAS curve up or down. Equally, a rise in real output will lead to a movement along the SRAS curve.

In the long run, however, there is a limit to how much firms can increase their supply. They run into capacity constraints. There is a limit to the amount of labour that can be hired in an economy. Capital equipment is fixed in supply. Labour productivity has been maximised. So it can be argued that in the long run, the aggregate supply curve is fixed at a given level of real output, whatever the price level. What this means is that the long-run aggregate supply curve is vertical on a diagram showing the price level and real output.

Figure 3 shows such a vertical **long-run aggregate supply curve** or LRAS curve. The LRAS curve shows the productive potential of the economy. It shows how much real output can be produced over a period of time with a given level of factor inputs, such as labour and capital equipment, and a given level of efficiency in combining these factor inputs. It can be linked to three other economic concepts.

FIGURE 3

The classical long-run aggregate supply curve
Classical economics assumes that in the long run, wages and prices are flexible and therefore the LRAS curve is vertical. In the long run, there cannot be any unemployment because the wage rate will be in equilibrium where all workers who want a job (the supply of labour) will be offered a job (the demand for labour). So, whatever the level of prices, output will always be constant at the full employment level of income.

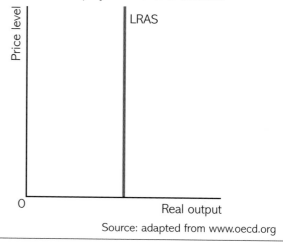

Source: adapted from www.oecd.org

- The LRAS curve is the level of output associated with production on the production possibility frontier of an economy. In Figure 4, any point on the boundary AB is one that shows the level of real output shown by the LRAS curve.

FIGURE 4

A production possibility frontier
Any point on the production possibility frontier AB shows the potential output of the economy when all resources are being used. The LRAS curve also shows the potential output of the economy. At any point in time, if the economy is operating on its LRAS curve, then it will be operating at one of the points along the production possibility frontier.

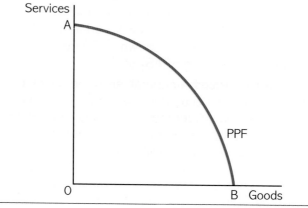

FIGURE 5

The trend rate of growth for an economy

At any point in time, the level of output shown by the LRAS is on the line of the trend rate of growth of output.

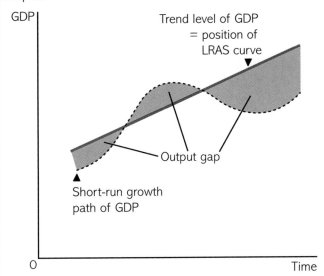

FIGURE 6

The trend rate of growth for an economy

Rate of growth (£ billion, 2010 prices)

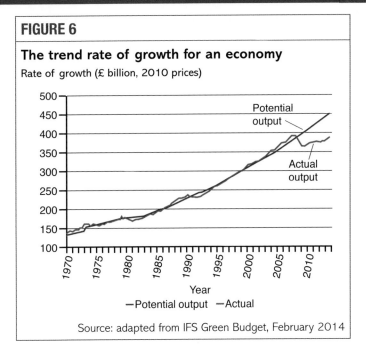

Source: adapted from IFS Green Budget, February 2014

- The LRAS curve is the level of output shown by the trend or long-term average rate of growth in an economy. When output is above or below this long-term trend level, an output gap is said to exist. In Figure 5, the economy is growing along the trend rate of growth. There are short-term variations in actual output above and below the trend rate. This shows that actual output can be above or below that given by the LRAS curve. When actual output is above the trend rate on Figure 5 in the short run, and so to the right of the LRAS curve in Figure 3, economic forces will act to bring GDP back towards its trend rate of growth. Equally, when it is below its trend rate of growth, and so to the left of the LRAS curve in Figure 3, the same but opposite forces will bring it back to that long-run position. For example, the UK economy was operating close to its LRAS curve for most of the period shown in Figure 6. However, from 2008, the UK experienced a deep and long recession. Actual output is significantly below potential output. In this period there was a relatively large negative output gap.

- The LRAS curve shows the level of **full capacity** output of the economy. At full capacity, there are no underused resources in the economy. Production is at its long-run maximum. In the short run, an economy might operate beyond full capacity, creating a positive **output gap**. However, this is unsustainable and the output in the economy must fall back to its full capacity levels.

SHIFTS IN THE LONG-RUN AGGREGATE SUPPLY CURVE

The LRAS curve is likely to shift over time. This is because the quantity and quality of economic resources changes over time, as does the way in which they are combined. These changes bring about changes in the productive potential of an economy.

Technological advances Improvements in technology allow new products to be made or existing products to be produced with fewer resources. Increases in capital productivity (output per unit of capital employed) shift the LRAS curve to the right. Improvements in technology will also increase labour productivity. If workers have access to better capital equipment, output per worker will increase.

Changes in relative productivity to competing economies An increase in productivity for an economy will increase its productive potential. The production possibility frontier will shift outwards. This means the LRAS will shift to the right. The LRAS of the world economy will increase if there is increased specialisation between economies, allowing production to be located in the cheapest and most efficient place in the world economy.

Changes in education and skills Improvements in education and skills of workers will raise their productivity (output per worker), so increasing LRAS.

Changes in government regulations Changes in government regulations can lead to an increase in LRAS. For example, making it simpler to set up a company could encourage more entrepreneurs to create companies, and in turn more output and jobs.

Imposing regulations on supermarkets to deal fairly with their suppliers could reduce the number of suppliers going into administration and reducing the productive potential of the economy.

Demographic changes and migration Demographic (population) changes that increase the size of the workforce are likely to increase LRAS. For example, an increase in immigration of people of working age will increase the productive potential of the economy. A population where the number of people of working age is shrinking will reduce LRAS.

Competition policy Government policies that increase competition among firms is likely to increase LRAS. Competition is likely to force firms to be more productive and reduce their costs, or more innovative producing new products and new ways of producing goods and services. However, less competition can sometimes be beneficial if it encourages investment and innovation. For example, without patent and copyright laws, firms that spend on research and development would find their results being copied by other firms.

Enterprise and risk taking Economies where enterprise and risk taking are encouraged are likely to see increases in their LRAS. The creation of new firms will increase output now and in the future when some of them grow in size. Enterprise and risk taking also encourage competition which in itself might increase LRAS.

Factor mobility Increases in factor mobility are likely to increase LRAS. For example, in the European Union, movements of workers from Poland or Estonia to work in Germany or France are likely to increase the productive potential of Germany, France and the EU.

Economic incentives Improvements in economic incentives can increase aggregate supply. For example, giving tax incentives for the unemployed to take a job can reduce unemployment and increase output.

The institutional structure of the economy The institutional structure of an economy refers to the political system, laws, the educational system, the banking system, and other systems that determine how an economy works. For example, if there is a strong tradition of paying bribes or other corruption within an economy, then making the system better governed by the rule of law is likely to increase LRAS. Equally, if the banking system is weak, saving and borrowing will be affected. A stronger banking system can encourage households to save and make funds more available to firms, again increasing long-run aggregate supply.

Figure 7 shows how a growth in potential output is drawn on an aggregate supply diagram. Assume that the education and skills of the workforce increase. This should lead to labour becoming more productive, in turn leading to an increase in the productive potential of the economy at full employment. The LRAS curve will then shift from $LRAS_1$ to $LRAS_2$, showing that at a given level of prices, the economy can produce more output. A fall in potential output, caused for instance by a fall in the size of the labour force, would be shown by a leftward shift in the curve, from $LRAS_1$ to $LRAS_3$.

A shift to the right in the LRAS curve shows that there has been economic growth. On a production possibility frontier (PPF) diagram, it would be represented by a movement outwards on the boundary. In Figure 5, it would be shown by a movement up along the trend rate of growth line. A shift to the left in the LRAS curve would show that the productive potential of the economy has fallen. On a PPF diagram, the boundary would shift inwards. On a trend rate of growth diagram, there would be a movement down the trend rate of growth line to the left.

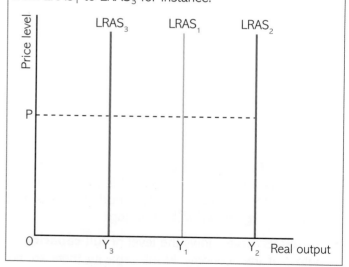

FIGURE 7

A shift in the long-run aggregate supply curve
An increase in the productive potential in the economy pushes the LRAS curve to the right, for instance, from $LRAS_1$ to $LRAS_2$. A fall in productive potential, in constrast, is shown by a shift to the left of the curve, from $LRAS_1$ to $LRAS_3$ for instance.

THE CLASSICAL AND KEYNESIAN LONG-RUN AGGREGATE SUPPLY CURVES

The vertical LRAS curve is called the classical LRAS curve. It is based on the classical view that markets tend to correct themselves fairly quickly when they are

ACTIVITY 3   SKILLS ANALYSIS, REASONING

CASE STUDY: THE OUTPUT GAP

Table 1 gives estimates of the output gap (deviation of actual GDP from potential GDP as a percentage of potential GDP) for a few different economies in the OECD for 2016.

Greece	−12.967
Hungary	0.426
Italy	−4.194
Japan	0.532
Portugal	−3.056
Spain	−5.158
UK	−0.529
USA	−1.193

▲ Table 1 Output gap, selected OECD countries, 2016

(a) Which economy was operating the closest to its LRAS curve?

(b) Which economies were operating to the left of their LRAS curves?

(c) Which economy experienced the greatest negative output gap? Comment on whether you would expect unemployment to be high or low for that economy.

(d) Which economies were operating to the right of their LRAS curves? Suggest how it may be possible for an economy to operate at this level in the short run.

pushed into **disequilibrium** by a shock. In the long run, product markets like the markets for oil, cameras or meals out, and factor markets like the market for labour, will be in equilibrium. If all markets are in equilibrium, there can be no unemployed resources. Hence, the economy must be operating at full capacity on its production possibility boundary.

Keynesian economists, however, point out that there have been times when markets have failed to clear for long periods of time. Keynesian economics was developed following the Great Depression of the 1930s when large-scale unemployment lasted for 10 years. If it had not been for the Second World War, high unemployment could have lasted for 20 or 30 years. John Maynard Keynes famously said that 'in the long run we are all dead'. There is little point in studying and drawing vertical LRAS curves if it takes 20–30 years to get back to the curve when the economy suffers a demand-side or supply-side shock.

Keynesian economists therefore suggest that the LRAS curve is the shape shown in Figure 8. At an output level of Y_2, the LRAS curve is vertical, as with the classical LRAS curve. Y_2 is the full capacity level of output of the economy. It is when the economy is on its production possibility boundary.

At an output level below Y_1, the economy is in a deep and prolonged depression. There is mass unemployment. In theory, unemployment should lead to wages falling. If there is too much supply of labour, the price of labour will fall. However, in a modern economy, there are many reasons why wages may not fall. There might be a national minimum wage that sets a floor for wages. Trade unions might fight to maintain wage levels. High unemployment might continue in one area of the country when there is full employment in another area because of labour being unable to move. Firms may not want to lower wages because this could lead to less motivated staff and thereby lower productivity. So at output levels below Y_1, markets, and in particular the labour market, fail to clear. Firms can hire and fire extra workers without affecting the wage rate. Wages are stuck and there is long-run disequilibrium. Hence, there is no pressure on prices when output expands.

FIGURE 8

The Keynesian long-run aggregate supply curve
Traditional Keynesian economists argue that, even in the long run, unemployment may persist because wages do not necessarily fall when unemployment occurs. When there is mass unemployment, output can be increased without any increases in costs and therefore prices. As the economy approaches full employment, higher output leads to higher prices. At full employment, the economy cannot produce any more ,whatever prices firms receive.

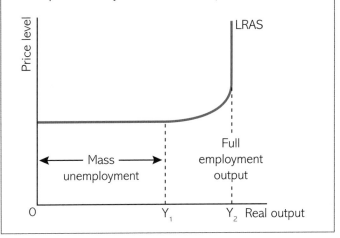

At an output level between Y_1 and Y_2, labour is becoming scarce enough for an increase in demand for labour to push up wages. This then leads to a higher price level. The nearer output gets to Y_2, the full employment level of output, the greater the effect of an increase in demand for labour on wages and therefore the price level.

ACTIVITY 4

 **SKILLS** COMMUNICATION, REASONING, ANALYSIS

CASE STUDY: A MINIMUM WAGE

High unemployment in an economy should push down wages, but at the bottom end a minimum wage exists in many advanced economies. In June 2015, the Fair Works Commission in Australia raised its minimum wage by an above inflation 2.5 per cent. From July 2015, 1.86 million workers must be paid a weekly wage of at least AUD 656.90. This is equivalent to AUD 17.29 per hour and is one of the highest minimum wage levels in the world. However, even in countries whose legal minimum wage is lower than this, there is growing pressure for firms to pay a 'living wage'. For example, US campaigners have successfully campaigned for Walmart®, McDonald's® and several cities and states to adopt a minimum wage above the national US$7.25 rate. In the UK, the living wage is calculated according to the basic cost of living and is set higher than the national minimum wage. Employers choose to pay on a voluntary basis. Arguments for a living wage focus on reducing inequality, improving incentives to work, reducing absences and helping to retain staff. Critics argue that firms need flexibility to lower wages to remain competitive and keep them in business.

1. Explain why a living wage might:

(a) prevent the labour market from clearing

(b) lead to a long-run aggregate supply curve (LRAS) that is not vertical.

THINKING LIKE AN ECONOMIST

THE CASE OF OIL

Oil price changes and inflation

Between 1970 and 2014, there were three periods when the price of oil on world markets jumped significantly, as can be seen from Figure 9. The first two were caused by political events. In 1973, a conflict in the Middle East saw Arab oil-producing countries restrict supplies to Western countries that supported their opponents. It was also the first time that OPEC, the oil cartel, used its market power to restrict supply and raise prices. In 1978, political upheaval in Iran brought a Shia Muslim government to power. Iran was a major oil producer at the time.

When it severely restricted supplies of oil to the market, the oil price increased dramatically. Finally, there was a significant rise in the price of oil from 2003 to 2012. The first two oil shocks were caused by a sudden fall in the supply of oil. The last was caused by increased demand for oil, particularly from China. In the early 2000s, Chinese demand for commodities such as oil saw a large increase fuelled by its average 10 per cent growth rate per year. As Figure 9 shows, there was sharp fall in the price of oil in 2008 and 2009 as Europe and the USA suffered recessions due to a banking crisis. Their demand for oil fell.

However, demand from fast-growing emerging countries such as China and India continued to grow. By 2010, oil prices had recovered significantly before falling again in 2013 as growth in China fell. In 2014, a sudden increase in the production of oil and a simultaneous fall in global demand for oil caused oil prices to plunge. The price of crude oil was trading at US$115 a barrel in June 2014, but this had fallen to as low as US$27 a barrel by January 2016.

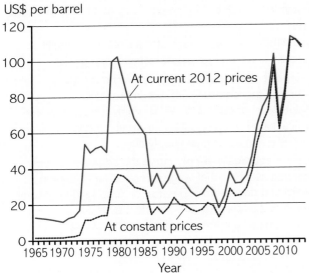

▲ **Figure 9 Spot oil price[1], US$ per barrel at current and constant (2011 US$) price, 1965–2014**
1. 1965–83 Arabian Light, 1984–2011 Brent
Source: adapted from BP Statistical Review of World Energy, 2014

The impact on the short-run aggregate supply curve

The three periods of sharp oil prices all had an important effect on the short-run aggregate supply curve of economies, including the UK. Oil price rises increase the costs of firms. Businesses as different

as farming and clothes manufacture use materials made from oil. So as oil prices rise, material costs for many firms also went up. Oil prices also increase transport costs for firms, so a change in the price of oil will have a significant impact on an economy. So at any given level of output, firms need to charge higher prices to cover their costs. As a result, the short-run aggregate supply curve shoots upwards, as shown in Figure 10. For the UK, the oil price rises of 1973–75 and 1979–81 were a major contributor to the inflation in those periods. However, the large increases in the oil price between 2003 and 2007 and then 2009–12 had far less impact on inflation. One reason was that the average amount of oil used to generate £1 of GDP was far less between 2003 and 2012 than in 1975 or 1981. Greater energy efficiency and the decline of the manufacturing industry were the main reasons for this. Another reason for the small impact of the oil price was that UK firms found it much more difficult to pass on price rises to their customers than in 1975 or 1981.

The economic climate was more competitive and firms tended to absorb oil price rises rather than pass them on. The severe and prolonged recession and weak recovery of 2009 to 2012 also meant that firms found it hard to pass on oil prices rises to customers.

The recent fall in the price of oil, since 2014, will cause costs for firms to fall. This will shift the SRAS curve downwards (an increase in aggregate supply). Emerging economy oil importers are likely to be the main winners. They are likely to use more oil to generate each dollar of their GDP. The fall in oil prices will also be beneficial to economies who are dealing with high inflation. India, for example, has seen a fall in inflationary pressures as oil import prices have fallen.

The impact on the long-run aggregate supply curve

There may also be an effect on the LRAS curve if there is a sustained rise in oil prices. Many economists argue that the oil price rises of 1973–75 and 1979–81 reduced the productive potential of the UK economy, shifting the LRAS curve to the left, as shown in Figure 10. The rise in the oil prices meant that some capital equipment that was oil intensive became too expensive to run. This equipment was left unused and then scrapped, leading to a permanent fall in the amount of capital in the economy.

Because the economy was far less oil dependent by 2003, this scrapping of equipment was less significant. Firms had become reluctant to invest in equipment using oil when there were good substitutes because they were afraid of a large rise in oil prices.

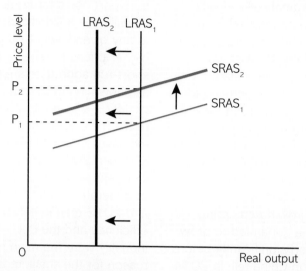

▲ Figure 10 The effect of steep rises in oil prices on aggregate supply

CHECKPOINT

1 If the price of oil increases, what happens to costs in the economy?

2 State three reasons why the SRAS curve might shift to the right (downwards).

3 What might happen to the exchange rate to shift the SRAS to the left (upwards)?

4 State how the LRAS relates to the PPF.

5 What is meant by the term 'trend rate of growth'?

6 How do technological advances influence the LRAS?

7 State three reasons why the LRAS might shift to the right.

8 Create a Keynesian long-run aggregate supply curve.

SUBJECT VOCABULARY

aggregate supply curve the relationship between the average level of prices in the economy and the level of total output.

disequilibrium a loss or lack of equilibrium or stability, especially in relation to supply, demand and prices.

full capacity the level of output where no extra production can take in the long run with existing resources. The full capacity level of output for an economy is shown by the classical long-run aggregate supply curve or the vertical part of a Keynesian aggregate supply curve.

long-run aggregate supply curve the aggregate supply curve that assumes that wage rates are variable, both upward and downwards. Classical or supply side economists assume that wage rates are flexible. Keynesian economists assume that wage rates may be 'sticky downwards' and hence the economy may operate at less than full employment even in the long run.

output gap the difference between actual level of GDP and the productive potential of the economy (actual output less trend output).

productivity output per unit of input employed.

short-run aggregate supply curve the upward sloping aggregate supply curve that assumes that money wage rates are fixed.

supply-side shock a factor, such as changes in wage rates or commodity prices, that causes the short-run aggregate supply curve to shift.

EXAM PRACTICE

AGGREGATE SUPPLY 2007–13

SKILLS REASONING, INTERPRETATION

Q

1 In 2014 the average annual OPEC crude oil price was US$96 per barrel. However, by late 2014, the price of oil started to collapse and continued on this downward trend. In 2016, the average price of oil per barrel was only US$41 per barrel. Explain the likely impact on the short-run aggregate supply curve for a net oil importer economy.

(4 marks)

2 Disappointing productivity for the USA

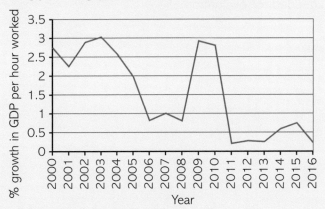

▲ Figure 11 US labour productivity, 2000–16

Source: OECD

Multifactor productivity is measured as an index, 2010 = 100. Multifactor productivity reflects the overall efficiency with which labour and capital inputs are used together in the production process.

Year	Multifactor productivity
2000	89.2
2006	96.8

Year	Multifactor productivity
2010	100
2016	101.8

▲ Table 1 Multifactor productivity in the USA between 2000 and 2006 and 2010 and 2016.

Source: OECD

Extract A: Low productivity remains a barrier

US labour productivity was forecast to increase by 1 per cent in 2017, but this was still below the growth in productivity experienced in the USA in the early 2000s. Since 2008–09, most economies have suffered from a slowing rate of productivity growth. In comparison, the major emerging economies were expected to experience a 3.3 per cent labour productivity growth in 2017, but this was still below the 4.9 per cent average growth between 1999 and 2006.

The productivity weakness in recent years seems to reflect the impact the global financial crisis had on firms appetite to invest. For the USA, total investment (gross fixed capital formation) grew by 6.3 per cent in 2000. At the height of the crisis, 2009, the annual growth in investment was −13.1 per cent. By 2016, investment growth was just 0.6 per cent. In the USA this is a double blow, because low labour productivity growth is coming at the same time as a slowing down in the size of the labour force.

However, for many developed economies with an ageing population, migration can increase the growth of the labour force. The McKinsey report on migration found that North America and the continent of Australia perform better than most European countries in integrating migrants into labour markets. So, policies to promote migration rather than reduce it may be beneficial. An article by economists in the IMF's research department argues a 1 percentage point increase in the share of migrants in the adult population of a developed country can raise GDP per capita by 2 per cent over the long term. Both high- and low-skilled migrants provided a boost.

(a) Using Table 1, calculate the percentage change in multifactor productivity for the USA between 2000 and 2006 and between 2010 and 2016. **(4 marks)**

(b) With reference to the extract, explain how immigration will likely affect the long-run aggregate supply curve for an economy. **(4 marks)**

(c) With reference to Figure 11 and the extract, discuss the likely impact on the long-run aggregate supply curve for the USA of the fall in 'firms appetite to invest' since the global financial crisis. **(14 marks)**

EXAM HINT

Use the extract to identify the effect of a fall in investment. Make reference to data in Figure 11. Explain clearly the impact a fall in investment is likely to have on the LRAS – think about how investment will affect productivity and productive potential. To evaluate, consider whether the effect of the fall in investment is likely to have a significant effect on the LRAS for the USA. Are there any other factors likely to affect the position of the LRAS curve, mentioned in the extract, or from your own knowledge?

3 People in emerging markets keen to use new technology

Citizens of developing nations are making use of technology and online resources to train themselves, increasing the stock of skilled people. This is particularly noticeable in China, where there is a rapid increase of fast growing digital companies that provide tuition to users in subjects including IT. The Internet is allowing skills to be acquired across China and not just in the larger cities.

The public sector is also helping Asian students advance their education using technology. For example, in Indonesia the government has encouraged universities to set up online courses, and digital resources also help to keep costs down for students who struggle to afford expensive text books.

However, it can be hard for education in technology to be funded adequately. In India, companies are struggling to find graduates with the necessary skills in advanced fields such as data analysis. Formal education is struggling with this. It is up to individual companies to invest heavily in extended training for new employees if the skills gap is to be filled.

(a) With reference to the extract above, examine the likely impact on the long-run aggregate supply curve for emerging economies of the increasing use of technology in education and training. **(8 marks)**

EXAM HINT

Use the extract to help identify the impact of the use of technology. Explain clearly how the use of technology in this example will influence long-run aggregate supply. Draw a relevant diagram. The extract also identifies a reason why the impact might be limited; this would help to get the two marks needed for evaluation.

NATIONAL INCOME

This section introduces the term 'the circular flow of income' and explains the difference between injections and withdrawals. It introduces the concept of equilibrium level of real national output. The section analyses the impact of changes in aggregate demand and aggregate supply using aggregate demand/supply diagrams. It uses the multiplier process to explain why initial changes in injections or withdrawals will lead to a greater impact on national income.

32 CIRCULAR FLOW OF INCOME

LEARNING OBJECTIVES

- Understand the circular flow of income.
- Understand the distinction between income and wealth.
- Understand the distinction between injections and withdrawals.
- Understand the impact of net injections into, and net withdrawals from, the circular flow of income.

GETTING STARTED

Get a sheet of paper and put your name in a box. Put arrows into the box showing your (or your family's) sources of income. Put arrows out of the box showing what you (or your family) do with that income. Group all spending under one category, 'expenditure'. Now think of how your (or your family's) outgoings are linked to your (or your family's) income, perhaps through the wages of your parents, the taxes they pay, which are spent by government or even through the international economy.

INCOME, OUTPUT AND EXPENDITURE

Macroeconomics is concerned with the economy as a whole. A key macroeconomic variable is the level of total output in an economy, often called **national income**. There are three ways in which national income can be calculated. To understand why, consider a very simple model of the economy where there is no foreign trade (a **closed economy** as opposed to an **open economy** where there is foreign trade) and no government. In this economy, there are only households and firms, which spend all their income and revenues.

Households own the **wealth** of the nation. They own the stock of land, labour and capital used to produce goods and services. They supply these factors to firms in return for **income**. These incomes are rents, wages, interest and profits – the rewards to the factors of production. They then use this money to buy goods and services.

Firms produce goods and services. They hire factors of production from households and use these to produce goods and services for sale back to households.

The flow from households to firms is shown in Figure 1. The flow of money around the economy is shown blue and red. Households receive payments

FIGURE 1

The circular flow of income in a simple economy
Households supply factors of production to firms in return for rent, wages, interest and profit. Households spend their money on goods and services supplied by firms.

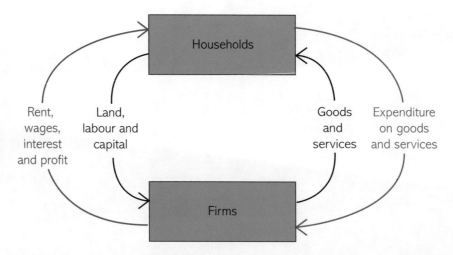

for hiring their land, labour and capital. They spend all that money on the goods and services produced by firms (consumption). An alternative way of putting this is to express these money payments in real terms, taking into account changes in prices. The real flow of products and factor services is shown in black. Households supply land, labour and capital in return for goods and services. The **circular flow of income model** can be used to show that there are three ways of measuring the level of economic activity.

National output (O) This is the value of the flow of goods and services from firms to households. It is the black line on the right of Figure 1.

National expenditure (E) This is the value of spending by households on goods and services. It is the red line on the right of the diagram.

National income (Y) This is the value of income paid by firms to households in return for land, labour and capital. It is the blue line on the left of the diagram.

So income, expenditure and output are three ways of measuring the same flow. To show that they must be identical and not just equal, we use the ' $\equiv$ ' sign.

$$O \equiv E \equiv Y$$

INJECTIONS AND WITHDRAWALS

The simple circular flow of income model in Figure 1 can be made more realistic by adding **injections** and **withdrawals or leakages**. An injection into the circular flow is spending that does not come from households. There are three injections.

- Investment is spending by firms on new capital equipment like factories, offices and machinery. It

is also spending on stocks (or inventories) of goods that are used in the production process.
- Government spending is spending by central and local government as well as other government agencies.
- Exports is spending by foreigners on goods and services made in the economy.

Withdrawals or leakages from the circular flow are spending that does not flow back from households to firms. There are three withdrawals that correspond to the three injections.

- Saving by households is money that is not spent by households. Equally, firms do not spend all of their money on wages and profits but may save some of it.
- Taxes paid to the government take money from both households and firms.
- Imports from abroad are bought by both households and firms. The money paid in taxes then does not flow back round the circular flow.

A circular flow diagram that includes injections and withdrawals is shown in Figure 2.

In equilibrium, when there is no tendency to change, injections must equal withdrawals. When this happens, output, expenditure and income flowing round the circular flow remain the same. When injections are greater than withdrawals, national income will rise to reflect the greater spending. Equally, when injections are less than withdrawals, spending will fall. For example, a rise in investment will increase spending in the economy. A rise in saving will reduce spending.

FIGURE 2

Injections and withdrawals and the circular flow
Investment, government spending and exports are injections into the circular flow. They raise spending. Saving, taxes and imports are withdrawals and reduce spending.

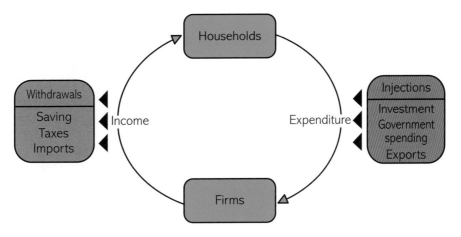

ACTIVITY 1   SKILLS   REASONING, COMMUNICATION, PROBLEM-SOLVING

CASE STUDY: EFFECTS ON NATIONAL INCOME

Assume an economy is initially in equilibrium, with injections equal to withdrawals.

(a) What will be the effect on national income for each of the following? State, for each one, whether injections/withdrawals are rising or falling.

- a rise in government spending
- a fall in taxation
- a rise in savings
- a rise in the value of the currency on foreign exchange markets (exchange rate)
- a fall in interest rates.

THINKING LIKE AN ECONOMIST

INCREASING GOVERNMENT SPENDING

The global financial crisis caused recessions in many countries, including the USA and UK. In the USA in 2009, President Barack Obama launched a stimulus plan, worth almost 6 per cent of GDP. Taxes for businesses were cut and government spending on health, education, social security and infrastructure rose. Money was injected into the circular flow to increase national output, income and expenditure. Between 2010 and 2012, the USA was reporting growth figures consistently higher than the UK.

In contrast, although the UK government had increased some government spending and reduced the rate of VAT in 2009, the stimulus was less significant. By 2010, the new coalition government decided the priority was to reduce the budget deficit (the difference between government spending and taxation). The government raised taxes and reduced government spending. The circular flow model shows that this will shrink the size of income, output and expenditure flowing round the economy. Critics argue that this policy was a mistake and explains why UK growth between 2010 and 2013 was weak compared to that of the USA. The UK economy only expanded slightly in this period due to small increases in investment and exports. Some argue that a better policy would have been for the government to increase its spending on investment goods, because this type of spending would increase the LRAS curve as well as inject money into the circular flow.

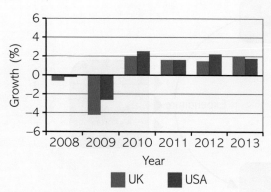

▲ **Figure 3 US and UK growth rates, 2008–13**

Source: OECD Economic Outlook: Statistics and Projections

CHECKPOINT

1 Sketch a circular flow of income diagram.
2 State the difference between income and wealth.
3 State the three injections into the circular flow of income.
4 State the three withdrawals from the circular flow of income.

(Questions 5–8 assume the economy is initially in equilibrium.)

5 What happens to national income if investment rises?
6 What happens to national income if investment falls?
7 What happens to national income if savings rise?
8 What happens to national income if imports fall?

SUBJECT VOCABULARY

circular flow of income a model of the economy that shows the flow of goods, services and factors and their payments around the economy.

closed economy an economy in which there is no foreign trade.

income rent, interest, wages and profits earned from wealth owned by economic actors.

injections in the circular flow of income, spending that is not generated by households including investment, government spending and exports.

national income the value of the output, expenditure or income of an economy over a period of time.

open economy an economy in which there is trade with other countries.

wealth a stock of assets that can be used to generate a flow of production or income. For example, physical wealth such as factories and machines is used to make goods and services.

withdrawals or leakages in the circular flow of income, spending by households that does not flow back to domestic firms. It includes savings, taxes and imports.

EXAM PRACTICE

 SKILLS PROBLEM-SOLVING, COMMUNICATION, REASONING

Q

1 Figure 4 shows exports and imports for China as a percentage of GDP in 2016.

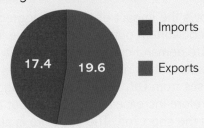

- Imports
- Exports

17.4   19.6

▲ **Figure 4 Chinese exports and imports as a percentage of GDP, 2016**

(a) Explain the difference between an injection and a withdrawal from the circular flow of income.
(4 marks)

2 South Korea needs a boost

Extract A

In June 2016, the South Korean government was facing growing calls for a stimulus package to boost South Korea's GDP. The shipbuilding and shipping industries were expected to lay off workers and the UK's Brexit vote was creating uncertainty for South Korea. In 2017, the government announced a record US$380 billion government spending programme for 2018. The spending plan was a 7 per cent increase from the 2017 budget and was the biggest year on year increase since 2009, when South Korea was hit by the global financial crisis.

Extract B

South Korea's exports, which make up about one-half of the country's US$1.38 trillion gross domestic product, had fallen for a 17th consecutive month in May 2016. The government had forecasted a 4.7 per cent fall in exports in 2016, compared to 2015.

Source: adapted from © the *Financial Times*, 'S. Korea plans stimulus boost in wake of Brexit', 28.6.2016 and 'Seoul plans biggest spending splurge since financial crisis', 30.8.2017, All Rights Reserved.

(a) With reference to extract A, explain the term 'injection into the circular flow of income'.
(4 marks)

(a) With reference to extract B, explain the likely impact on South Korea's national income of the fall in exports. **(4 marks)**

33 EQUILIBRIUM LEVELS OF REAL NATIONAL OUTPUT

LEARNING OBJECTIVES

- Understand the concept of equilibrium level of real national output.
- Understand the causes of changes in equilibrium levels of real national output as a result of shifts in AD and/or AS curves.
- Understand the causes of changes in the price level as a result of shifts in AD and/or AS curves.
- Understand the differences between the classical and Keynesian models.

GETTING STARTED

Price and equilibrium output in a market are fixed by the forces of demand and supply. So in the whole economy, price and output are fixed by the aggregate demand (AD) and aggregate supply (AS). Give two factors that are currently in the news that affect either AD or AS. Explain what impact these are having on overall prices and output in the economy as a whole.

EQUILIBRIUM OUTPUT IN THE SHORT RUN

Chapters 27 and 31 outlined theories of aggregate demand and aggregate supply. Both **Keynesian economists** and **classical economists** agree that in the short run the aggregate demand curve is downward sloping while the aggregate supply curve is upward sloping. The **equilibrium level of output** in the short run occurs at the intersection (crossing) of the aggregate demand and aggregate supply curves. In Figure 1, the equilibrium level of income and output is OY. The equilibrium price level is OP.

An increase in aggregate demand will shift the aggregate demand curve to the right. Aggregate demand is made up of consumption, investment, government spending and export minus imports. So an increase in aggregate demand will result from an increase in one of these components. For example:

- a fall in interest rates will raise both consumption and investment
- a fall in the exchange rate will boost exports and reduce imports

- a lowering of income tax will raise consumption because households will now have higher disposable income.

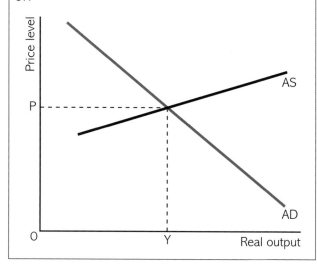

FIGURE 1

Equilibrium output
The equilibrium level of national output is set at the intersection of the aggregate demand and supply curves at OY. The equilibrium price level is OP.

Figure 2 shows the impact of a rise in aggregate demand on equilibrium output and the price level. The aggregate demand curve shifts from AD_1 to AD_2. Equilibrium output then rises from OY_1 to OY_2 while the price level rises from OP_1 to OP_2. A rise in aggregate demand therefore increases both real output and the price level in the short run. The opposite is also true. A fall in aggregate demand will lead both to a fall in real output and a fall in the price level.

A fall in short-run aggregate supply (SRAS) will shift the SRAS curve upwards and to the left. A variety of factors could bring about a fall in SRAS. For example:

- wages of workers might rise
- raw material prices might go up
- taxes on goods and services might be raised by the government.

FIGURE 2

A rise in aggregate demand in the short run
A rise in aggregate demand, shown by the shift in the aggregate demand curve from AD_1 to AD_2, leads to a rise in both equilibrium real output from OY_1 to OY_2 and the price level from OP_1 to OP_2.

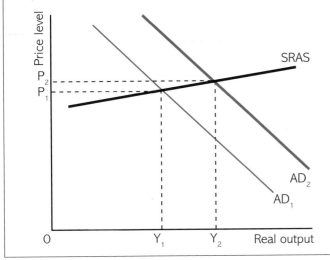

Figure 3 shows the impact of a fall in aggregate supply on equilibrium output and the price level. The SRAS curve shifts from $SRAS_1$ to $SRAS_2$. Equilibrium output then falls from OY_1 to OY_2. At the same time, the price level rises from OP_1 to OP_2. A fall in SRAS therefore leads to a fall in output but a rise in the price level in the short run. The opposite is also true. A rise in aggregate supply, shown by a downward shift to the right of the SRAS curve, will lead to a rise in equilibrium output and a fall in the price level.

FIGURE 3

A fall in aggregate supply in the short run
A fall in SRAS, shown by the shift in the SRAS curve from $SRAS_1$ to $SRAS_2$, leads to a fall in equilibrium real output from OY_1 to OY_2 and a rise in the price level from OP_1 to OP_2.

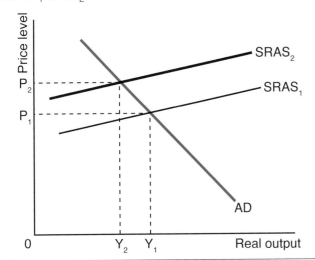

ACTIVITY 1   SKILLS ▷ REASONING, COMMUNICATION

CASE STUDY: STRIKE ACTION

What would be the effect on equilibrium income in the short run if the workers in the photograph were (a) successful or (b) unsuccessful with their demands?

ACTIVITY 2   SKILLS ▷ COMMUNICATION, REASONING, ANALYSIS

CASE STUDY: SOARING COMMODITY PRICES

By 2010, an increase in demand, particularly from China and emerging economies, was causing commodity prices, such as wheat, metals and oil, to increase quickly. This increased the cost of importing raw materials across many countries.

(a) Using a short-run AD/AS, explain the effect of this supply-side shock on real GDP and the price level.

EQUILIBRIUM OUTPUT IN THE LONG RUN

In the long run, the impact of changes in aggregate demand and supply are affected by the shape of the long-run aggregate supply (LRAS) curve. Classical economists argue that in the long run the aggregate supply curve is vertical, as shown in Figure 4. **Long-run equilibrium** occurs where the LRAS curve intersects with the aggregate demand curve. Hence equilibrium output is OY and the equilibrium price level is OP. Associated with the long-run equilibrium price level is a SRAS curve that passes through the point where LRAS = AD. The LRAS curve shows the supply curve for the economy at **full employment**. Hence there can be no unemployment in the long run according to classical economists.

FIGURE 4

Long-run equilibrium in the classical model
Long-run equilibrium output is OY, the full employment level of output, since wages are flexible both downwards as well as upwards.

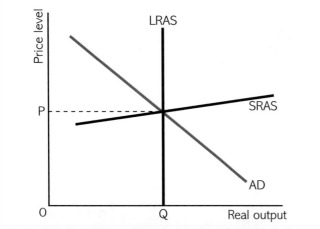

Keynesian economists argue that the LRAS curve is as shown in Figure 5. The economy is at full employment where the LRAS curve is vertical at output OY$_2$ – a point of agreement with classical economists. However, the economy can be in equilibrium at less than full employment.

In Figure 5 the equilibrium level of output is OY$_1$ where the AD curve cuts the LRAS curve. The key point of disagreement between classical and Keynesian economists is the extent to which workers react to unemployment by accepting real wage cuts.

FIGURE 5

Long-run equilibrium in the Keynesian model
Long-run equilibrium output OY$_1$ may be below the full employment level of output OY$_2$ because real wages may not fall when there is unemployment.

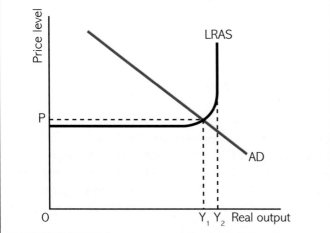

Classical economists argue that a rise in unemployment will rapidly lead to cuts in real wages. These cuts will increase the quantity demanded of labour and reduce the quantity supplied, returning the economy to full employment quickly and automatically. Keynesian economists, in contrast, argue that money wages are unlikely to fall. Workers will refuse to take money wage cuts and will resist cuts in their real wage. The labour market will therefore not clear except perhaps over a very long period of time, so long that it is possibly even not worth considering.

Having outlined a theory of equilibrium output, it is now possible to see what happens if either aggregate demand or aggregate supply changes.

A RISE IN AGGREGATE DEMAND

Assume that there is a rise in aggregate demand in the economy with LRAS initially remaining unchanged. For instance, there may be an increase in the wages of public sector employees paid for by an increase in the money supply, or there may be a fall in the marginal propensity to save and a rise in the marginal propensity to consume (as explained in Chapter 28). A rise in aggregate demand will push the AD curve to the right. The classical and Keynesian models give different conclusions about the effect of this.

The classical model A rise in aggregate demand, in the classical model, will lead to a rise in the price level but no change in real output in the long run. In Figure 6, the aggregate demand curve shifts to the right from AD$_1$ to AD$_2$. This could have been caused by a fall in interest rates, for example. The equilibrium price level rises from OP$_1$ to OP$_2$ but equilibrium real output remains the same at OY. In the classical model, no amount of extra demand will raise long-run equilibrium output. This is because the LRAS curve shows the maximum productive capacity of the economy at that point in time.

FIGURE 6

A rise in aggregate demand in the classical model
A rise in aggregate demand in the long run will shift the aggregate demand curve from AD$_1$ to AD$_2$. The equilibrium price level will rise from OP$_1$ to OP$_2$ but there will be no change in equilibrium real output, Y.

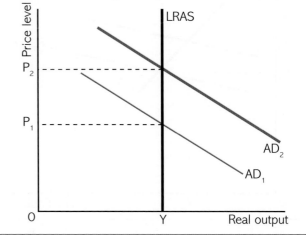

The movement from one equilibrium point to the next can also be shown on an AD/AS diagram. Assume there is a rise in aggregate demand, which shifts the aggregate demand curve from AD_1 to AD_2. In the short run, this will result in a movement up the SRAS curve. In Figure 7, output will rise from OY_1 to OY_2 and there will also be a small rise in the price level from OP_1 to OP_2. This will move the economy from A to B.

FIGURE 7

The classical model in the short and long run

A rise in aggregate demand shown by a shift to the right in the AD curve will result in a movement along the SRAS curve. Both output and prices will increase. In the long run, the SRAS curve will shift upwards with long-run equilibrium being re-established at C. The rise in demand has led only to a rise in the price level.

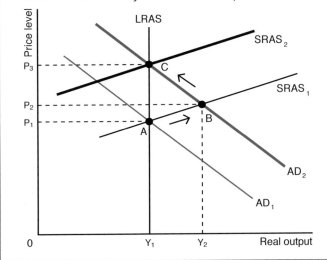

However, the economy is now in **long-run disequilibrium**. The full employment level of output is OY_1, shown by the position of the LRAS curve. The economy is therefore operating at over-full employment. Firms will find it difficult to recruit labour, buy raw materials and find new offices or factory space. They will respond by making higher offers for wages and other costs. The SRAS curve is drawn on the assumption that wage rates and other costs remain constant. So a rise in wage rates will shift the SRAS curve upwards. Short-run equilibrium output will now fall and prices will keep rising. The economy will only return to long-run equilibrium when the SRAS curve has shifted upwards from $SRAS_1$ to $SRAS_2$ so that aggregate demand once again equals long-run aggregate supply at C.

The conclusion of the classical model is that increases in aggregate demand will initially increase both prices and output (the movement from A to B in Figure 7). Over time prices will continue to rise but

output will fall as the economy moves back towards long-run equilibrium (the movement from B to C). In the long term, an increase in aggregate demand will only lead to an increase in the price level (from A to C). There will be no effect on equilibrium output. So increases in aggregate demand without any change in LRAS are purely inflationary.

The Keynesian model In the Keynesian model, the LRAS curve is shaped as in Figure 8. Keynesians would agree with classical economists that an increase in aggregate demand from, say, AD_4 to AD_5 will be purely inflationary if the economy is already at full employment at OY_4.

However, if the economy is in deep depression, an increase in aggregate demand will lead to a rise in output without an increase in prices. The shift in aggregate demand from AD_1 to AD_2 will increase equilibrium output from OY_1 to OY_2 without raising the price level from OP as there are unused resources available.

The third possibility is that the economy is a little below full employment, for instance at OY_3 in Figure 8. Then a rise in aggregate demand from AD_3 to AD_4 will increase both equilibrium output and equilibrium prices.

In the Keynesian model, increases in aggregate demand may or may not be effective in raising equilibrium output. It depends on whether the economy is below full employment or at full employment.

FIGURE 8

The Keynesian model

If the economy is already at full employment, an increase in aggregate demand in the Keynesian model creates an inflationary gap without increasing output. In a depression, an increase in aggregate demand will increase output but not prices. If the economy is slightly below full employment, an increase in aggregate demand will increase both output and prices.

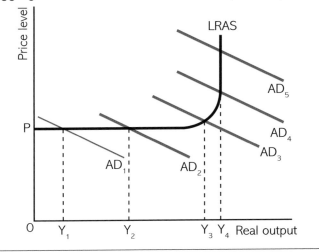

ACTIVITY 3 SKILLS COMMUNICATION, REASONING, ANALYSIS

CASE STUDY: US STIMULUS PLAN

In response to lower aggregate demand, caused by the global financial crisis in 2007–08, President Barack Obama launched a stimulus plan in 2009, worth almost 6 per cent of GDP. In the USA, taxes for businesses were cut and government spending on health, education, social security and infrastructure rose. It was hoped that this would take the USA out of its recession.

(a) Explain why Keynesians would support Barack Obama's policy for increasing real GDP in the USA in 2009.

A RISE IN LONG-RUN AGGREGATE SUPPLY

A rise in LRAS means that the potential output of the economy has increased. Rises in LRAS that are unlikely to shift the aggregate demand curve might occur if, for instance, incentives to work increased or there was a change in technology.

The classical model In the classical model, an increase in LRAS will lead to both higher output and lower prices. In Figure 9 a shift in the aggregate supply curve from $LRAS_1$ to $LRAS_2$ will increase equilibrium output from OY_1 to OY_2. Equilibrium prices will also fall from OP_1 to OP_2. Contrast this conclusion with what happens when aggregate demand is increased – a rise in prices with no increase in output. It is not surprising that classical economists are so strongly in favour of supply-side policies.

FIGURE 9

An increase in aggregate supply in the classical model
A shift to the right of the LRAS curve will both increase equilibrium output and reduce the price level.

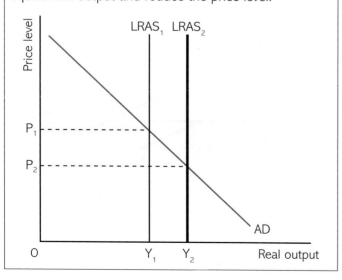

FIGURE 10

An increase in aggregate supply in the Keynesian model
The effect of an increase in LRAS depends upon the position of the aggregate demand curve. If the economy is at or near full employment, an increase will raise output and lower prices. However, if the economy is in depression at Y_D, an increase in LRAS will have no impact on the economy.

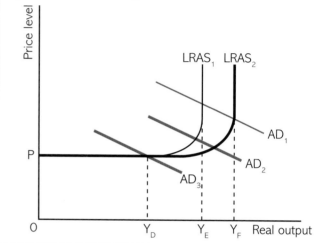

The Keynesian model In the Keynesian model, shown in Figure 10, an increase in aggregate supply will both increase output and reduce prices if the economy is at full employment. With aggregate demand at AD_1, a shift in the aggregate supply curve from $LRAS_1$ to $LRAS_2$ increases full employment equilibrium output from Y_E to Y_F. If the economy is at slightly less than full employment, with an aggregate demand curve of AD_2, then the shift to the right in the LRAS curve will still be beneficial to the economy, increasing output and reducing prices. However, Keynesians disagree with classical economists that supply-side measures can be effective in a depression. If the aggregate demand curve is AD_3, an increase in aggregate supply has no effect on equilibrium output. It remains obstinately stuck at Y_D. Only an increase in aggregate demand will move the economy out of depression.

It is now possible to understand one of the most important controversies in the history of economics. During the 1930s, classical economists argued that the only way to put the millions of unemployed during the Great Depression back to work was to adopt supply-side measures – such as cutting unemployment benefits, reducing trade union power and cutting marginal tax rates and government spending. John Maynard Keynes attacked this mainstream view by suggesting that the depression was caused by a lack of demand and suggesting that it was the government's responsibility to increase the level of aggregate demand. The same debate occurred again in the UK in the early 1980s. This time it was Keynesians who represented mainstream thinking.

They suggested that the only quick way to get the millions officially unemployed back to work was to expand aggregate demand. In the budget of 1981, the government did precisely the opposite – it cut its predicted budget deficit, reducing aggregate demand and argued that the only way to cure unemployment was to improve the supply-side of the economy.

INCREASING AGGREGATE DEMAND AND SUPPLY

In microeconomics, factors that shift the demand curve do not shift the supply curve as well and vice versa. For instance, an increase in the costs of production shifts the supply curve but does not shift the demand curve for a good (although there will of course be a movement along the demand curve as a result).

However, in macroeconomic aggregate demand and aggregate supply analysis, factors that shift one curve may well shift the other curve as well. For instance, assume that firms increase their planned investment. This will increase the level of aggregate demand. However, in the long run it will also increase the level of aggregate supply. An increase in investment will increase the capital stock of the economy. The productive potential of the economy will therefore rise. We can use aggregate demand and supply analysis to show the effects of an increase in investment.

An increase in investment in the classical model will initially shift the aggregate demand curve in Figure 11 to the right from AD$_1$ to AD$_2$. There will then be a movement along the SRAS curve from A to B. There is now long-run disequilibrium. How this will be resolved depends on the speed with which the investment is brought online and starts to produce goods and services. Assume that this happens fairly quickly. The LRAS curve will then shift to the right, say, from LRAS$_1$ to LRAS$_2$. Long-run equilibrium will be restored at C. Output has increased and the price level fallen slightly. There will also be a new SRAS curve, SRAS$_2$. It is below the original SRAS curve because it is assumed that investment has reduced costs of production.

Not all investment results in increased production. For instance, a business that refits a shop but then goes bankrupt within a few months will increase

aggregate demand but not LRAS. The LRAS curve will therefore not shift and the increased investment will only be inflationary. Equally, investment might be poorly directed. The increase in aggregate demand might be greater than the increase in LRAS. Here there will be an increase in equilibrium output but there will also be an increase in prices. The extent to which investment increases output and contributes to a lessening of inflationary pressure depends on the extent to which it gives a high rate of return in the long run.

FIGURE 11

An increase in investment expenditure
An increase in investment will increase aggregate demand from AD$_1$ to AD$_2$, and is likely to shift the LRAS curve from LRAS$_1$ to LRAS$_2$. The result is an increase in output and a small fall in prices.

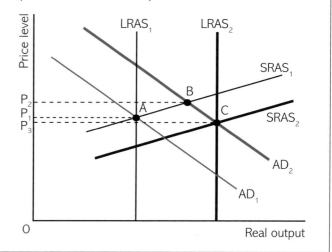

ACTIVITY 4   SKILLS ▶ COMMUNICATION, REASONING, ANALYSIS

CASE STUDY: EFFECTS ON AGGREGATE SUPPLY AND DEMAND

Using a classical model of the economy, explain the effect of the following on: (i) aggregate demand; (ii) short-run aggregate supply; (iii) output and prices in the long run:

(a) a 10 per cent rise in earnings

(b) an increase in real spending by government on education and training

(c) an increase in the average long-term real rate of interest from 3 per cent to 5 per cent.

THINKING LIKE AN ECONOMIST

THE GLOBAL FINANCIAL CRISIS

A demand-side shock to the global economy

The downturn of 2008–13 was caused by a banking crisis in 2007–08. The catalyst for the financial crisis came from the USA. Banks there had given large numbers of mortgages to low-income households (so called 'sub-prime' borrowers) on deals that fixed low repayments for a few years. This was irresponsible lending. It was clear that when these households came to pay the full rate of interest on their loans, many would not be able to afford the repayments. While this was happening, banks, which had given mortgages, were bundling mortgages together and selling packages of mortgages to other banks or investors. In the bundle would be mortgages from 'prime' borrowers, who were almost certainly going to be able to repay their loan, and mortgages from sub-prime borrowers who were likely to be unable to repay (they were likely to default). However, the US banks were selling these bundles as if all the mortgages were prime mortgages. Banks outside the US were buying these, without realising the risk, and selling them on in global financial markets.

At the same time, the housing bubble burst in the USA. This meant house prices were falling. The value of the loans taken out on mortgaged houses now

exceeded the value of the house in too many cases. The assets that banks were buying were now worth less than the price at which they had been bought. If a bank had bought too many of the 'bundled' mortgages, there was a risk the bank might collapse, since these assets had become 'bad debts'. However, individual banks did not know to what extent they were vulnerable and which other banks might be vulnerable. Banks stopped lending to each other, afraid that they might lose the money if the other bank collapsed. The UK, Ireland, Spain and Portugal were just some of the other countries affected.

In the USA, the authorities allowed Lehman Brothers, an investment bank, to fail in 2008. This caused widespread panic and individuals feared bank after bank would be allowed to fail, leading to losses for savers. Governments realised that they had to step in to prop up their banking systems. For example, in the UK, the government, having bought Northern Rock, proceeded to buy most of the Royal Bank of Scotland and part of Lloyds Bank. In Ireland, the government was forced to buy two main Irish banks. By the time the Irish government had pumped money into banks to cover their losses, it had cost the Irish taxpayer €56 billion. Many bank bailouts took place across Europe.

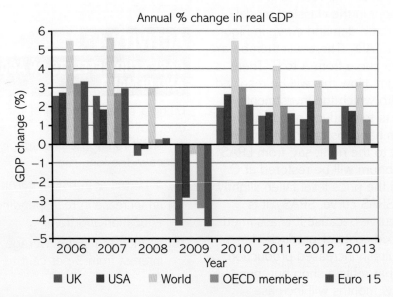

▲ Figure 12 Annual real GDP percentage change, various countries and grouping, 2006–13

Source: OECD

Note: Euro 15 – data provided by OECD for 15 countries in eurozone as an aggregate for comparative purposes in this period (Austria, Belgium, Estonia, Finland, France, Germany, Greece, Ireland, Italy, Luxembourg, Netherlands, Portugal, Slovak Republic, Slovenia, Spain).

Even though governments propped up the banking system, bank lending fell sharply, so consumption and investment fell. These components of aggregate demand also decreased because business and consumer confidence fell to rock bottom levels. Real GDP fell and unemployment rose in many economies. When an economy goes into recession, with aggregate demand falling, the demand for imports will also tend to fall. This means trading partners will see a fall in their exports. For example, the UK's main trading partners are the EU and USA. With recession in Europe and the USA, it was clear that export growth in the UK would remain weak. The economic slowdown in the USA and across Europe, caused by the financial crisis, would also effect economies that depended on exporting to the west. Since economies are linked through trade, a slowdown in one will cause a slowdown in another. Both developing and emerging economies suffered as their exports declined. Figure 12 shows the impact of the crisis on the global economy. The sharp fall in real GDP occurred throughout the global economy, but negative economic growth was concentrated more in the USA, UK and the rest of Europe. However, a slowdown in growth in many emerging and developing economies can still have devastating effects for keeping people in poverty.

The impact of the demand-side shock caused by the global financial crisis is shown in Figure 13 and Figure 14. Figure 13 shows the classical model and Figure 14 the Keynesian model.

In Figure 13, a fall in aggregate demand in the short run will cause the price level to fall from P_1 to P, and real GDP to fall from Y_1 to Y_2. The economy will move from point A to point B. At point B, the economy is in long-run disequilibrium and is operating at under-full employment. With rising unemployment, workers will have less wage bargaining power, so wages should be pushed downwards. This was clearly seen in the UK where many individuals saw a fall in their wages over this period. A fall in wages will shift the SRAS curve to the right (downwards). Prices continue to fall, so this also puts downwards pressure on wages. Equilibrium will be restored when the SRAS has shifted downwards from $SRAS_1$ to $SRAS_2$, so that aggregate demand once again equals LRAS at C. Real GDP moves from Y_2 to Y_1 and the price level moves from P_2 to P_3.

In Figure 14, a fall in aggregate demand will cause real GDP to fall if the economy is not operating at full employment. A fall in aggregate demand from AD_1 to AD_2 shows real GDP falling from Y_1 to Y_2 and the price level falling from P_1 to P_2. According to the Keynesian view, wages are 'sticky downwards' (this means money wages do not tend to fall, even if unemployment is rising). This means the economy will stay at Y_2 until aggregate demand increases again. Keynesians believe governments should actively step in and increase their own spending to increase aggregate demand.

In practice, a mix of the two views might be viewed as acceptable. Wages did fall during this period, but it is likely that without governments implementing policies to increase aggregate demand, the global recession might have lasted considerably longer. There is always great debate on which view has more credibility.

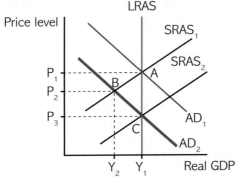

▲ **Figure 13 Impact of demand-side shock: classical model**

Source: OECD

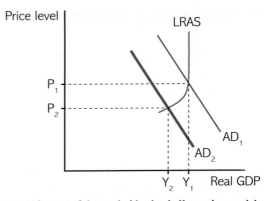

▲ **Figure 14 impact of demand-side shock: Keynesian model**

Source: OECD

CHECKPOINT

1 Create a short-run AD and AS diagram to show equilibrium level of real national output.

2 State three reasons why the AD curve might shift to the right.

3 State two reasons why the SRAS curve might shift to the left (upwards).

4 Create a short-run AD and AS diagram to show the effect on the real output and price level of a shift in the aggregate demand curve to the right.

5 Create a short-run AD and AS diagram to show the effect on the real output and price level of a shift in the SRAS curve to the left (upwards).

6 Sketch a diagram showing the classical LRAS curve. Show the effect of a rise in aggregate demand, in both the short run and long run, on the real output and price level.

7 Sketch a Keynesian LRAS curve.

8 Show the effect of a rise in aggregate demand on real output and the price level.

9 Using the classical model, create a diagram to show the effect on real output and the price level, of an increase in investment.

SUBJECT VOCABULARY

classical economists economists who hold the view that the long-run aggregate supply curve (LRAS) is vertical. So an increase in aggregate demand, in the long run, will be purely inflationary unless the LRAS curve shifts to the right.

equilibrium level of output the level of real national output (real GDP) when aggregate demand equals aggregate supply.

full employment the level of real national output (real GDP) where the LRAS curve is vertical.

Keynesian economists economists who hold the view that an increase in aggregate demand may or may not cause real national output to rise. It depends on whether the economy is below full employment or at full employment.

long-run disequilibrium a term used by classical economists when the short-run equilibrium level of real GDP is either below or above the level of real national output (real GDP) where the LRAS curve is vertical.

long-run equilibrium when aggregate demand equals long-run aggregate supply.

EXAM PRACTICE

SKILLS ANALYSIS, REASONING, CRITICAL THINKING

1 In April 2014, Japan raised its sales tax from 5 per cent to 8 per cent. The rise to 10 per cent has been delayed until 2019. (This tax is also called the consumption tax and is known in other countries as VAT. It is a tax on goods and services.)

Source: adapted from © the *Financial Times*, 'Japan's Shino Abe admits deflation fears with sales tax delay', 1.6.2016, All Rights Reserved.

Draw a short-run AS and AD diagram to show the effect of a rise in the sales tax on the price level and real output. **(4 marks)**

2 In 2015 and 2016, both Brazil and Russia were in a recession. It was felt that their economies could grow without causing pricing pressures.

Source: adapted from © the *Financial Times*, 'Emerging market inflation approaches turning point, 8.9.2017, All Rights Reserved.

Draw a Keynesian AS curve to show the effect of an increase in aggregate demand, on the price level and real output, if the economy is operating well below full employment. **(4 marks)**

3 The OECD outlook for South Korea in 2016–17 was positive. A rise in world trade growth was expected to boost South Korean exports and business investment. Consumption was also forecast to rise as individuals earn higher incomes and the savings ratio falls.

Source: OECD Economic Survey 2016, Korea

Draw a short-run AS and AD diagram to show the likely effect on the price level and real output for Korea, over this period. **(4 marks)**

4 The impact of China

Extract A

In 2016, the International Monetary Fund (IMF) expected China to account for almost 18 per cent of world economic activity. China is the world's largest economy, according to the IMF, measured by GDP adjusted for purchasing power parity. This means a slowdown in China's growth rate will have a significant impact on other economies. In 2010 China's growth rate was 10.6 per cent, by 2015 its growth rate was 6.92 per cent.

A fall in China's economic growth rate will reduce the export growth of economies that are dependent on Chinese demand for oil, metals, materials and capital equipment. Neighbouring economies, such as those of South Korea and Japan, who share integrated supply chains, are significantly affected. Of the European economies, Germany feels the greatest impact since it exports many capital goods to China.

In 2015, South Korea's economy was hit by two shocks. First, a new illness called Middle East Respiratory Syndrome caused consumption to fall in the second quarter. Second, a slowdown in economic growth in China and other Asian economies caused a fall in export growth. Exports to China and the other Asian economies account for one-half of South Korea's exports. South Korea is heavily reliant on exports as a component of aggregate demand. In 2012, exports of goods and services represented 56.3 per cent of GDP and its exports of goods to China accounted for 10 per cent of GDP in 2014.

Source: adapted from © the *Financial Times*, 'World economy feels the impact when China takes a knock', 7/1/2016, All Rights Reserved; OECD Economic Survey, Korea, 2016.

With reference to the extract and Figures 15 and 16, discuss the likely impact of the two shocks in 2015 on the price level and real output for South Korea.   **(14 marks)**

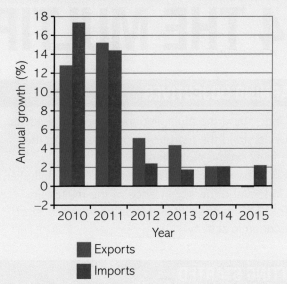

▲ **Figure 15 South Korean annual export and import growth rates (%), 2010–15**

Source: OECD

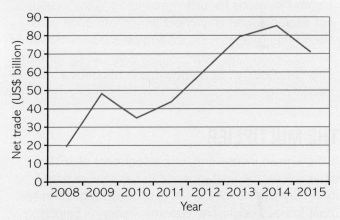

▲ **Figure 16 South Korean net trade in goods and services (US$ billion), 2008–15**

Source: OECD

EXAM HINT

A 'discuss' question requires knowledge, application, analysis and evaluation. Explain how aggregate demand is affected for each of the shocks. Link this with the data given in Figures 15 and 16. Make sure you use a short-run AD/AS diagrams to illustrate the effects on the price level and real output in South Korea. For the evaluation, consider to what extent South Korea might be affected – use the extract to support your answer.

34 THE MULTIPLIER

LEARNING OBJECTIVES

- Understand the multiplier and multiplier process.
- Understand the marginal propensities and their effects on the multiplier.
- Know how to calculate the value of the multiplier.
- Understand the significance of the multiplier for shifts in aggregate demand and the level of economic activity.

GETTING STARTED

A supermarket chain has decided to build a small local store in your area. Draw a chart showing five ways in which this investment in your local community leads to further spending in the economy. For example, one way could be: construction workers spend their wages → spending on food → increased output by food packager → more output by farmers. This illustrates what is known in economics as the multiplier process.

THE MULTIPLIER

If there is an increase in, say, investment of MYR 1, what will be the final increase in national income? John Maynard Keynes, a UK economist, argued in his most famous book, *The General Theory of Employment, Interest and Money*, published in 1936, that national income would increase by more than MYR 1 because of the **multiplier effect**.

To understand why there might be a multiplier effect, consider what would happen if Malaysian firms increased spending on new factories by MYR 100 million. Firms would pay other companies to build the factories. This MYR 100 million would be an increase in aggregate demand. The building company would use the money in part to pay its workers on the project. The workers would spend the money on everything from food to holidays. This spending would be an addition to national income. Assume that MYR 10 million is spent on food. Food manufacturers would then pay their workers who would spend their incomes on a variety of products, increasing national income further. Keynes argued that this multiplier effect would increase jobs in the economy. Every job directly created by firms through extra spending would indirectly create other jobs in the economy.

This process can be shown using the circular flow of income model. Assume that households spend 90 per cent of their gross income. The other 10 per cent is either saved or paid to the government in the form of taxes. Firms increase their spending by MYR 100 million, money that is used to build new factories. In Figure 1, this initial MYR 100 million is shown in stage 1 flowing into firms. The money then flows out again as it is distributed in the form of wages and profits back to households. Households spend the money, but remember that there are withdrawals of 0.1 of income because of savings and taxes. So only MYR 90 million flows back round the economy in stage 2 to firms. Then firms pay MYR 90 million back to households in wages and profits. In the third stage, MYR 81 million is spent by households with MYR 19 million leaking out of the circular flow. This process carries on with smaller and smaller amounts being added to national income as the money flows round the economy. Eventually, the initial MYR 100 million of extra government spending leads to a final increase in national income of MYR 1 billion. In this case, the value of the **multiplier (or national income multiplier or Keynesian multiplier or real multiplier)** is 10.

If leakages from the circular flow in Figure 1 (on page 247) had been larger, less of the increase in investment would have continued to flow round the economy. For instance, if leakages had been 0.8 of income, then only MYR 20 million (0.2 × MYR 100 million) would have flowed round the economy in the second stage. In the third stage, it would have been MYR 4 million (0.2 × MYR 20 million). The final increase in national income following the initial MYR 100 million increase in investment spending would have been MYR 125 million.

The multiplier model states that the higher the leakages from the circular flow, the smaller will be the increase in income that continues to flow round the economy at each stage following an initial increase in spending. Hence, the higher the leakages, the smaller the value of the multiplier. Leakages are what is not spent. So, another way of saying this is that the multiplier is smaller when the ratio of consumption to income is lower.

The multiplier effect works too when investment, government spending or exports fall. If government spending, for example, falls by MYR 3 billion and the multiplier is 2, then the final fall in national income will be MYR 6 billion.

FIGURE 1

The circular flow of income

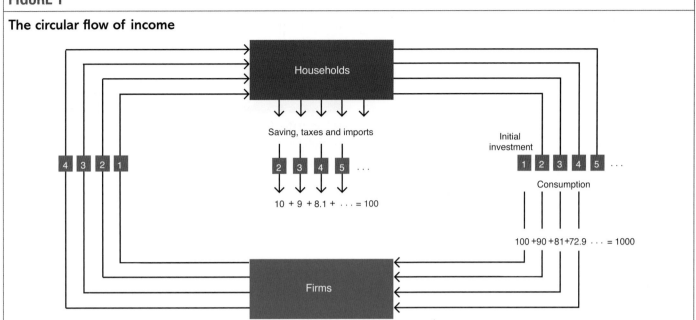

CALCULATING THE MULTIPLIER

The value of the multiplier can be calculated by using a formula involving a number of variables (C or consumption; S or saving; T or taxation, M or imports, W or total withdrawals) and their marginal propensities.

- The marginal propensity to consume (MPC), which is the increase in consumption (ΔC) divided by the increase in income (ΔY) that caused it (i.e. $\Delta C \div \Delta Y$).

- The **marginal propensity to save (MPS)**, which is the increase in saving divided by the increase in income that caused it (i.e. $\Delta S \div \Delta Y$).

- The **marginal propensity to tax (MPT)**, which is the increase in tax revenues divided by the increase in income that caused them (i.e. $\Delta T \div \Delta Y$).

- The **marginal propensity to import (MPM)**, which is the increase in imports divided by the increase in income that caused them (i.e. $\Delta M \div \Delta Y$).

- The **marginal propensity to withdraw (MPW)**, which is the increase in withdrawals from the circular flow ($S + T + M$) divided by the increase in income that caused them (i.e. $\Delta W \div \Delta Y$); this is the same as the sum of the marginal propensity to save, tax and import ($MPS + MPT + MPM$).

The formula for the multiplier is:

$$1/1 - MPC$$

which is equal to

$$\frac{1}{(MPS + MPT + MPM)} \text{ or } \frac{1}{MPW}$$

ACTIVITY 1   SKILLS   PROBLEM-SOLVING

CASE STUDY: CALCULATING THE MULTIPLIER

The following examples would relate to an economy in the eurozone. Calculate the value of:

(a) the MPC if consumption increases by €100 million and income increases by €200 million

(b) the MPS if saving increases by €200 million and income increases by €2 billion

(c) the MPT if tax increases by €50 million and income increases by £150 million

(d) the MPM if imports fall by €300 million and income falls by €1 billion

(e) the MPW if savings fall by €100 million, taxes fall by €300 million, imports fall by €600 million and income falls by €2.5 billion.

MATHS TIP

A multiplier example

Assume the following

$MPC = 0.4$

$MPS = 0.1$

$MPT = 0.2$

$MPM = 0.3$

The marginal propensity to withdraw (which is $MPS + MPT + MPM$) is therefore 0.6.

The value of the multiplier ($1 \div MPW$) is therefore $1 \div 0.6$ or 1.66.

Alternatively, it can be calculated from $1 \div (1 - MPC)$, which is $1 \div (1 - 0.4)$ or 1.66. So if injections increase by MYR 100 million, the final increase in national income is MYR 166 million (MYR 100 million x 1.66).

THE MULTIPLIER EFFECT AND INJECTIONS

Investment is an injection into the circular flow. The multiplier effect shows the impact on aggregate demand and income of a *change* in an injection. So if the multiplier were 2, then a MYR 100 million increase in investment would lead to an increase in national income of MYR 200 million.

Investment is not the only injection into the circular flow. Government spending and exports are also injections. So a rise in government spending of, say, MYR 200 million would lead to a rise in national income of MYR 800 million if the multiplier were 4. A fall in exports of MYR 500 million would lead to a fall in national income of MYR 1500 million if the multiplier were 3.

THE MULTIPLIER EFFECT AND WITHDRAWALS

Changes in the marginal propensities to consume, save, tax and import will change the value of the multiplier. An increase in the marginal propensity to consume, which must occur because one or more of the marginal propensities to save, tax or import have fallen, will lead to a rise in the value of the multiplier. This is because a rise in the MPC, which means a fall in the MPW, reduces the number on the bottom of the fraction:

$$1/1 - MPC \quad \text{or} \quad \frac{1}{MPW}$$

used to calculate the multiplier. For example, a fall in the marginal propensity to withdraw from 0.5 to 0.25 would increase the value of the multiplier from 2 ($1 \div 0.5$) to 4 ($1 \div 0.25$).

However, a fall in the MPC, which must be associated with a rise in the MPW, will lead to a fall in the value of the multiplier.

ACTIVITY 2   SKILLS   PROBLEM-SOLVING

CASE STUDY: CALCULATING THE MULTIPLIER AND CHANGE IN INCOME

Calculate (i) the value of the multiplier and (ii) the change in income if there is:

(a) an increase in investment of €1 billion and the MPC is 0.5

(b) a fall in government spending of €10 billion and the MPW is 0.8

(c) an increase in exports of €5 billion and the MPC is 0.6

(d) a fall in investment of €20 billion and the MPW is 0.25

(e) a fall in exports of €7 billion and the MPS is 0.1, the MPT is 0.2 and the MPM is 0.2

(f) a fall in government spending of €20 billion and the MPS is 0.2, the MPT is 0.3 and the MPM is 0.2

(g) a rise in government spending of €10 billion and the MPS is 0.2, the MPT is 0.3 and the MPW is 0.7

(h) a fall in investment of €30 billion and the MPS is 0.1, the MPM is 0.3 and the MPC is 0.5.

THE MULTIPLIER AND THE AGGREGATE DEMAND CURVE

An increase in investment, exports or government spending of, for example, MYR 1 billion will increase aggregate demand by MYR 1 billion. The multiplier effect, assuming the multiplier is greater than 1, will lead to a further increase in aggregate demand. If the multiplier is 1.5, then the final increase in aggregate demand will be the MYR 1 billion increase in I, X or M plus an additional MYR 500 million, making a total of MYR 1500 million.

Figure 2 (on page 249) shows an initial aggregate demand curve of AD_1 with a Keynesian aggregate supply curve. An increase in exports of Y_1Y_2 initially shifts the aggregate demand curve to AD_X. The multiplier effect then leads to a further increase of aggregate demand of Y_2Y_3, shifting the aggregate demand curve to AD_2. The total increase in aggregate demand is Y_1Y_3.

A fall in investment exports or government spending will lead to a shift to the left of the AD curve. The size of the fall in equilibrium national income will be the value of the fall in injections times the multiplier.

ACTIVITY 3　SKILLS ⟩ REASONING, ANALYSIS

CASE STUDY: EFFECTS ON AGGREGATE DEMAND

Explain, using a diagram, the likely effect of the following on the aggregate demand curve for the following economies.

(a) The 4 per cent fall in real household consumption expenditure in the UK between 2007 and 2011.

(b) The fall in bank base interest rates in the UK from 5.5 per cent in 2007 to 0.5 per cent in 2010.

(c) A fall in income taxes, proposed by US President Trump, in 2017.

(d) The 40 per cent fall in London Stock Exchange prices between October 2007 and February 2009 (UK economy).

(e) The rise in Russia's household savings ratio from 4 per cent in 2012 to 7 per cent in 2015.

(f) In August 2016, the Japanese government announced an increase in new government spending of JPY 4.6 trillion (Japanese yen), for the fiscal year 2016.

(g) The value of the sterling (pound) fell 16 per cent against the currencies of the UK's main trading partners between the start of 2016 and September 2017.

FIGURE 2

The multiplier effect on aggregate demand

An increase in exports of $Y_1 Y_2$ leads to a final increase in equilibrium output of $Y_1 Y_3$ due to the multiplier effect.

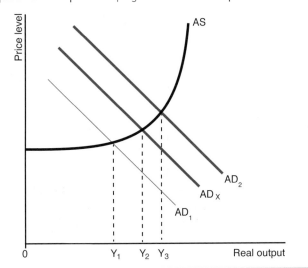

EFFECTS OF THE ECONOMY ON THE MULTIPLIER

The value of the multiplier is determined by the marginal propensities to consume, save, tax and import. These marginal propensities can change in value if other variables in the economy change.

Any change in a factor that affects the proportion of income spent will change the value of the multiplier. For example, the marginal propensities to consume and save are likely to change if there is a significant change in interest rates. A large rise in interest rates is likely to discourage consumption and encourage saving, leading to a fall in the MPC and a rise in the

MPS. Consequently, a large rise in interest rates is likely to lead to a fall in the value of the multiplier. Equally, a rise in household wealth is likely to raise the marginal propensity to consume and so lead to a rise in the value of the multiplier.

Government changes to taxes paid by households will affect the multiplier. A rise in taxes that increases the proportion of income paid in tax at the margin will increase the MPT. Hence the value of the multiplier will fall. A fall in marginal tax rates will lead to a rise in the value of the multiplier.

Any factor apart from income that changes imports will also change the value of the multiplier. For example, an improvement in the quality of imported goods, which encourages households to buy more imports, will increase the MPM and so reduce the value of the multiplier.

GOVERNMENTS AND THE MULTIPLIER

Governments in the past have used changes in government spending to influence national income and macroeconomic variables such as unemployment and inflation. It would be very helpful if governments, for example the Malaysian government, knew that an extra MYR 1 in government spending would produce an extra, say, MYR 2 in national income. However, in practice, it is not so simple.

● It is difficult to measure the exact size of the multiplier. Sophisticated statistical models have to be used that describe the workings of the economy. They are not completely accurate. Equally, changes can happen in an economy that can alter the size of the multiplier from one period to the next.

- The multiplier effect is not immediate. A MYR 100 increase in government spending today does not increase national income by MYR 200 today. It takes time for the money to flow round the circular flow. So there are time delays between the increase in the government spending and the final increase in national income.

- Economists disagree about the exact size of the multiplier. However, in general it is considered to be relatively low in high income countries, such as the UK and the USA.

THINKING LIKE AN ECONOMIST

IMF AND OECD ENCOURAGES INVESTMENT IN INFRASTRUCTURE

European countries, including the UK, face major infrastructure problems. In the UK, for example, a lack of investment in new or upgraded road and rail links is increasing journey times and transport costs for firms. A failure to invest sufficiently in new housing is one cause of house price inflation. In Europe, transport links too are a major problem. The German Institute for Economic Research (DIW Berlin) estimated that Germany spent 40 per cent less on transport infrastructure between 2006 and 2011 than needed to maintain the existing system in good working order. The fall in investment can be seen in Figure 3. Extra investment of €10 billion a year would be needed to make up the shortage. Energy is another area suffering from lack of investment. In the UK, a failure to invest in new electricity sources such as gas-fired power stations or renewable energies means that the margin needed to prevent loss of power in some areas at peak demand times in winter is now dangerously small. In Europe, building new power lines between countries could reduce electricity costs for consumers and firms. Spain and Italy are ideally suited to produce solar-powered electricity. The north of Germany is ideally suited to produce wind energy. But getting that electricity to middle Europe needs investment in new transmission lines.

The IMF argued in 2014 that infrastructure spending increases national output by US$3 for every US$1 of investment. By borrowing money at current very low rates of interest, governments in Europe and the USA can provide a fiscal stimulus, which will increase both aggregate demand and aggregate supply. Infrastructure spending will in part use resources that are currently unemployed, such as unemployed or underemployed workers. It will increase economic growth both in the short term and the long term. Extra infrastructure spending in itself

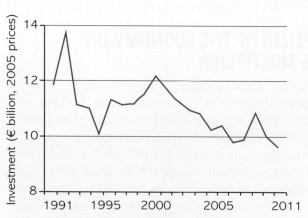

▲ **Figure 3 Falling investment in roads and bridges in Germany**

Source: adapted from DIW Berlin, 2013

will increase the rate of growth of GDP in the year in which the money is spent. It will also increase growth in the long term because the productive capacity of the economy will have grown.

Currently, many governments are committed to reducing government spending and raising taxes to reduce their budget deficits. John Maynard Keynes argued in the 1930s that such policies at times of high unemployment were self-defeating. Cutting government spending leads to cuts in national income magnified by the multiplier effect. National income at best stagnates, as do tax revenues. At worst, both income and tax revenues fall, making the situation worse. Many economists today believe that spending cuts are recreating the problems of the 1930s. The solution is for governments in Europe and the USA to spend more on infrastructure and create economies that can grow at the rates seen in previous years.

Source: adapted from IMF, 'World Economic Outlook', October 2014; © the *Financial Times*, 10.7.14, 9.9.14, 7.10.2014, All Rights Reserved.

CHECKPOINT

1 What is the multiplier effect?

2 What happens to the value of the multiplier, the higher the level of leakages (withdrawals) at each stage in the multiplier process?

3 If the value of the multiplier is 2, how much does national income increase if the government increases its spending by US$100 million?

4 State the formulas for the multiplier.

5 What is the value of the multiplier if the MPC = 0.6?

6 What happens to national income if investment falls?

7 State what is meant by the marginal propensity to import.

8 What happens to the value of the multiplier if the tax rate on income falls?

9 What happens to the value of the multiplier if interest rates fall?

10 State two reasons why the exact value of the multiplier may be difficult to know in practice.

SUBJECT VOCABULARY

marginal propensity to import (MPM) the increase in imports divided by the increase in income that caused them (i.e. $\Delta M \div \Delta Y$).

marginal propensity to save (MPS) the increase in saving divided by the increase in income that caused it (i.e. $\Delta S \div \Delta Y$).

marginal propensity to tax (MPT) the increase in tax revenues divided by the increase in income that caused them (i.e. $\Delta T \div \Delta Y$).

marginal propensity to withdraw (MPW) the increase in withdrawals from the circular flow $(S + T + M)$ divided by the increase in income that caused them (i.e. $\Delta W \div \Delta Y$); this the same as the sum of the marginal propensity to save, tax and import $(MPS + MPT + MPM)$.

multiplier (or national income multiplier or Keynesian multiplier or real multiplier) the figure used to multiply a change in an injection into the circular flow, such as investment, to find the final change in income (assuming the injection is not determined by income). It is the ratio of the final change in income to the initial change in an injection. It can be calculated as

$$1/1 - MPC \ \text{or} \ \frac{1}{(MPS + MPT + MPM)} \ \text{or} \ \frac{1}{MPW}$$

multiplier effect (or process) an increase in investment or other injection will lead to an even greater increase in income (assuming the injection is not determined by income).

EXAM PRACTICE

SKILLS REASONING, ANALYSIS, COMMUNICATION

Q

1 GDP growth in Indonesia reached 4.9 per cent in 2015. This was largely driven by a 7.3 per cent rise in public spending. The rise in public spending should set off a powerful multiplier effect beyond just the immediate pick-up in demand for goods and services from the government projects.

Source: adapted from © the *Financial Times*, 'Indonesia GDP growth accelerates amid public spending boost', 5.2.2016 All Rights Reserved.

With reference to the information above, explain the term 'the multiplier effect.' **(4 marks)**

2 In August 2016, the Japanese government launched an increase in actual new government spending of JPY 4.6 trillion. The stimulus plans are expected to include JPY 2.5 trillion in welfare spending, which includes a welfare payment of JPY 15,000 each to 22 million low-income individuals.

Source: adapted from © the *Financial Times*, 'Japan launches $45bn stimulus package', 2.8.2016. All Rights Reserved.

Explain the likely impact on Japan's national income of this change in government spending. **(4 marks)**

EXAM HINT

Think about the impact the increase in welfare payments for low income families will have on the value of the multiplier.

3 The economic growth rate of the UAE fell from 5.8 per cent in 2013 to 3.0 per cent in 2016. Around three-quarters of GDP is now from sources other than oil as the UAE has made its economy more diverse by investing in industry, tourism and financial services. However, the oil slowdown in this period had hit sectors dependent on the oil industry and construction. Both consumer confidence and employment levels fell.

The chief economist at Abu Dhabi Commercial Bank said in 2016, 'We will see a pick-up in non-oil GDP, from 2.3 per cent in 2016 to 2.8 per cent in 2017, largely on more investment activity in the run up to Expo 2020 (the world fair that Dubai will host that year). But the multiplier effect from this recovery will be weaker than in previous investment cycles.'

Source: adapted from © the *Financial Times*, 'Emirates pour concrete to fight a global slowdown', 10.12.2016 All Rights Reserved.

(a) Define the term 'multiplier effect'. **(2 marks)**

(b) With reference to the extract, examine the likely impact on the level of real GDP of the increase in investment in the run up to Expo 2020. **(8 marks)**

EXAM HINT

Include a short-run AD and AS diagram. Use the extract to identify predicted impact. Explain the multiplier. What is the likely value of the multiplier, high or low? Use the extract to find evidence for this. For evaluation you may like to briefly discuss why it is difficult to predict the precise impact on the level of real GDP.

4 An economy estimates the marginal propensity to consume for its consumers is 0.6. Which one of the following is the correct value of the multiplier?

(a) 2.5

(b) 1.6

(c) 0.6

(d) 0.4. **(1 mark)**

5 For an economy, the MPS = 0.1, the MPT = 0.3 and the MPM = 0.2. Calculate the increase in national income if the level of injections increases by US$100 million.

(4 marks)

ECONOMIC GROWTH

This section starts by distinguishing between actual and potential growth. It then uses these definitions to introduce the concept of output gaps. Economic growth is an essential driver of changes in living standards, so the causes of economic growth need to be understood by policy makers. This section explores the causes of economic growth and then considers the impact of economic growth. It discusses both the benefits and costs of economic growth.

35 CAUSES OF ECONOMIC GROWTH AND OUTPUT GAPS

LEARNING OBJECTIVES

- Understand the distinction between actual and potential growth.
- Know that actual growth is caused by an increase in the components of aggregate demand.
- Understand the importance of international trade for export-led growth.
- Understand the causes of potential growth.
- Understand the importance of productivity for the rate of economic growth.
- Understand the difference between actual growth rate and long-term trends in growth.
- Understand the distinction between positive and negative output gaps.
- Know the characteristics of positive and negative output gaps.
- Understand the difficulties of measuring output gaps.

GETTING STARTED

What is the current rate of growth of an economy of your choice? How does this compare to Germany, the USA and China? Research what factors are affecting the growth rate of these economies.

ACTUAL GROWTH

Economies change in size over time. For example, the Chinese economy doubled the value of its production roughly every seven years between 1990 and 2010. The UK economy has seen its production grow at an average of 2.5 per cent per annum for the past 60 years.

Growth in the quantity of goods and services produced is measured by the percentage change in real GDP. This is actual growth. For example, Brazil's real GDP contracted by 3.6 per cent in 2016; so its economic growth rate was −3.6 per cent. This means Brazil's output fell by 3.6 per cent over 2016.

In contrast, the US economy grew by 1.62 per cent in 2016. Its actual growth was positive, so output in the US economy increased by 1.62 per cent over 2016.

Actual growth means that real output has increased. It therefore also means that spending in the economy, or aggregate demand, has increased since national output must equal national expenditure. In turn, this means that the overall total of $C + I + G + X − M$ has increased.

FIGURE 1

Positive actual growth 1

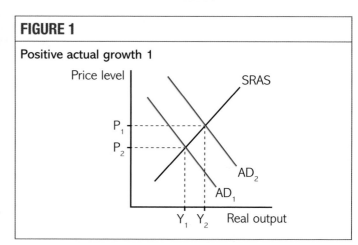

FIGURE 2

Positive actual growth 2

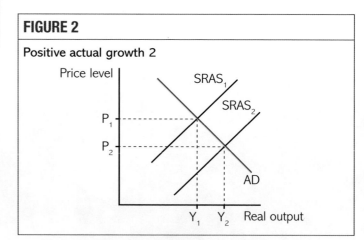

Both Figures 1 and 2 illustrate positive actual growth. Real GDP increases in both diagrams from Y_1 to Y_2. In Figure 1, an increase in consumption, investment, government spending or net exports will lead to a shift in the aggregate demand curve from AD_1 to AD_2. Real output increases from Y_1 to Y_2. In Figure 2, a shift to the right of the short-run aggregate supply (SRAS) curve (for example, caused by a rise in productivity or a fall in global commodity prices) causes a movement along the AD curve as the price level in the economy falls. Real GDP increases from Y_1 to Y_2, which shows the combined total of the components of aggregate demand has risen.

Some economies rely heavily on international trade to achieve actual growth. For example, China and Germany are often used as examples of economies that run high current account surpluses. For these economies, net trade (exports – imports) is a significant component of aggregate demand. If exports rise for any economy, then this will cause **export-led growth**. An over reliance on export-led growth is likely to cause problems when there is a **downturn** in the global economy. This is because a recession in one economy, with falling national income, means import spending will fall in that economy. This therefore means the demand for another economy's exports will fall.

POTENTIAL GROWTH

Potential growth measures the increase in the productive capacity of an economy over a year. It directly links with the **production possibility frontier** (PPF) and how much the **productive potential** of the economy is increasing over time. Potential growth means the PPF is shifting to the right. The maximum potential output of the economy is increasing. The productive potential is determined by the factors of production available to an economy, such as labour and capital. The productive potential of an economy is also shown by the **long-run aggregate supply (LRAS)** curve. Potential growth is shown by a shift to the right of the PPF and the LRAS curve.

In Figure 3 the movement from C to D shows potential growth. In this case the productive potential of the economy has increased because the economy has increased its maximum output over a period of time. The productive potential of an economy can only increase if more factors of production become available to an economy or more efficient methods can be used, or a combination of the two. An increase in potential growth does not necessarily mean there

has been any actual growth. Additionally, actual growth does not necessarily mean there has been an increase in potential growth. For example, the PPF may currently be at PPF_1. If the economy moves from A to B, B to C or A to C, then these movements all illustrate positive actual growth. Real GDP has increased. Because the productive potential remains at PPF_1, there has been no potential growth. However, some causes of actual growth are also causes of potential growth. For example, an increase in investment means aggregate demand increases. This will cause actual growth. An increase in investment also causes potential growth if the stock of capital goods in the economy increases or productivity increases.

The phrase **economic growth**, if it is not made more specific, can mean either actual growth or potential growth. Which of these two it refers to depends on the context in which the phrase is being used.

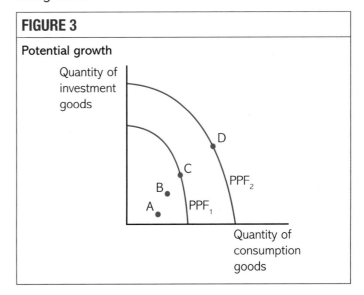

FIGURE 3

Potential growth

A PPF can also be used to show the conflict between investment and consumption. One major source of potential economic growth is investment. All other things being equal, the greater the level of investment, the higher will be the rate of potential growth. However, increased production of investment goods can only be achieved by a reduction in the production of consumption goods if the economy is at full employment. So there is a trade-off to be made between consumption now and consumption in the future. The lower the level of consumption today relative to the level of investment, the higher will be the level of consumption in the future.

ACTIVITY 1 SKILLS REASONING, ANALYSIS

CASE STUDY: FISCAL POLICY

Fiscal policy refers to government spending and taxation decisions by the government. US President Trump had been expected to reduce taxes and increase government spending on infrastructure investment to boost the US economy. However, this was not happening as much or as quickly as the IMF had originally expected.

Source: IMF World Economic Outlook, update July 2017

(a) Explain the likely impact of a fall in taxes and a rise in government spending on aggregate demand in the US economy. (Hint: use terminology such as circular flow of income, withdrawals/injections and the multiplier effect as part of your explanation.)

(b) Explain why an increase in infrastructure investment spending in the USA should increase both actual and potential US economic growth. (Hint: go back to Chapter 33 to recap the impact of an increase in investment on the AD and AS curves. Link this to actual and potential growth.)

TREND GROWTH RATE

The **trend rate of growth** is the long-run average rate of growth of the productive potential of an economy over time. Because it is not possible to measure the productive potential of an economy directly, the trend rate of growth is assumed to be an approximation of the average actual rate of growth of GDP over a period of time. However, in any one year, the actual economic growth rate is likely to be above or below the trend rate. The path of actual economic growth tends to fluctuate around the long-run real GDP growth path. This is shown in Figure 4.

CAUSES OF FLUCTUATIONS IN SHORT-RUN GROWTH RATE

There are many different reasons why the short-run rate of growth of real GDP may vary around its long-term trend. But they can be classified into two main types: **demand-side shock** and **supply-side shock**.

Demand-side shocks are shocks that affect aggregate demand. Examples of demand-side shocks include the following.

- A housing market bubble may burst. This occurs when house prices rise to too high a level and suddenly there is a collapse in demand for housing and a sharp fall in house prices. This reduces consumer confidence, leading to less consumer spending and few new houses being built, which affects output and employment.

- The stock market may crash, perhaps if stock market prices are too high. A stock market crash reduces the wealth of individuals who are then likely to reduce their spending and save more to rebuild their wealth. This reduces aggregate demand, causing recession.

- The central bank may sharply raise interest rates, perhaps to combat rising inflation. This reduces consumer spending on durables and investment spending, sending the economy into recession.

- The government may sharply raise taxes or cut government spending, perhaps to address rising inflation or balance its budget. This leads to lower aggregate demand and a recession.

- The world economy may go into recession, hitting an economy's exports sharply and so sending the economy into a recession too.

- There may be a sharp rise in the value of a currency against other currencies. This reduces the competitiveness of the economy, sending exports down and imports up. The subsequent fall in aggregate demand sends the economy into recession.

Supply-side shocks are shocks that affect aggregate supply. Examples of supply-side shocks include the following.

- A large rise in world commodity prices could both raise the price level in an economy and lead to a rise in import values if demand for the commodity is price inelastic. The rise in import costs will reduce aggregate supply, leading to lower output.

- An increase in trade union activity could see large wage increases that will raise the price level substantially and reduce aggregate supply, leading to recession.

The examples given above are all negative shocks that could move the economy into a negative output gap. However, a shock can also be positive. For example, a sharp fall in oil and other commodity prices would increase the SRAS curve. If an economy is a net importer of oil and other commodities. The equilibrium level of real GDP will increase. The economy will be operating at a level of real GDP above the LRAS in the short run. There will be a positive output gap while the price of oil and other commodities remains low, assuming the economy had originally been operating on its LRAS curve.

THE OUTPUT GAP

The difference between the actual level of real GDP and its estimated long-term value at a point in time is known as the **output gap**. In Figure 4, the straight line is the trend rate of growth in real GDP over a long period of time. It is assumed that this shows the level of real GDP associated with the productive potential of the economy. The actual level of real GDP varies around the trend growth line. The output gap is an economic measure of the difference between the actual output of an economy and its potential output. Economists also refer to potential output as trend output or the productive capacity of an economy. A negative output gap occurs when actual output is less than potential output. The economy is operating inside the PPC. Actual output is less than what the economy could produce at full capacity. A negative output gap means there is **spare capacity**, or slack, in the economy due to weak aggregate demand. A positive output gap exists when the economy is operating beyond full capacity. This can only be achieved in the short run, since that level of production could not be sustained in the long run. For example, workers may be taking on unsustainable extra hours at work or machinery will be over used.

Neither positive or negative gaps are ideal. A negative output gap means some factors of production in the economy are being underutilised. Weak demand suggests there is demand deficient unemployment. There may also be a risk of deflation if aggregate demand is falling too much. In contrast, a positive output gap means factors of production are being over utilised. There is excess demand in the economy. The main problem will be rising demand-pull and cost-push inflation. The problems caused by output gaps will be more significant if the size of the output gap is large.

Output gaps can also be illustrated using an aggregate demand and aggregate supply curve diagram. In Figure 5, the long-run equilibrium output of the economy is OY_1. This is shown by the vertical LRAS curve. However, in the short run, equilibrium is higher at OY_2, because this is where short-run aggregate supply and aggregate demand are equal. There will therefore be a positive output gap in the economy of $Y_1 Y_2$. This positive output gap will be filled either through long-run economic growth moving the LRAS curve to OY_2, or through a recession shifting aggregate demand downwards. A central bank is likely to raise interest rates to reduce aggregate demand in order to reduce the demand-pull inflation. If the positive output gap persists, then workers are likely to bargain for higher wages to compensate for the rising inflation. This will increase costs in the economy and shift the SRAS upwards. This will cause cost push inflation but will move the economy back to the trend growth rate.

FIGURE 4

The output gap
The trend rate of growth of GDP is similar to the growth in productive potential of the economy. When actual GDP falls below this or rises above it, there is said to be an output gap. When actual GDP growth falls below this, there is a negative output gap. When actual GDP growth rises above it, there is a positive output gap.

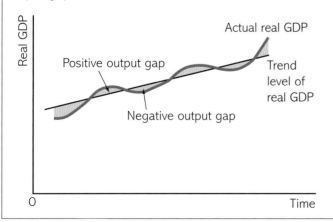

FIGURE 5

A positive output gap
The positive output gap is $Y_1 Y_2$, shown by the difference between the actual level of output of Y_2 and the long-run potential output of the economy at Y_1.

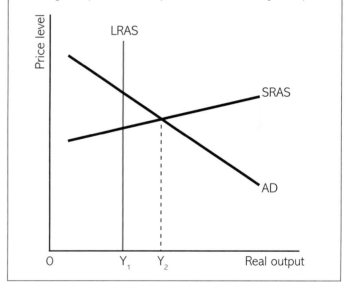

Figure 6 shows a negative output gap. LRAS is to the right of the short-run equilibrium output level of OY_1. The negative output gap is therefore $Y_1 Y_2$. To close the gap, aggregate demand is likely to rise faster than the long-run growth in the economy shown by the shifts to the right of the AD and LRAS curves. Governments are likely to intervene in the economy with policies to boost aggregate demand if the negative output gap is too large.

FIGURE 6

A negative output gap

The negative output gap is Y_1Y_2, shown by the difference between the actual level of output of OY_1 and the long-run potential output of the economy at OY_2.

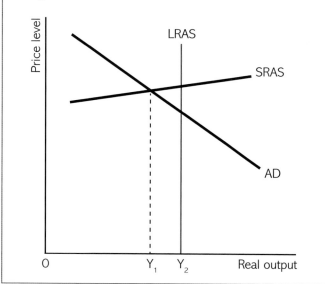

ACTIVITY 2   SKILLS   REASONING, ANALYSIS

CASE STUDY: POSITIVE AND NEGATIVE OUTPUT GAPS

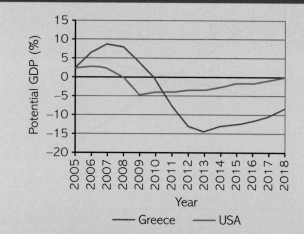

▲ Figure 7 US and Greek output gaps, 2005–18

Note: If the line is above zero, it shows a positive output gap and below zero a negative output gap.

Source: OECD Economic Outlook, June 2017

(a) Explain the terms positive and negative output gaps.

(b) Compare the state of the Greek and the US economies over the period shown.

DIFFICULTIES IN MEASURING OUTPUT GAPS

It might seem that the size of any output gap is easy to estimate. In practice, it can be difficult to assess. This is mainly because economists do not know exactly the position of the LRAS curve. For example, following the lengthy recession and very low recovery rate in the UK between 2008 and 2013, economists revised downwards their estimates for the long-run rate of growth of the economy. By 2014, the negative output gap on the average 2008 estimate of the trend rate of growth was above 15 per cent of GDP. By reducing the trend rate of growth, this had been revised down to a few per cent in 2014 estimates. The other problem in estimating the output gap is that initial estimates of GDP, showing where SRAS and demand are equal, are almost always inaccurate. GDP figures are constantly revised. There can be quite major changes to figures one or two years after the period being measured. Some economists believe that output gaps are so difficult to measure that they are not a valid concept to use for the purpose of economic policy.

HYSTERESIS

Figure 8 might suggest that there is little cost associated with variations in the level of activity. Output lost in a recession is regained during a boom, leaving the economy no better or worse off in the long term. However, there are possible other costs.

- Those made unemployed during a recession, however mild, suffer a loss in their income even if the majority of workers are unaffected.

- Those on fixed incomes suffer in a boom if inflation rises. Their spending power is reduced because of higher prices.

- Some economists argue that in a deep recession, economies do not bounce back to their previous trend level of growth. This is an example of **hysteresis**. Instead, the economy remains at a lower level of output, though still growing at its previous trend rate. In Figure 8, the economy starts off on a trend growth path of AA. However, a deep recession with its slump at OR means that the economy only booms at a level consistent with a lower growth path of BB. The economy then suffers another deep recession with a slump at OS. The trend line of growth shifts down to CC. After this, the business cycle is much shallower and actual output varies around the trend line of CC. One reason why an economy may fail to recover fully from a deep recession is that there is a permanent loss of human capital. In a recession, millions can lose their jobs. Some take early retirement, with

FIGURE 8

Hysteresis

The trend rate of growth of an economy can shift downwards if there is a deep recession because of permanent losses of human and physical capital.

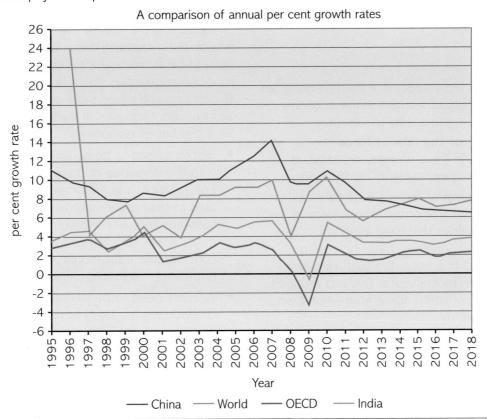

A comparison of annual per cent growth rates

— China   — World   — OECD   — India

a consequent loss of output for the economy. Others suffer long periods of unemployment and lose their skills. They are therefore less productive than before. Another reason is that there can be a permanent loss of physical capital. In a recession, firms reduce their investment. If they fail to make this up in the next boom, there is less physical capital in the economy than would otherwise have been the case. Potential output must then fall.

THE CAUSES OF POTENTIAL GROWTH

Variations in the level of real GDP around the trend rate of growth are caused by demand- and supply-side shocks. However, what explains increases in the productive potential of the economy over time?

All economists would agree that an increase in LRAS supply will increase the potential level of output in an economy. LRAS can increase if there is an increase in the quantity or quality of the inputs to the production process. Output can also be increased if existing inputs are used more efficiently. Increasing the quality of the inputs to the production process or using existing inputs more efficiently will increase

productivity. Productivity is output per unit of factor input employed. The terms capital productivity and labour productivity are often used by economists. Capital productivity is output per unit of capital employed. Labour productivity is output per worker. An increase in productivity means more output can be produced for a given quantity of factor inputs. An increase in productivity will therefore increase long-run economic growth. This can be expressed in terms of a production function:

Output = f (land, labour, capital, technical progress, efficiency)

Each of these factors will now be considered.

LAND

Different countries possess different types and amounts of land. Land in economics is defined as all natural resources, not just land itself. Some countries, such as Saudi Arabia, have experienced large growth rates almost solely because they posess rich natural resources. Without oil, Saudi Arabia today would almost certainly be a poor developing country. Other countries have received large unexpected income. The UK, for instance, only started to exploit its oil and gas resources in the mid-1970s. However, most economists argue that the exploitation of raw materials is unlikely to be a significant source of growth in developed economies, although it can be vital in developing economies.

LABOUR

Economic growth is likely to occur if there is either an increase in the quantity of workers in the economy or there is an increase in the quality of labour.

Growth in the size of the labour force can result from changes in the birth rate, increases in participation rates and increases in immigration.

Changes in demography Today's birth rate has a knock-on effect on the size of the labour force in 20 years' time. Countries that have a high birth rate, such as many African countries, have increasing numbers of workers. In Europe, the birth rate has been relatively low in recent years. This has reduced the size of the current labour force from what it would otherwise have been.

Changes in participation rates Participation rates are the proportion of the population of a certain age who are either in work or seeking work. Increases in the proportion of young people staying on in education have reduced the size of the labour force over the past few decades for many economies. At the opposite end of the age range, two contradictory forces have been at work. More workers can afford to take early retirement, particularly in high income countries, than 30 years ago. In contrast, the pushing up of the state pension age in countries such as the UK is seeing a growing number of workers work beyond the traditional ages of retirement for men of 65 and women of 60. Lastly, more and more women have entered the labour force in many economies, encouraged by higher wages, better childcare arrangements and more labour saving devices in the home.

Immigration A relatively easy way of increasing the labour force is to employ migrant labour. For example, according to an OECD report 2017, G20 countries population increased by 10 million between 2010 and 2015 due to net migration, which is at its highest level since the early 1950s. Over the past 10 years, migrants accounted for about 50 per cent of the increase in the workforce in the USA and 70 per cent in Europe.

It should be noted that increasing the size of the labour force may increase output but will not necessarily increase economic welfare. One reason

is that increased income may have to be shared out among more people, causing little or no change in income per person. If women come back to work after having children, they have to give up time with their children to do so. This reduces the increase in economic welfare that they experience.

Increasing the size of the labour force can increase output, but increasing the quality of labour inputs is likely to be far more important in the long run. Labour is not homogeneous (i.e. it is not all the same). Workers can be made more productive by education and training. Increases in human capital are essential for a number of reasons.

- Workers need to be sufficiently educated to cope with the demands of the existing stock of capital. For instance, it is important for lorry drivers to be able to read, personal assistants to use computer software and shop workers to operate tills. These might seem very low-grade skills but it requires a considerable educational input to get most of the population up to these elementary levels.

- Workers need to be flexible. On average in the UK, workers are likely to have to change job three times during their lifetime. Increasingly workers are being asked to change roles within existing jobs. Flexibility requires broad general education as well as in-depth knowledge of a particular task.

- Workers need to be able to contribute to change. It is easy to see that scientists and technologists are essential if inventions and new products are to be brought to the market. What is less obvious, but as important, is that every worker can contribute ideas to the improvement of techniques of production. An ability of all workers to take responsibility and solve problems will be increasingly important in the future.

A 2017 OECD report highlighted how migrants, as well as adding to the size of the labour force, can also bring new skills into an economy. The report stated that more than one in four migrants in the G20 has a tertiary level of education. The emigration of highly educated women to the G20 has increased particularly rapidly in recent years.

DOMESTIC INVESTMENT

Domestic investment refers to investment by domestic firms, or the government of an economy, on capital goods. The stock of capital in the economy needs to increase over time if economic growth is to be sustained. This means that there must be sustained investment in the economy. However, there is not necessarily a connection between high investment and high growth. Some investment is not growth related. For example, it is often argued that investment in new housing does not lead to future increases in real GDP. Investment can also be wasted if it takes place in industries or projects that fail to be commercially successful.

However, most investment is normally assumed to increase the productive potential of an economy if the stock of capital goods is increasing over time. An increase in the stock of investment will cause potential growth. Investment in new capital goods, which incorporate the latest technological advances, will also increase productivity and reduce unit costs for firms. This means the SRAS will shift to the right as well as the LRAS. Technological progress cuts the average costs of production. For instance, a machine that performed the tasks of a simple scientific calculator was unavailable 100 years ago. Fifty years ago, it needed a large room full of expensive equipment to do this. Today calculators are portable and available for a few pounds. Technological progress also creates new products for the market. Without new products, consumers would be less likely to spend increases in their income. Without extra spending, there would be less or no actual economic growth.

FOREIGN DIRECT INVESTMENT

Foreign direct investment (FDI) can also drive economic growth. FDI refers to flows of money between countries where one firm buys or sets up another firm in another country. FDI can inject money into the circular flow of income and increase aggregate demand. This would set off a positive multiplier effect and cause actual growth.

FDI is also a cause of potential growth. A foreign company may introduce new technology or management practices to a workforce. There is likely to be better training for local workers. New technology knowledge and other acquired skills will start to spill over into the economy, so more firms gain. These advantages are particularly significant for developing countries. Both capital and labour productivity are likely to rise. A foreign firm setting up may also increase competition in an industry. With more competitive pressures, local firms are forced to become more efficient to survive. If they have the sources of finance, they will be keen to invest in new capital and better training for their workers to remain competitive; this further promotes potential growth. However, if FDI destroys local competition then the overall impact on potential growth may be limited.

INNOVATION

Innovation is also a driver of potential growth. **Product innovation** is the creation of new or better products. **Process innovation** is when more efficient methods for producing goods and services are developed. Process innovation will increase productivity, so the PPF shifts outwards. The creation of new ideas will encourage firms to invest in new technology. Product innovation may increase productivity if new capital is required to create the new products. Even if this is not the case, product innovation ensures consumers want to spend. This keeps actual growth buoyant. Innovation requires sources of finance. The government can promote innovation directly by introducing tax credits for research and development or by reducing tax rates generally for firms. It can also spend money directly on research and development as well as maintaining high quality education and training. This means workers will have the skills needed to become innovators in the future.

EFFICIENCY AND COMPETITION

The way in which the factors of production are used together is vital for economic growth. Increased efficiency in the use of resources in itself will bring about rises in output.

In a market economy, competition should lead to greater efficiency. Firms that use more efficient production techniques will drive less efficient firms out of the market. Firms that develop new, better products will drive old products out of the market. So economic growth can come about because of government policies that promote competition and protect innovation. For example, policies such as privatisation, deregulation and control of monopolies should increase competition. Laws that protect patents and copyright will encourage innovation.

Markets promote efficiency but they can also fail. So government may have to step in to deal with market failure. In the past, some have argued that market failure is so widespread that the government should own most, if not all, of industry. This socialist or communist view is mostly rejected today. The problem was that in communist countries, like Russia, government failure became so great that it outweighed any benefits from the correction of market failure. However, some countries today are more likely to intervene in markets than others. France and Germany, for example, intervene more in markets than, say, the USA.

In low- and middle-income economy many of the features of a functioning market economy may be missing. Resources are then combined inefficiently. For example, laws may not exist that protect property

ACTIVITY 3  SKILLS REASONING, INTERPRETATION

CASE STUDY: INCREASING POTENTIAL GROWTH

The OECD Economic Survey in April 2016 mentioned recommendations for how Germany might increase productivity and cope with the challenges of an ageing population.

Although research and development spending by German firms is high compared to other OECD countries, other investment spending called 'knowledge-based capital', such as software and management skills, which promotes innovation, is lower. Investment in 'knowledge-based capital' spending would be particularly beneficial for Germany. There is growing evidence that this type of investment is a key determinant of long-term productivity growth. It has been estimated that this accounts for one-fifth to one-third of labour productivity growth in the USA and EU economies.

The size of the labour force is also set to fall faster than the population due to the growing ageing population. Providing more incentives and opportunities for women and older workers would help to solve this. Immigration and the large inflow of refugees would also add to the labour force. These extra workers will need training to make sure they have the skills needed to be productive.

Source: OECD Economic Survey, April 2016

(a) Using the passage, discuss how Germany could increase its potential growth rate.

rights, or laws may exist but the state may take assets away from private citizens and businesses through corruption, bribery and a justice system that does not enforce the law. If property rights are not protected, citizens and firms have little incentive to save and invest in the long term. Widespread bribery leads to resources being taken by a few individuals rather than being used in the most efficient manner across the economy. Another problem is that there may be no properly functioning capital markets. Farmers in rural areas, for example, may have no access to banks. They are then cut off from access to relatively cheap loans to expand their businesses. If there is a complete breakdown of government or a widespread natural disaster, then this will lead to negative growth. For example, widespread extreme flooding will destroy both the physical and human assets of an economy.

THE IMPORTANCE OF PRODUCTIVITY FOR THE RATE OF ECONOMIC GROWTH

Actual economic growth, with no corresponding potential growth, will push production closer to the PPF. However, once the economy is operating close to its productive potential, an increase in aggregate demand can no longer cause any significant increases in real GDP. The economy might experience a positive output gap in the short run, but, in the long run, real GDP is limited by the position of the LRAS. High growth rates can now only be achieved if the PPF is shifting outwards (LRAS shifting to the right). One of the key drivers of potential growth is an increase in productivity.

Causes of potential growth that focus on improving the quality of factors of production, such as improving the skills of workers or technological advances that improve the quality of capital goods, will increase productivity. Also, an increase in the efficiency with which existing factors of production are used, for example, through process innovation, also increases productivity in the economy. Other causes of potential growth, such as increasing the size of the labour force or finding new natural resources are often limited in scope, particularly for developed economies where birth rates are often lower and natural resources have already been fully exploited.

An increase in productivity is therefore often vital for increasing the trend growth rate (long-term growth rate). It will also impact on actual growth since a fall in unit costs causes a shift in the SRAS to the right, with more output and employment.

In a report by Christine Lagarde for the IMF in April 2017, the productivity slowdown over the previous 10 years was examined. In advanced economies, for example, productivity growth has dropped to 0.3 per cent, down from a pre-crisis average of about 1 per cent. This trend has also affected many emerging and developing countries, including China. Another 10 years of weak productivity growth would seriously impact global living standards.

AGGREGATE DEMAND

Many economists argue that aggregate demand can also affect the long-run growth rate of an economy. For example, over the past 70 years, many politicians and economists in the UK have recommended export-led growth. They have seen the success of Germany, Japan and China and linked that to the strength of their exports. A rise in exports will initially increase aggregate demand rather than aggregate supply.

However, a permanent increase in exports, all other things being equal, will force UK firms to invest in equipment and lead to a rise in the demand for labour to satisfy the increased demand. The rise in investment will lead to a rise in the productive potential of the economy and hence impact on economic growth. The other impact of export-led growth is on competitiveness and efficiency. To export, UK firms have to have a competitive advantage over domestic firms in foreign markets. For example, their prices have to be lower, or the goods have to better designed or of better quality. Becoming more export focused therefore forces firms to become more efficient. Greater efficiency leads to an increase in LRAS and economic growth.

Some economists also argue that increases in aggregate demand in general, through its influence on investment, impacts on aggregate supply. When an economy goes into a moderate to severe recession, firms react by cutting their investment. Lower output means they do not need as much capital as before. Lower sales also reduce the amount of cash firms have to use for investment. If the economy bounces back quickly, firms will tend to overinvest in the next boom, making up for the loss of investment in the recession. However, in a prolonged recession, the loss of investment and the fall in human capital can lead to long-run aggregate supply being permanently lower. This is the problem of hysteresis described above.

What if the economy fails to recover even within, say, 20 years and runs permanently below its productive potential? This is an important current issue because of the experience of Japan and a

ACTIVITY 4   SKILLS ▸ REASONING, ANALYSIS

CASE STUDY: UK DRIVERS OF GROWTH

Figures from the Office for National Statistics (ONS) show the main drivers of growth over the period 2000–13. Throughout the period, the impact of a better-educated workforce, shown by 'Labour composition' in Figure 9, has made a positive contribution to economic growth. For the most part, so too has the number of hours worked. On the whole, this has not come from individual full-time employees working longer hours. It has come from an expanding labour force particularly due to immigration from the EU, and from part-time workers increasing their hours perhaps to full time.

Capital input too has made a positive contribution to growth. This is made up of new investment, but also past investment in capital goods, buildings and infrastructure.

Worryingly, however, since the recession, which started in 2008, the efficiency (called multifactor productivity by ONS) with which the factors of production are combined has tended to be negative. The worst-performing sector of the economy in terms of efficiency has been North Sea oil where aging oil fields have made it harder to extract oil despite greater capital investment, and the employment of more and better-qualified workers.

The ONS estimates that before 1997, Britain's growth was driven by a more rapidly growing capital stock. Since 1997, the most important driver for growth has been the improvement in the education of the labour force.

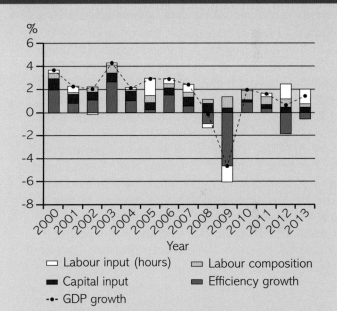

▲ **Figure 9 Decomposition of UK annual growth, 2000–13**
Source: adapted from www.ons.gov.uk

(a) Using the data, explain why GDP fell in 2009.

(b) How can (i) more workers and (ii) a better educated workforce contribute to economic growth?

(c) If firms invested more in North Sea oil production, discuss whether this would raise the rate of economic growth for the UK.

number of countries in the eurozone such as Italy. In a number of eurozone countries, for example, there are unemployment rates of 10–25 per cent that have lasted over a number of years. Supply-side economists would argue that this shows that supply-side reforms need to be implemented in the labour market. Reducing workers' rights in areas such as the ability of employers to sack workers will encourage employers to take on more workers and so solve the problem. Other economists would argue that there will be no extra jobs if aggregate demand remains depressed. Government policies of fiscal austerity, for example, which reduce aggregate demand, are contributing to low or zero growth rates in the economy. This would suggest that a necessary condition of economic growth is that there is adequate aggregate demand to stimulate investment and employment of unused resources.

ACTIVITY 5   SKILLS ▶ REASONING, ANALYSIS

CASE STUDY: GERMANY'S ECONOMIC GROWTH

Europe's biggest economy, Germany, topped 2016 as the fastest growing advanced economy. Output grew by 1.9 per cent, its best in five years. Its growth rate was higher than the UK's 1.8 per cent and outpaced other counties in the eurozone and the USA. Actual growth was powered by the growth of exports compared to imports, as well as a rise in consumption. The recovery in the eurozone, as well as the depreciation of the euro largely compensated for the weakening growth in emerging economies. The German economy depends more on world trade than most, because exports are a significant component of aggregate demand. The current account surplus in 2016 was a record 8.7 per cent of GDP.

Source: adapted from © the *Financial Times*, 'Germany ends 2016 as world's fastest growing advanced economy', 23.2.2017; and OECD Economic Survey, April 2016, Overview, All Rights Reserved.

(a) Using an AD/AS diagram, explain how the growth of exports compared to imports will cause an increase in actual growth in Germany in 2016.

(b) Explain how export-led growth might cause potential growth for Germany over time.

FOUR DISTINCTIONS

Economic growth is typically measured by the rate of change of output or GDP. When measuring GDP, four important distinctions should be made.

- Economic growth is typically measured by the rise in the output of goods and services over time. Economic growth is changes in **real GDP** and not changes in **nominal GDP**, which also includes increases in prices. Real GDP over time has to be measured using one year's prices. So, for example, in 2015 real economic growth was measured by the UK statistical service, the Office for National Statistics, using 2011 prices.

- Real GDP is a proxy measure used to represent the volume of goods and services produced. It is equal to the quantity produced in an economy. The value of goods and services produced is volume times the average price. So a proxy measure of the volume of goods produced can be calculated by taking the nominal value of GDP and dividing it by the price level.

- Total GDP is the total amount of GDP produced in an economy. However, when comparing living standards, it is often more important to compare **GDP per capita** or total GDP divided by the size of the population. Similarly, growth in GDP per capita, which takes into account both change in GDP and the change in population, is often more useful when comparing living standards than simply using growth in total GDP.

- Falling economic growth does not mean that the level of real GDP itself is falling. China grew at 10 per cent per annum between 1980 and 2010. If its growth rate fell to 2 per cent per annum, its GDP would still be rising by 2 per cent each year. A falling rate of growth simply means that GDP is not rising as fast as before. So it is very important to distinguish between the *level* of GDP and the *rate of growth* of GDP. Only if the rate of growth of GDP became negative would GDP be falling.

THINKING LIKE AN ECONOMIST

AFRICA – HOPE FOR THE FUTURE

The year 2016 was one of mixed performances in economic growth across the African continent. Nigeria and South Africa, which account for half of sub-Saharan Africa's GDP, were at or close to recession. Other resource-rich countries, including Angola, Mozambique and Zambia, suffered low growth as commodity prices fell. This reduced export-led growth in these economies. Growth in the region overall is forecast to be 3 per cent.

However, Kenya enjoyed relative success. In 2016, Kenya was one of the best performing economies in sub-Saharan Africa. The government expects growth to increase from 5.6 per cent in 2015 to 6.1 per cent in 2016. Some of the key drivers for Kenya's growth include low fuel prices, a growing middle class and rising incomes, which will increase consumption, as well as increased public investment in energy and transport.

Despite this, Mr Njoroge, the Kenyan Central Bank governor, has some worries. In 2016, he said he was particularly concerned about the effect the UK leaving the EU (Brexit) would have on Kenyan exports. The EU, and especially the UK, has been a big market for Kenyan flowers and vegetables. Addressing challenges of low investment and low productivity will also be vital to achieve sustained economic growth for Kenya.

There is some optimism for the long-term prospects of African economies. The McKinsey Report of 2016 sets out some positives. Over the next decade, nearly 190 million more Africans will be living in cities. By 2034, Africa will have one of the world's biggest working-age populations. This is an asset when many other economies across the world are facing problems of an ageing population. McKinsey's research suggests that job creation is outpacing labour force growth at 3.8 per cent versus 2.8 per cent. This means household spending is predicted to grow by 3.8 per cent a year to reach US$2.1 trillion by 2025.

African economies will also benefit from the advancement of technology. His report states, 'Technological change can unlock growth and leapfrog the limitations and costs of physical infrastructure.' By 2020, the percentage of the population using smartphones is expected to rise from 18 per cent in 2016 to 50 per cent. The use of mobile money is enabling new firms to set up.

McKinsey sees the potential for new technology to transform health and education.

However, critics argue that the benefits of new technology are exaggerated. It is vital that governments increase investment in basic infrastructure, such as roads, electricity generation and access to power. Otherwise, potential growth will be limited.

Sources: World Bank Overview Kenya, © the *Financial Times*, 'Kenya bucks Africa's economic trend', 23.5.2016 and 'Africa is growing in fits and starts', 14.9.2016, All Rights Reserved.

CHECKPOINT

1 What is the distinction between actual growth and potential growth?

2 Sketch a short-run AD/AS diagram to show how an increase in aggregate demand causes actual growth.

3 What is meant by export-led growth?

4 State two reasons why the short-run rate of growth may fluctuate around its long-term trend.

5 What is meant by the term 'output gap'?

6 State the characteristics of a negative output gap.

7 Sketch an AD/AS diagram to illustrate a positive output gap.

8 State four possible causes of potential growth.

9 What effect will an increase in productivity have on the rate of economic growth?

10 State a difficulty of measuring the size of an output gap.

SUBJECT VOCABULARY

actual growth economic growth as measured by recorded changes in real GDP over time.

demand-side shock a sudden and large impact on aggregate demand.

downturn a period when either economic growth or GDP itself is falling.

economic growth a rise in output in an economy that can be either actual growth or potential growth.

export-led growth a rise in aggregate demand caused by a rise in exports.

foreign direct investment flows of money between countries where one firm buys or sets up another firm in another country.

GDP per capita GDP divided by the number of people in the population. GDP per capita is GDP per person.

hysteresis the process whereby a variable does not return to its former value when changed. In terms of the trade cycle, it is used to describe the phenomenon of an economy failing to return to its former long term trend rate of growth after a severe recession.

LRAS (long-run aggregate supply) shows the productive potential of an economy.

nominal GDP GDP valued at current prices (i.e. GDP unadjusted for the effects of inflation)

output gap the difference between the actual level of GDP and the productive potential of the economy. There is a positive output gap when actual GDP is above the productive potential of the economy and it is in boom. There is a negative output gap when actual GDP is below the productive potential of the economy.

production possibility frontier (PPF) a curve that shows the maximum potential level of output of one good, given a level of output for all other goods in the economy.

productive potential the maximum output of an economy at a point in time if all its resources are fully and efficiently utilised.

potential growth economic growth as measured by the changes in the productive potential of the economy over time.

process innovation when more efficient methods for producing goods and services are developed.

product innovation the creation of new or better products.

real GDP GDP valued at constant prices (i.e. GDP adjusted for inflation).

spare capacity for a whole economy, this exists when long-run aggregate supply is greater than aggregate demand and so there is a negative output gap.

supply-side shock a sudden and large impact on aggregate supply.

trend rate of growth the long-run average rate of growth of the productive potential of an economy over time.

EXAM PRACTICE

SKILLS ANALYSIS, INTERPRETATION, COMMUNICATION, CRITICAL THINKING

Q

1 Figure 10 shows the output gap for Hungary for the years 2012–18

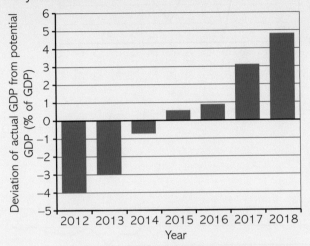

▲ **Figure 10 Hungarian positive and negative output gaps, 2012–18**
Source: OECD Economic Outlook No. 101, June 2017

Which one of the following can be deduced from Figure 10?

(a) Unemployment is likely to have risen between 2012–18.

(b) In 2018, the economy will be at full employment.

(c) In 2018, the economy has the most spare capacity.

(d) Between 2015–18, the economy is likely to be experiencing demand-pull inflation and cost-push inflation. **(1 mark)**

2 In 2016, an IMF report stated that there were several challenges for Jordan's economy. Real GDP growth was below potential and unemployment was high and rising.

Source: IMF Jordan: 'Staff concluding statement of the 2016 Article IV Mission and First-Review under the Extended Fund Facility', 14 November 2016

With reference to the information above, explain the term 'output gap'. **(4 marks)**

3 In 2016, foreign direct investment in the aerospace sector seemed to be increasing again. If Singapore is included, over one-half of the top ten most popular inward investment destinations over the past five years were made up of emerging economies. China came in at third place, Mexico fourth, India fifth and Brazil ninth.

Source: adapted from © the *Financial Times*, 'Emerging markets gain from revival in aerospace FDI', 15.7.2016
All Rights Reserved

Explain the likely impact on potential growth of an increase in inward foreign direct investment for an emerging economy. **(4 marks)**

4 Since 2014, Spain has enjoyed an economic recovery with actual growth figures hitting positive values after five years of recession. As with most EU countries, the fall in the price of oil helped. In 2015, it was believed that this alone contributed at least half a percentage point to Spain's growth.

Source: OECD data, 'Spain: Recovery position (2015)', Financial Times, 22 October. All rights reserved

Draw a short-run AS and AD diagram to show the effect of the fall in the price of oil on the price level and real output. **(4 marks)**

5 Spain's improved export performance

Extract: A

What makes Spain stand out has been its improved export performance. In 2009 exports accounted for 22.7 per cent of GDP. By 2016 this had risen to 33.1 per cent of GDP. Imports as a per cent of GDP have also risen, but less so.

Spain's export growth can be explained by several factors. Its cost competitiveness has improved, partly because of structural reforms in 2012, which helped to push down wage costs. This, combined with rising productivity in the export-led manufacturing industries, means Spain has regained its price competitiveness abroad. 'The combination of moderate wages, productivity and product quality makes Spanish goods attractive for many EU and North American and Latin markets.' Spain has also attracted multinationals to set up in certain industries, such as vehicle manufacture, pharmaceuticals and chemicals. This has also boosted export led growth.

However, to keep the economic recovery going more is needed. In general, Spain's productivity per hour worked is low by international comparisons. Stronger productivity growth is needed. More money needs to be spent on research and development, education and training.

Source: OECD data, 'Spain: Recovery position', 22.10.2015, © the *Financial Times*, 'How Spain seized economic growth as others missed out', 30.11.2016. All Rights Reserved

(a) With reference to Figure 12, explain the term 'export-led growth'. **(4 marks)**

(b) With reference to the information provided, discuss the importance of international trade for Spain's economic recovery. **(14 marks)**

EXAM HINT

Use the passage to explain why demand for exports has risen. Use Figure 12 to show how the data supports this. Integrate an AD/AS diagram to show the impact of an increase in exports on real GDP. To evaluate, use Figures 11 and 12 to see if there seems to be a direct link between an improvement on the current account and higher economic growth rates. If not, what other factors might also explain Spain's economic recovery? Use the passage to explain what other causes of growth will be important for Spain's sustained recovery.

(c) With reference to Figure 13 and the extract, analyse the likely effect on Spain's potential growth if it increases its spending on research and development. **(6 marks)**

EXAM HINT

Spending on research and development is likely to increase innovation. Analyse how innovation increases potential growth. Use the concept of productivity in your answer. Use the extract and Figure 13 to suggest how Spain's economy has been affected by a lack of spending on R&D. This can be used to support your argument for why increasing spending on R&D will be beneficial.

6 Evaluate the importance of productivity for the rate of economic growth. **(20 marks)**

EXAM HINT

Although this question is a 'stand-alone' question, use of the extract above identifies how productivity can be related to export-led growth. Productivity can also be linked to actual and potential growth. Make sure AD/AS diagrams are included in your analysis. Evaluation requires a discussion on why productivity is particularly important, compared to other causes of growth. Are other causes of growth important too?

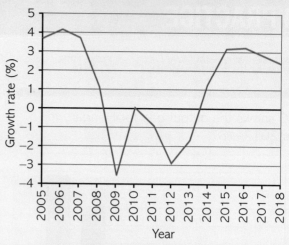

▲ Figure 11 Spanish annual growth rate (%), 2005–18

Source: OECD

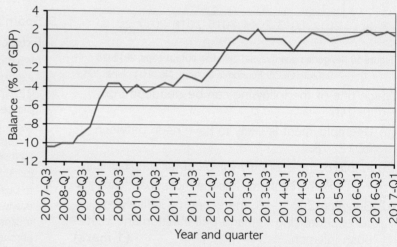

▲ Figure 12 Spanish current account balance (% of GDP), 2007:Q3–17:Q1

Source: OECD

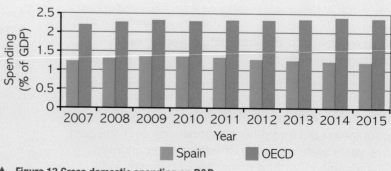

▲ Figure 13 Gross domestic spending on R&D

Source: OECD

36 THE BENEFITS AND COSTS OF ECONOMIC GROWTH

LEARNING OBJECTIVES

- Understand the possible benefits of growth.
- Understand the possible costs of growth.

GETTING STARTED

What was life like 100 years ago in an economy of your choice? Find ten facts that relate to people's standard of living 100 years ago. Were people better off then than now?

ECONOMIC GROWTH

The rate of **economic growth** of the world economy has accelerated, historically, in the last 50 years. Even 500 years ago, most people would have seen little change in incomes over their lifetimes. In Victorian England, the economy grew at about 1 per cent per annum. Between 1948 and 2014, UK real GDP grew at an average of 2.7 per cent per annum. Between 1979 and 2014, China's economy grew at nearly 10 per cent per annum on average. Growth in the developed world, in Western Europe, the USA, Japan and other countries, has led to enormous wealth. In China, while hundreds of millions of its 1.3 billion inhabitants are still very poor, many are now leading 'Western' life styles.

To see the importance of economic growth, consider Table 1. It shows by how much MYR 100 will grow over time at different rates. At 1 per cent growth per annum, income will roughly double over the lifetime of an individual. At 2 per cent, it will increase by four times over a lifetime. At 3 per cent, it is doubling every 25 years. At 5 per cent, it only takes about 14 years to double income. At 10 per cent, it only takes about seven years to double income.

According to an OECD report in 2016, Malaysia is one of the most successful Southeast Asian economies. It has sustained rapid average growth of over 6.4 per cent per year since 1970. It aims to become a high-income country by 2020. A low and stable rate of inflation is desirable. If inflation is stable then this makes it easier for individuals, firms and governments to plan for the future.

ACTIVITY 1   SKILLS   INTERPRETATION, REASONING, ANALYSIS

CASE STUDY: BENEFITS OF GROWTH

The photographs show a modern kitchen and a kitchen at the start of the 20th century.

(a) To what extent do they show that economic growth has been desirable?

Year	Annual growth rates				
	1%	2%	3%	4%	5%
0	100	100	100	100	100
5	105	110	116	128	161
10	110	122	134	163	259
25	128	164	209	339	1084
50	164	269	438	1147	11,739
75	211	442	918	3883	127,189
100	271	724	1922	13,150	1,378,061

▲ Table 1 compound growth rate of MYR 100 over time

THE BENEFITS OF ECONOMIC GROWTH

Economic growth is likely to have a positive impact, which can bring enormous changes to individuals and society.

Living standards are likely to rise. Economic growth means real GDP is rising in the economy. If population grows at a slower rate, then real GDP per capita will increase. This is used as a measure of living standards. In Malaysia, in 2016, real GDP per capita was 5.5 times bigger than it was in 1970. This suggests that Malaysian citizens are over 5.5 times better off.

Figure 1 shows how Malaysia's rapid economic growth has led to higher real GDP per capita between 1990 and 2016. This is then compared to an advanced economy, the USA, over the same period. Using GDP per capita as the measure of living standards, the average US citizen seemed to be approximately 3.5 times better off than an average Malaysian citizen in 1990. However, following Malaysia's rapid economic growth, this had narrowed to just over 2 times better off by 2016.

A rise in income tends to improve aspects of well-being. For example, life expectancy in Malaysia rose from approximately 71 years in 1990 to 75 years in 2015.

Standards of education tend to rise too as income rises in an economy. This helps individuals improve their life satisfaction as well as promoting further growth. The average (mean) years in schooling for Malaysian children increased from 6.5 in 1990 to 10.1 in 2015.

Health tends to be better. Not only do people live longer on average, but the quality of their life improves if they are healthy. Housing standards also improve as income rises.

FIGURE 1

US and Malaysian GDP per capita, constant 2011 US$, 1990 and 2016

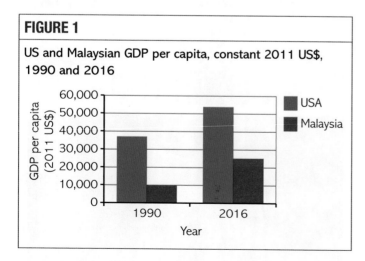

GROWTH IS UNSUSTAINABLE

Perhaps the most serious anti-growth argument is that growth is unsustainable. **Sustainable growth** can be defined as growth in the productive potential of the economy today that does not lead to a fall in the productive potential of the economy for future generations. Consider again Table 1. If a country grows at an average 3 per cent per annum, then in 25 years' time national income will be twice as large as it is today; in 50 years' time, it will be over four times as large; in 75 years' time, it will be nine times as large; and in 100 years' time it will be 19 times as large.

Each extra percentage increase in national income is likely to use up non-renewable resources such as oil, coal and copper. It is argued that the world will soon run out of these resources and there will then be economic collapse. Increases in national income are also argued to be associated with greater pollution. The greatest threat we currently face is from global warming. The worst-case outcome is that within 100 years, the earth will be so warm and sea levels will have risen to such an extent that much of the world will be uninhabitable. Again, a collapse in the world economy is forecast.

Economic theory suggests that the future may not be as hopeless as this analysis suggests. In a market economy, growing scarcity of resources, such as oil, results in a rise in price. Three things then happen. First, demand and therefore consumption falls – the price mechanism results in conservation. Second, it becomes profitable to explore for new supplies of the resource. Third, producers and consumers switch to substitute products. For example, it is likely that within the next 50 years, electric or hydrogen-powered cars will have replaced vehicles powered by scarce and more polluting oil.

Governments too respond to pressures from scientists and the public. The activities of industry are far more regulated today in the western world than they were 30 years ago. Individual governments, for example, have introduced strict controls on pollution emissions and regulated disposal of waste. Western European governments have also introduced strict greenhouse gas emission limits.

What is worrying, however, is that the market mechanism and governments are frequently slow to act. Governments and markets are not good at responding to pressures that might take many years to build up but have consequences suddenly at the end of that time period. Some scientists have predicted that global warming is now already impossible to reverse. If this is true, the problem that we now face is how to change society to cope with this. There is no clear agreement as to how we could reverse economic growth, consume less, and cope with the coming disaster without creating an economic nightmare with mass starvation.

INCREASING INEQUALITIES

Some economists have argued that economic growth is increasing inequalities in income and wealth. Karl Marx, the founder of communism in the 19th century, argued that workers would live on subsistence wages while all the benefits of economic growth would go to the owners of capital. The history of the 20th century in rich countries, like the UK and the USA, seemed to disprove this Marxist view. Inequalities broadly narrowed and both manual workers and the rich enjoyed rising incomes. Equally, since the 1990s, there has been a narrowing of income differences between developing countries and rich western countries. For example, with China growing at up to 10 per cent per year and Western economies at 2.5 per cent, the narrowing has been quite dramatic. Today, many developing countries are targeting growth rates of 5 or 6 per cent, while the developed world considers itself lucky if it can achieve 2.5 per cent.

However, certainly in the UK and the USA, inequalities have been growing in recent years. In the case of the USA, the average (median) worker has seen almost no growth in income over the past 25 years at a time when the US economy has been growing on average by 2.5 per cent per year. One explanation is that the average worker today is competing for jobs not within an economy, but globally. A worker in UK manufacturing is competing for a job with a worker in China or Bangladesh. Technology gives the UK worker some competitive advantage. But often using state of the art technology is not enough to make the UK competitive. In the non-traded sector, workers, such as healthcare assistants or hotel staff, are competing with a steady supply of new immigrant labour. In the UK, this might mean other European workers. In the USA, it might be migrants from Central America. At the top of the pay scale, demand is pushing up wages for what are seen as the best workers. In the middle and the bottom, increases in the supply of workers are leading to stagnating wages. The benefits of economic growth are therefore taken by the highest earners, particularly the top 1 per cent. None of the benefits is being seen by middle and lower income households. Whether this continues into the future remains to be seen.

However, the rise in inequality, experienced by some economies as they have grown, is not true for others. For example, although Malaysia has enjoyed high economic growth rates since 1970, **income inequality** has fallen over this period.

GROWTH AND HAPPINESS

Some economists argue that higher average incomes do not necessarily make individuals happier. Using psychological surveys from across the world (cross-sectional surveys), they have found that happiness and income are positively related at low levels of income but higher levels of income are not associated with increases in happiness. The idea that increases in GDP do not lead to increases in happiness is called the Easterlin Paradox, after Richard Easterlin, an economist who identified the problem in a 1974 research paper. The argument is that an increase in consumption of material goods will improve well-being when basic needs are not met, such as adequate food and shelter. But once these needs are being met, then increasing the quantity of goods consumed makes no difference to well-being. Having a new high-definition television or a new car when you already have a reasonable, functioning television or car does not increase your well-being in the long term.

Rather than concentrate on increasing GDP, governments of high-income countries, such as the UK, should concentrate on factors that contribute to happiness. These include improving the quality of human relationships, working fewer hours, ensuring adequate healthcare for all and giving all citizens a minimum income.

▲ Richard Easterlin

THE ANTI-GROWTH LOBBY

One point to note is that supporters of the anti-growth lobby tend to be people who are relatively rich. Cutting their consumption by 25 per cent, or producing environmentally friendly alternative technologies, might not create too much hardship for them. However, leaving the mass of people in the developing world today at their present living standards would lead to great inequality. A small minority would continue to live below the absolute poverty line, facing the continual threat of having insufficient food. A majority would not have access to services such as education and healthcare, which people in the West take for granted. Not surprisingly, the anti-growth lobby is stronger in the West than in the developing world.

THE IMPACT OF ECONOMIC GROWTH

The impact of economic growth is felt by a number of different groups and on different issues. There are costs and benefits that arise from economic growth.

Consumers Economic growth should allow households to see rising incomes over time. They can then afford to buy more goods and services. These households will experience higher living standards. However, if the economic benefits of economic growth are received by only the richest in society, then average households will see no gain. This has been the experience of US households for the past 30 years. Also, there is debate about whether buying more goods and services leads to rising living standards and rising levels of happiness. If the Easterlin Paradox is correct, economic growth will bring no benefits to consumers in terms of happiness in rich industrialised countries.

Firms Economic growth may provide opportunities for existing firms to increase sales as buyers have rising incomes. Many firms will be able to make higher profits. These extra profits can be retained by the firm to fund investment or distributed to the owners. If investment rises, then this will help to support further actual and potential growth. However, economic growth is accompanied by changes in the structure of the economy. Changing technologies mean that some firms will find their markets disappearing. Economic growth also provides opportunities for new firms to establish themselves.

The government Rising incomes means that government tax revenues should rise. Rising private sector spending also tends to lead to demands for similar rises in public sector spending. After all, if consumers are going on more holidays, buying more computer equipment or going out to restaurants more often, they also want to see better education for their children, better roads on which to drive their cars or better healthcare for themselves. So the quality of public services and infrastructure should improve. This also helps to promote further growth. An increase in the quality of educational opportunities and good quality healthcare also contributes positively to well being scores for individuals. However, the response to rising tax revenues depends upon parties in power.

Right-wing governments are more likely to reduce rates of tax and reduce government services than left-wing governments.

The environment In rich developed countries, economic growth is likely to lead to less pollution and a cleaner environment. Economic actors are likely to spend on technologies and projects to improve the environment. In developing countries, growth in primary and secondary industries is likely to increase pollution and damage the environment. China, for example, has a serious pollution problem because of the growth of its heavy industries in recent years. However, further growth should lead to a cleaning up of the environment in these countries.

The economy Growth in GDP results in a larger economy. The possible impact on consumers, firms and government has already been described. In terms of jobs, growth may result in more jobs being created or there may be fewer if existing workers become more productive.

For example, in Malaysia, job creation has averaged 270,000 jobs per year over the last 30 years. The majority of these were in manufacturing and services. Actual growth increases real GDP, so demand-deficient unemployment should fall as the economy moves closer to full employment. Negative output gaps will reduce in size. A fall in unemployment and underemployment will benefit individuals. The overall impact on unemployment will depend on how much the increase in goods and services demanded increases the demand for labour. For some industries, it may be that advances in technology mean there is limited impact on employment. An increase in aggregate demand is also likely to cause demand-pull inflation. This will be more significant as the economy approaches full employment or is operating in a positive output gap.

Once prices start to rise, workers will experience a fall in their real wages unless their nominal wages also rise. If wage bargaining is successful, this will also trigger cost-push inflation.

The balance of trade in goods and services on the current account will also be affected by economic growth. As incomes rise, the level of imports will rise (the marginal propensity to import). So there is more chance that the balance of trade will move into a deficit. The overall impact on the balance of trade will depend on how an economy's growth rate compares with other countries. It will also depend on what has caused the economic growth in the economy. For example, Germany is a high-income economy, but it has a current account surplus. It was export-led growth that was largely responsible for Germany's high economic growth rate in 2016. Germany has a relatively high savings ratio, so spending on imports remains relatively low.

Current and future living standards The impact of economic growth on living standards depends on who receives the benefit of that economic growth. If it is only the richest in society, then it will have no impact on the majority of households. However, in developing countries, everyone in society is more likely to benefit from economic growth. The debate about the link between rising GDP and living standards must also be taken into account. The weaker the link, the less economic growth will benefit households and individuals.

OPPORTUNITY COSTS OF GROWTH

Potential growth is the change in the productive potential of the economy over time. Potential growth requires an increase in the quantity or quality of factors of production. There is a potential conflict between consuming now and economic growth fuelled by investment. An economy may wish to increase its potential growth. Assuming the economy is currently operating on its production possibility frontier, if it chooses to devote more of its resources to the production of capital goods, in order to increase its stock of capital goods, then producing more capital goods today means diverting some resources away from the production of consumer goods. This means short-run living standards will be lower than what they might otherwise have been. Therefore, in the short run there is an opportunity cost of growth. However, in the long run the PPF will shift further to the right. This means both more capital and consumer goods can be produced. Living standards in the long run will be higher than they would have been without the extra investment today.

ACTIVITY 2   **SKILLS**   REASONING, ANALYSIS, CRITICAL THINKING

CASE STUDY: MALAYSIA – THE IMPACT OF GROWTH

Malaysia's rapid economic growth, averaging 6.4 per cent per year since 1970, has brought huge benefits. And many have gained, not just the few. Income inequality has actually fallen over the period. In 1970, the mean gross income ratio of the top 20 per cent of households, compared to the bottom 40 per cent, was nearly 10. By 2014, this had fallen to approximately 6.

However, as with any economy, there are still those who do not benefit significantly. Income support for disadvantaged persons such as the unemployed, single parents, disabled and elderly, is poorly targeted. Support is also inadequate to ensure basic living standards. Government expenditure on social protection is still lower than in all Southeast Asian countries, for which data is available.

There are also large differences in GDP per capita per region. In 2014, Kelantan had the lowest GDP per capita at MYR 11,820, with Kuala Lumpur the highest at MYR 91,100. The income gap between the richer and poorer states has widened over the last five years. However, steps have been taken to improve access to quality healthcare for low income urban and rural residents. The 11th Malaysia Plan includes objectives to extend the provision of rural basic infrastructure, including road, water and energy supply.

(a) From the case study, to what extent have the gains of growth been shared?

(b) How might economic growth improve public services so that the benefits of growth are shared with all levels of society?

THINKING LIKE AN ECONOMIST

ECONOMIC GROWTH – WHO GAINS?

One of the costs of economic growth might be rising inequality. This is not a surprise. Innovation and investment decisions often carry the risk of failure. So the incentives of financial rewards are vital to promote these engines of growth. In this situation, the increase in real GDP will clearly benefit some individuals more than others; it is their reward for taking the risk. However, other causes of growth, such as the promotion of competition, may lead to a more equal share of the increased real GDP.

Interestingly, the IMF, in 2015, published a paper that suggests lower inequality would boost economic growth. Their research suggests that a higher share of income for the top 20 per cent drags down growth, but a higher share of income for the poorest 20 per cent boosts growth. One argument is that access to skills and better health becomes more affordable for poorer individuals, if they receive a higher share of income. This boosts productivity and therefore promotes growth.

So the issue of inequality is not just one about fairness. Inequality today may affect growth rates tomorrow. However, perhaps the crucial debate should be on whether economic growth is necessarily desirable.

For developing countries, the evidence does suggest that rapid and sustained growth is the single most important way to lift people out of poverty. In a paper published by the UK's Department for International Development, a study in the 1990s of 14 countries found that a 1 per cent increase in per capita income reduced poverty by 1.7 per cent. The poverty reduction in Vietnam was particularly dramatic – between 1993 and 2002, the poverty rate fell from 58 per cent to 29 per cent.

In a new study by the Boston Consulting Group, the increase in GDP per capita for different African countries (between 2007 and 2012) was studied in relation to whether levels of well-being had actually improved. As well as income per person (which reflects average living standards), levels of well-being also included jobs, the quality of government (trustworthiness), health and inequality.

In Zambia, despite growth in income per person of more than 5 per cent since 2007, well-being scores were low. Ordinary Zambians had largely missed out on the benefits of economic growth. However, those African countries that reported the most improvement in well-being also enjoyed rapid growth in GDP per person. Countries such as Angola, Congo, Ethiopia and Malawi fell into this category. They have successfully translated strong growth into improved well-being. So for these countries, economic growth has brought significant benefits.

This debate is vital. It seems that economic growth can bring benefits – it is perhaps a necessary way to improve well-being, but it does not seem to be sufficient on its own. Who gains from economic growth, and, to what extent, are likely to remain widely discussed issues.

CHECKPOINT

1 State three benefits of economic growth.

2 State three costs of economic growth.

3 Why might economic growth lead to higher levels of investment?

4 State why public services are likely to improve after a period of rapid economic growth.

5 Why might economic growth cause inflation to rise?

6 Why might economic growth cause a balance of trade deficit?

7 State a reason why economic growth may lead to environmental costs.

8 Does everyone gain from economic growth?

SUBJECT VOCABULARY

economic growth a measure of how much output has increased by over a 12-month period. It is expressed as a percentage.

income/wealth inequality when income/wealth is shared out unevenly between different groups in society.

sustainable growth growth in the productive potential of the economy today that does not lead to a fall in the productive potential of the economy for future generations.

EXAM PRACTICE

CHINA'S RAPID ECONOMIC GROWTH

SKILLS ▸ REASONING, ANALYSIS, CRITICAL THINKING

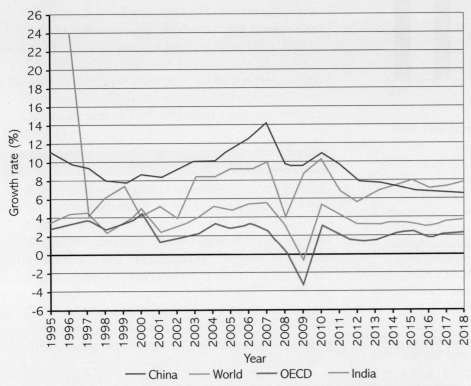

▲ Figure 2 Comparison of annual growth rates, selected countries and groupings (%), 1995–2018

Year	Number
1984	75.76
1996	42.05
2005	18.75
2013	1.85

▲ Table 2 Chinese poverty headcount ratio at US$1.90 a day (2011 PPP, % of population), selected years

Year	percentage of people
1982	65.5
2015	96.4

▲ Table 3 Chinese literacy rate, adult aged 15+ (% of population), 1982 and 2015

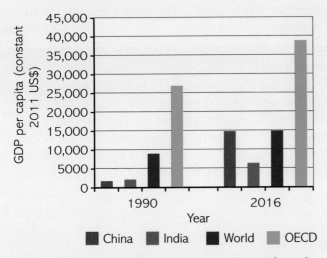

▲ Figure 3 Comparison of GDP per capita, selected countries and groupings (PPP, constant 2011 US$), 1990 and 2016

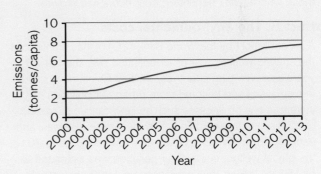

▲ Figure 4 Chinese CO_2 emissions (metric tonnes per capita), 2000–13

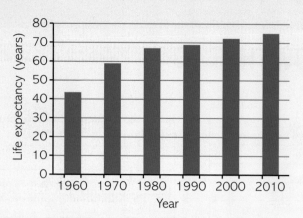

▲ Figure 5 Chinese life expectancy at birth (years), 1960–2010

Extract A: Inequality in China

According to a report from Peking University's Institute of Social Science, among the world's 25 largest countries by population, only South Africa and Brazil had greater inequality than China. Even the USA recorded a more even distribution of income. In the 1980s, China had far greater income equality. Income distribution has widened significantly over the last 30 years as real GDP has increased rapidly.

China's leadership has promised to address inequality. 'We want to continuously enlarge the pie, while also making sure we divide the pie correctly', said a government representative. One way to achieve this would be to raise taxes on income from those on higher incomes and use welfare payments to increase the income of those who haven't benefitted from economic growth.

Extract B: The environmental costs

A recent report by the World Bank (2016) has highlighted the soaring welfare cost of air pollution over the last 25 years as developing countries, such as China, have rapidly industrialised and become more urban. Air pollution increases risk of illnesses such as lung cancer, strokes, heart disease and chronic bronchitis. These diseases, and early deaths from them, create an economic cost. In 2013, the global welfare costs of air pollution was estimated to be US$5.1 trillion (by comparison, in 1990, the global welfare cost was only US$2.6 trillion, in 2011 dollar terms at PPP). Low- and middle-income countries accounted for 59 per cent of the global welfare loss in 2013, with the majority coming from Asia. Wealthier regions, such as Europe and North America, also suffer significant costs from air pollution, although these have decreased slightly over the last 10 years. Urashi Narain, who led the World Bank team said, 'Countries are definitely acting on this agenda. China has declared a war on pollution. We've seen action from India as well.'

Q

1 With reference to Figure 5 and Table 2, explain how rapid economic growth will likely affect life expectancy for low- or middle-income economies.
(4 marks)

2 With reference to Figure 2 and Table 3, analyse one reason why economic growth is likely to improve the quality of education. **(6 marks)**

3 With reference to the information provided, discuss the likely impact of continued rapid economic growth on living standards for Chinese citizens.
(14 marks)

EXAM HINT

Consider both positive and negative impacts. Has previous economic growth in China benefited Chinese citizens? Use the data to provide evidence for this. To what extent will further rapid economic growth increase living standards? Use the data and the passage to highlight any costs of economic growth that impact living standards. Can future growth minimise these costs? It is useful to reflect whether the costs are a necessary cost of growth or whether they can be minimised by government intervention.

4 In 2016, the annual percentage change in real GDP for the UK was 1.8 per cent, Ethiopia 7.6 per cent, China 6.7 per cent and Malaysia 4.2 per cent. Evaluate the benefits of economic growth for an economy. **(20 marks)**

EXAM HINT

Analyse the likely benefits. To evaluate, consider whether economic growth will necessarily lead to some of the benefits you have analysed. Under what circumstances might the gains from economic growth be greater? Do any costs of growth offset the gains? Conclude by giving an overall judgement.

MACROECONOMIC OBJECTIVES AND POLICIES

Macroeconomic objectives, introduced in the first section, are developed further. This section explains why policymakers will find it hard to achieve all these objectives at any one time and explores the conflicts between macroeconomic objectives. The section finishes by looking at a range of demand and supply-side polices, which are used by governments and central banks to help improve the performance of an economy. It discusses the strengths and weaknesses of different polices.

37 MACROECONOMIC OBJECTIVES

LEARNING OBJECTIVES

■ Understand that macroeconomic objectives for an economy are typically:
- economic growth
- low and stable rate of inflation
- low unemployment
- balance of payments equilibrium on current account
- balanced government budget
- greater income equality.

GETTING STARTED

Find out the current rate of economic growth, the rate of unemployment, the inflation rate and the level of the current account deficit on the balance of payments. In your country, why might a high rate of economic growth benefit you and the household in which you live? Why might a high rate of inflation impose costs on you and your household? Why might a high rate of unemployment affect you in the future?

GOVERNMENT OBJECTIVES

Governments attempt to influence the economy so as to improve its economic performance. Different economies perform in different ways. So what is possible for the Malaysian economy might be very different from what is possible for the Chinese economy, the Afghan economy or the Serbian economy. However, governments typically have macroeconomic objectives relating to four variables: **economic growth**, **unemployment**, **inflation** and the **current account** on the balance of payments. They will also have objectives in relation to government budgets, the environment and income inequality.

ECONOMIC GROWTH

In most circumstances, governments attempt to maximise the growth rate of their economies. For low- and middle-income countries like China, Uganda or Brazil, it may be possible to reach annual growth rates of up to 10 per cent or even more. For high-income countries such as the UK, the USA or Germany, an annual growth rate of 2.5 per cent might be possible.

High rates of growth in low-and middle-income countries can be achieved, for example, by moving large numbers of workers from low-productivity agriculture to higher-productivity manufacturing. Using modern technology can also significantly increase output per worker.

High-income countries, however, have already been through an industrialisation process and will have already introduced most technological developments. Moreover, a number of high-income countries, including Japan and Italy, face a rapidly ageing population where the number of workers in the economy is falling. Achieving even a 2.5 per cent growth rate is now seen as challenging in these circumstances.

UNEMPLOYMENT AND EMPLOYMENT

Governments would like to see unemployment as low as possible without there being inflationary pressure in the economy. It is impossible to have no unemployment in a market economy because there is always frictional and seasonal unemployment. Most governments have no official target for unemployment. Whether an unemployment rate is high or low, for an economy, depends on many factors. For example, unemployment rates in the 1950s and 1960s for the UK, in an era of full employment, were around 1.5 per cent. Over the past 20 years, the best unemployment figure was a 4.8 per cent rate achieved in 2004. Under present circumstances, a 5 per cent rate would be seen as a considerable policy achievement for the UK, in economy.

Most governments are keen to expand employment. Higher employment should increase tax revenues and reduce welfare benefits to the unemployed and those on low incomes. Getting people out of unemployment and off benefits is often a major policy objective in recent years.

INFLATION AND DEFLATION

Central banks and governments in the industrialised world have tended to set inflation targets of around 2 per cent. This is low but positive inflation. Higher inflation is seen as undesirable, particularly because of the fear that inflation will then increase even further. Nonetheless, governments want to avoid **deflation**.

Deflation is seen as being linked to recession and low or negative economic growth. A low and stable rate of inflation is desirable. If inflation is stable then this makes it easier for individuals, firms and governments to plan for the future.

THE BALANCE OF PAYMENTS ON CURRENT ACCOUNT

Governments aim for the balance of payments on current account to be broadly in balance over time. Economies where the current account is regularly in surplus are seen to be 'strong' economies while those running persistent deficits are seen to be 'struggling' or 'weak' economies. However, the reality is far more complex than these initial judgements. Countries can run regular surpluses, for example, and have low economic growth rates. Other countries can run regular deficits and grow very fast over time without significant economic problems.

Very large current account deficits, measured as a percentage of **GDP** can, however, be very dangerous. If borrowers in these countries reach a point where they can no longer repay their loans, as Argentina did in 2001 or Greece in 2009, then there will be an economic crisis and a sudden large fall in GDP.

GOVERNMENT BUDGETS

A government broadly aims to have a **balanced government budget**. This is when government spending is equal to its revenue. There may be some years when the government chooses to have a budget (fiscal) deficit (for example, to actively inject money into the circular flow of income), but any borrowing must be sustainable over time. Since the financial crisis of 2008, the importance of fiscal (i.e. government) budget deficits as a major economic objective has grown. If a country is growing at around 2.5 per cent per year and there is 2 per cent inflation and low interest rates, then a fiscal deficit of around 3 per cent per year will probably maintain a stable level of national debt (the sum total of all outstanding government borrowing) as a percentage of GDP.

Following the financial crisis of 2008, a number of countries including the USA, Greece and Spain saw their fiscal deficits grow to over 10 per cent of GDP. These levels are unsustainable in the long term because it means that governments have to borrow far more money than they expect to repay with interest in the future. In the short term, however, large fiscal deficits that increase the national debt from, say, 40 per cent of GDP to 100 per cent of GDP, are sustainable so long as the fiscal deficit is reduced to manageable levels over time.

Economists disagree about the path to long-term equilibrium. Some argue that fiscal deficits should be cut as quickly as possible, even if this means negative economic growth and significant increases in unemployment. Others argue that cutting fiscal deficits at a slower pace is better because it allows the economy to grow faster, leading to quicker rises in tax revenues and falls in welfare payments to the unemployed.

THE ENVIRONMENT

There is no simple measure of the impact of economic activity on the environment. Governments therefore have a wide variety of objectives in relation to the environment. These might range from global warming to pollution on beaches to air quality in cities. There is a range of opinion about whether economic growth is good or bad for the environment.

Environmentalists tend to be anti-growth, arguing that any increased economic activity will damage the planet. Pro-growth economists tend to argue that increases in output and improvements in technology allow economies to clean up their environments and reduce pollution.

INCOME DISTRIBUTION

Economists and politicians disagree about income distribution policies. Very broadly, right-wing economists and politicians tend to argue that inequality is positive because it increases incentives to work and take economic risks. This increases economic growth rates, raising incomes for all in society. They therefore are against policies that reduce inequalities, particularly increases in taxes on higher earners and businesses.

Left-wing economists and politicians tend to argue that, on principles of fairness, everyone in society should have access to a certain standard of living and that free markets lead to high levels of inequality. Therefore, governments need to intervene to reduce inequality. They can intervene in markets, for example, by setting minimum wages or maximum prices for essential goods. They can also provide goods such as healthcare and education free to every citizen and fund this through raising taxes, particularly on high earners. They can also transfer income directly through taxes and benefits. Left-wing economists would tend to argue that high levels of inequality do not lead to higher economic growth. Individuals will work and take risks even if marginal rates of tax are high.

There are many variations on these views. So while economists and politicians would usually agree, for example, that fiscal deficits need to be contained over time or that low unemployment is desirable, there is no general agreement about objectives for **income equality**.

ACTIVITY 1

CASE STUDY: SAUDI ARABIA'S PLANS TO TRANSFORM ITS ECONOMY

In June 2016, the National Transformation Plan was released, setting out Saudi Arabia's 'Vision 2030'. The fall in oil prices over the previous 18 months, causing a sharp fall in oil revenue, had meant less income for the government. This had resulted in government spending cuts, with many government projects put on hold. The slowdown had pushed real GDP growth to as low as 1 per cent of GDP.

The plan aims to make Saudi Arabia less dependent on oil, with a more diverse economy with greater private sector activity. It is hoped that industrial development, in particular an expansion of manufacturing, which makes up one-quarter of non-oil activity, will help the private sector increase from 45 per cent to 60 per cent of GDP and reduce unemployment from 11.6 per cent to 7 per cent.

Saudi Arabia also plans to cut public wages. This would mean a decrease in total salaries from SAR 480 billion (Saudi riyal) to SAR 456 billion by 2020. About two-thirds of Saudi workers are state-employed. Other targets include raising non-oil revenues for the government to SAR 530 billion by 2020, from SAR 163.5 billion in 2015. This would be done by increasing taxes, including a sales tax, income taxes on non-Saudi residents and taxes on harmful products, such as tobacco. The objective is to balance the budget by 2020. The budget deficit in 2015 was 16 per cent of GDP.

(a) Use the extract to explain Saudi Arabia's current main macroeconomic objectives. How do they intend to achieve these?

THINKING LIKE AN ECONOMIST

A TALE OF FOUR ECONOMIES – BEFORE, DURING AND AFTER THE GLOBAL FINANCIAL CRISIS

The USA, Germany, Japan and the UK are four of the largest economies in the world. Their governments are all committed to achieving a high rate of economic growth for their economies.

Figures 1 and 2 show how well they have achieved that over the period 2001 to 2014. Looking at the data, it is clear that none of the four economies was able to avoid the impact of the 2008 financial crisis. In 2009, for example, the US economy shrank by 2.8 per cent while the German economy shrank by 5.6 per cent.

Figure 3 shows the percentage change in GDP at purchasing power parities over the whole period 2001–08. This shows that over these eight years, the performance of the UK and US economies were significantly better than Japan or Germany. Japan faced particular problems. An ageing population, a high savings rate and prices at times falling rather than rising (deflation) caused a reduction in the growth of domestic demand.

Growth in exports, the main driver of the Japanese economy in the 1960s, 1970s and 1980s, was disappointing as Japanese companies lost competitive advantage to lower cost countries such as China and South Korea. Germany, in the early 2000s, was still suffering from the costs of the reunification of East and West Germany in 1990.

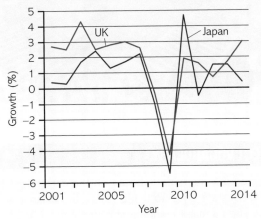

▲ Figure 1 Annual % growth rate in GDP, Japan and the UK, 2001–14

Source: adapted from www.oecd.org

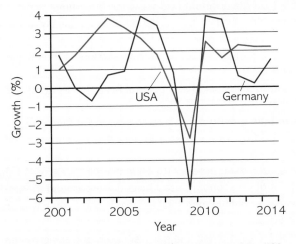

▲ Figure 2 Annual % growth rate in GDP, Germany and the USA, 2001–14

However, Figure 3 shows the disastrous cost of the 2008 financial crisis. In five years, 2009–13, the four economies barely achieved what might have been one year's growth in the period 2001–07. It also shows the poor relative performance of the UK economy compared to the US economy. In the USA, the government adopted a much looser fiscal policy than the UK in order to increase demand and reduce unemployment. The UK, from 2010, saw significant government spending cuts and rises in taxes designed to reduce the government budget deficit. However, it had the effect of reducing demand in the UK economy and lowering economic growth. The UK government chose to prioritise cutting its budget deficit over its aim to achieve the long-term growth rate for the economy.

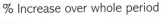
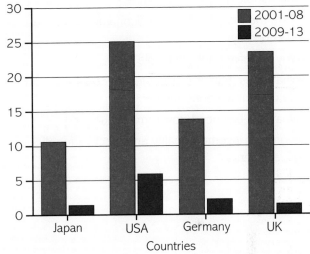

▲ Figure 3 Percentage growth in real GDP (at PPPs), 2001–08 and 2009–13

JAPAN

GERMANY

UK

USA

CHECKPOINT

1 Why are economic growth rate targets likely to be lower for advanced economies compared to low- and middle-income economies?

2 State the main likely macroeconomic objectives for an economy.

3 Why is deflation undesirable?

4 What does 'balance of payments equilibrium on the current account' mean?

5 What is a balanced government budget?

6 Is greater income equality an objective for all governments?

SUBJECT VOCABULARY

balance of payments equilibrium on the current account where credits are equal to debits. Since the balance of trade is often a major component of the current account, equilibrium is broadly when the value of exports equals the value of imports.

balanced government budget when government spending is equal to its revenue over a period of time, usually a year.

current account part of the balance of payments account. A major component of the current account is the balance of trade.

deflation a sustained and general fall in prices across an economy.

economic growth a measure of how much output has increased by over a 12-month period. It is expressed as a percentage.

gross domestic product (GDP) a standard measure of the output of an economy, used by countries around the world.

income equality when total income in the economy is shared out equally.

inflation a sustained and general rise in prices across an economy.

unemployment occurs when individuals are without a job but are actively seeking work.

EXAM PRACTICE

THE WAY FORWARD FOR FRANCE

SKILLS REASONING, ANALYSIS, CRITICAL THINKING

In May 2017, Emmanuel Macron was elected France's new president. In many ways, the French economy he has taken on performs well. The purchasing power of France's GDP per capita was the same as the UK's in 2016, but 12 per cent below Germany's. French labour productivity per hour was the same as Germany's and 28 per cent above the UK's. Its distribution of income was more equal than the UK and USA, and similar to Germany. It has excellent infrastructure and public services.

Because France is a member of the eurozone, the control of inflation is the responsibility of the European Central Bank (ECB). The ECB aims to keep the inflation rate in the eurozone below, but close to 2 per cent.

The French government faces three key economic challenges. Its unemployment is high, it has a low rate of economic growth and government spending is too high.

Macron has said that he aims to keep France's budget deficit within the EU's limit of 3 per cent of GDP. In June 2017, it was expected that France's deficit would be 3.2 per cent of GDP by the end of the year. The government would need to find savings of €4 billion to meet the target.

	France	Germany	UK
Unemployment rate March 2017 (%)	10.1	3.9	4.5
Employment rate (15–64) quarter 4, 2016 (%)	64.2	75	73.7
Government spending as a percentage of GDP 2016	56	44	39

▲ **Table 1 French, German and UK selected economic indicators, 2016 and 2017**

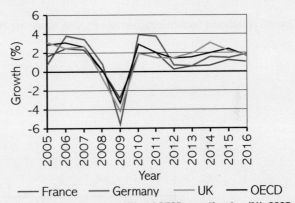

▲ **Figure 4 French, Germany, UK and OECD growth rates (%), 2005–16**

Source: adapted from www.oecd.org

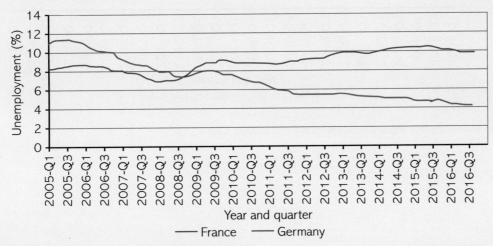

▲ **Figure 5 French and German unemployment rates (%) 2005Q1–16Q3**

Source: adapted from www.oecd.org

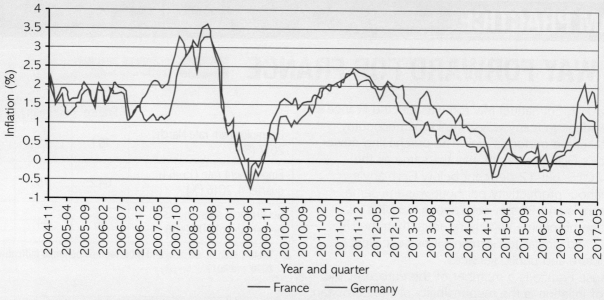

▲ **Figure 6 French and German inflation rates (%, CPI), November 2004–May 2017**

Source: adapted from www.oecd.org

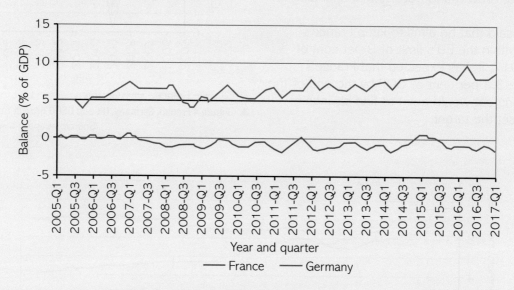

▲ **Figure 7 French and German current account balances (% of GDP), 2005Q1–17Q1**

Source: adapted from www.oecd.org

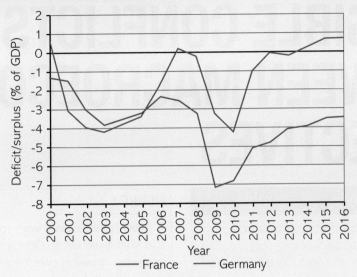

▲ **Figure 8 French and German government deficit/surplus (% of GDP), 2000–16**

Source: adapted from www.oecd.org

Q

(a) With reference to Figure 8, explain the macroeconomic objective 'balanced government budget'. **(4 marks)**

(b) With reference to the extract, Table 1 and Figure 4, analyse why increasing economic growth might be an important macroeconomic objective for the French government in 2017. **(6 marks)**

EXAM HINT

Figure 4 shows France's economic growth compared to other economies. How do they compare? The passage identifies three key challenges for France's economy. Explain why increasing economic growth might help to reduce unemployment and government spending (or help to reduce the budget deficit via increasing tax revenues).

(c) With reference to the information provided, discuss how well the French government met its possible macroeconomic objectives, compared to Germany, between 2005 and 2016. **(14 marks)**

EXAM HINT

First outline the possible economic objectives, for both France and Germany, over the whole period. Take each objective and comment on the relative performance of France and Germany – identify any trends in the data where these seem to exist. Comment on why the performance of the economies were particularly bad for some of the period shown. In your conclusion, make an overall judgement as to whether France or Germany is more likely to have met their objectives successfully. Identify any areas where you might not have enough information to conclude.

38 POSSIBLE CONFLICTS BETWEEN MACROECONOMIC OBJECTIVES

LEARNING OBJECTIVES

- Understand the possible conflicts that can occur between the following macroeconomic objectives:
  - inflation and unemployment, including the short-run Phillips curve
  - economic growth and protection of the environment
  - economic growth and equilibrium on the current account of the balance of payments
  - inflation and equilibrium on the current account of the balance of payments
  - economic growth and income equality.

GETTING STARTED

Use the Internet or newspapers to find examples of inflation and unemployment data moving in opposite directions. Look at the OECD website and go to the data section. For an economy of your choice, look up inflation and unemployment data over the last 20 years. Are there some years within this period where the inflation rate has risen and the unemployment rate has fallen (or vice versa)?

MACROECONOMIC OBJECTIVES

Governments have a number of macroeconomic objectives, which were explained in Chapter 37. These include:

- high and sustainable economic growth
- low unemployment
- low inflation
- a sustainable current account equilibrium on the balance of payments
- a sustainable fiscal position
- environmental objectives, such as reducing pollution and greenhouse gas emissions
- objectives relating to income and wealth equality.

A SUCCESSFUL, SUSTAINABLE ECONOMY

What might a successful economy look like for a developed country such as Germany, where the government was achieving all its macroeconomic objectives?

FIGURE 1

A growing economy with low inflation
The shift from OA to OB can show a successful economy growing over time with full employment and mild inflation.

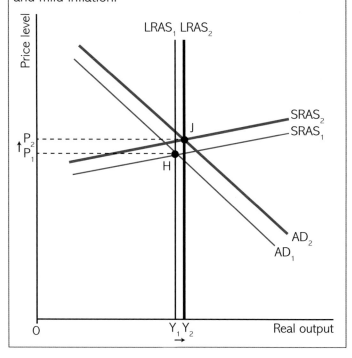

Consider Figure 1. At the point H, the economy is in both short-run and long-run equilibrium. Aggregate demand is equal to SRAS and LRAS. At OY, there may be structural unemployment, but here we will assume that there is full employment in all regions and all industries in the economy. The economy is growing at 2.5 per cent per year, the average for developed countries before the 2007–08 financial crisis. Over time, aggregate demand is increasing, shown by the shift in the aggregate demand curve to the right. This is matched by an increase in both SRAS and LRAS. At J, there is a new equilibrium. Output is higher. There is also very mild inflation, shown by the increase in the price level from OP_1 to OP_2. This is caused by aggregate demand rising slightly faster than SRAS and LRAS. Figure 1 cannot be used to show that there is a sustainable fiscal equilibrium or that there is a sustainable current account equilibrium on the balance of payments. Again, assume that these two equilibria exist. Nor can Figure 1 say anything about income and wealth inequality. However, assume that growth in the economy is partly being used to finance environmental improvements, such as a shift towards renewable energy.

CONFLICTS BETWEEN MACROECONOMIC OBJECTIVES

Inflation and unemployment Assume that the rate of inflation is too high. One way to reduce the rate of inflation is to reduce aggregate demand, for example, by cutting consumer spending or government spending. However, reducing aggregate demand is likely to lead to recession and cyclical unemployment. This illustrates the **trade-off** between inflation and unemployment.

In the same way, if the rate of economic growth is too low, one way to increase it in the short term is to raise aggregate demand. This will lower unemployment but increase inflation. The trade-off or conflict between inflation and unemployment exists in the short run. Both the Phillips curve and SR AD/AS analysis can explain why a trade-off exists in the short run.

THE SHORT-RUN PHILLIPS CURVE

One example of a trade-off between two macroeconomic objectives is the short-run Phillips curve. A W Phillips was an economist who published a paper in 1958 showing that there was a statistical relationship between the rate of unemployment and the rate of change of money wages between 1861 and 1957 in the UK. This relationship, called the Phillips curve, is shown in Figure 2. The money wages paid to workers are the most important single cost of production in the UK economy. When money wages go up faster than the increase in output per worker (their productivity) then costs increase for firms. They respond by putting up prices. The rate of increase in money wages is, therefore, a good proxy (or substitute) variable for the rate of increase in the price level i.e. the rate of inflation.

FIGURE 2

The short-run Phillips curve
The **short-run Phillips curve** shows there is a trade-off between high unemployment rates and higher rates of change of money wages, a proxy measure for inflation.

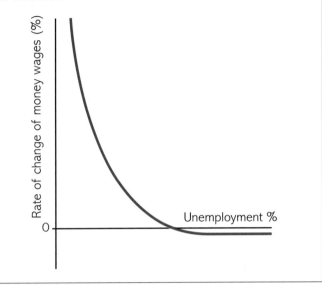

So the Phillips curve shows that there is a trade-off between unemployment and inflation. The lower the rate of unemployment, the higher the inflation rate. This trade-off can be seen on an aggregate demand and supply curve diagram. In Figure 3, the economy is at OA in short-run equilibrium. There is an increase in aggregate demand from AD_1 to AD_2. Real output rises from OA to OB. Higher output means more jobs and less unemployment. But the fall in unemployment comes at a cost of a rise in the price level of EF. In the long run, with a vertical long-run aggregate supply curve, there is no trade-off between unemployment and inflation because, in the long run, there is no unemployment. This trade-off is a short-run trade-off. It results from a movement up or down the short-run aggregate supply curve.

The trade-off between inflation and unemployment would not exist if supply-side policies were used (Chapter 39). Supply-side polices increase the LRAS, so the price level falls and real GDP rises. A rise in real GDP means unemployment will fall, since more output requires more labour. Classical economists also argue that the LRAS curve is vertical. So, whatever the level of aggregate demand and therefore price level, real output will always end up at the full employment level. With this view, there is no trade-off between inflation and unemployment in the long run.

FIGURE 3

The trade-off between unemployment and inflation

The movement up the short-run aggregate supply curve leads to higher real output, lower unemployment but higher prices.

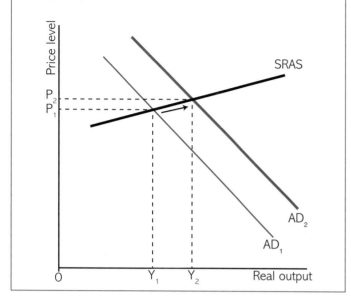

ECONOMIC GROWTH AND EQUILIBRIUM ON THE CURRENT ACCOUNT OF THE BALANCE OF PAYMENTS

If economic growth is too low, in the short run the government might increase aggregate demand. This is likely to lead to a rise in imports because increased incomes will lead to extra demand for imported goods. If there was originally an equilibrium on the current account of the balance of payments, then this will cause a deficit.

Similarly, if imports are far greater than exports, there might be difficulties for a country in financing this deficit. Cutting imports by reducing domestic consumption and investment will also reduce demand for domestically produced goods in the economy. Real GDP will fall and unemployment will rise. So again, trying to achieve one macroeconomic objective conflicts with achieving another.

However, if the current account is in deficit, the use of supply-side polices (policies to increase the LRAS) would achieve growth, lower inflation and reduce the current account deficit. This is because domestic goods would become more price competitive in international markets. In this case there is no conflict between these macroeconomic objectives.

Economic growth and income equality Correcting inequalities may involve direct government intervention by redistributing income through taxes and government spending. Direct provision of better educational outcomes for low-achieving students should lead, in the long term, to them being able to earn higher wages. Correcting inequalities may also involve intervening in markets, for example, by setting minimum wages or giving trade unions more power. Economists disagree about the outcomes of these measures. However, reducing inequality, for example by large rises in benefits for the unemployed, is likely to have some disincentive effect to work and this then raises long-term unemployment and reduces long-term growth. Equally, a failure to correct inequalities in education between children from rich and poor households is likely to reduce long-term economic growth.

As seen in Chapter 36, a rise in inequality is often viewed as a cost of economic growth. In other words, a rise in economic growth widens income inequality. However, in reality the situation is more complex, because there are many causes of economic growth.

Some might even reduce income inequalities. For example, government spending on education, directed at disadvantaged children, might increase social mobility. However, some policies that promote growth do conflict with equality. For example, many free market supply-side policies, such as reducing trade union power, making wages more flexible and making it easier for firms to sack workers are all likely to put downward pressure on wages. In this case, economic growth conflicts with income equality.

ACTIVITY 1 · · · SKILLS · REASONING, COMMUNICATION

CASE STUDY: ARE EASTERN EUROPEAN COUNTRIES HEATING UP?

In February 2017, economists were predicting that Eastern European central banks would soon be announcing interest rate rises. Inflation had risen across Hungary, the Czech Republic and Poland from an average of −1 per cent in 2014, to 1.5 per cent in February 2017, with expectations of further increases. Much of this seemed to be driven by wage pressures rising. Labour shortages had been increasing across all three countries, but particularly in Hungary. In Hungary, the labour shortage had already led to a 15–25 per cent increase in the minimum wage. Wage growth across the region was now greater than productivity growth. The unemployment rate of Hungary had fallen from a high of almost 12 per cent in 2013 to just 4.4 per cent. Similarly, unemployment in the Czech Republic had fallen from 8.7 per cent in 2014 to 5.2 per cent. Poland's unemployment had fallen from 14.3 per cent in 2013 to 8.3 per cent.

(a) Explain why labour shortages cause wage pressures to build.

(b) Explain how the data illustrates a trade-off relationship between inflation and unemployment. Use the Phillips curve to illustrate the data.

Economic growth and protection of the environment

In developing countries, growth in primary and secondary industries is likely to increase pollution and cause other environmental problems. For these economies, the main macroeconomic objective will be to achieve high economic growth rates. This is crucial to lift their population out of poverty. At this stage of their development, they do not have the technology or resources available to promote environmental protection. Governments will have limited taxation income to invest in environmental improvements. However, in rich developed economies, economic growth should further improve environmental protection. Advanced technology, sophisticated regulation from governments and government support of environmental quality investment, should all help to achieve this.

However, there may still be critics who argue that policies, designed to improve environmental protection, will conflict with economic growth. If environmental indicators are deteriorating, the government can introduce policies to reverse these trends. As with inequalities, economists disagree about the impact of policies designed to correct environmental failures. However, investing in cleaner technologies might lead to lower economic growth because investment resources are being diverted into resources that do not contribute to economic growth. Tightening environmental regulation might discourage investment, leading to lower growth and high unemployment. In contrast, investing in, say, wind farms or pollution-reducing equipment might lead to an increase in investment and therefore aggregate demand. This might raise growth and reduce unemployment.

In some cases, environmental policies can force inefficient firms to become more efficient, for example by recycling more of their waste or forcing them to think about whether it would be more profitable to replacing aging equipment. Environmental policies can also increase LRAS from what it might otherwise have been if the cost of those environmental policies is less than the costs arising from environmental market failure that would otherwise have occurred. For example, assume it costs US$20 billion to implement environmental policies. Then assume the environmental cost of doing nothing is US$30 billion. Environmental policies have then gained the economy US$10 billion.

INFLATION AND EQUILIBRIUM ON THE CURRENT ACCOUNT OF THE BALANCE OF PAYMENTS

Assume the current account balance of the balance of payments is currently in equilibrium. If inflation is too high, the central bank of an economy is likely to raise interest rates. This will reduce aggregate demand and therefore reduce demand-pull inflation. A fall in aggregate demand will also reduce demand for imports. This will cause the current account to move into surplus. The surplus will also arise because a fall in inflation will make domestic goods more price competitive on international markets. This will increase the demand for exports. If the government's objective was to achieve an equilibrium on the current account, then there has been a conflict between achieving the inflation target and this objective.

In the same way, if inflation is too low, a central bank will lower interest rates. Aggregate demand will increase and so demand-pull inflation will rise. This causes domestic goods to be less price competitive with those abroad. Exports will fall. The rise in aggregate demand will also increase the demand for imports (this is linked to the concept of the marginal propensity to import). The combined effect means the current account will deteriorate. If the current account was originally in equilibrium, it will now be in deficit. If there was already a deficit on the current account, then the deficit will worsen.

ACTIVITY 2   SKILLS   REASONING, CRITICAL THINKING

CASE STUDY: WILL IMPROVED GROWTH THREATEN THE ENVIRONMENT?

China's economy grew at an annual rate of 6.9 per cent in the first quarter of 2017, its fastest in 18 months, according to official data. This follows a four-year slowdown in growth. This seems like good news, but some are worried about the impact this will have on the environment. Already, the economic recovery has contributed to a rise in smog in northern China and the southern manufacturing areas, after three years of improving air quality and falling coal consumption. This is likely to cause concern that environmental regulations are not tight enough to prevent pollution rising when economic growth is strong. An acceleration in economic growth creates a greater increase in pollution from heavy industry. When the economy slows, smaller factories that burn dirtier coal and are less efficient, shut down. But when economic growth picks up, they start up again as it is possible to make profit.

(a) Explain why economic growth might cause environmental problems.

(b) What might be the impact of stronger environmental regulations on future economic growth in China?

THINKING LIKE AN ECONOMIST

HAS THE PHILLIPS CURVE GONE FLAT?

It has long been accepted by central banks and economists that falls in unemployment will at some point start to cause inflation. However, despite decent economic growth and low unemployment rates across many advanced economies, inflation rates remain mysteriously low.

This is particularly the case for the USA. In June 2017, as the economy approached 'full employment', both unemployment and inflation remained low. In June 2017, the unemployment rate was 4.4 per cent and core inflation, which excludes food and energy price changes, had still not hit the Federal Reserve Bank's 2 per cent inflation target since 2012. In June 2017, wage growth and inflation remained surprisingly low. In June 2017 prices, excluding food and energy were only 1.5 per cent higher than the year before.

By comparison, after the financial crisis, unemployment peaked at 10 per cent in October 2009. However, the rate of inflation was only 1.3 per cent, just a little lower than in 2017. This shows how surprising it was, in June 2017, that there seemed to be no evidence inflation was about to rise. Some critics were beginning to argue that the Phillips curve had gone missing, perhaps never to return. However, despite recent events, most economists and policymakers still believe a short-run trade-off between inflation and unemployment exists. There are three reasons that might explain why the Phillips curve should not be abandoned.

- The effects of unemployment on inflation can get lost when there are sudden changes in prices charged in specific markets. For example, better mobile phone deals have reduced consumer-price inflation by over 0.2 percentage points over the last year. This would mean a given level of unemployment would be associated with a lower inflation rate.

- It is possible that inflation and wage growth will begin suddenly and sharply when unemployment gets too low, rather than gradually as unemployment falls.

- It might be that wage growth is remaining temporarily low because workers do not believe that low unemployment is here to stay. If they think inflation will remain low, they would only need modest pay rises to cover their expected increased living costs. They would not want to bargain for much higher wages if that meant a higher risk of losing their jobs. However, once workers believe unemployment will remain low, they will have the confidence to bargain for higher wages. This will push up costs and cause cost-push inflationary pressures to rise.

So, once these factors settle down, it is expected that the relationship between inflation and unemployment, as shown by the short-run Phillips curve, will continue to hold.

CHECKPOINT

1 What are the main macroeconomic objectives?

2 If aggregate demand increases, what happens to the inflation rate and unemployment rate?

3 Create a Phillips curve – make sure you label the axis carefully.

4 Give one reason why economic growth might conflict with the protection of the environment.

5 Name one cause of economic growth that might increase inequalities.

6 If the current account is in equilibrium, state why a central bank, raising interest rates to reduce inflation, is likely to cause the current account to move into surplus.

7 Why doesn't the trade-off between unemployment and inflation exist, in the LR, according to classical economists?

SUBJECT VOCABULARY

short-run Phillips curve shows the relationship between the rate of unemployment and the rate of change of money wages (a proxy measure for inflation). The short-run Phillips curve shows the short-run trade-off between unemployment and inflation.

trade-off when achieving one macroeconomic objective conflicts with achieving another.

EXAM PRACTICE

SKILLS REASONING, COMMUNICATION, CRITICAL THINKING

Q

1 Which one of the following is most likely to explain the current account of the balance of payments moving into deficit?

(a) Productivity increases in the economy.

(b) Inflation rises sharply.

(c) Aggregate demand falls sharply as household spending falls.

(d) The value of the exchange rate has fallen and has remained low over recent months.

(1 mark)

2 In Brazil between November 2016 and April 2017, inflation had fallen from approximately 9 per cent to 4.5 per cent. Brazil's economy had shrunk by 3.6 per cent in 2016, after declining 3.8 per cent in 2015, leading to rising unemployment. Draw a short-run Phillips curve to show the effect of the recession on unemployment and inflation.

(4 marks)

3 **The Czech Republic – inflationary pressures are picking up**

Extract A:

In August 2017, Central European countries reported strong growth, for example, real GDP in the Czech Republic increased by 4.5 per cent, year on year, in the second quarter of 2017. This is partly because of the increase in demand from the rest of the eurozone driving export-led growth. It is also because consumption had picked up, as low unemployment pushed up wage increases and encouraged households to spend. With rising house prices too, inflationary pressures are building up.

With reference to extract A, examine the likely impact on inflation of the low level of unemployment in the Czech economy. **(8 marks)**

EXAM HINT

Question 3 has 6 marks for knowledge, application and analysis, and 2 marks for evaluation. For analysis, it would be useful to include a short-run AD/AS diagram to explain the trade-off between inflation and unemployment. Use the passage to explain why aggregate demand has risen. Using the Phillips curve would also be useful to show the trade-off. For evaluation, consider the difference between the short and long runs.

4 **US fiscal policy plans**

Extract B:

In the USA, the government is set to promote economic growth. There are plans for the government to increase its spending on infrastructure and cut taxes. The fiscal deficit (government budget) will increase by 3 per cent of GDP.

Top individual income tax rates are set to fall to 33 per cent and the corporate tax rate from 35 per cent to 15 per cent. The highest income taxpayers (0.1 per cent of the population with incomes over US$43.7 million [2016 $]) will receive an average cut of more than 14 per cent of their after-tax income. The poorest fifth's taxes will fall by an average of 0.8 per cent of taxed income. There will be concern that these tax cuts will increase income inequality.

Even though the concentration of tax cuts on the wealthiest will limit how much aggregate demand increases (because a smaller proportion of extra income for a rich person is spent), economic growth should rise.

The Trump government has a goal of 4 per cent growth, but there are fears that if aggregate demand increases too much, it might trigger inflation.

With reference to extract B, discuss the likely impact of the US tax cuts and infrastructure spending plans on the US economy. **(14 marks)**

EXAM HINT

Consider the impact on the macroeconomic objectives. Analyse the effect on aggregate demand. Discuss whether the multiplier effect of the tax cuts is likely to be large. If actual growth rises, what might be the impact on other measures of economic performance? Under what circumstances might the impact on the different measures of economic performance be beneficial? To what extent might there be a conflict between the macroeconomic objectives? Is there likely to be an impact on the LRAS? If so, how might this affect your judgement of this policy?

5 An estimate by Statistics Portugal said GDP increased from 1.5 per cent in 2016 to 2.7 per cent in 2017, driven mainly by an increase in domestic demand, especially investment. The economic recovery in Portugal began in 2014. The Portuguese economy has been growing for 15 consecutive quarters.

Source: *Financial Times*, 'Portugal grows at fastest rate since 2000', 14.2.2018

(a) With reference to the extract and Figure 4, analyse the short-run relationship between inflation and unemployment for Portugal from 2014 onwards. **(6 marks)**

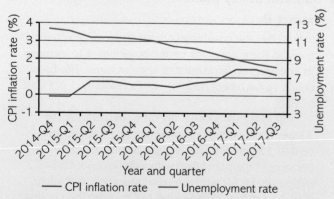

Year and quarter

—— CPI inflation rate   —— Unemployment rate

▲ **Figure 4 Portugal's inflation and unemployment rate**

Source: OECD

6 In the USA, since 1960, CO_2 emissions per capita peaked in 1973. By 2014 they had fallen by 27 per cent. In contrast, China's are still on an upward trend. Similarly, the percentage of the population exposed to air pollution levels greater than the World Health Organization guidelines, for high income countries fell from 84.1 per cent in 1990 to 61.8 per cent in 2015. For low- and middle-income countries, the average percentages were above 98 per cent.

Evaluate the view that conflict between economic growth and the protection of the environment only exists for countries on low- or middle-incomes, such as China or India. **(20 marks)**

EXAM HINT

Use Chapter 36 (which dealt with the costs of growth on the environment) as well as this chapter for reference. To support the view, consider why economic growth for poorer countries may cause environmental problems. Why are richer economies able to reduce the impact of growth on the environment? To what extent does more growth even improve the environment? It is also useful to consider whether government policies to protect the environment, typically used by more advanced economies, may actually reduce the growth rate for these economies.

39 MACROECONOMIC SUPPLY-SIDE POLICIES

LEARNING OBJECTIVES

- Understand supply-side policies designed to increase productivity, competition and incentives.
- Understand free market policies.
- Understand interventionist policies.
- Understand strengths and weaknesses of different supply-side policies.

GETTING STARTED

Research some local job adverts that are targeted at jobs which offer a fairly low wage rate per hour. Think about an individual's decision to accept this job. If the tax rate on labour income was currently 20 per cent, and then rose to 50 per cent, how would this affect an individual's decision to take the job? Do you think there is a minimum rate of pay before an individual will take on a job? What might this depend on?

SUPPLY-SIDE POLICIES

Supply-side economics is the study of how changes in long-run aggregate supply will affect variables such as GDP. The long-run aggregate supply curve shows the productive potential of the economy. At any point in time, there is only so much that an economy can produce from a given set of resources.

Over time, there are likely to be **supply-side improvements**. Firms will invest, for example, and there will be innovation through technological progress, which will allow capital to produce more goods and services from a given input. The quality of labour is likely to increase as education and training standards improve. The productivity of labour is likely to rise due to higher capital stock and better skills. These supply-side improvements can be illustrated by a rightward shift in the long-run aggregate supply curve, as shown in Figure 1, from LRAS$_1$ to LRAS$_2$. They can also be shown as a movement outwards of the production possibility frontier on a PPF diagram. Alternatively, Figure 2 shows the impact of successful supply-side policies, assuming a Keynesian aggregate supply curve.

FIGURE 1

Supply-side policies
Effective supply-side policies push the long-run aggregate supply curve to the right. This increases economic growth and reduces inflationary pressures. It may also bring about a reduction in unemployment and lead to higher exports and lower imports.

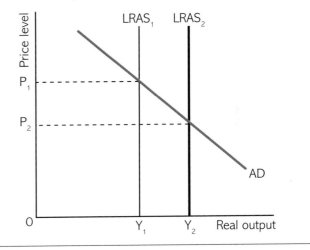

FIGURE 2

Supply-side policies the Keynesian aggregate supply curve
Assuming a Keynesian aggregate supply curve, successful supply-side policies will shift the aggregate supply curve to the right, from LRAS$_1$ to LRAS$_2$. In equilibrium, real output will rise from Y$_1$ to Y$_2$ while the price level will fall from P$_1$ to P$_2$.

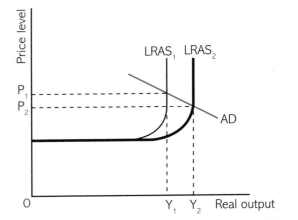

Supply-side improvements often come from the private sector and are independent of government. However, governments can attempt to further increase output through **supply-side policies**. These are government policies designed to increase the rate of economic growth. They may act broadly across the whole economy. They may also act specifically in certain markets to remove **bottlenecks** that prevent the economy from growing faster.

Supply-side policies mainly work through their impact on individual markets. The policies therefore are aimed to improve the microeconomic performance of different individual markets. These, in turn, improve the macroeconomic performance of the economy.

The objective of an individual supply-side policy is likely to focus on increasing productivity, competition or incentives (some will impact on more than one).

MARKET BASED AND INTERVENTIONIST APPROACHES

Supply-side policies can be split into two types.

- **Free market policies (or market-based policies)** are policies designed to remove barriers to the efficient working of free markets. These barriers limit output and raise prices. For example, in the labour market, they might reduce the willingness of workers to take jobs or to take risks. In the goods market, they might lead to inefficient production, high prices or a lack of innovation.
- Interventionist policies are policies designed to correct market failure. This means the government intervening in free markets to change the outcome from that which it would otherwise have been. For example, free markets may underprovide education and so the government has to step in and deliver this service. Firms may be short-termist, only interested in maximising short-run profits and failing to invest for the future. The government might step in to encourage firms to invest.

We will now consider a range of supply-side policies designed to improve the performance of the economy.

EXAM TIP

You should be able to explain, for each supply-side policy, how it helps to achieve supply-side objectives. For example, what impact does it have on efficiency, productivity or incentives? You should also be able to explain specific disadvantages (weaknesses) of different supply-side polices. This helps with evaluation in questions.

FREE MARKET POLICIES
1. PROMOTING COMPETITION

Markets can fail because of a lack of competition. Typically this means there will be higher prices for goods because firms will exploit customers and earn higher profits. Output will be lower because customers will buy less at the higher price. Promoting competition will incentivise firms to use resources efficiently. This is because profits can only be made in competitive markets if firms minimise costs, while maintaining a high-quality product. Firms will be under more pressure to innovate in order to compete successfully with other firms. Shareholders will be more willing for some funds to be spent on research and development (R&D), rather than being distributed as profits to shareholders, since this will be more necessary to help the firm remain competitive. There are a number of different supply-side policies that governments use to promote competition.

Deregulation of product market Deregulation is the process of removing government controls from markets. Deregulation of product markets means removing government controls from the markets of goods and services. For example, a local government might remove restrictions on the number of taxis for hire in their area. The government might allow any bus company to offer services along a route. The government might relax planning controls on the building of new houses. The aim is to encourage more firms to provide goods and services. This will increase output and lower prices.

A major problem with deregulation is that it encourages 'creaming' of markets. This means firms only providing services in the most profitable areas of the market. For example, in the UK postal market, the Royal Mail is against deregulation because it argues that competitors will be able to offer postal services in urban areas more cheaply, thereby taking away revenue and profit that effectively subsidise postal services to rural areas.

Privatisation Privatisation is the sale of government organisations or assets to the private sector. Over the past 50 years, the UK government privatised many previously state-owned organisations, including airline companies, gas companies, prisons and hospitals. Free market economists argue that government-run organisations have little incentive to cut costs or innovate. There is therefore government failure. Selling assets to the private sector enables those assets to be used more efficiently by private sector firms that are incentivised by the profit motive. Critics would argue that private firms put profit before providing a good or service. It is also the case that many privatised firms, at least in the short run, end up operating in markets where there is little competition. This means they can raise prices to make more profit. There will be some fall in output which actually means the supply-side policy may reduce growth. Privatisation will be more effective as a supply-side policy if there is a well developed competition policy in an economy.

Competition policy Competition policy is designed to increase competition in markets, reducing the power of monopolies and making cartels and price fixing agreements illegal. By reducing prices and increasing output, competition policy should raise output in the economy and so increase aggregate supply.

ACTIVITY 1   SKILLS   REASONING, ANALYSIS

CASE STUDY: CHINA'S SUPPLY-SIDE REFORMS

In 2015, China's economic planners promised to have more flexible policies in an attempt to boost its economic growth rate, which had fallen to its lowest in a quarter century. Chinese officials promised to cut **red tape** and lower taxes. Many manufacturers based in China had argued that they faced costs comparable to, if not higher, than those in the USA and Europe.

State owned enterprises also need reforming. Many of these state-owned enterprises are inefficient. However, the government stopped short of privatising state-owned enterprises, putting the focus, instead, on reorganising them. The Chinese government promised greater willingness for private sector companies to operate in some areas of the economy. An official stated, 'We will have deregulation, so more Chinese and foreign firms can enter different sectors.'

(a) Explain why deregulation of product markets might help to boost economic growth in China.

---

2. A REDUCTION IN TAXATION

Taxes on income High taxes on income will discourage individuals from working. This could mean taking a job, working extra hours or working hard at a job. High taxes for employers will discourage them from hiring workers. The key variable is not average tax rates, but marginal tax rates. If workers work an extra hour, how much will they be taxed on the earnings from that extra hour and how much will they take home after tax? If the marginal rate of income tax is 60 per cent, and a worker is paid US\$10 an hour, then US\$6 will go in tax and US\$4 will be left. If the marginal tax rate is 20 per cent, then US\$2 goes in tax and US\$8 will be left.

Free market economists believe that the elasticity of supply of labour is high. Cutting the marginal rate of tax from 20 per cent to 15 per cent will lead to a significant increase in the desire to work. Other economists argue that small changes in marginal tax rates will have little effect on incentives. They point out that many workers are paid salaries and don't receive either overtime payments or bonuses. These workers cannot respond to changes in marginal tax rates except in the long term by changing jobs or leaving the workforce. For those who are not on a fixed salary, a change in tax from US\$2 to US\$2.30 or US\$1.50 on US\$10 earned will have almost no effect on incentives.

Another problem of cutting marginal rate of taxes on income is that the difference between low and top income earners will widen. Some research suggests that this may significantly reduce well-being or happiness for those on lower incomes, even if their real income improves over time. It is the 'income gap' that creates the problem.

Taxes on profit Many countries tax company profits. This is called corporate tax or corporation tax. Free market economists argue that high marginal rates of taxes on profits discourage firms from investing and from being successful. Tax taken from a company is not available to be reinvested in the firm to help it to survive and grow. High rates of tax also encourage firms to distribute profits to shareholders rather than invest for the future. This is because future profits after tax will be low and so the rate of return on investment made now will be lower than if taxes were lower. A high tax on companies profits might also mean employee wages are kept lower than would otherwise be. This might reduce labour productivity, since workers may be less motivated. A lack of investment in technology would also reduce productivity. As with income tax, critics of this view would argue that there would be little or no effect on incentives to invest if the marginal rate of tax were 30 per cent or 20 per cent. If marginal tax rates were 80 per cent, then there could be some impact if they were brought down to 20 per cent. So large changes could have some impact, but small changes will have little, if any, impact.

ACTIVITY 2 · SKILLS · REASONING, ANALYSIS

CASE STUDY: FRANCE SET TO GET BUSINESS BUZZING

In 2017, the newly elected French president, Mr Macron, launched a bid to make France more business friendly. 'Our guiding principle is to create a business environment in which companies can succeed', said Mr Le Maire, his finance minister. The country has particular potential in sectors set for rapid growth, such as machine learning, artificial intelligence and big data. This all reflects the strength of France's engineering schools. Macron plans to reduce the corporate tax rate from 33 per cent to 25 per cent over the next five years, and reduce the taxes paid by employers on the wages of their staff.

The new French government also promised to lower taxes for banks and cut red tape, in a move to attract financial services companies from London after the UK leaves the EU (Brexit). The prime minister, Mr Phillippe, stressed this was part of a broader set of pro-business reforms designed to restore the competitiveness of France.

(a) Explain why the measures announced by the French government should:
  (i) increase employment
  (ii) increase the long-run aggregate supply curve.

ACTIVITY 3 · SKILLS · REASONING, ANALYSIS

CASE STUDY: ITALIAN UNEMPLOYMENT

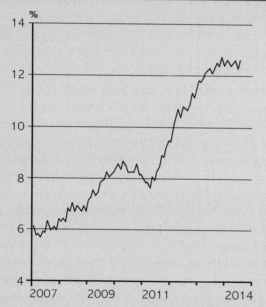

▲ Figure 3 Italian unemployment rate (%)

Source: adapted from Thomson Reuters Datastream; © the *Financial Times*, 15.1.2014, All Rights Reserved

In 2014, the Italian prime minister, Matteo Renzi, was planning to change the country's labour laws. Workers on permanent contracts had huge benefits, including rights that made it difficult for employers to make them redundant. In contrast, those on temporary contracts had almost no employment rights. Not surprisingly, very few young workers had permanent contracts. The government planned to establish a single contract for new workers that would gradually replace the old system. The new contract would have few protections in the first years of employment, but more in later years. There would also be a move to an unemployment insurance system that compensated laid-off workers for their lost salaries rather than keeping them technically employed at their old company with no hours and greatly reduced wages. Further, there would be tight links between unemployment benefits, job training and job searches.

Source: adapted from © the *Financial Times*, 15.1.2014, All Rights Reserved.

(a) Explain why Italian employers in 2014 might have been reluctant to take on workers on permanent contracts.

(b) Explain why the Italian government's proposals might reduce unemployment in the long term.

3. CHANGING THE LEVELS OF WELFARE PAYMENTS

Welfare benefits Incentives to work will be low if welfare benefits received by those not in work are too high in relation to the wages they could receive if they took a job. Hence, welfare benefits can reduce the level of aggregate supply because more workers remain unemployed. One solution is to cut state unemployment benefits to encourage workers to take typically low-paid jobs. This can mean cutting rates of benefit paid to increase the ratio of pay to benefits. Or it could mean stopping benefits altogether if those out of work fail to seek work actively or take on jobs that are offered.

The combination of marginal rates of income tax and withdrawal of benefits can lead to poverty and unemployment traps. The **poverty or earnings trap** occurs when a low-income working individual or household earns more, for example by gaining promotion, getting a better-paid job or working more hours, but the net gain is little or even negative. It occurs because as income increases, welfare benefits are withdrawn. Equally, the individual or household might start to pay tax. For example, if an individual loses £0.50 in benefits when earning an extra £1, and then pays income tax and National Insurance contributions at 30 per cent, then the net gain from earning the extra £1 is only £0.20 (£1 − 0.50 − 0.30). The effective marginal rate of tax here is 80 per cent. If the benefit lost were £0.90 in the pound, the individual would be £0.20 worse off. The effective marginal rate of tax here would be 120 per cent. The poverty trap is a major disincentive for those working and receiving benefits to work harder or increase their skills. The unemployment trap occurs when an individual is little better off or is even worse off getting a job than staying unemployed because of loss of benefits and taxation. The **unemployment trap**, where it occurs, is a major disincentive for the unemployed to find work. One solution to both kinds of trap is to lower welfare benefits, but this increases poverty. The other solution is to reduce taxes on income and the rate of welfare benefit withdrawal as incomes increase. This is a more expensive solution for the government and the taxpayer.

One way to incentivise workers to take on work or work extra hours is to subsidise them for working. In the UK, low-paid workers can claim income tax credits. Instead of paying income tax, they receive tax refunds from the government. These are designed to reduce the effective marginal tax rates that occur when low-paid workers pay tax and lose benefits. They help reduce the impact of the poverty trap.

4. CUTTING THE COSTS OF BUREAUCRACY FOR FIRMS

Free market economists tend to argue that the state should be as small as possible. Rules and regulations (sometimes called red tape) governing markets should be light. Unnecessary bureaucracy or red tape pushes up costs for firms, leading to higher prices for consumers and lower output. They may also provide a disincentive for entrepreneurs to set up. However, critics would argue that some regulation actually protects citizens, such as procedures to improve health and safety in product design. It is important to distinguish between unnecessary form filling and regulation which benefits society.

5. DEREGULATION OF LABOUR MARKETS

Deregulation of labour markets is the process of removing government controls from labour markets. This means removing any regulations that make labour less flexible, such as removing minimum wage laws and reducing trade union power. Free market economists believe the effect of making labour markets more flexible will be to either increase the labour supply and/or increase labour productivity. This means the impact of deregulating labour markets will be to shift the LRAS curve to the right.

Labour market flexibility is the degree to which demand and supply in a labour market respond to external changes and return to a new market equilibrium. More flexible labour markets, such as in the UK and the USA compared to many EU countries, are associated with lower unemployment and a higher participation rate with a larger proportion of the population working. However, they are also associated with lower average wages. There are more jobs, but those in work, on average, are paid less. There are many different types of flexibility.

Geographical flexibility refers to the willingness of workers to move area to get a job, or the willingness of firms to relocate to take advantage of healthier labour markets.

External numerical flexibility refers to the ability of firms to adjust their workforce according to their needs. For example, in some EU countries like Spain and Italy, it is very difficult to sack permanent workers, even when they are no longer needed by a firm. Firms get around this by hiring workers on a temporary basis or replacing workers by capital equipment.

Internal numerical flexibility refers to the ability of firms to adjust the working hours of staff to suit their needs. In the UK, for example, there is a growing trend for firms to offer zero hour contracts, where workers are employed by a firm, but are not guaranteed any work. Effectively, they become perfectly flexible, working only as and when the firm needs them. Another trend is to sign contracts with self-employed workers or contractors rather than taking on permanent members of staff. If they are not needed, self-employed workers and contractors can simply not be given any more work. With permanent staff, it is much more costly to make them redundant.

Functional flexibility occurs when a firm can move a worker from one job to another. Functional flexibility requires workers to be multi-skilled. This often requires firms to train workers. The cost of training has to be offset against the gains from more flexible working on the part of workers.

Wage flexibility occurs when firms are able to adjust wages up and down according to the forces of demand supply in the labour market. In practice, most workers are on fixed wage contracts. However, wage flexibility can be achieved if bonuses form part of a worker's pay package. Equally, the weaker the power of any trade unions in a firm, the more likely it is that a firm could impose pay cuts.

Deregulation of labour markets to increase labour market flexibility will involve abolishing minimum wage laws as well as reducing the legal power of trade unions. Other laws will also need to be changed to make labour markets more flexible.

Minimum wages In many countries there is a national **minimum wage**. In the USA, individual states can also set a higher minimum wage for their state than the national minimum wage set in Washington, the capital. It would be equivalent to paying a different minimum wage in London than in the rest of the UK. Free market economists argue that minimum wages create unemployment and tend to argue that they should be abolished. The higher the wage rate, the less demand there will be for workers from employers. This would therefore limit the supply-side of the economy.

However, other economists argue that the impact on employment depends on the level at which the minimum wage is set. For the UK, there is little evidence to suggest that minimum wage levels create any significant unemployment. There is also an argument that a higher minimum wage can lead to supply-side improvements. Higher minimum wages encourage employers to train their low paid workers to be more productive in order to justify the expense of employing them. It also encourages firms to invest in physical capital to replace low-paid workers. If the economy is at full employment, higher investment will lead to higher economic growth.

Trade unions The purpose of a trade union is to organise workers into one bargaining unit. The trade union then becomes a monopolist, the only seller of labour, and prevents workers from competing among themselves in the job market. Economic theory predicts that if trade unions raise wage rates for their members, then employment and output will be lower in otherwise competitive markets. So free market economists argue that government must intervene to limit the power of trade unions. Company-level agreements on things such as wages, overtime pay and working hours should exist rather than industry level agreements. Free market economists argue that the ability of trade unions to strike should also be limited.

It is changes in legislation that reduce the power of trade unions. Reducing the power of trade unions increases the flexibility for firms and helps them be more productive and competitive. However, certainly

in some economies, it could be argued that trade unions have little industrial power. Reducing their power further would then have almost no impact on improving the efficiency of the labour market. Critics would also argue that reducing trade union power leaves some groups at risk of exploitation. For example, zero hour contracts have been criticised for their lack of job security and their contribution to the problem of under-employment for these workers.

Other changes to legal employment laws Examples of other laws that would help to deregulate labour markets include making it easier to hire and fire workers. This would involve reducing compensation payments awarded to employees by law courts for unfair dismissal. Other examples of law changes free market economists would argue for include increasing the time an employee needs to have worked for a firm before it is covered by laws on redundancy pay, increasing the ability for firms to have flexible hour contracts and removing maximum working hours per week. Again, critics would argue that at-risk groups in society may be exploited by reducing legal protection. Free market economists might oppose this with the claim that employment will rise as the economy gains from supply-side growth.

Another issue is migration policy. Countries will have laws that determine who and how many immigrants are allowed into an economy. For example, within the EU there is freedom of movement for workers between member countries. Countries outside the EU often need visas or work permits. Some have argued that economies could benefit more from net immigration by targeting particular types of immigrants. This type of policy is used in countries such as the USA and Canada where those applying for visas to work in the country are more likely to be granted a visa if they have desirable skills and qualifications. This might mean skills and qualification in occupations where there is a shortage of workers; or it might mean high levels of skills, such as having a university degree. In a rich developed economy, supply-side benefits are more likely to come having well-educated and highly skilled workers than having low-skilled workers.

INTERVENTIONALIST POLICIES

1. INVESTMENT IN EDUCATION, TRAINING AND SKILLS

A more productive workforce with higher levels of human capital will raise the level of long-run aggregate supply. Over time, the human capital of workers can be raised through education and training.

Education The United Nations set eight Millennium Development goals to be achieved by 2015. Goal 2 was to ensure that, by 2015, children everywhere, boys and girls alike, would be able to complete a full course of primary schooling. Enrolment in primary education in developing regions reached 91 per cent in 2015, up from 83 per cent in 2000. Economies throughout the world aim to provide state education. Increasing educational levels of students can be affected by the amount of money spent on education. One reason why average achievement levels in advanced economies are higher than in, say, Kenya or India is because education is far better funded. Public spending on education is generally a significant proportion of total government spending for economies. Economies with higher GDP per capita are likely spend more on the education system, per pupil, than poorer countries. Equally, the length of time students spend in full-time education is likely to affect educational achievement. A population where the majority have studied to 21 are more likely, assuming that other factors remain the same, to be better educated than one where only a small minority study beyond 18. Although students tend to finance higher education themselves, the cost of this is often subsidised by the government to make it cheaper than it would otherwise be. However, education standards are also affected by what students learn and how they are taught. An interventionist approach is for the government to set a curriculum, specify teaching methods and then set targets to raise standards.

Training Training may lead to market failure. Firms are responsible for training their own workers. This is a cost to the firm and they may provide less training than best level of training for the whole economy. For this reason, governments tend to intervene in the training market. It can do this by the government directly providing training courses itself, for example through further education colleges. It could also set up training schemes working in co-operation with firms. The government could also choose to give subsidies to firms for training.

Although economists are likely to agree that government spending on education and training is essential, there is still discussion on the extent governments should make all decisions in this area. Some economists believe there is a role for 'free market policies' to be used in a limited way. For example, it may be beneficial, in a state funded system, to allow schools to compete for pupils, set their own curriculum and decide on teaching methods. It is argued, by those who hold these views, that efficiency increases in such a system.

2. INCENTIVES TO ENCOURAGE INVESTMENT

An important example of investment spending is research and development. This is because R&D often leads to technological progress and encourages innovation. An interventionist policy, to encourage investment, would be to use tax incentives or subsidies. These are targeted specifically on investment. For example, a government might offer tax relief on investment spending. This means a firm would get a reduction in taxation that is dependent on how much they spend on investment. Only investment spending would qualify for the tax reduction. For example, a company might make US$100 million profit. If they had spent US$20 million on R&D then they would only have to pay a profits tax on US$80 million. This differs from the free market policy of reducing corporation tax rate to promote investment. Even with a reduction in corporation tax, a company could also decide to distribute more profits to shareholders. In this case, the company can choose how this tax reduction affects their behaviour. However, providing a tax incentive to invest is interventionist, since the government is deciding how it wants to direct resources. Subsidies linked to investment spending would also have a similar effect. Critics might argue that the administrative costs might be high to run these. The government will want to make sure that the money is being spent on investment. If the government can only pick some investment projects, because there are limited funds available for investment, then there is scope for government corruption. Critics might also argue that a system of tax incentives (tax relief) or subsidies can be complicated to administer and may lead to waste of resources. It could also cause 'wasteful' investment, if firms do not fully assess the costs and benefits of investment spending.

3. INFRASTRUCTURE INVESTMENT

Infrastructure is important to promoting economic growth. Poor roads, for example, lead to longer journey times for goods being transported and for workers getting to work. This adds costs to firms, making them less internationally competitive and creates labour immobility. A lack of good school buildings can harm education. Poor hospitals lead to more illness and deaths of workers, destroying the human capital of the economy. Infrastructure spending tends to be the responsibility of government. They have to set priorities for spending, deciding which projects will go ahead and which will be abandoned.

For many economies, the amount spent on infrastructure is often limited by the funds available for public spending. However, a lack of infrastructure spending will cause supply-side constraints. For example, poor road networks may disrupt production for firms or an inability to distribute goods effectively to markets. Developing countries, in particular, suffer from poor infrastructure. Even within a developed economy, such as Germany, there may be regional differences causing some supply-side constraints.

Critics often argue that project management of infrastructure projects needs to be improved. Often infrastructure projects end up costing much more than originally expected. This means other essential areas of public spending need to be cut, or taxes need to be raised.

4. FINANCE FOR START-UPS

Small- and medium-sized businesses are important in the economy because they can provide new jobs and become the big businesses of tomorrow. Governments tend to encourage the setting up of new businesses through various schemes such as providing training or benefits to those who become self-employed. Governments may also, directly or through the banking system, offer loans at better than commercial terms to small- and medium-sized businesses.

However, critics may argue that many small businesses fail within the first few years of setting-up. If taxpayers have helped to fund the setting up of these businesses, then this money might not have been well spent. This might be minimised if better training and support is provided to entrepreneurs.

5. REGIONAL POLICY

Regional policy aims to improve regions of low growth and low income within an economy. These regions have often suffered because a key industry in the region, which often employed a large majority of the region's workforce, went into decline. Regional policy refers to government policies that focus on specific regions to improve job creation, the growth of new businesses and to improve business competitiveness. The overall objective is to improve the quality of life in regions that are often disadvantaged. Governments may intervene by providing grants for firms who set up in these regions, tax incentives, government spending on infrastructure in these regions etc. Critics may argue that some government spending may cause a misallocation of resources; for example, if the government gives funding to firms who are unlikely to be profit making without the government support.

STRENGTHS AND WEAKNESSES OF DIFFERENT SUPPLY-SIDE POLICIES

As already discussed, each of the different supply-side policies have their own strengths and weaknesses. However, in general, the strengths and weaknesses of the different policies focus on the following issues.

Targeting the supply-side problem The strength or weakness of a supply-side policy will depend partly

on whether that policy helps to address the problem in the economy that is constraining supply-side growth. For example, workers might be long-term unemployed. Is the problem that they are being paid too much in benefits to incentivize them to get a job? If so, reducing welfare payments would be effective. Or is the problem that they lack work skills needed to get them a job? If so, policies to increase investment in education, training and skills would be effective. Firms might spend too little on investment. Is the problem that they are taxed too highly on their profits? If so, reducing corporate tax rates would help to address this. Or is it that they are subject to intense pressure from shareholders to deliver short-run profits at the expense of long-run growth? If so, providing tax relief for investment spending might help to address this problem.

VIEWS ABOUT THE ROLE OF THE STATE

Economists disagree about whether market-based policies or interventionist policies are most effective. The debate about market-based policies versus interventionist policies is part of a wider disagreement about the role of the state. Free market economists tend to argue that the state should be as small as possible. They often highlight the problem of government failure, when governments intervene too much. Rules and regulations governing markets should be light. As many goods and services as possible should be provided by the private sector rather than the public sector. Taxes should be as low as possible. Taxes discourage work and enterprise and reduce the productive potential of the economy. Proponents of market-based policies argue that incentives are vital for markets to function effectively. If incentives are too small, or even worse, encourage the wrong economic decisions, then long-run aggregate supply will suffer.

Economists who support interventionist approaches argue that market failure is common. Free markets, left to themselves, will create an inefficient allocation of resources leading to lower economic growth. Hence, the state needs to intervene to regulate markets and, where necessary, provide goods and services directly. Poorly directed taxes can discourage work and enterprise, but an economy where taxes are 50 per cent of GDP will not grow any less quickly than an economy where taxes are 30 per cent of GDP, all other things being equal.

Distribution of income Some market-orientated, supply-side policies lead to a widening of the distribution of income. For example, abolishing minimum wages, cutting welfare benefits to the unemployed and reducing trade union power while at the same time cutting marginal rates of tax for the top 10 per cent of income earners are all supply-side policies but will lead to a growing gap between high-

ACTIVITY 4  SKILLS   REASONING, ANALYSIS

CASE STUDY: ASIAN ECONOMIES NEED TO PLUG THE INFRASTRUCTURE GAP

An Asian Development Bank (ADB) analysis said Southeast Asian countries need to spend 5.7 per cent of GDP between 2016 and 2030 on infrastructure – a level most have not come close to reaching in the past. The ADB's priority areas were transport, power and other projects to link countries to regional and global markets.

Although Malaysia has a well-maintained motorway network and has created a new airport to replace the out-of-date 1960s facility that served its capital Kuala Lumpur, it still suffers a rural urban divide on infrastructure. However, work on the East Coast Rail Line (ECRL), filling some of the infrastructure gap, has now started (MYR 55 billion). Chinese state-owned companies will finance and help build this line. The ECRL will reduce transport costs between the west and east coast. It will boost jobs, encourage investment in towns on the route and help the tourism sector too, such as in Kelantan.

In Indonesia, Southeast Asia's largest economy, President Joko Widodo has made infrastructure spending a priority after years of underinvestment. Spending on infrastructure collapsed during the Asian financial crisis, which started in 1997, and has stayed low since.

In Vietnam, the country's recent historical annual infrastructure spending of more than 5 per cent of GDP has been much greater than its regional peers. But Vietnam has seen its fiscal deficit rise, and is short of private investment to make up for more constrained state activity.

(a) Explain why spending on transport links would increase long-run aggregate supply.
(b) Explain why infrastructure spending also sets off a positive multiplier effect, boosting aggregate demand and actual growth.
(c) Explain what limits how much governments might be able to spend on infrastructure.

---

income and low-income earners. Privatisation and deregulation too tend to lead to growing inequality because workers in the industries affected tend to see their wages fall in real terms after privatisation and deregulation have taken place. Free market economists would argue that rises in GDP caused by supply-side policies will benefit everyone.

There will be more jobs and higher incomes. However, recent UK and US experience suggests that many of the new jobs will be low paid. At the same time, those on very high incomes tend to appropriate most of the increase in GDP, leaving those on low and middle incomes with almost no increase. Technically everyone benefits, but very high-income earners benefit disproportionately.

STRENGTHS AND WEAKNESSES OF SUPPLY-SIDE POLICIES IN GENERAL

Supply-side policies have an effect on the macroeconomic performance of an economy but they have both strengths and weaknesses.

Economic growth Supply-side policies are designed to maintain or increase the rate of growth of the economy. Figure 5 shows a growing economy. Without supply-side policies, the productive potential of the economy would grow from $LRAS_1$ to $LRAS_2$ because of supply-side improvements occurring in the private sector, such as use of better technology. However, with successful supply-side policies, the productive potential of the economy grows from $LRAS_1$ to

$LRAS_3$. Extra output of Y_2Y_3 can be obtained through successful supply-side policies. The extra productive potential is dependent on the success of the policies in place. Individual supply-side policies may not work and, at worst, could reduce the growth rate.

FIGURE 4

The impact on growth of supply-side policies
Supply-side improvements push the LRAS curve from $LRAS_1$ to $LRAS_2$. The movement from $LRAS_2$ to $LRAS_3$ shows the additional impact of supply-side policies.

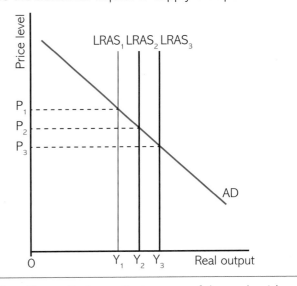

Inflation Figure 5 shows that successful supply-side policies have the effect of reducing the price level. This assumes that aggregate demand is constant. In

a growing economy, however, aggregate demand will be increasing too. Figure 6 shows an economy where over time aggregate demand is growing, shown by the rightward shift in the AD curve from AD_1 to AD_2 and AD_3. In this economy, there will be no inflation if long-run aggregate supply is also increasing from $LRAS_1$ through to $LRAS_3$. To maintain a 2 per cent inflation rate, the inflation target for the Bank of England, supply-side policies need to be pushing the LRAS curve to the right at a slightly slower pace than the increase in aggregate demand, as shown in Figure 7.

FIGURE 5

Long-run aggregate supply and aggregate demand growing by the same amount
Supply-side improvements push the LRAS curve from $LRAS_1$ to $LRAS_2$. The movement from $LRAS_2$ to $LRAS_3$ shows the additional impact of supply-side policies.

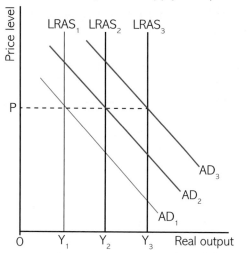

Unemployment Many supply-side policies are aimed at reducing unemployment and encouraging employment. However, supply-side policies on their own cannot guarantee low unemployment. Figure 8 shows an economy where, in the short run, output is OY_1 because this is where aggregate demand equals short-run aggregate supply. This is below the full employment output of long-run aggregate supply of OY_2. Increasing long-run aggregate supply will not reduce unemployment unless there is a larger increase in aggregate demand.

The current account on the balance of payments
Successful supply-side policies in general could lead to an improvement, a worsening or have no effect on the current account balance. It depends on their impact on exports and imports. However, supply-side policies can be directed at increasing exports, which should improve the current account balance. Equally, if an economy's supply-side policies are more successful at lowering prices than their main trading partners, then this should improve their price competitiveness

on international markets. This should increase their exports, causing export-led growth. The same would be true if supply-side policies led to greater technological advances compared to other economies.

Distribution of income As already discussed, free market supply-side polices tend to lead to a widening of the distribution of income. Even though everyone has a chance to be better off, some will gain more than others.

FIGURE 6

Achieving a small positive rate of inflation
If aggregate demand grows slightly more than long-run aggregate supply then there will be a small increases in the price level over time and so there will be low inflation.

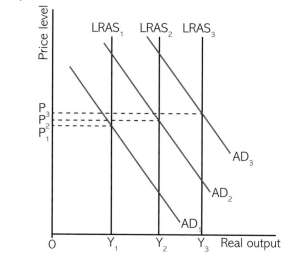

FIGURE 7

Unemployment despite growing long-run aggregate supply
If short-run equilibrium output is at OY_1 below its full employment level of OY_2, increasing aggregate supply through supply-side policies will not help achieve full employment. To do this, aggregate demand must rise faster than long-run aggregate supply.

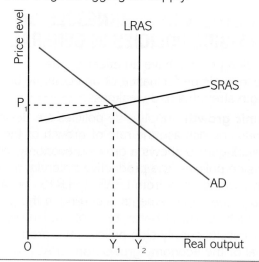

ACTIVITY 5   SKILLS ▶ REASONING, ANALYSIS

CASE STUDY: HOW FLEXIBLE SHOULD WAGES BE?

Further cuts in real wages in countries whose labour markets have been hardest hit by the economic crisis would risk creating deflation and deepening poverty, the OECD has warned. It said that reforms to increase competition in product and service markets, rather than more wage adjustments, were needed. The priority now was to foster the creation of not just more jobs but also better jobs. Wage adjustment had played an important part in helping labour markets weather the deep downturn by improving competitiveness and reducing job losses. Any further reduction of wages risks being counter-productive, because economies would run into a vicious circle of deflation, lower consumption and lower investment. Policies such as minimum wages, progressive taxation and in-work benefits could help to share the costs of economic adjustments more fairly

Source: adapted from © the *Financial Times* 4.9.2014, All Rights Reserved.

(a) Explain why supply-side adjustments in the labour market could lead to a fall in consumption, investment and economic growth.

(b) Why might higher minimum wages improve the macroeconomic performance of an economy following a deep and prolonged recession?

THINKING LIKE AN ECONOMIST

SOUTH AFRICA: A WALK ON THE 'SUPPLY-SIDE'

In June 2017, it was reported that South Africa was once again in recession. Unemployment had risen to its highest rate since 2003, at 27 per cent, and GDP per capita had been declining for several years.

In fact, there have been many problems with the economy in recent years. In 2014, strikes at platinum mines caused five months of labour unrest, as disputes between unions and mining bosses intensified. Power shortages, under Eskon, the failing state utility, also dampened manufacturing. By 2017, power production had improved, but there were still many supply-side constraints on the economy.

In the July 2017 South Africa OECD Economic survey report, it was noted that economic growth had fallen markedly since 2011. The poor performance of the South African economy is, in part, due to constraints on the supply side.

The OECD report highlights key problems and recommendations. On the supply-side, examples include the following.

• More investment in education, training and skills is vital. Skills shortages and mismatches persist. The report highlights the need for expansion of second chance programmes for early school leavers, an increase in entrepreneurial education and work placements in the post-16 education system and the development of apprenticeships. There is also a need to make higher education

more accessible. All these recommendations have the objective of improving labour productivity and making sure individuals have the skills firms need. The OECD report states that, if public spending is made more effective (i.e. less money is wasted), this would free up resources for infrastructure and education spending by the government.

• Lowering barriers to entrepreneurship and improving the business environment is also highlighted. Free market policies in the report include recommendations for introducing reforms to reduce red tape for firms, which create large burdens for entrepreneurs and small firms, as well as opening up telecommunications, energy, transport and services to more competition. It says the regulation of network sectors and services remains high, adversely affecting quality, prices and job creation.

• A key recommendation is that special economic zones should be provided with better infrastructure. A regional fund should be created for infrastructure and private firms should be more involved in these projects.

What is clear from the report is the importance of supply-side reform; only then can South Africa's economy significantly improve.

Source: OECD Economic Survey South Africa, July 2017 overview and 'Dark days ahead', *The Economist*, 28.5.2015

CHECKPOINT

1 What are the objectives of supply-side policies?

2 What is the difference between free-market supply side policies and interventionist supply-side policies?

3 List three free-market and three interventionist supply-side policies.

4 Why might privatisation improve efficiency?

5 What does deregulation mean?

6 How might a government use the tax system to encourage investment?

7 Give a weakness or problem of the government cutting marginal rates of income tax.

8 Which supply-side policies cause a widening of income distribution?

9 How might the government encourage new entrepreneurs?

SUBJECT VOCABULARY

bottlenecks supply-side constraints in a particular market in an economy that prevent higher growth for the whole economy.

deregulation the process of removing government controls from markets.

free market policies or market-based policies government policies designed to promote economic growth by reducing barriers to the efficient working of free markets.

interventionist policies government policies designed to correct market failures that are reducing the growth rate of the economy.

labour market flexibility the degree to which demand and supply in a labour market respond to external changes (such as changes in demand for a product or in population size) to return the market to equilibrium.

minimum wage the least amount an employer can pay one of its workers, usually expressed as an hourly wage rate.

poverty or earnings trap occurs when an individual is little better off or even worse off when gaining an increase in wages because of the combined effect of increased tax and

benefit withdrawal.

privatisation the sale of government organisations or assets to the private sector.

red tape rules and regulations issued by government, that firms must follow to operate legally.

supply-side economics the study of how changes in aggregate supply will affect variables such as national income; in particular, how government microeconomic policy might change aggregate supply through individual markets.

supply-side improvements changes in individual markets, such as investment by firms or improvements in the skills of workers, which lead to an increase in long-run aggregate supply without necessarily the intervention of government.

supply-side policies government policies designed to increase the productive potential of the economy and push the long-run aggregate supply curve to the right.

unemployment trap occurs when an individual is little better off or even worse off when getting a job after being unemployed because of the combined effect of increased tax and benefit withdrawal.

EXAM PRACTICE

SKILLS REASONING, ANALYSIS, CRITICAL THINKING

1 Donald Trump, the president of the USA, has proposed to cut corporation tax from 35 per cent to 15 per cent.
   Which one of the following is most likely to result from this change?
   (a) Real GDP will fall and the price level will fall.
   (b) The LRAS will shift to the right, as investment by firms increases.
   (c) There will be more withdrawals from the circular flow of income.
   (d) Real GDP will fall, but the price level will rise.

(1 mark)

2 In 2017, the French government announced labour market reforms. The reforms will benefit employers, giving them more flexibility if they want to agree specific working arrangements with their unions or employees, rather than keeping sectoral collective agreements. A sectoral collective agreement applies to all workers in a sector and not just the workers in one firm. A sectoral collective agreement would regulate a wide range of terms and conditions, such as pay or dismissal procedures, for all firms in that sector.
   The 2017 labour market reforms are likely to reduce trade union power. The reforms will

also make it easier for firms to cut jobs, easier to increase working hours and cheaper to dismiss employees.

Source: *Financial Times*, 'France's labour minister promises speedy reform of welfare system', 4.9.2017

With reference to the information above, explain the term 'deregulation of labour markets'.

(4 marks)

3 The government of Argentina, in 2017, is investing in new infrastructure. There is a need to improve the road network. The infrastructure programme is investing US$33 billion; it is hoped one-quarter of this will be financed by the private sector and the rest by public spending.

Source: *Financial Times*, 'Argentina Election-Macri uses infrastructure programme to woo voters', 31.7.2017

Explain how an increase in infrastructure spending will likely affect the level of real GDP. **(4 marks)**

4 **Extract A: Mexico: A new wave of entrepreneurs**

In 2017, it was reported that Mexico was experiencing a rise in entrepreneurs wanting to set up and start their own businesses. The government is encouraging them, with interventionist policies actively being used. The government is injecting funding into entrepreneurship and technology development with grants, loans and direct investment into start-ups. It is hoped the entrepreneurial boom will create high-value jobs, improve distribution of income, generate innovation and improve competitiveness.

Source: *Financial Times*, 'Mexico - Innovation and Technology - Comment - Why the country is ripe for a start-up boom', 21.6.2017

Extract B: Industrialised countries are cutting taxes

In 2016, many industrialised countries were starting to cut taxes in order to boost actual and potential growth. In particular, five OECD countries cut corporate tax rates in 2015 and four announced tax rate cuts in the coming years. In Norway and Japan, a reason for cutting corporate taxes was to support investment. In 2015, Austria, Belgium and the Netherlands all cut taxes on labour income.

Source: *Financial Times*, 'Tax policies have turned from austerity to growth, says OECD', 22.9.2016

(a) With reference to extract A, explain the term 'interventionist supply-side policies'. **(4 marks)**

(b) With reference to extract B, examine the likely impact on the LRAS of the reduction in tax rates.

(8 marks)

EXAM HINT

A question with the command word 'examine' has 2 marks for evaluation. You must provide some evaluative comments to score more than 6 marks out of 8. In this case, consider what might limit the impact on the LRAS.

5 Economists disagree about whether free market policies or interventionist policies are most effective in promoting supply-side growth. Evaluate the view that free market supply-side policies are more effective than interventionist supply-side policies for improving the potential growth of an economy.

(20 marks)

EXAM HINT

It is important to consider both sides of the argument. Take a view and analyse it. However, present the opposing view. For evaluation, compare the two views and make a judgement about which is more likely to be correct or better. Think about why some economists have a strong view supporting one side. What might determine whether a particular supply-side policy is likely to be effective? In your answer consider a broad range of different types of supply-side polices.

40 MACROECONOMIC DEMAND-SIDE POLICIES

LEARNING OBJECTIVES

- Understand the term 'demand-side' policy.
- Understand the distinction between fiscal and monetary policy.
- Understand the distinction between reflationary and deflationary policies.
- Understand fiscal and monetary policy instruments and how they influence an economy.
- Understand the role of central banks in the conduct of monetary policy.
- Understand the strengths and weaknesses of different demand-side policies.

GETTING STARTED

Aggregate demand is equal to consumption plus investment plus government spending plus net exports (X–M). How, in theory, could the government attempt to increase each individual component of aggregate demand? Use the Internet to find out one way in which the government has attempted to increase consumption, investment and net exports over the past two years.

MONETARY AND FISCAL POLICIES

Governments have a number of key macroeconomic and microeconomic objectives. At a macroeconomic level, these include promoting economic growth, having low inflation and unemployment and achieving a sustainable balance on the current account of the balance of payments. At a microeconomic level, these include reducing market failures, such as environmental externalities.

To achieve these objectives, governments use monetary and fiscal policies.

- **Monetary policy** is the manipulation by government of monetary variables, such as interest rates and the money supply, to achieve its objectives.
- **Fiscal policy** is the use of taxes, government spending and government borrowing to achieve its objectives.

If the government or central bank is using a policy to manipulate aggregate demand, it is called a **demand-side policy**.

Fiscal or monetary policies aimed at increasing aggregate demand are called *reflationary policies*. Fiscal or monetary polices aimed at reducing aggregate demand are called *deflationary policies*.

MONETARY POLICY

Governments can, to some extent, control the rate of interest and the amount of money circulating in the economy. They can also influence the amount of borrowing or credit available from financial institutions like banks and building societies.

The variables that the government is attempting to control are known as the **instruments of policy**. So interest rates, the money supply, tax rates or government spending on roads are all examples of instruments of policy.

In recent years, six central banks, including the Federal Reserve Bank (USA), the Bank of England (UK) and the European Central Bank (ECB), have used two main monetary policy instruments to influence the economy as a whole: interest rates and **quantitative easing**. They have been used to get their respective economies out of the deep and prolonged global recession that occurred after the financial crisis of 2008.

EXAM TIP

Make sure you do not get confused between the terms 'fiscal' and 'monetary' policy. If fiscal or monetary policy is being used as a demand-side policy, then the objective will be to influence aggregate demand. However, remember that both policies can also affect aggregate supply, particularly if they affect investment spending. This could be considered as an evaluative comment.

INTEREST RATES AS A MONETARY POLICY INSTRUMENT

The **rate of interest** is the price of money. Lenders expect to receive interest if money is supplied for loans to money markets. Equally, if money is demanded for loans from money markets, borrowers expect to have to pay interest on the loans.

The rate of interest affects the economy through its influence on aggregate demand (AD). The higher the rate of interest, the lower the level of AD. There is a variety of ways in which interest rates affect the AD curve.

Consumer durables Many consumers buy consumer durables, such as furniture, kitchen equipment and cars, on credit. The higher the rate of interest, the greater the monthly repayments will be for any amount borrowed. Hence, high interest rates lead to lower sales of durable goods and hence lower consumption expenditure.

The housing market Houses, too, are typically bought using a mortgage. The lower the rate of interest, the lower the mortgage repayments on a given sum borrowed. This makes houses more affordable. It might encourage people to buy their first house or to move house, either trading up to a more expensive house or trading down to a smaller property. There are three ways in which this increases AD. First, an increase in demand for all types of housing leads to an increase in the number of new houses being built. New housing is classified as investment in national income accounts. Increased investment leads to increased AD. Second, moving house stimulates the purchase of consumer durables, such as furniture, carpets and kitchens. This increases consumption. Third, moving house may release money that can be spent. A person trading down to a cheaper house will have access to the value of money that was previous tied up in their home. Those trading up may borrow more than they need for the house purchase and this may be used to buy furniture or perhaps even a new car.

Wealth effects A fall in rates of interest may increase asset prices. For instance, falling interest rates may lead to an increase in demand for housing, which in turn pushes up the price of houses. If house prices rise, all homeowners are better off because their houses have increased in value. This may encourage them to increase their spending. Equally, a fall in interest rates will raise the price of government bonds. Governments issue bonds to finance their borrowing. They are sold to individuals, assurance companies, pension funds and others who receive interest on the money they have loaned to government. Like shares, bonds can go up and down in value. Rises in the price of bonds held by individuals or businesses will increase their financial wealth, which again may have a positive impact on consumer expenditure.

Saving Higher interest rates make saving more attractive compared to spending. The higher the interest rate, the greater the reward for delaying spending now and spending more in the future. This may lead to a fall in AD at the present time.

Investment The lower the rate of interest, the more investment projects become profitable. Hence the higher the level of investment and AD. Equally, a rise in consumption, which leads to a rise in income will lead, in turn, to a rise in investment. Firms will need to invest to supply the extra goods and services being demanded by consumers.

The exchange rate A fall in the interest rate is likely to lead to a fall in the value of the domestic currency (its exchange rate). For the USA, a fall in the value of the dollar means that foreigners can now get more dollars for each unit of their currency. However, US residents have to pay more dollars to get the same amount of foreign currency, such as Japanese yen. This means that goods priced in dollars become cheaper for foreigners to buy, while foreign goods become more expensive for US firms to buy. Cheaper US goods should lead to higher exports as foreigners take advantage of lower prices. In contrast, US buyers find foreign goods less price competitive. Greater export levels and fewer imports will boost AD.

ACTIVITY 1   SKILLS   REASONING, ANALYSIS, COMMUNICATION

CASE STUDY: THE CZECH CENTRAL BANK MAKES THE FIRST MOVE

In August 2017, the Czech central bank raised its main policy interest rate from 0.05 per cent to 0.25 per cent. This was the first time interest rates had been raised by the bank since the financial crisis in 2008. With unemployment at historically low levels and strong economic growth, inflationary pressures had been building. An analyst at Citi, a large global bank, commented, 'This is the first central European bank to accept the reality of rising wage growth, closing of output gaps and positive export performance.' The governor of the Czech central bank said that the bank could raise interest rates further in the future, but this would depend on the development of key indicators, not just inflation but others as well.

Source: 'Czech central bank lifts interest rates', *Financial Times*, 3.8.2017

(a) What evidence is there from the passage that aggregate demand is high?

(b) Explain the effect a rise in interest rates is likely to have on the inflation rate.

QUANTITATIVE EASING AS A MONETARY POLICY INSTRUMENT

In response to the financial crisis of 2008, governments through their central banks, including the USA, pushed interest rates to their minimum levels. However, historically low interest rates failed to stimulate AD sufficiently. Six central banks have used quantitative easing. These are the US Federal Reserve, the European Central Bank, the Bank of Japan, the Bank of England, along with Swiss and Swedish central banks. Quantitative easing is a monetary policy instrument where the central bank buys financial assets in exchange for money in order to increase borrowing and lending in the economy.

For example, a commercial bank in an economy might hold (i.e. own) bonds. Bonds are loans issued either by governments or by firms. With quantitative easing, the central bank buys bonds from banks in exchange for money. The commercial bank now holds fewer bonds, or loans, and more money. It can then lend out that money to customers. Those customers might be firms wanting to borrow to invest in new equipment. It might be households wanting to buy a car or a new kitchen. Higher investment and higher consumption then increases AD.

Quantitative easing also has the effect of lowering interest rates further and so encouraging borrowing. Central banks have a headline rate of interest that is meant to influence other rates of interest in the economy. In the UK, this is called the **base rate**. It is the rate of interest that the Bank of England charges if a bank borrows money from it overnight. Other central banks might use the term 'benchmark' interest rate. There are a large number of different interest rates in the economy, some of which are highly influenced by

base rate and others that have little connection to base rate. Quantitative easing lowers interest rates for any type of financial asset that the central bank buys as part of its policy of quantitative easing. For example, in the UK, it lowers interest rates on bonds issued by government and firms because the Bank of England effectively has increased demand for these bonds. It also indirectly influences other interest rates. For example, it allows commercial banks to offer very low interest deals to their borrowing customers because the Bank of England is providing them with so much cash to lend out.

There is also an effect on the exchange rate. By lowering interest rates, the exchange rate of a country falls. For example, if the European Central Bank (ECB) begins a programme of quantitative easing, interest rates in the eurozone fall. This encourages international investors to switch their money out of eurozone assets and into other assets in other countries. This leads to a fall in demand for the euro and a rise in its supply, so causing a fall in the price of the euro against other currencies. A lower exchange rate will make exports more competitive and imports less competitive.

CHANGES IN LENDING CRITERIA

Risky lending by financial institutions was one of the main factors that caused the global financial crisis in 2007–08. Risky lending is when there is an above average probability, compared to all loans, that the borrowers won't be able to afford the repayments. Since the global financial crisis, central banks have played a greater role in supervising banks, to ensure the banking system can cope with difficult economic situations. Central banks want to make sure that banks lend responsibly to customers. If necessary, they

Quantitative easing seems to have succeeded at boosting growth and lifting inflation. Martin Weale, a member of the Bank of England's interest-rate setting Monetary Policy Committee, has found that asset purchases worth 1 per cent of national income boosted UK gross domestic product by about 0.18 per cent and inflation by 0.3 per cent.

Quantitative easing has been a monetary policy tool used by Japan, the USA and the UK. The European Central Bank has now decided to launch quantitative easing too. It has announced it will buy

€1.1 trillion worth of bonds to increase economic growth and reduce the risk of deflation in the eurozone.

Source: adapted from © the *Financial Times*, 21.1.2015, 23.1.2015, All Rights Reserved.

(a) Explain how quantitative easing might have boosted UK gross domestic product.

(b) Why might quantitative easing by the European Central Bank combat the threat of deflation in the eurozone?

may intervene to change lending criteria rules, which banks must adopt. This is a monetary policy tool, since availability of loans in the economy can be changed and this will affect the money supply.

For example, in June 2017, the Bank of England announced new rules on mortgage availability in its Financial Stability Report. A mortgage is a loan to buy a property. The central bank wanted to reduce the number of 'risky' loans that banks were offering. With current interest rates low, there was a greater risk that a borrower may not be able to afford loan repayments if the interest rate was to rise over time. The central bank changed the rules to require a lender (banks) to apply an interest rate test to check that a borrower could afford to pay a higher rate. The Bank of England's Prudential Regulation Authority, in July 2017, also announced that banks must show they have loan risks under control. There has been a rapid growth in consumer credit, in the UK on car finance, over the last few years since the financial crisis.

RESERVE ASSET (LIQUIDITY) REQUIREMENTS

When customers of a bank have bank deposits, this money shows up as a liability for a bank. This is a liability for the bank because it is money that it owes to others. On a day-to-day basis, most money in deposit accounts doesn't move out of these accounts. This gives commercial banks the opportunity to lend out this money to other customers and earn a profit.

Central banks are often concerned that commercial banks will lend out too much of the money they have borrowed from their customers. Commercial banks need to keep enough **liquid assets** to repay their customers when they demand repayment. Assets are items that a bank owns and have a monetary value. Liquid assets are assets that can quickly and at little cost be turned into money, such as bank deposits or cash. If a bank doesn't have enough liquid assets on a day when its customers make particularly heavy withdrawals, it can go bankrupt. So central banks fix liquidity ratios. A liquidity ratio is the proportion of liquid assets to total assets for a commercial bank.

The financial crisis of 2007–08 involved a **liquidity crisis**. Before the financial crisis, banks seemed to have enough liquidity. However, during the crisis, many bank assets turned out to be a lot less 'liquid' than expected. In fact, some 'assets' turned out to be 'bad debts', which meant they became worthless.

Commercial banks lend to each other to ensure they have enough liquidity to meet day to day customer needs. In the financial crisis, this 'interbank lending' froze. This is because banks were worried about which other banks it was safe to lend to after it became clear the extent of the 'bad debts' banks were

holding as assets. Many central banks were forced to step in and support the banks in their own country. Otherwise, some of these banks would have been unable to meet the monetary needs of their customers who wanted to withdraw their deposits. This could then have led to banks going bankrupt. The liquidity problem meant that banks cut back on their lending. This slowed down aggregate demand, causing a recession.

The difficulties experienced by some banks were due to poor liquidity risk management. In response to the crisis, the Basel Committee on Banking Supervision proposed, in 2010, an international standard on bank regulation called the liquidity coverage ratio (LCR). The objective of the LCR is to ensure that banks hold enough liquid assets to survive a significant 'stress scenario' lasting for one month. This will become fully effective from 2019. In 2013, most big banks in Europe already met the liquidity requirements required by 2019. For instance, the UK introduced liquidity rules for banks in 2010.

As well as this, **capital requirements** for banks were also set up by financial regulators. A bank's capital represents its own funds and includes the value of its shares (equity). Capital is recorded as a liability of the bank, since it has been funded by its owners. If a bank suffers 'bad debts', then it has lent out money that will never be repaid. This lending, which was recorded as an asset for the bank, must be written off because it is now worthless. Having enough capital means the bank can absorb this loss, without becoming insolvent. Insolvency would mean that a bank, even if it sold all its assets (for example, the value of all its loans and its reserves), it would still be unable to pay all its liabilities (e.g. customer deposits). This would cause a serious banking crisis, so banks must now hold sufficient capital as part of the new financial regulations. This is set as a capital ratio to assets. For example, if the capital ratio is 5 per cent, then a bank needs £5 of capital to support £100 of loans (most bank's assets are loans to others).

THE ROLE OF CENTRAL BANKS IN THE CONDUCT OF MONETARY POLICY

A key role of central banks is to implement monetary policy to achieve price stability (low and stable inflation) and help manage fluctuations in real GDP. Central banks will manipulate monetary variables, such as interest rates and the money supply, to achieve its objectives.

INFLATION TARGETING

Since the late 1980s, many central banks have adopted a monetary framework called inflation targeting. This is when a central bank publishes a 'target' inflation rate, and then attempts to steer actual inflation towards that target, using monetary tools such as interest rate changes. The monetary policy committee of a central bank will make these decisions. It takes a period of time for a change in interest rates to have their full effect on the price level in an economy. For example, the multiplier effect on aggregate demand will take time. A change in interest rates today will therefore affect the inflation rate in a later period. This time lag means a central bank will need to keep forecasts of future inflation, assuming no changes have been made to current interest rates. These forecasts are then compared to the target inflation rate. If forecasted inflation is higher than the target inflation rate, the central bank will raise its interest rate (sometimes called the base rate or benchmark rate). This will start to reduce demand-pull inflation as aggregate demand starts to fall. This means the future inflation rate will remain in target. A forecasted inflation rate below the target inflation rate means the central bank is likely to lower interest rates today.

Many central banks from advanced, emerging and developing economies have adopted inflation targeting. Most countries have chosen an inflation target that covers a range. For example, the South Africa Reserve Bank has a CPI inflation target of 3–6 per cent, the National Bank of Poland has an inflation target of 2.5 per cent ±1 per cent. An inflation target does not mean a central bank will be able to keep inflation at that level every month. The aim is normally to keep inflation back at the target range within a reasonable time period (over the medium term). This means monetary policy can also be used to sort out other short-run objectives, such as smoothing out short-run real GDP fluctuations. Central banks will differ on the extent that the inflation target is their prime focus; some may use monetary policy to achieve employment objectives as well as low inflation. For example, from March 2009, the Monetary Policy Committee of the Bank of England kept the base rate at a record low of 0.5 per cent. It recognised that any inflation above 2 per cent (its target) was most unlikely to be caused by excess demand. This was because unemployment was high and economic growth very weak. Monetary policy became more focused on the objectives of boosting economic growth and reducing unemployment.

AS BANKER TO THE GOVERNMENT

Most central banks act as a banker to their governments. An exception is the European Central Bank, where there is no national European government for it to serve in this role. The exact nature of the services offered by central banks differs from country to country. Central banks may handle the accounts of government departments and make short-term advances to the government.

AS BANKER TO THE BANKS – LENDER OF LAST RESORT

Central banks tend to force the largest banks that operate in their country to deposit money with them. In some countries, this is used to balance the accounts of banks at the end of each day. So, if bank X owes bank Y US$50 million because bank X's customers have paid a net US$50 million more in cheques to bank Y customers, this US$50 million is debited from bank X's account at the central bank and transferred to bank Y's account.

The key role, though, of central banks in relation to other banks is to act as lender of last resort. Banks can face liquidity crises for two reasons.

- A bank at the end of a day's trading can run out of liquid assets to pay money it owes. For example, a bank may one day experience a withdrawal of US$50 million more than expected by its customers. It has more than enough assets to cover this but they are illiquid, i.e. difficult if not impossible to sell immediately, and therefore turns to the central bank as the lender of last resort and either borrows the US$50 million or sells some of those illiquid assets. This is a short-term liquidity problem and does not mean that the bank is in fundamental trouble.

- The bank may face fundamental problems because too many of its assets have fallen in value. For example, it may have lent money to customers and too many of those loans turn into bad debts, never to be repaid. In the 2007–08 financial crisis, banks, for example, found that too many of their mortgage assets were in default. Poor lending combined with a housing bubble left many banks exposed to bad debts. The central bank then becomes the lender of last resort in the sense that it lends money to banks to prevent them from collapsing.

Some argue that acting as lender of last resort results in moral hazard. Banks know that they can engage in highly profitable, high-risk activities in the short term because if they ultimately make large losses, then the central bank will bail them out. However, if the central banks did not act as lender of last resort, banks could fail. One bank failing would almost certainly see customers of other banks trying to get their money out: this is known as a 'run on the banks'. The whole banking system could fail because banks only keep a small fraction of their assets in relatively liquid assets. There is no way a single bank could pay back in cash in one day every single amount deposited with it. The cost to the economy of the whole banking system failing would be larger than the cost of a central bank bailing out one or two banks that were in difficulties.

ACTIVITY 3   SKILLS   REASONING, COMMUNICATION

CASE STUDY: THE BANK OF JAPAN KEEPS MONETARY POLICY LOOSE

▲ Head office of the central Bank of Japan in Tokyo

In July 2017, the Bank of Japan cut its inflation forecast for the year to March 2018 from 1.4 per cent to 1.1 per cent. This means inflation would be below the bank of Japan's target of 2 per cent. As a result, the Bank has signalled that monetary policy will remain 'loose'. The bank will carry on using quantitative easing to stimulate the economy. The purchase of assets would continue at a pace of about JPY 80 trillion a year.

(a) Explain the term 'quantitative easing'.

(b) Using an SR AS and AD diagram, explain how quantitative easing should help the Bank of Japan achieve its inflation target.

FISCAL POLICY

AD can also be affected by government fiscal policy. The main areas of public spending for most governments include health, defence, education and roads. In addition, a government often spends large sums of money on welfare payments, such as unemployment benefits or state pensions. All of this is financed mainly through taxes, such as income tax, taxes on spending, such as VAT, or taxes on companies profits (corporation or corporate tax).

Since 1945 many governments have rarely balanced their budgets (i.e. they have rarely planned to match their expenditure with their receipts). In most years, they have run **budget or fiscal deficits**, spending more than they receive. If, for a particular year a government spends less than it has received in receipts, then it has run a **budget or fiscal surplus**. If a government has a persistent budget deficit over time, this can build up too much national debt (the total accumulated borrowing of a government that remains to be paid to lenders).

The government has to make decisions about how much to spend, tax and borrow. It also has to decide on the composition of its spending and taxation. Should it spend more on education and less on defence? Should it cut income tax by raising taxes on spending? These decisions about spending, taxes and borrowing are called the fiscal policy of the government.

FISCAL POLICY AND AGGREGATE DEMAND

Both fiscal policy and monetary policy can be used to influence AD, $C + I + G + X - M$.

With constant tax revenues, a rise in government spending will increase AD. In the formula for aggregate demand, a rise in G leads directly to a rise in AD. The rise in AD is shown by a rightward shift in the AD curve in Figure 1 on page 312, leading to a high equilibrium level of national output at OY_2.

If government spending is kept constant but tax rates fall, equally there will be a rise in AD. If the government cuts income tax, the disposable income of households will increase, which will lead to an increase in consumption, although there will also be a rise in imports. If the government cuts VAT or excise duties, prices of consumer goods should fall again, leading to a rise in consumption. If governments cut taxes on company profits, this might encourage firms to increase investment.

The government could also increase AD by raising both government spending and taxes, but raising taxes by less than the increase in government spending. Equally, a cut in taxes but a smaller cut in government spending will lead to a rise in AD.

In general, a rise in the budget deficit or a fall in the budget surplus is likely to increase AD. This would be called **expansionary fiscal policy**. Fiscal policy is said to loosen as a result. In contrast, **contractionary fiscal policy** occurs when there is a fall in the budget deficit or a rise in the budget surplus. Fiscal policy is said to tighten as a result. In Figure 2 on page 312, if the shift to the left in the AD curve were caused by tighter fiscal policy, equilibrium real output would fall from OY_1 to OY_2. So the **fiscal stance or budget position** of the government could be expansionary or contractionary. It could equally be neutral. **Neutral fiscal policy** is when changes to government spending and taxation leave the overall budget surplus or deficit unchanged and have no effect on AD.

A rise in government spending will not just increase AD by the value of the increase in G. There will be a multiple increase in AD. This multiplier effect will be larger, the smaller the leakages from the circular flow. In a modern economy, where leakages from savings, taxes and imports are a relatively high proportion of national income, multiplier values tend to be small. However, Keynesian economists argue that they can still have a significant effect on output in the economy if the economy is below full employment.

MONETARY POLICY AND AGGREGATE DEMAND

Monetary policy can be used to influence AD. **Expansionary monetary policy**, or a loosening of monetary policy works, for example, through lowering interest rates or increasing quantitative easing.

FIGURE 1

Expansionary demand-side policies and aggregate demand

Expansionary policies, such as a rise in government spending or a fall interest rates, will shift the AD curve to the right from AD_1 to AD_2. In the short run, equilibrium output will rise from Y_1 to Y_2 but there will also be an increase in the price level from P_1 to P_2.

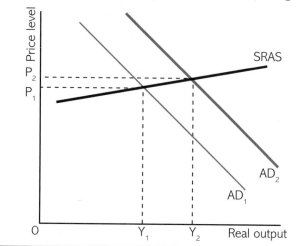

Contractionary monetary policy, or a **tightening** of monetary policy works, for example, through raising interest rates or reducing quantitative easing.

In Figure 1, a fall in the rate of interest leads to a rise in consumption and investment. This increase in AD is shown by a shift to the right in the AD curve.

Equilibrium output increases from OY_1 to OY_2. In Figure 2, a rise in the rate of interest leads to a fall in consumption and investment, causing a fall in AD. This is shown by a shift to the left in the AD curve. Equilibrium output falls from OY_1 to OY_2.

FIGURE 2

Contractionary demand-side policies and aggregate demand

Contractionary policies, such as a fall in government spending or a rise in interest rates, will shift the AD curve to the left from AD_1 to AD_2. In the short run, equilibrium output will fall from Y_1 to Y_2 but there will also be a fall in the price level from P_1 to P_2.

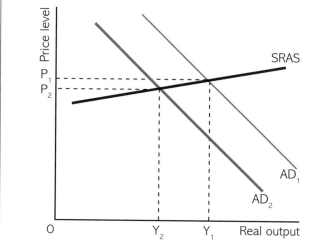

STRENGTHS AND WEAKNESSES OF DEMAND-SIDE POLICIES

Economists are divided about the effectiveness of demand-side policies and their strengths and weaknesses. Keynesian economists tend to favour the use of both fiscal and monetary demand-side policies

---

ACTIVITY 4   **SKILLS** › REASONING, INTERPRETATION, COMMUNICATION

CASE STUDY: TRUMP'S FISCAL EXPANSION

In November 2016, the OECD improved its growth forecast for the US economy in light of President Trump's spending and tax plans. Trump's team had pledged to invest US$550 billion in infrastructure. At the time, the increase in government spending, mostly on public infrastructure, was expected to create a stimulus worth 0.25 per cent to 0.5 per cent of national income in the second half of 2017. Expected tax cuts would create a further stimulus of 1 per cent or so in 2018. Among the tax cut proposals was a fall in the corporation tax rate from 35 per cent to 15 per cent. The OECD also said there

was room for fiscal expansion in the UK, Germany, France, Belgium and Russia, but recommended that China and Hungary (among others) should move to a tighter budgetary stance.

(a) Explain, using a short-run AS and AD diagram, the impact the changes in the US government spending and taxation plans will have on real GDP in the US economy.

(b) Explain what the OECD might have meant by 'room for fiscal expansion' in the UK, Germany, France, Belgium and Russia.

ACTIVITY 5   SKILLS ▸ PROBLEM-SOLVING, REASONING

CASE STUDY: THE BEST WAY TO REVIVE THE EUROZONE

Economists polled by the *Financial Times* have said that a massive quantitative easing programme by the European Central Bank would fail to revive the eurozone economy. Dario Perkins, economist at Lombard Street Research, said it would help lift inflation expectations and reduce the value of the euro against other currencies but would not be a 'total game changer'. Several respondents said government bond buying would not prevent disappointing growth. The biggest impact would come if governments at the same time were allowed to start a deficit-financed investment programme. However, borrowing to fund new roads, railway links and housing is unlikely to

'ever happen in the euro area' according to Carsten Brzeski of ING DiBa, a bank.

(a) The European Central Bank wants to raise growth in eurozone countries through quantitative easing. The economists polled by the *Financial Times* think this is unlikely to work. Put forward one argument that would support the European Central Bank view and one argument to support the view of the economists polled by the *Financial Times*.

(b) Why might a deficit-financed investment programme help economic growth?

when the economy is in recession or is growing so fast that inflation begins to increase. Classical economists tend to argue that fiscal policies are ineffective and governments should rely only on monetary policy to influence AD, if at all.

Speed of adjustment Economists are divided about how quickly an economy can return to long-run equilibrium. Keynesian economists tend to argue that an economy could be in short-run disequilibrium for years and even longer periods because of a lack of demand. If consumers, firms and governments all spend less than is needed to get the economy to full employment, then the economy can remain depressed for a long time. Classical economists tend to argue that economies adjust very quickly. If there is long-term unemployment, for example, with no economic growth, this is not because there is recession in the economy. It is because there are supply-side problems in the economy. Using demand-side policies to get a stagnant economy moving again will have no effect.

Conflicting policies If there is high unemployment and the economy is in recession, Keynesian economists would argue that governments should use both expansionary fiscal and monetary policies to get the economy back to growth. However, since 2008, some economists have argued that fiscal policy should be contractionary, while monetary policy should be expansionary. This is because they argue that the costs of increasing the national debt from expansionary fiscal policy are greater than any benefits to AD that might result. Some might go further and argue that fiscal policy has no impact on AD and so raising taxes and cutting government spending is not contractionary.

The national debt In a recession, expansionary fiscal policy can be used as a demand-side policy to

increase AD. However, it will increase the size of the national debt. Some economists argue that the benefit of increased AD in the short term is outweighed by the negative impact of increasing the national debt. Keynesian economists argue the contrary. So long as a government can print money to finance its deficit without raising inflation or borrow money from the financial markets, then the national debt is not a problem in the short term. Nearly all economists, however, would argue that, in the long term, large national debts can be a problem, particularly if they are financed mainly by borrowing money from foreigners.

The rate of interest In a recession, economists agree that the central bank should cut interest rates to stimulate AD. However, following the financial crash of 2008, many central banks effectively reduced interest rates to 0 per cent and found it had little impact on AD. It was because of this that they started programmes of quantitative easing. So interest rates have limitations on their effectiveness.

Quantitative easing Economists disagree about the effectiveness of quantitative easing. Some economists argue that it significantly boosts AD because households and firms borrow to spend on real goods and services. Other economists argue that it mainly pushes up asset prices such as houses or stocks and shares. Households and firms borrow money but instead, for example, of buying or building new houses, they instead buy second-hand houses, pushing up their price but not increasing AD.

Reserve asset (liquidity) requirements Using a required reserve ratio to manipulate the amount of lending by banks, and therefore the money supply, is used by some central banks as a main focus of their monetary policy. However, many others prefer to have their focus on interest rate setting to achieve their inflation targets or other macroeconomic objectives. This is because, in practice, changes in the required reserve ratio have not always led to predictable changes in the amount banks lend to their customers. So, the use of a required reserve ratio is often considered to be ineffective.

The size of the multiplier Economists disagree about the size of the multiplier. Classical economists tend to argue that it is virtually zero even in the short term. They argue that extra government spending crowds out (or forces out) private sector spending. Cuts in tax financed by government borrowing mean that the private sector can borrow less money. An increase in the budget deficit financed by printing money only leads to inflation, not extra output.

Keynesian economists, in contrast, argue that the multiplier is positive and can be large if government spending and tax charges are carefully targeted. For example, if there is large-scale unemployment in the construction industry, extra government spending on building new social housing could work its way quickly through the economy to increase AD.

Time lags Demand-side policies can have significant time lags or time delays. For example, if a government announces plans to build new motorways, high-speed rail links or nuclear power stations to stimulate the economy, then the policy will fail. This is because there is at least a five-year time lag between announcement and spending taking place on big infrastructure projects. By the time the project begins, the economic situation is likely to have changed significantly. Demand-side policies need to be focused on changing AD within a very short period of time to be effective in responding to problems in the economy today.

Fine-tuning In the 1950s and 1960s, Keynesian economists thought that demand-side policies could move the economy to a very precise level of national income. Today, most economists agree that such precise control is impossible. There are too many small, or indeed large, random shocks to the economic system and too little precision about the tools of demand-side policy for this to work.

THINKING LIKE AN ECONOMIST

UNWINDING THE MONETARY STIMULUS

In July 2017, the US central bank (the Federal Reserve) signalled that it was ready to unwind its crisis-era stimulus programme as soon as its next meeting in September. This means putting its quantitative easing (QE) programme in reverse.

Over the past decade, since the financial crisis of 2008, six central banks have used quantitative easing as a monetary policy instrument to boost AD. This involved the central banks buying bonds and securities on a large scale from commercial banks. The objective was to help firms and individuals have access to finance at a time when the supply of credit was scarce. The effect of quantitative easing was to reduce long term borrowing costs. This helped to stimulate more investment and consumer spending at a time when economic growth rates were negative or at very low levels. In August 2017, it was reported that the US Federal Reserve held US$4.47 trillion of assets, the European Central Bank US$4.9 trillion, the Bank of Japan US$4.53 trillion and the Bank of England, along with Swiss and Swedish central banks making up the total of more than US$15 trillion assets purchased as part of the QE programme.

By July 2017, US unemployment was at a low of 4.4 per cent and the US economy was viewed to be in, good health, with both consumption and business investment continuing to expand. Interest rates had already been raised four times by the Federal Reserve Bank since December 2015, as growth prospects had improved. By July 2017, it was anticipated that other countries might soon follow with rate rises.

By May 2017, the global recovery was evident with most rich countries growing close to their long-term trend rates. Most central banks were now beginning to focus on when to tighten monetary policy, rather than maintaining or trying to boost AD. There was now more danger of overheating as economies were moving close to full employment. Reversing QE and putting up interest rates would dampen AD, so that full employment could be achieved, but without spiralling inflation. QE was originally only supposed to be a temporary emergency measure, but had been used more as a mainstream policy since the financial crisis. Although it is viewed by most to have been successful in helping to reflate economies after the financial crisis, it had not been without its critics.

One main concern of QE is that it has caused inequality. The purchase of assets by a central bank will push up the price of these assets. This means household wealth will increase for those already viewed as wealthy. The associated fall in interest rates also causes more investment in the stock market; benefitting those who hold wealth in shares. The fall in interest rates also disadvantages savers; some of these will be struggling pensioners who rely on interest to support their income.

So, it seems that quantitative easing may finally be taking a back seat. The only recent puzzle among many central banks has been why inflation has remained so low, despite jobs growth and strong economic growth. This includes the USA, where, in July 2017, inflation was running below 2 per cent. Inflation was also below target for Canada and the eurozone, despite strong AD.

Source: *Financial Times*, 'US Fed signals readiness to unwind crisis-era stimulus from next meeting', 27.7.2017, 'Decade of QE leaves big central banks owning fifth of public debt', 16.8.2017, 'Economies can take a lot more stimulus without overheating', 23.5.2017, 'Monetary policy-cheap money - Canada set to join retreat from stimulus', 11.7.2017

SUBJECT VOCABULARY

balanced budget government statement of spending and income plans where spending is equal to its receipts, mainly tax revenues.

base rate the rate of interest charged by central banks to other financial institutions, to borrow money overnight. The base rate is the most important interest rate in an economy's financial system, because it influences all other interest rates in the economy, such as lending and savings rates offered by banks.

budget a statement of the spending and income plans of an individual firm or government.

budget deficit a deficit that arises because government spending is greater than its receipts. Government therefore has to borrow money to finance the difference. The term 'fiscal deficit' is also used.

budget surplus (or fiscal surplus) a government surplus arising from government spending being less than its receipts. Government can use the difference to repay part of the National Debt.

capital requirements the capital that a government says that a financial institution must have in relation to the amount that it lends, so that it can operate safely.

contractionary fiscal policy fiscal policy that leads to a fall in aggregate demand.

contractionary monetary policy monetary policy that leads to a fall in aggregate demand.

demand-side policies policies used by the government or central bank to manipulate aggregate demand.

expansionary fiscal policy fiscal policy that leads to an increase in aggregate demand.

expansionary monetary policy monetary policy that leads to a rise in aggregate demand.

fiscal policy the use of taxes, government spending and government borrowing by government to achieve its objectives.

fiscal stance or budget position whether fiscal policy is expansionary, contractionary or neutral.

instruments of policy economic variables, such as the rate of interest, income tax rate or government spending on education, that are used to achieve a target of government policy.

liquid assets assets that can easily be converted into cash.

liquidity when a business or a person has money or goods that can be sold to pay debts.

liquidity crisis a situation where depositors demand larger cash withdrawals than normal on such a scale that there is a risk that the bank may not have enough liquid assets to meet the demand. A liquidity crisis is often unpredictable and caused by a lack of confidence in a specific bank.

monetary policy government changes to monetary variables, e.g interest rates and the money supply, to achieve its objectives.

neutral fiscal policy when changes to government spending and taxation leave the overall budget surplus or deficit unchanged and have no effect on aggregate demand.

quantitative easing a monetary policy instrument where the central bank buys financial assets in exchange for money in order to increase borrowing and lending in the economy.

rate of interest the price of money, determined by the demand and supply of funds in a money market where there are borrowers and lenders.

reserve asset (liquidity) requirement a reserve asset ratio as a percentage of the bank's total deposits that must be kept as reserves. This is either because they are needed to satisfy customer liquidity requirements or because a central bank forces banks to keep them to manipulate the money supply.

CHECKPOINT

1 Give definitions for both fiscal and monetary policy.
2 State three different ways a rise in interest rates would affect aggregate demand.
3 How does quantitative easing work?
4 What is expansionary fiscal policy?
5 What is contractionary monetary policy?

6 What is inflation targeting?
7 What is a reserve asset liquidity requirement?
8 What are two general problems of using demand-side policies?
9 State one advantage of using quantitative easing.
10 What is one possible problem of using expansionary fiscal policy?

EXAM PRACTICE

SKILLS PROBLEM SOLVING, REASONING, INTERPRETATION, ANALYSIS, CRITICAL THINKING

Q

1 In February 2016, the People's Bank of China cut the required reserve ratio – or the share of customer deposits that banks must hold in reserves – by 0.5 percentage points. The cut will inject about CNY 690 billion (US$106 billion) into the banking system. This brings the ratio for big banks to 17 per cent.

Which one of the following is the most likely effect to result from the cut in the reserve asset requirement ratio?

(a) Real output will fall and the price level will rise.

(b) Real output will rise and the price level will rise.

(c) The money supply will fall.

(d) Aggregate demand will remain unchanged.

(1 mark)

▲ **The People's Bank of China**

2 In August 2017, India's central bank reduced its benchmark interest rate from 6.25 per cent to 6 per cent. This was the lowest rate it had been for six and a half years. Draw a short-run AS and AD diagram to show the effect of this reduction in interest rates on the price level and real output.

(4 marks)

3 Quantitative easing had been introduced by the European Central Bank in 2015 to help stimulate the eurozone. However, in 2017 it was reported that the European Central Bank was likely to scale back or gradually phase out its €60 billion a month bond buying programme (known as quantitative easing). This was likely to take effect at the start of 2018.

Explain how the phasing out of the quantitative easing programme in the eurozone is likely to affect the price level.　　**(8 marks)**

4 In April 2017, Brazil's central bank cut its benchmark interest rate (the Selic rate) from 12.25 per cent to 11.25 per cent, as Latin America's biggest economy tries to recover from the worst recession on record. Brazil's economy contracted by 3.6 per cent in 2016 after declining by 3.8 per cent in 2015, leading to soaring unemployment. The fall in interest rate was possible since inflation had fallen by one-half over the previous 6 months, to levels close to the centre of the central bank's target band of 4.5 per cent, plus or minus 1.5 percentage points.

The central bank has forecast inflation to be 4.1 per cent by the end of 2017. The country's largest private bank said, following the central bank's announcement, it would pass on the rate cut in full to customers with personal loans and overdrafts, or small business borrowing.

(a) Define the term 'inflation'. **(2 marks)**

(b) With reference to the extract, examine the likely impact on the Brazilian economy of the reduction in the benchmark interest rate by Brazil's central bank. **(8 marks)**

(c) With reference to the extract and Figures 3 and 4, discuss the likely impact of an expansionary (reflationary) fiscal policy on an economy.
(14 marks)

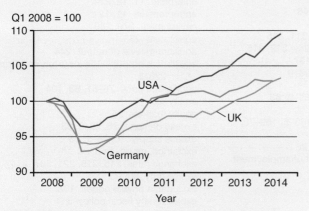

Q1 2008 = 100

▲ Figure 3 GDP, 1st quarter 2008 = 100, Germany, USA and UK, 2008–14

Source: adapted from Capital Economics

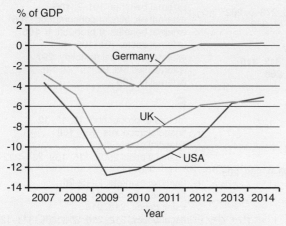

% of GDP

▲ Figure 4 Government budget balance, Germany, USA and UK, percentage of GDP, 2007–14

Source: adapted from www.oecd.org

Make sure you clearly explain the effect an expansionary fiscal policy will have on aggregate demand. Then discuss the likely effect on real GDP. Use Figures 3 and 4 carefully to see if the data suggests that an economy, whose government increases government spending relative to taxation, has a faster rise in real GDP over that time period. Will there be any other positive or negative impacts on other measures of economic performance? For evaluation you might consider some of the different views economists have on the effectiveness of fiscal policy or the difficulties of using fiscal policy. You might also discuss under what circumstances expansionary fiscal policy might be particularly beneficial.

6 By 2017, there was a growing sense that quantitative easing had been over used. With interest rates still low in many advanced economies, any future recession might require a greater role for fiscal policy to reflate an economy. Evaluate demand-side policies that would help an economy in a recession to increase actual growth. **(20 marks)**

INDEX

Page numbers in **bold** denote entries in subject vocabulary.